BANK ANALYST'S HANDBOOK

BANK ANALYST'S HANDBOOK

TRACY G. HERRICK
Bank of America, National Trust and Savings Association

A WILEY-INTERSCIENCE PUBLICATION

JOHN WILEY & SONS, New York • Chichester • Brisbane • Toronto

Library of Congress Cataloging in Publication Data:

Herrick, Tracy G 1933–
    Bank analyst's handbook

    "A Wiley-Interscience publication."
    Includes index.
    1. Banks and banking—Handbooks, manuals, etc.
I. Title.

HG1576.H47   332'.02'02   78-987
ISBN 0-471-02025-7

Printed in the United States of America

10 9 8 7 6 5 4 3 2 1

PREFACE

This is a handbook on banking. It is intended to be a practical book for persons who make business and investment decisions concerning banks. The aim has been to present information that would help these persons make better decisions.

The book is designed for use by an outsider of a bank who wants to learn whether a bank fulfills his or her needs. It is not a book on how banks manage themselves, although much of the information concerns this topic. It does not assume that an outsider has access to private information. In fact, all the information shown in the book is part of the public record. On the whole, the book indicates that banks reveal considerable information about themselves, more than is widely recognized.

Some readers may find that parts of the book appear to be conservative. Other parts point to ways of thinking that are new or may not have been rediscovered. My aim has not been to begin with either point of view. In fact, when considering banking over the past six centuries—from the Florentine merchant banks to the international banks of the present—I have never been sure which ideas are conservative and which are advanced banking practice. The terms fail me, and I believe that they miss the real issues.

People who use banks need to know what information they may rely on, even under strenuous circumstances. They need to know where they should place their resources or obtain commitments. This book is designed to fulfill these needs.

I have developed the book from conversations among a number of bankers, officials, businessmen, scholars, and others over the past decade. The book follows five basic steps. The initial step is to understand the financial data of a bank, and to trace its changes over time. The heart of the analysis is to probe the key policies of a bank. These policies provide the basis that a bank uses to organize knowledge within itself. The environment of a bank sets the limits of expansion. Finally, the way that a bank manages its strategies and controls its personnel indicates how effective it will be in accomplishing its goals. It is, I believe, a simple and complete picture.

There have been many late evenings and weekends. The understanding of my wife, Maie, and the hesitant but knowing acceptance of their dad's project by Sylvi and Alan were a constant strength. This work would never have appeared without their devotion.

Tracy G. Herrick

Palo Alto, California
February 1978

ACKNOWLEDGMENTS

This book reflects the help of many friends and has been enormously improved through their suggestions.

Several persons were helpful in forming the overall scope of the book. James G. Maletis lent a steady interest throughout the development of the book. Frank A. Plummer, chairman of First Alabama Bankshares Inc.; Eugene A. Leonard, first vice-president of the Federal Reserve Bank of St. Louis; and Raymond J. Doll, retired first vice-president of the Federal Reserve Bank of Kansas City were also helpful in forming the scope of the book during the informal faculty sessions at the Stonier Graduate School of Banking at Rutgers University. Discussions with Dr. Hans Haumer, chief executive of Erste Österreichische Spar-Casse and Jorge Aguilar Valenzuela of Banco National de Mexico, S.A., provided additional perspective. The particular interest of Thomas L. Chrystie, senior vice-president of Merrill Lynch & Co., Inc., was most helpful.

The first chapter was the most difficult, and I am deeply indebted to James R. Barker, chairman of Moore McCormack Resources, Inc.; Edward S. Shaw, professor emeritus of Economics of Stanford University; and Jack R. Shuman, vice-president and manager of the Shuman Agnew Advisory Group, for their suggestions for improving the original draft. In addition, Dr. Jean W. Nelson, senior social scientist of Stanford Research Institute International; Richard Shrieve of Stanford University Business School; and Clyde A. MacFie, executive vice-president of Ferro Corporation made numerous helpful suggestions.

The second chapter looks at sources of information. Norman Kost, vice-president of First National Bank of Chicago; and Arnold W. Spelker, vice-president of Chemical Bank, were helpful in sanding many rough edges.

The third chapter discusses the financial statements of J. P. Morgan & Co., Inc. Thomas G. Carr of the bank was a constant companion in working through the issues of the chapter, and Penelope A. Flugger was also generous and precise with her comments. Burton L. Sweeney, vice-president of Bank of America, added further perspective to this chapter, as well as to many others.

The fourth chapter reviews patterns of numerical data. Paul L. Smith, chairman of the Finance Committee of Security Pacific National Bank; David S. Conley, Jr., of Continental Illinois National Bank; and H. Peers Brewer, vice-president of Manufacturers Hanover Trust Company, gave many hours to the chapter.

The chapter on liquidity policy was, perhaps, the most difficult to present. John S. Albright, partner of Manley Bennett, Inc.; Alex E. Koutroubas of Irving Trust Company; G. Clarke Bean, chairman of Arizona Bank; Jeffrey D. Barr of Citicorp; and Yoshizo Kimota, director and general manager of Taiyo Kobe Bank, provided many thoughtful insights.

The chapter on credit risk policy covers problems that banks have faced in recent years. Ronald H. Mead, vice-president and treasurer, and Brian W. Bell of Rainier Bank; Jerry G. Weiner of Citizens and Southern National Bank; Herbert L. Mager, Jr., of Bank of America; and Noel A. McBride, vice-president of Cleveland Trust Company, were most helpful in their comments.

Interest rate policy is one of the most difficult policies to measure. Arthur M. Holter of Bank of America; and Charles E. Erickson, senior financial economist of Stanford Research Institute International, provided very useful comments. Lester J. Stephens Jr., vice-president of Chase Manhattan Bank, was most helpful with this, as well as with many other chapters.

The chapter on profitability has the broadest implications of all chapters that review policies. John A. Elorriaga, chairman of U.S. Bancorp; J. Robert Killpack, executive vice-president of Eaton Corporation; J. Richard Fredericks of Robertson, Colman, Siebel & Weisel; and Allan L. McKinnon, senior vice-president of First National Bank of Boston, were most helpful.

The chapter on capital policy looks at issues that are most controversial in banking. Douglas A. Hurd, group program manager of Stanford Research Institute International; Harold W. Bangert of Bangert, Dawes, Reade, Davis & Thom; William Roger Watson of the Federal Deposit Insurance Corporation; John J. Brine, executive vice-president of Western Bancorporation; John E. Ryan, acting director of the Division of Banking Supervision and Regulation of the Board of Governors of the Federal Reserve System; Paul James of the Comptroller of the Currency; and Selden Campen of Mellon Bank provided many insights into this complex issue.

The methods of comparing banks are in an early stage of development, and several approaches show promise. John Moriarty, president of Keefe Management Services Inc., helped keep the chapter in balance between the need for simplicity and the complicated nature of the subject. Jon R. Burke, vice-president of the Robinson Humphrey Company, Inc.; John S. Monroe, vice-president of the Bank Administration Institute; Robert Larson of Investors Management Sciences, Inc.; and David C. Cates, president of Cates, Lyons & Co., Inc., also provided assistance.

The chapter on economic influences benefited from comments by David B. Richard, vice-president of Wells Fargo Bank; and James M. Dawson, senior vice-president and economist of National City Bank of Cleveland.

Banking regulators have been particularly helpful in preparing the chapter on banking regulation. Douglas G. Paul, of the Federal Reserve Bank of San Francisco made many key technical suggestions in this chapter as well as other chapters. W. Gordon Smith, of the same bank, provided many insights. Joseph R. Bauer of the Federal Deposit Insurance Corporation was also helpful with this chapter and the chapter on capital policy.

Perhaps the most important chapter in the book, and the one literally with the fewest numbers, is the chapter that looks at strategies. There were many reviewers who made suggestions on the chapter, and the range of interest was the widest of all of the chapters. Gilbert F. Bradley, chairman of Valley National Bank, was most helpful with this chapter, as well as with suggestions for other parts of the book.

Control is the most sensitive issue in banking. I am grateful to Ralph J. Voss, chairman of Western Bancorporation, for his interest in the book and this issue. Charles Nagel, vice-president of Marine Midland Bank was also helpful with suggestions. Dr. Paul J. Brouwer, director and emeritus partner of Rohrer, Hibler & Replogle, helped keep the topic on course and provided valuable suggestions.

In looking at market valuations, Daniel D. Jackson, vice-president of First Boston Corporation; Roger B. Tallon Jr., of Standard & Poor's Corporation; Ivan W. Wing, vice-president of Weeden & Company; Edward J. Gibson, vice-president and secretary of the First Albany Corporation; and Fred W. DeBussey of Moody's Investors Service, Inc. were helpful with their suggestions.

Forecasts are a matter of almost universal interest. Robert B. Albertson of Smith Barney, Harris Upham & Co., Inc.; William M. Weiant, vice-president of First Boston Corporation; and John M. Boyle, vice-president, finance of Crocker National Corporation, offered numerous suggestions on the chapter.

Chapter 16 reviews the market valuation of a bank. Jesse Siff, president of Siff, Oakley Marks, Inc., was most generous with his thoughts, as were many others who are mentioned elsewhere.

The chapter covering the topic of composite valuation uses First National Bankshares as an example. Carl J. Stockdale, vice-president and controller, and Robert S. Raye, vice-president of the bank were generous with their time and suggestions, as was McKenzie Moss II, president.

One of the tasks of preparing the book was to give unity to diverse types of information. Seeing the book as a whole and reviewing the ways that it fulfills the needs of users was a formidable task. Robert A. McDonald, attorney; Edward J. Powers, vice-president, Research of M. A. Schapiro & Co., Inc.; Thomas H. Hanley of Salomon Brothers; William A. Wood of the America Bankers Association; William R. Fisher, vice-president of Donaldson, Lufkin & Jenrette, Inc; Charlkes Edward McConnell, vice-president of Keefe Bruyette & Woods, Inc.; James B. Monroe, vice-president of Morgan Guaranty Trust Co., Inc.; Philipp A. Frings, vice-president of Bank of America; and Joseph Asher of *Banking* were most generous with their help and comments. Jon d'Alessio, now with Kaiser Steel Corporation, lived with the development of the book as it progressed, chapter by chapter. Hardly a page has not been improved because of his thoughtful suggestions.

The deep interest of Alvin C. Rice, executive vice-president; Walter E. Hoadley, executive vice-president; and Leland S. Prussia, executive vice-president and cashier of Bank of America, underlies the writing of the book, as does that of James R. Robinson, vice-president, and Richard Puz, senior vice-president of the bank. I am particularly grateful to William Mack Terry, vice-president of the bank. The inspiration of his quick mind is woven into each page.

                                                                                          T. G. H.

CONTENTS

BANK ANALYST'S HANDBOOK

INTRODUCTION

Banks occupy a central position in the commercial life of perhaps more than three-quarters of all households in industrial countries. In addition, as is well known, banks aid businesses and governments through a wide range of financial services.

A central thread running through these activities is that banks are designed to be supportive of ownership positions. They permit people—individuals, companies, and governments—who lack funds to undertake programs that otherwise would be impossible to develop. For example, the development of virtually every industry has reflected companies with plans for development that were greater than the funds of those organizations. Banks provided a large portion of those funds. Banks were able to do this because large numbers of people, essentially middle class, had confidence that their money was safe when it was deposited.

The same pattern appears with the needs of individuals. For example, banks were the primary lenders to sales finance companies during their early development. These specialized lenders enabled persons of ordinary means to buy refrigerators, stoves, and automobiles. Banks have been important lenders to governments for a wide range of activities, from building roads to the teaching of skills.

Whenever banks have competed, they have sought those persons, companies, and governments that have shown promise of greater productivity. They have also sought those who wish to increase their present levels of consumption. More than any other institution, they have been engines of expansion.

This concept of banking appears at odds with the conventional image of a restrictive banker who is more concerned with protecting existing wealth of established friends than expanding opportunities in a community. In many areas of the world, even in areas of the United States, some banks have an effective monopoly on the banking business of a community. A traveler into the back roads of many states that do not permit widespread branch banking sometimes finds a bank in a small community that pays considerably less interest on savings deposits than is paid in cities where banks compete—a good sign of a monopoly position. Yet this is the exception in the industrial countries, and the conventional image of a restrictive banker is inaccurate.

Banks of the industrialized countries have become, in fact, challengers of established wealth. They have felt the hot breath of competition as well as the pressure of shareholders to increase earnings and dividends. They have looked for new types of customers and welcomed them, perhaps too eagerly.

Banks have often sought to be first in introducing banking activities, hoping to obtain a favored position. The list of new industries and markets is a long one and includes conglomerates, high technology, space, export financing, consumer installment lending, foreign currency trading, international corporate banking, revolving consumer credit, and real estate investment trusts, to name only a few. Most have been sound, profitable industries and markets.

Banks today are perhpas more important to the life of the people of the non-Communist world than ever before. Perhaps even this statement is too narrow, since the standard of living of many Communist countries has been subsidized by bank loans from the principal industrial countries. During high points of banking in the West, such as fourteenth-century Florence or seventeenth-century Amsterdam, the influence of banks did not permeate so deeply into the social fabric, because most persons in those periods lived on farms and participated in a commercial economy in only a limited way. Today, a large proportion of jobs is related to a world economy, which has become increasingly financed by banks.

Wherever the commercial way of life has failed—and any tourist to Florence will quickly recognize that the city today is not a major banking center—it has been the banks that failed first. Banks provide great mobility to funds. How funds are obtained and distributed, which is what this handbook is concerned about, is a force of great social pressure. The wise use of these funds so that the leadership of the West may be maintained is an issue that moves beyond the scope of this book. Nevertheless, we have a precious heritage in banking to pass on, if we wish, but it is in no way preordained that it will endure.

Banks seldom receive a pat on the back for a job well done. Whenever a project has been successfully completed, the role of banks is in the shadow, and that is perhaps as it should be. The nature of banking is supportive of others who receive congratulations. Few people can remember of hearing which banks assisted with the Marshall Plan or which banks aided in the building of the World Trade Center. Homeowners successfully obtain mortgages daily, and the fact that in the past year millions of deposits have been successfully paid at demand or when due appears as one of the least newsworthy facts imaginable.

The normal regularity of successful banking activities contrasts any transaction or development that does not run smoothly. In the past few years, banks appear to have received a wider press coverage than during earlier postwar years because of difficulties connected with banking. The chronicle is familiar to almost everyone and includes the failure of several large banks, widespread concern over the solvency of many real estate investment trusts which are major borrowers from large banks, news leaks about examiners' reports and concern that banks have accepted untested responsibilities in recycling OPEC funds to debtor nations, to name a few. Each of these issues may be answered in ways which show that the reports are exaggerated and do not show a balanced point of view. The rebuttals are entirely correct.

Yet concern still persists among many bank analysts that some banks are engaged in activities that are fundamentally different or are different in magnitude from activities of earlier years. For whatever reasons, there appears to have been a shift in the image of many large banks from conservative organizations which promote growth to growth companies themselves. These observers are interested in learning more about banks to judge for themselves the issues that they read about and hear discussed.

As a handbook, this publication is designed to be practical and for use by persons who have a business need to understand banks. The original handbooks in such fields as chemical processing, cabinetmaking, or porcelain enameling were small books that fitted into the hip pockets of foremen and plant managers. They were intended to bridge a gap between the scientific knowledge that was available in university laboratories and the intuitive sense of operatives on a line who would make judgments from the way a batch bubbled. Handbooks were also intended to bridge a gap between the needs of men on a line and the owners of a business. A handbook needed to be clear, easy to read, and above all, it had to contain information which could be used in discussions with both workingmen and businessmen.

This handbook is designed with these objectives in mind. It is intended to be a balanced book. The focus is not to present information for specialized exploratory insights. Nor is there an abundance of technical data, which a specialized legal or accounting specialist would use. There are no footnotes and no algebraic formulas. The balance of the handbook reflects its need to blend the essential parts of these more refined specialities into information needed by persons who are called on to act in an informed but nontechnical capacity.

The handbook is not designed to be read from cover to cover, although it may be read in that manner. Rather, it is intended to be used as a reference on a wide range of issues that affect a bank. It probably will be read by most readers in sections, as their needs and questions arise.

The one unifying interest of all users will often be the valuation of a bank. *Valuation* is the process of refining what is most important from what is least important and organizing the information in an understandable and conclusive manner. More than for any other purpose, the handbook aims to give the user an understanding of how to approach the valuation of a bank, which is the most fundamental purpose toward which any analysis of commercial life may be directed.

The handbook emphasizes case studies. These examples have been selected to illustrate the issues, as well as to heighten interest. No information may be useful if it is imprecisely preceived or forgotten, and anything that may be done to sharpen issues should help users.

Throughout the handbook, the term "bank" is used broadly to include both bank holding companies, as well as banks. This use is in line with ordinary conversation. However, wherever technical issues are discussed, the technical terms of banks and bank holding companies are used.

CHAPTER 1

WHO CAN USE THIS HANDBOOK

People use banks in many different ways, and in turn, their needs relate to banks in different ways. The users of a bank—who are described in this book as bank analysts—may be classified in many ways. This book shows seven groups of bank analysts, and most of the users of a bank are included in one of these seven categories. They are

Directors
Depositors
Borrowers
Shareholders (short-term interests)
Shareholders (long-term interests)
Debt holders
Employees.

These persons may represent large corporations, other banks, governments, partnerships, or their own interests. In the broadest meaning, these persons are bank analysts. This book is organized to enable these analysts to form their appraisal of a bank on a factual basis.

Other considerations, especially friendships, are important in banking relationships. Their importance should never be minimized or neglected. Nevertheless, an understanding of the strength and weaknesses of a bank is useful to bank analysts. This knowledge may be used to obtain full value in banking services or to determine whether one bank fulfills a bank analyst's present and future needs as well as its competitors.

Each of the analysts of a bank—directors, depositors, borrowers, short-term and long-term shareholders, debt holders and employees—has an overall concern in the welfare of the bank in which he or she may have an interest. Nevertheless, beyond this broad interest, considerable differences occur in the needs of the various groups of bank analysts. For example, in some instances, such as the interests of depositors and short-term shareholders, there could be conflicting needs. Each of these bank analysts is concerned with almost opposite interests and could evaluate a bank differently.

SUMMARY OF KEY INTERESTS OF BANK ANALYSTS

The table shows an overview of the seven types of band analysts together with the operating policies and other factors that have an important bearing on their performance. The weights shown for the policies and issues represent the author's estimate of how each group of bank analysts should rate their importance. Taken together, these ten factors provide a basis of a composite evaluation of a bank. Table 1 provides a display of the importance of various issues in evaluating banks among the seven groups of bank analysts.

The five policies include liquidity policy, credit risk policy, interest rate policy, profitability policy, and capital policy. These are the key operating policies of a bank. A quick review of the table shows that these policies carry the bulk of the weight in evaluating a bank. These policies represent areas of conducting business over which banks exercise considerable control. For example, the liquidity policy reflects a bank's preference in holding funds in near-cash equivalents, such as U.S. government securities. These policies may also be measured with some degree of precision. Each of these policies is reviewed in detail in succeeding chapters of the book.

The five issues used to form the basis of an evaluation of a bank include the future economic environment, regulatory environment, strategy, controls, and an evaluation of the accounting of the bank. These issues include the broadly based environment of a bank, as well as certain operating issues. Their measurement is not as precise as policies, and they include some degree of opinion. These issues are also discussed in later chapters.

The weights shown in the table for each type of bank analyst have been selected assuming that each of the analysts was familiar with all of the policies and issues. The weights are judgmental on the part of the author. Of course, various analysts may assign different weights, reflecting their point of view. Some would be more conservative, optimistic or rigorous in viewing their interests than is shown in the table.

DIRECTORS

The directors of a bank are responsible for the overall conduct of its affairs. Directors exercise this responsibility through their examination of the results of a bank's performance, especially its financial performance. They also are responsible for the selection of the management of a bank. Finally, they are responsible for the policies, strategies, and other issues that the management of a bank pursues.

The table suggests that directors are typically concerned about the broad scope of policies and issues of a bank in approximately equal weight. This

Table 1 Suggested Weights (%) in Valuing a Bank According to Seven Types of Bank Analysts

Observer	Liquidity Policy	Credit Risk Policy	Interest Rate Policy	Profit-ability Policy	Capital Policy	Future Economic Environ-ment	Regula-tory Environ-ment	Manage-ment Strategy	Manage-ment Controls	Evalua-tion of Account-ing	Total
1. Directors	10	10	10	10	10	10	10	10	10	10	100
2. Depositors	50	20	5	5	5	5	1	1	1	7	100
3. Borrowers	5	50	20	5	1	15	1	1	1	1	100
4. Shareholders— short term	2	30	30	2	2	30	1	1	1	1	100
5. Shareholders— long term	5	5	5	50	5	5	5	15	3	2	100
6. Debt holders	30	10	5	20	20	5	1	1	1	7	100
7. Employees	1	1	1	15	1	5	5	50	20	1	100

view reflects the fact that in many banks directors are not major shareholders of the organization and do not take the exclusive view of principal shareholders when they sit in board meetings.

For example, most directors are interested in maintaining adequate liquidity, but not so much as to impair earnings. They are interested in a credit risk policy that does not bring about major loan losses, but also does not draw lines on creditworthiness which would severely inhibit the expansion of loans. Directors are willing to give the management some latitude in interest rate policy, allowing them to adjust their portfolios of sources and uses of funds to take advantage of their expectations about the future of interest rates, but they would ordinarily tolerate only a limited interest rate speculation so as not to expose the bank to sudden or unexpected losses. Directors are usually interested in a profitability policy that balances earnings growth with asset growth. Finally, directors are interested in maintaining enough capital to satisfy regulators and liability holders, but not so much that shareholders may appear dissatisfied.

The future economic environment is a matter of interest to directors, since many of them will likely hold their position on the board when future developments reveal the wisdom of current policies. The regulatory agencies cover an area that directors often would prefer to avoid, since it suggests the hand of government regulations. Yet directors would also wish to avoid any legal liabilities from their position, and being in the good graces with regulators provides a kind of stamp of approval that they have acted in a prudent manner. Their interest is to keep the regulators satisfied and quiet.

Directors are interested in the strategy of a bank because they see it as a way of placing the key operating activities of a bank into perspective. Controls are important to directors to assure that policies and programs will be carried out effectively and that they will not be surprised by a sudden loss. As a final consideration, directors are concerned about the evaluation of their accounting and management information system. Before they make a decision, they want to be sure they are looking at information that is right and accurate.

The tendency to be accommodating with managements and the concern to look at the broad scope of a bank's activities describe the overriding tone of most board meetings. Nevertheless, some board members and a few boards take a more specialized view and place greater weight on one or more of the policies or issues. For example, one major bank in the East Coast places emphasis on its special skills in determining credit risks and purchasing liquidity. The bank also has indicated to the public it has special skills in forecasting the future economic and interest rate environment. Other policies and issues, including the regulatory environment, have been reduced in importance. The tone of the board is unique.

DEPOSITORS

The perspective of a typical depositor is much more narrowly focused than that of directors. Traditionally, depositors have looked on a bank first as a safe haven for funds and second as a place where funds earn interest. There also have been other factors, such as the convenience of offices and a personal feeling of affinity toward the bank. However, in the past 40 years, the widespread acceptance of the guarantees of the Federal Deposit Insurance Corporation have quelled the traditional concern of almost all depositors about the safety of their deposits. As a consequence, depositors have been guided by the other factors, such as small differences in interest rates and the convenience of banks.

In the past two years the pendulum appears to have begun to swing back to the traditional interest in safety of deposits. This interest does not reflect actual losses on the part of depositors. In fact, depositors have emerged unscathed from the bank mergers and failures during the past 40 years, especially during the more recent period of the demise of several larger banks. The interest in safety appears to have returned as an issue with the large depositors, including corporations and wealthy individuals. These depositors are not covered with Federal Deposit Insurance Corporation insurance for individual deposits over $40,000. The evidence of this trend reflects the discussions in banking circles and topics of magazine and newspaper publications.

The table in Figure 1 shows that depositors would ordinarily focus on the liquidity policy of a bank. In making this determination, it is assumed that depositors would be aware of the importance of the policies and issues indicated in the table and would have connected their interests with the categories of the table. Thus a depositor might not know exactly what the term "liquidity policy" meant, but he would be aware that he wanted to place his funds in banks which held enough near-cash assets that could easily and quickly be converted to cash.

The liquidity of a bank would be foremost in the thinking of major depositors because they would want assurance that they could obtain their funds in full measure either at demand or when the term of the deposit is completed. Banks with a comparatively large proportion of their funds in near-cash assets would presumably be able to repay depositors if there were conditions where depositors, as a group, wanted a large proportion of their funds returned. These banks would not have to take additional steps to obtain liquidity, such as obtaining new deposits to replace withdrawals or the sale of long-term assets to obtain funds. This is the traditional view of liquidity. There are other approaches to measuring liquidity which are discussed in the chapter on the topic, but all reflect ways of providing cash to depositors.

The second major consideration of depositors would be credit risk policy. Depositors customarily look at credit risks, which include loan losses and securities losses, as a major threat to earnings. A high level of losses can eliminate earnings, and the major losses can provoke a concern that a bank does not have full control over its lending and securities operations. Depositors would even be willing to accept the position that a bank which showed little earnings gains and few asset losses would be preferable to a bank with major earnings gains and large losses. Depositors do not share the fruits of the so-called programs of dynamic banking, although they could bear the brunt of any possible difficulties.

Most depositors would be interested in an evaluation of the accounting practices of a bank. They would look to accounting techniques as an indication of the temperament toward fair presentation and financial stewardship of the bank's management. Accounting is the principal language of banks. Depositors would look at an evaluation of accounting to determine whether the basic structure in which the numbers are cast would be sound and would therefore be presumed to accurately describe the financial facts about a bank.

BORROWERS

The position of a typical borrower is also narrowly focused. In most instances, borrowers view a bank as a source of funds and hope to keep borrowing costs as low as possible. Of course, other considerations, such as easy access to banking facilities, are also important to many borrowers. Since most banks have been able to accommodate most borrowers throughout the past 30 years, most of the interest of borrowers has been focused on the cost of a loan. The interest rate a bank charges a customer is determined in a large part by competitive forces and reflects the interest rate that other banks would be willing to apply. Nevertheless, it also reflects internal policies of a bank, which indicate the interest rate at which a bank can justify a loan.

For this reason, the credit risk policy of a bank would likely be the most important policy to borrowers. This policy looks at how a bank evaluates the creditworthiness of its borrowers. A bank which views the creditworthiness of borrowers in a liberal manner would give borrowers higher marks on their ability to repay loans. A bank with this type of credit policy would likely seek higher-risk loans or offer somewhat lower interest rates to borrowers who would be regarded as average credit risks. In the first instance, the bank might experience higher loan losses, and in the latter instance, the bank might find that its profitability was lower than other banks. These types of credit policies might reflect genuine convictions on the part of the bank's management, or they might be prompted by weak loan demand and a desire to obtain higher loan volume.

Both of these situations—which represent a type of a loss to a bank—would represent a gain to borrowers. Given the experience of the past 30 years, most borrowers would be interested in placing their loans with banks with these liberal credit risk policies, because the cost of loans could be cheaper than with other banks. Borrowers would tend to avoid banks that followed stringent credit policies. These banks would charge a comparatively higher price for loans, since they would tend to appraise credit risks as being greater and require a greater cushion for this perception of credit risk. Nevertheless, recently there has been a new trend of some borrowers to seek banks strong enough to survive any possible difficulties and pay the interest rates of these banks.

Closely tied with credit risk policy in the view of borrowers would be a bank's interest rate policy. This policy refers to how a bank balances the cost of its funds with the income from the use of those funds. Banks that appear to follow a policy of keeping the differential between these two factors fairly steady may be more likely to maintain whatever credit policy they choose. Banks that show a considerable mismatch from time to time may find that they could be forced to raise the cost of lending in order to avoid a severe squeeze on earnings. Thus the interest rate policy acts as an indication of the sustainability of credit risk policy of a bank. Combined, the credit risk policy and the interest rate policy represent the key issues to borrowers.

The issue that would rank third in importance is the future economic environment. The pattern of economic development in postwar years has given borrowers a considerable confidence that economic factors will not present any sudden new difficulties. The consensus opinion of most borrowers, as well as of most economists, is that the pattern of stability of a fairly steady economy will prevail, and neither excessive unemployment nor high inflation will confront borrowers and banks. Nevertheless, in recent years, the strength of this consensus opinion has faded somewhat.

This placid view of economic trends would represent a contrast to the view of borrowers during most of the years of this century prior to the postwar period. During most of those earlier years, borrowers were concerned about the ability of banks to weather a possible future economic crisis, because if they happened to have short-term loans with a bank that was faltering, their loans might have been called as the bank sought liquidity. These borrowers would have been hard pressed to replace the loans at another bank, except at extremely high interest rates. In the event that borrowers might again be concerned about the future economic environment, this issue would assume considerably greater importance.

SHAREHOLDERS WITH SHORT-TERM INTERESTS

Shareholders with short-term interests include participants who acquire shares of a bank in anticipation of gains in the price of the bank's stock in a relatively short period. These analysts would be interested in obtaining the benefit of rapid gains in earnings per share. Overall, these shareholders would be expected to be principally concerned with the three policies and issues that directly affect reported earnings per share. They would be concerned about other issues only to the extent that there might be public reports of problems connected with earnings.

Short-term shareholders would be interested in the credit risk policy of a bank, because changes in this policy represent one way that a bank can quickly boost earnings in the short term. A bank may lower its credit standards in the belief that a future period of strong gains in the economy will keep even marginal borrowers in healthy financial condition. It may do so also with the belief that the policy change is necessary to gain entry into a new market and accepting higher risks for a limited period would be a way of accomplishing this objective. There could be many other reasons which would make such a credit risk decision plausible. Whatever the reason, the effect would be to bring in a considerably higher interest income within a relatively short period.

The possible losses from the loans of higher credit risk usually require a longer period to develop. It would not be unusual for a three- to five-year lag to occur between the initial benefit of higher-interest income revenues and the subsequent higher expenses of the loan loss provision to cover the losses. During this interval, earnings could be boosted, because the higher level of interest revenues would flow through to earnings immediately without the costs associated with losses.

It is also possible that this arrangement of credit risk policy could be continued beyond a three- to five-year period. Nevertheless, this interval was selected because most loan and securities difficulties are related to the business cycle and occur during periods of late recession and early expansion. A bank could continue to expand its volume of loans for a much longer period and expand its business so that losses would regularly trail the expansion in loans. It is also possible that a reverse situation could occur, where tighter credit risk policies could lead to lower earnings gains. Short-term investors would likely become disenchanted with the earnings prospects of such a bank.

Short-term shareholders would receive the maximum benefit during the initial shift in credit risk policy. It is then that short-term shareholders would find the largest gap between their expectations of major earnings gains and the past slower earnings performance of a bank. These shareholders could begin to think of a bank as an undervalued situation. The change in expectations of earnings, as the result of the new credit risk policy became widely known, would provide the impetus to the change in price of the bank's stock.

The interest rate policy would be of importance to short-term shareholders. Banks may mismatch their sources and uses of funds and speculate on interest rates. A speculation which might turn out as expected would provide an unusual benefit to earnings. For example, a bank that borrowed funds on a short-term basis and lent those funds on a long-term basis would benefit earnings if interest rates declined over the future period. The bank would then fund its long-term loans from progressively less expensive sources while it would continue to receive interest income from loans which were ongoing throughout the period. The expansion in net interest income would enhance earnings. This speculation could work in reverse, of course, and earnings would then suffer.

Gains or losses in earnings from this source tend to be relatively short-lived, usually lasting only as long as a swing in interest rates. This duration typically runs from two to five years. A bank can, of course, change its interest rate position as interest rates shift from a rising to a declining phase or vice versa. Yet the likelihood of a bank or anybody else having such prescience on a consistent basis is slim. Moreover, there would be considerable difficulty for a bank to shorten or lengthen the maturity of its loan portfolio with the speed that would be necessary to capture the benefits of an interest rate swing. Thus it would be unusual for a bank to show a record of successfully positioning itself for several interest rate swings. Short-term shareholders would be interested in learning of a bank's interest rate policy to determine whether changes in earnings would be expected to last beyond the duration of a particular interest rate swing. The implication to these shareholders would be to buy or sell shares when they believed the interest rate swing had come to full term.

SHAREHOLDERS WITH LONG-TERM INTERESTS

Shareholders with a long-term interest in the equities of a bank include bank analysts seeking a sustainable dividend return and those who consider their responsibilities to be similar to owners of a bank. These persons would be interested in pursuing developments that could be maintained or expanded on a regular basis and would avoid programs that would appear to be transitory. Long-term shareholders are dedicated to the appreciation of their capital, the buildup of net worth, and the return from these gains that has tangible value. It is difficult to indicate precisely the time horizon of these shareholders, but they would likely consider their personal long-term outlook as being similar to their equity outlook.

Long-term shareholders would be most interested in the profitability of a bank. They would view strong profitability as the central policy to accomplish their goal of dividend expansion. Profitability is sometimes mistakenly viewed as being the same as profits. The two terms actually refer to two different measures of a bank's performance. Profitability refers to the return on assets employed and is most basically measured by dividing earnings by assets. Profits refer only to earnings.

By being a ratio, profitability is immune to one of the illusions of earnings growth. This illusion refers to an expansion in earnings that proceeds at a slower pace than an expansion in assets, still allowing earnings per share to expand at a rapid rate. The bank would have expanded its operations, but would have lowered its earnings per dollar of assets. Eventually, this program of expansion in size of operations would reach limits where additional profits would be minimal despite an expansion in assets. This limit represents one restraining limit of low profitability.

Long-term shareholders view strong profitability as a policy that provides the greatest number of opportunities for a bank to expand dividends on a sustainable basis. A high level of profitability indicates that a bank can undertake new programs with a cushion of earnings. It is also an indication that a bank is an efficient organization and is able to meet competitor banks successfully. Finally, long-term shareholders would look at strong profitability as a source of internally generated capital.

The strategy of the management of a bank would be of major interest to long-term shareholders. Strategies refer to how a bank uses its personnel and directs its activities with its customers and its public. A banking strategy represents a combination of its approach to marketing, operations, and personnel activities. Long-term shareholders would be interested in the strategy of a bank because it represents how that bank approaches the efficiency of its operations. If a bank organizes itself so that it is the most efficient supplier of banking services to its customers, it would likely show greater earnings from its efforts than its competitors and a higher return on assets. Long-term shareholders would tend to view profitability and management strategy as two sides of the same coin.

DEBT HOLDERS

Debt holders include persons who hold short-term notes, capital notes, and all other types of debentures. They tend not to be traders of these securities to the extent of shareholders and thus are discussed here as holders of securities to maturity. These bank analysts are interested in seeing a bank repay their claims at a future due date. Debt holders share a common interest with depositors on the ability of a bank to repay its liabilities. Nevertheless, debt holders would be more interested in the ability of a bank to show a good record in its operations than depositors, because debt holders are concerned about the ability of a bank to repay obligations that usually are due many years in the future. Most banks have only a small proportion of their liabilities in debt instruments. Nevertheless, debt instruments have expanded fairly rapidly in the decade of the 1970s, as some have been regarded as a partial substitute for equity capital by the Comptroller of the Currency Federal Deposit Insurance Corporation and the Federal Reserve Board.

Debt holders would be concerned about liquidity, but not to the extent of depositors. Liquidity would be important to debt holders because they eventually would be paid out of liquidity or a sinking fund, and the present liquidity of a bank would provide a measure of assurance that a bank recognizes the importance of liquidity policy. Of course, the debt of a bank might be rolled over and never be repaid, as old debt would be replaced with new debt. Even so, the ease by which the old debt could be rolled over would reflect, in part, the ease by which the old debt might be repaid if no new debt were to be issued. The adage that nothing attracts a lender quicker than evidence that a borrower doesn't need a loan applies to banks, as well as to their customers.

Debt holders are also interested in the capital policy of a bank. They stand in line just ahead of shareholders—in the event of liquidation. Yet the line separating them is the widest chasm in accounting. Shareholders share in the varying fortunes of a bank and have an opportunity to share in benefits beyond those that might be known at the time of purchase of shares. Debt holders do not share in this possible benefit.

Most current discussions about the liabilities of banks tend to give little attention to liquidation. They stress various deposit guarantees by government agencies and the commitment of the U.S. government to a strong economy that would make bank liquidations unnecessary. Yet forced mergers of banks have occurred in recent years, and the effect on debt holders of a weak bank has not been unlike that of liquidation.

Debt holders are interested in the profitability policy of a bank, because strong profitability represents the best way a bank can provide sustained earnings over a long period. Debt holders are more likely to be repaid by a profitable bank. More important, strong profitability represents a symbol of independence from debt, which, of course, increases the interest of holders of funds to place them with such banks.

Credit risk policies are of interest to debt holders because they would be regarded as an important factor in the long-term ability of a bank to continue showing a profit. A bank which would appear to lower the standards of its credit-risk policies might have begun a program which could have long-term implications on its ability to service its debt. Of course, depending on the type of change, new credit-risk policies could have favorable as well as unfavorable implications to prospective debt holders.

EMPLOYEES

Among all bank analysts, employees are perhaps the most concerned. They spend more hours working with the bank's problems than other analysts. They also usually tend to take a long-term view of their employment with a bank. Their commitment does not involve the size of funds of depositors or the reputation of directors or the well-being of large enterprises of borrowers. Rather, their interests in a banking company are personal.

The major issue to employees is the strategy of the bank. These bank analysts see a bank's outlook in terms of the development of their talents and promotional possibilities. They are concerned about the future of their bank, which is their employer, because it is the vehicle for their own advancement. They would consider that an expanding, profitable bank would provide greater opportunities for personal development and advancement than a bank which might appear to be static.

Employees are usually well aware of the strategies of the bank that employs them. They are also aware that relatively few banks have management strategies which are effective in ways that are fully beneficial to them. The strategies of most banks are not effective in accomplishing this goal, and although employees are usually aware of this shortfall, they usually do not know how to correct it. Nevertheless, they remain interested in strategies and hopeful that somehow a superior strategy will be developed.

Management controls are the second issue that would be important to employees. These controls include all the ways that the work of employees is directed and reviewed. Banks with effective controls, for example, are likely to require that supervisors understand employees' needs and talents and match those with available more challenging positions. These banks are also likely to quickly recognize different levels of job performance and make clear distinctions among categories of work ratings. Thus management controls would provide both a way of insuring that the bank's business would be properly handled and also a way of giving greater identity to the efforts of the employees.

These analysts would be interested in a bank's profitability policy. This policy is linked with management strategy and represents the means by which the success of a strategy is measured. Profitability also provides the basis of making a long-term assessment of whether the bank would have the resources to provide positions for the personal advancement many employees would hope to achieve.

This brief review illustrates that there are common policies and issues uniting all bank analysts. It also shows that various analysts would perceive the importance of these policies and issues differently. This book next looks at sources of information, each of these policies and issues, and then in the chapter on composite valuation applies the various points of view in an example.

PART ONE
GATHERING
THE DATA

CHAPTER 2

SOURCES OF INFORMATION

This chapter provides an overview of the public information concerning banks. Many bank analysts often overlook the large quantity of information provided by most banks. Moreover, as will be discussed in later chapters, much of this information can be used to provide useful approximations concerning important undisclosed information.

The source of all basic information concerning a bank is the organization itself, and the bank analyst can obtain most of this information directly from the bank. Most major banks now have designated an officer for investor relations who acts as a liaison between the bank and shareholders, as well as other persons who are interested in the organization. In smaller banks the chief financial officer usually acts as the liaison with the public.

THE ANNUAL REPORT

The annual report is an important document for information. Some larger banks publish large booklets for their annual report, others provide a statistical supplement to the report, while most medium and small-sized banks provide relatively few pages of information. The following comments cover the six key sections comprising a typical annual report, available from the secretary of the bank.

Shareholders' Letter

This letter is often written by the chief executive officer (usually the chairman), although it sometimes includes the signatures of several principal officers of the bank. This letter is usually written either by the chief executive officer or is extensively rewritten by him and may be regarded as the closest document available to bank analysts that reflects the thinking, selection of important information, and mode of expression of this person. For these reasons, the shareholders' letter provides a special insight into the thinking of a bank.

The typical letter to shareholders begins with a brief review of the financial performance of the bank, which represents a repeat of the financial highlights. It then discusses the past year's developments in the United States economy, trends in the banking industry, and selected measures of strength of the bank. This section usually has a touch of low-pressure selling and is an interesting reflection of the skill in which it is presented.

The shareholders' letter may present a point of view on one or more subjects, such as disclosure, legislation, or the philosophy of banking. This polemical part of the shareholders' letter, if it should occur, should be read with care, because it is the one part of the letter where the bank's chief executive is alone on stage. In this part of the letter the chief executive does not have the support of audited numbers or well-recognized historical events. Rather, he is describing what he is most worried about so far as the well-being of the bank is concerned. The bank analysts can test the way a chief executive approaches problems, the values that he regards most highly, and how adroitly he handles himself in an adversary relationship. These observations form an important part of a bank analyst's evaluation of management. The final part of the shareholders' letter usually ends with a brief salute to optimism, the future, or the staff.

The letter to the shareholders of the 1975 Annual Report of Continental Illinois Corporation illustrates the four principal sections (Figures 1 and 2). The most interesting section of this letter discusses the issues of disclosure and proposed changes in the structure of financial institutions and may be regarded as the polemical section. The discussion begins with the second paragraph of the second page of the letter. It presents the view of a management that weighs the need for more complete disclosure against the practical issue of moving toward increased disclosure at a moderate pace. Nevertheless, there is always the impression of a steady interest in more complete disclosure. A second polemical issue covers the proposals to change the banking and financial services environment in the United States. Here, the review is strongly one of caution, and the reasoning stresses the importance of looking at the record from a practical point of view.

The review of the language and thinking of these four paragraphs may be used as a reflection of the type of thinking of management which may be presumed to occur concerning many issues affecting the bank that are not open to public view. These four paragraphs set an image of thoughtfulness and steadiness of purpose which pervade all of the numbers in the annual report which follow this letter.

The letter to shareholders of the 1972 Annual Report of the Beverly Hills Bancorp shows a different perspective of a bank's management (Figures 3–5). No section of this letter discusses polemical issues, and a bank analyst is left with no indication of the manner in which management thinks through an issue. The bulk of the letter consists of a review of the past year's operations, statements of philosophy, and indications of future activities. The philosophy

to the shareholders:

Nineteen seventy-five was a good year for Continental Illinois Corporation in spite of widely publicized problems affecting the banking industry.

Earnings before security transactions reached a record of $118,997,000 for a 24 per cent increase over 1974. This represented a five-year compound growth rate of 12.5 per cent and a 14.9 per cent return on average shareholders' equity. Per-share earnings before security transactions were $6.84, up from $5.53 last year. During the fourth quarter, earnings before security gains were 10.8 per cent above the record level achieved in the comparable period in 1974. The 1975 performance is described in detail in the Financial Review section beginning on page 19 of this report.

These increases were especially gratifying in view of trouble spots that persisted in the economy and in banking during the year. As is true for the industry in general, we are continuing to work our way through a number of difficult financial problems that developed in the course of the deepest and most prolonged recession in almost 40 years. Loan charge-offs reached $68.9 million in 1975, compared with a $75 million charge against earnings to provide for these loan losses and add further to reserves. At year-end our loan valuation reserves totaled 1.33 per cent of outstanding loans, compared with 1.24 per cent a year ago. This important ratio continues to be the highest of the ten largest bank holding companies in the country, and our record of relatively low loan charge-offs over the years continued in spite of the higher dollar amounts involved.

The problems faced and taken in stride by Continental in 1975 were common, in varying degrees, to all major banks in the United States, which were the focus of much public attention. In fact, the repeated disproportionate emphasis on isolated instances of troubled banks or on troublesome financial areas has itself proved to be one of the industry's major concerns.

Prominent among the areas that have been highly publicized were lending relationships with the real estate industry, including the real estate investment trusts; certain losses (in which we did not share) in the foreign exchange trading markets; the unusual failures of two large banks in 1974, which have continued to serve as a source of gloomy speculation about the industry; and the relatively high level of loan charge-offs during 1975 for the industry as a whole. More recent subjects of public attention have been loans to the shipping industry, a part of which was hit by the world-wide recession while in a period of capacity expansion, and the difficulties that some of the developing nations could encounter in

servicing the increased debt loads they have assumed in recent years. Too often the public analyses of these and other problems have been marked by an unfortunate lack of badly needed perspective and balance and have failed to give due credit to the industry for the progress it has made toward solutions during this recession period.

We agree that our industry, indispensable to the nation's economy and vital to the well-being of every citizen, should be subject to careful and continuing scrutiny and should be given substantial, fair treatment in the press, in the Congress, in the regulatory agencies, and in the state legislatures. The danger is that a lack of adequate understanding of this complex industry might produce an unwarranted impairment of the public's confidence and so render a disservice to the public itself.

The financial system of this country, as well as that of the entire free world, is based on public trust that has been earned over the years by a continuing, if not completely unblemished, record of successful banking service to all segments of the public. The real need, therefore, is for a fuller understanding of how this rapidly changing system functions and a comprehension of the record, along with a better balanced, more informed examination of it. In spite of the current emphasis on problems, banking's record of achievement and strength is clear.

Even with sizeable loan charge-offs last year, bank holding companies' earnings overall continued strong and in many cases at a record level. In general, reserves not only absorbed the losses but were actually increased. Among the ten largest U.S. bank holding companies, the ratio of valuation reserves to loans outstanding at the end of the year was, in every case, larger than at the beginning of the year, even after substantial charges to absorb losses.

These few key facts suggest that the industry is handling these difficult areas successfully. We hope it will become more widely recognized that many of the attention-getting reports have tended to focus on problems that by now are far from new and are being worked on aggressively by bank managements and the regulatory authorities. Many of them are on the way to solution while, of course, many others are still ahead. It also should be recognized that in banking some losses are always inevitable. This is in the nature of the business. As long as banks continue to do their job in meeting the credit needs of the economy, they will find it necessary to take risks and will continue to suffer some small proportion of losses. The alternative is for banks to fail to fulfill their

Figure 1

obligation to help finance the economy.

Throughout the recession and the ensuing period of slow recovery that began last spring, the banking industry generally maintained an even-handed, statesmanlike posture in dealing with the serious weaknesses in the general economy as well as in confronting trying situations within the industry that arose out of some excesses during the earlier protracted expansionary period. For example, the highly publicized problems of the real estate investment trust industry were and continue to be serious. Nevertheless, there now are encouraging early signs as the gradual recovery takes place in the economy. Much of the success that has been and is yet to be achieved must be attributed to the constructive attitude of banks, which determined to maintain credit life-lines to these companies as they work through their problems, and to the positive approach of the regulatory authorities. This same kind of supportive behavior has helped out in many other areas.

In a related development, many of these issues and events have condensed in the Congress and in the press in the form of questions regarding public disclosure by the banking industry. Interest and misunderstanding both have been heightened by the publication of so-called problem bank lists compiled for the internal use of government regulators and by the illegal leaking of several confidential bank examination reports.

The banking industry has moved rapidly in recent years toward the kind of disclosure that would seem to be appropriate to the public interest without creating problems in necessarily confidential relationships. Popularly perceived needs for information must be weighed carefully against actual needs and the consideration that the public interest also is well served by maintaining a correct degree of confidentiality within the banking system. The judicious development of sound policies and procedures to deal with this issue will and should take time. It especially will require an intimate understanding based on a thorough review of the historic role and performance of banks and on a comprehensive knowledge of the workings of the industry. This process appears to be well under way by an inter-agency committee of federal regulators over recent months.

Forming still another aspect of the public attention to the banking industry is a series of proposals, now moving through Congress, for major restructuring of the financial industry, particularly banks and various types of thrift institutions. We believe many facets of these proposals are constructive; they also currently include a number of controversial ideas. We are concerned about the possible development of an overly hasty climate of opinion that could lead to major changes being made in a crisis mood under the pressure of a desire to do something immediately, rather than in the thoughtful atmosphere that is called for by current circumstances.

In this context, we are disturbed by the many proposals for major restructuring of the federal bank regulatory agencies. A constructive attitude toward examining the need for change is always in order. In our opinion, however, these agencies have proved their flexibility by making changes in their approaches and procedures in order to be responsive to the needs of the times as they have emerged. Their record on the whole has been good. While some evolutionary modifications in these agencies may be desirable, and indeed are already in progress, the case for radical change is not convincing and in any event needs considerably more sober analysis.

We do not intend to leave an impression that the problems of the banking system are over. No doubt further sizeable charge-offs against loans will be made in 1976, and it is possible that earnings could be depressed somewhat from recent levels by a decline from last year's very favorable spreads between the return on assets and the cost of funds. In our own case, we enter 1976 recognizing that during the year we will be making quarter-to-quarter comparisons with record 1975 earnings.

While there are challenges ahead of us, we nevertheless have reason to be encouraged. With the economic recovery well under way and the accomplishments that the industry in general and our Corporation and its excellent staff in particular have made, we look to the future with confidence.

Chairman of the Board   President

February 6, 1976

Figure 2

22

**To Our
Shareholders:**

Beyond the 54% increase in operating income achieved in 1972, the
significance of the year for Beverly Hills Bancorp is continued growth
consistent with the plan established in 1968.

Completion of the first five year segment of that plan has, we believe,
proved the validity of the concept which is the basis for the Company's
present one bank holding company structure. Quoting our 1968 Annual
Report, "Transformation...to a one bank holding company will provide
maximum flexibility in the establishment...of new financial services,
outside the traditional limitations of banking. Management looks forward
to growth as a financial congeneric corporation, with an ultimate range
of activities that may span the full spectrum of the financial services
industry."

At 1972 year end, our position in relation to that of 1968 was as follows:

   Operating income up from $261,767 to $1,998,622

   Per share operating income up from $.28 to $1.55 after 3 for 2 stock
   splits and issuance of 300,000 additional shares.

   Direct assets under management up from $68 million to
   $164 million.

   Capital base up from $4 million to $12.8 million.

   Operations expanded from Western Los Angeles to National and
   International Markets.

   Products and services increased from six in the field of banking to
   over 40 major products covering the gamut of financial services to
   individuals and businesses.

The operating strategy of Bancorp is to innovate and to evolve new
service businesses rather than acquire; to look for opportunity areas not
already covered by the banking industry that could be developed for
our own customers and for other banks and institutions, and to obtain
the best talent available to implement these programs.

Management's primary objective is to continue to insure the quality of
earnings while at the same time establishing a pattern of persistency in
the non-banking operations which will help to stabilize the cyclical
pattern of our business. Until the contribution of earnings from
Western Diversified Equities is balanced by additional earnings from our
newer financial operations, earnings will be weighted toward the third
and fourth quarters reflecting the historical year-end demand for real
estate investments. We are, however, pleased with the quality of earnings
from Western Diversified Equities. Unlike many companies in the real
estate industry, Western Diversified Equities has established a pattern of
operation, which in 1972 resulted in the bulk of its profits being in cash.

Figure 3

and plans appear commendable, but with the exception of one paragraph,
there is no indication of the management's reasoning processes, nor is there
any indication of the limits of management's scope or control of events.

The exception is the third paragraph from the end of the letter, an
important paragraph. This paragraph says that leasing activities were discontinued and that the reason for the difficulties with leasing activities
stemmed from the capital intensive nature of leasing and the error of competing with giants. The paragraph should have disturbed bank analysts. Leasing is
not a capital intensive business, as is the steel or mining business. Rather, it is
another form of financial intermediation, and it is a leveraged business that is

Throughout Bancorp, we continue to demand innovation and development of strategies that will support our continued future growth.

At Beverly Hills National Bank, we are seeking to continue to develop
a large deposit base and to expand programs for sound, high yielding
loans such as accounts receivable financing, term loans and various
types of loan programs for corporate executives, entertainers, athletes
and professional men. We believe that the Bank can continue its
projected growth without incurring the expense of establishing new
branches.

A major undertaking in 1973 by Western Diversified Equities, the realty
services subsidiary of Beverly Hills Bancorp, will be a 707-unit apartment
complex on 10 acres in Pasadena. This project is part of the 158 acre
Pasadena Downtown Redevelopment Project which is designed to
revitalize the downtown area through a coordinated program of new
development as well as rehabilitation of a number of existing buildings.

The project will offer a wide range of apartments from studios to three
bedroom with den layouts. A major portion of the site will be devoted to
open landscaped areas and recreational facilities including tennis courts,
swimming pools and children's play areas. Total value of the apartment
project is estimated to be in excess of $15 million.

Western Diversified Equities will continue to develop quality real estate
investments for placement with sophisticated private and institutional
investors while maintaining a sensitivity to changes in demand for
different types of projects in various geographic locations.

The objective of Fund of the West remains the generation of a steady
volume of management consulting contracts and fees with emerging
growth companies.

Overseas Diversified Equities represents an opportunity for Beverly Hills
Bancorp in the international market. We believe that throughout the
world there are voids which represent banking opportunities for an
organization with our philosophy. The present base for ODE is Israel
and in 1973 activities there will be accelerated while other areas are
studied for future penetration. ODE is an international reflection of all
activities of the Company.

Beverly Hills Bancorp's successful entry into the thrift & loan industry
highlights our ability to recognize an emerging trend and to blend that
need with in-house expertise. Golden State Thrift & Loan ended the year
in the black with approximately $6 million in deposits and $7 million in
loans outstanding. Our 1973 objectives are two additional offices in other
parts of California and deposits in excess of $18 million. At March 1,
1973, deposits exceeded $8 million.

Figure 4

comparatively sparse in its use of capital. Perhaps the meaning was that leasing
takes more capital than the fee-based services of Beverly Hills Bancorp's other
subsidiaries. At best, calling leasing a capital intensive business is an unclear
statement. But the inability to carry on leasing operations because of
entrenched giants provides even more problems of understanding. Leasing is
one of the more unconcentrated industries in the United States, with literally
hundreds of lessors in all parts of the country. Moreover, the fourth paragraph of the shareholders' letter states that the strategy of the bank is to innovate, and this implies the ability to compete with larger firms in an industry by
specializing its services.

All the stated explanations of the inability of Beverly Hills Bancorp to

Golden State Thrift & Loan is one of the activities of our subsidiary, Funding Services, Inc. Its others include the sale of insurance and the brokerage of loan packages generated by Beverly Hills National Bank to smaller banks throughout the west and mid-west.

Our newest financial service is Dimensional Planning Group. This subsidiary provides a comprehensive personal financial planning service for high net worth individuals and for the key executives of major corporations across the country. Although we have entered an area in which others are already active, we feel that by bringing a measure of objectivity and a high degree of sophistication to our planning approach, we can capture a significant share of a market which is just beginning to emerge.

In 1972 we discontinued operations of Spectrum Leasing. With Spectrum, we entered a highly competitive capital intensive industry. This experience has demonstrated the validity of our over-all program of being in the vanguard of new services rather than attempting to compete on unequal terms with many entrenched giants.

As we critique the past, the direction for the second five year plan clearly emerges. Build people, carefully control growth and emphasize long term stability. We will continue to be pragmatic and innovative in the operation and development of the financial services we offer to individuals, corporations and institutions.

On behalf of the Board of Directors and officers of the Company, we wish to express our appreciation to all of those employees and stockholders whose continued support, interest and hard work has made it possible for Beverly Hills Bancorp to achieve prominence as a fully integrated financial services company.

Sincerely yours,

David H. Rowen

David H. Rowen
Chairman

John H. Rauch

John H. Rauch
President
March 20, 1973

Figure 5

compete in leasing are not satisfactory. The point is important, because the ability of any organization to handle its difficulties is one of the key tests of management. Although the paragraph reads smoothly at first glance, it does not appear to describe clearly the facts of the business world, and there are problems with the reasoning process, since it challenges rather than affirms the thinking of other sections of the shareholders' letter. Because of liquidity difficulties, Beverly Hills Bancorp, for all practical purposes, ceased operations in the spring of 1974.

Discussion of the Year's Activities

Many annual reports include a section that describes a bank's activities throughout the year and serves as a feature article about the bank. Often the discussion is based on a theme, such as the international business of the bank, a commitment to consumers, or planning.

This section of the annual report usually includes many photographs, shows few figures, and is often written by a public relations staff rather than bankers. It shows the image that the bank wishes to project to the public. A review of the annual reports of several years shows whether the bank projects a consistent image. This information is useful to compare with the financial statements to see if the bank possesses a clear perception of its own position or if it is engaging in hopes or fantasies.

The section is also useful because it usually includes considerable descriptive information about the new and ongoing programs of the bank. The new programs are often carried forward by ad hoc committees that include persons from many different parts of the bank. They sometimes pinpoint the areas of the bank which the chief executive officer would like to change. Sometimes the section gives reasons to explain why the programs were begun. These explanations may be regarded has having been carefully proofed by the chief executive officer and reflect his thinking.

Core Financial Statements

These financial statements will be reviewed in the following chapter.

Management's Review of Financial Operations

This section attempts to interrelate all of the financial information available in the annual report and use this information to explain the financial results shown in the core financial statements. This section usually appears after the accountant's opinion and is unaudited. However, in some recent annual reports, this review precedes the core financial statements, emphasizing the importance of reviewing this section and the core financial statements as a whole.

In recent years many banks have expanded the management's review of financial operations from a one-page summary to a more thorough analysis of the year's developments. The section usually reviews the trend in earnings over recent years, looks at the components of earnings, reviews loan demand and loan losses and the securities portfolio, as well as other parts of the financial statements. It most likely will emerge as one of the most useful parts of the annual report within a few years.

Supplementary Financial Information

This section usually includes a wide range of historical financial information and is probably the most convenient source of most financial information concerning the bank. The section usually shows income statements and balance sheets for the previous five years and shows restatements of data. The section often includes averages for each item in the balance sheet and shows average yields on assets and rates on liabilities. The section also often gives detailed information concerning the balance sheet, the maturity of investment securities, and details of loan losses, as well as a review of the bank's stock price. Many sections also show ratios of several of these series.

Directory of Key Personnel and Location of Offices

This section shows the names and titles of the personnel that the bank believes should be recognized by the public. (In some annual reports, these names appear on one of the initial pages.) There are often the addresses of branches. The section often shows an indication of the presence of the bank in various financial fields.

This part of the annual report also shows the names and often the business affiliation of the bank's board of directors, the group that determines how the bank will be managed. A careful review of the responsibilities and background of these persons serves as one of the few visible indications of the philosophy of the management that runs the organization.

Most outside directors of banks know little or nothing about the banking business, and most bank managements do not provide directors with information in a way that would enable them to easily become informed about operations. Moreover, it is not unknown for banks to make their financial statements available to directors only during directors' meetings. These limitations to the effectiveness of directors can be lessened or overcome if four simple tests are successfully met.

The first test is whether the directors include a large proportion of chief executive officers, who are charged with general management responsibilities of other organizations. The temperment, attitude, and an ability to bear final responsibility sets chief executives apart from all other officers of an organization, no matter how large the title or salary may be for persons of lesser rank. Banks include lower-level corporate officers of major corporations on their board, and these associations help business relations. Nevertheless, the toughest, most astute board members of a bank are chairmen or chief executive officers of other organizations.

A second test of the effectiveness of a board is whether it includes at least one person who is outside the mainstream of the business of the bank. Often these persons include a physician or an educator. Lawyers do not qualify for this group, since banks are many lawyers' best clients. A physician or educator may serve on a board and function as a representative of values other than commercial success. They may represent the human limits of a program, taking a personal or social conscience as the measure of success rather than earnings alone. This view has importance, since banks provide a major social service and may be regarded as being part of a socially regulated industry.

A third test of the effectiveness of a board is whether it is predominantly an outside board. Inside boards can provide great support to the programs of management simply by their presence. These boards can squelch questioning from outside board members, who may feel overwhelmed by arrays of statistics and the prepared positions of the inside board members. The presence of frequent, searching questions is in the long-term interests of a bank.

A fourth test is whether the board includes many persons who may have a clear conflict of interest. These persons may represent companies they can promote for acquisition by the bank. They may use their board membership to promote their interests, rather than the best interests of the bank. Moreover, their board membership gives them potential access to information that could work against the best interests of the bank's shareholders. The presence of persons who represent a potential acquisition reflects a management that might compromise too easily or too quickly.

A comparison of the board of directors of Franklin New York Corporation and Security Pacific Corporation provides an interesting comparison of how the philosophies of banks is reflected in boards.

The 1973 Annual Report of Franklin New York Corporation and Franklin National Bank showed twenty members of both boards of directors (Figure 6). Ten of these persons were Franklin officers, giving insiders a strong position of one-half of the seats. Of the remaining ten directors, only one was a chief executive officer of a company that was not involved in either acquiring or being acquired by Franklin. Thus only one of the nineteen directors could be regarded as viewing the management of Franklin from the position of an independent chief executive officer. The presumption may be made that Franklin's management was not often challenged by its board. In the spring of 1974 Franklin was overwhelmed with difficulties and was sold to the European-American Bank and Trust Company.

The 1975 Annual Report of Security Pacific Corporation and Security Pacific National Bank showed twenty-four members of both boards of directors (Figure 7). Four of these persons were or had been operating officers of Security Pacific (two were retired) giving insiders a relatively weak position and outside board members a relatively strong position. Of the remaining eighteen directors, twelve or two-thirds showed titles of chairman, chief executive officer, or president of a commercial organization. Thus this bank has a strong showing of men who may be presumed to have the opinions and attitudes of a chief executive. Security Pacific also showed one physician as a director.

THE QUARTERLY REPORT

In recent years the quarterly report of many major banks has grown in size and detail. In addition, many medium-sized banks now provide comments concerning quarterly operations.

The larger banks have patterned their quarterly reports after their annual reports. Some of the quarterly reports have expanded considerably and now show a president's letter, news highlights, financial statements, a feature story, management discussion, and a statistical supplement. The quarterly report is available from the secretary of the bank.

FORM 10-K

Form 10-K (usually referred to as the 10-K report) is one of the most useful documents for bank analysts (Figure 8). This report is filed with the Securities

FRANKLIN NEW YORK CORPORATION
FRANKLIN NATIONAL BANK

Board of Directors

* Raymond T. Andersen
Senior Vice-Chairman

Joseph A. Beisler
Vice-President
Cyrus J. Lawrence, inc.

△ Carlo Bordoni
Managing Director
Banca Unione

Howard D. Crosse
Vice-Chairman

* Harold V. Gleason
Chairman of the Board
and Chief Executive Officer

William J. Hogan
Director, Executive Vice-President
and Chief Financial Officer
The Interpublic Group of Companies, Inc.

Sol Kittay
Chairman of the Board
NCC Industries, Inc.

Charles H. Kraft
Vice-President and Treasurer
The Anaconda Company

William B. Lewis, Jr.
Senior Executive Vice-President

* Paul Luftig
President and Chief Administrative Officer

* Michael J. Merkin
Vice-Chairman

* Norman B. Schreiber (Elected in 1974)
Chairman. Executive Committee
Franklin New York Corporation

Robert N. Sears
Senior Vice-President
Phillips Petroleum Company

△ Peter R. Shaddick
Executive Vice-Chairman

△ Michele Sindona
Chairman
Banca Privata Finanziaria

James C. Slaughter
Chairman and Chief Executive Officer
Talcott National Corporation

† James G. Smith
Vice-Chairman

John J. Tuohy
Chairman of the Board
and Chief Executive Officer
Long Island Lighting Company

Frank G. Wangeman
Executive Vice-President and General Manager
Waldorf-Astoria Corporation and
Senior Vice-President
Hilton Hotels Corporation

Harold A. Webster
Chairman Emeritus
T. Frederick Jackson, Inc.

△ On Board of Franklin New York Corporation only.
† On Board of Franklin National Bank only.
* Member of the Executive Committee of the
Board of the Franklin New York Corporation.

Senior Officers

Harold V. Gleason
Chairman of the Board and Chief Executive Officer

Norman B. Schreiber (Elected in 1974)
Chairman, Executive Committee
Franklin New York Corporation

Paul Luftig
President and Chief Administrative Officer

Peter R. Shaddick
Executive Vice-Chairman

Raymond T. Andersen
Senior Vice-Chairman

Howard D. Crosse
Vice-Chairman

Michael J. Merkin
Vice-Chairman

James G. Smith
Vice-Chairman

William B. Lewis, Jr.
Senior Executive Vice-President

Harry P. Barrand, Jr.
Executive Vice-President

William G. Barry
Executive Vice-President

George H. Becht
Executive Vice-President and Secretary
Franklin New York Corporation

John Sadlik
Executive Vice-President and Cashier

Martin A. Simon
Executive Vice-President

Environment

For the fourth consecutive year, the pages of this report have been
printed on recycled paper because of our continuing concern
for environmental problems.

Figure 6

29

**Directors of
Security Pacific Corporation and
Security Pacific National Bank**

Robert Anderson	*President and Chief Executive Officer, Rockwell International Corporation (multi-industry company)*
Richard C. Bergen	*Partner, O'Melveny & Myers (law firm)*
J. G. Boswell II	*President, J. G. Boswell Co. (agribusiness)*
Thornton F. Bradshaw	*President, Atlantic Richfield Company (integrated oil company)*
Sidney F. Brody	*President, Brody Management Company (real estate development and property management)*
Walter W. Candy, Jr.	*Investments*
*Peter Colefax	*Consultant and Director, Kerr-McGee Corporation (oil, gas, uranium and chemical producer)*
Edwin H. Corbin	*Executive Vice President of the Bank, Retired*
Charles E. Ducommun	*Chairman of the Board, Ducommun Incorporated (multi-industry fabricator and distributor)*
Richard J. Flamson III	*President of SPC and Vice Chairman of the Board of the Bank*
Carl E. Hartnack	*Vice Chairman of the Board of SPC and President and Chief Operating Officer of the Bank*
Robert C. Jackson	*Chairman, Teledyne Ryan Aeronautical (aerospace)*
Fred C. Jennings	*Investments and Property Development*
William M. Keck, Jr.	*Director, The Superior Oil Company*
A. Carl Kotchian	*President, Lockheed Aircraft Corporation (aerospace)*
Frederick G. Larkin, Jr.	*Chairman of the Board and Chief Executive Officer of SPC and the Bank*
Oscar T. Lawler	*Chairman of the Executive Committee of the Bank*
Glen McDaniel	*Chairman of the Executive Committee, Litton Industries, Inc. (multi-industry manufacturer)*
*Carl K. Schieck	*Executive Vice President of the Bank, Retired*
H. Russell Smith	*Chairman of the Board, Avery Products Corporation (diversified office products company)*
Dwight L. Stuart	*President, Carnation Company (food and related products processor)*
*Milton M. Teague	*Chairman of the Board, Limoneira Company (citrus and avocado industry)*
Richard R. Von Hagen	*President, Lloyd Corporation, Ltd. (oil production and property development)*
John Cree Wilson, Jr., M.D.	*President, The Hospital of the Good Samaritan*

*Advisory Director of
Security Pacific National Bank*

Director Changes

We were pleased to have attracted H. Russell Smith to our board of directors in 1975. He brings additional strength to the board both in terms of his successful business experience and his long time participation in community affairs.

1975 also brought about the loss of some directors who will be sorely missed. We were saddened by the untimely death on November 17 of R. Stanley Dollar who had been a director since 1968. Walter B. Gerken resigned from the board and Franklin Stockbridge, vice chairman, and member of the office of the chairman, retired after serving the Bank and the Corporation since 1947.

In addition, the following eight advisory directors of Security Pacific Bank retired in accordance with the Bank's retirement policy: Robert J. Cannon, Leland A. Doan, Philip S. Fogg, George D. Hart, Clifford V. Heimbucher, Robert A. Lurie, John R. Niven and Robert N. Pomeroy.

Figure 7

and Exchange Commission and is available to the public within 90 days following each year-end or fiscal year-end for a few banks which report on that basis. The report is usually available free of charge from the bank. A copy is always available at $0.10 per page from the Securities and Exchange Commission, Public Reference, 500 North Capital Street, N.W., Washington, D.C. 20549, telephone 202-523-5506.

A principal attraction of the 10-K report is its clear language. virtually all 10-K reports are written in simple declarative English, with an absence of adjectives and adverbs. The reports make no effort to be persuasive or interesting, and the bank analyst can usually find essential information presented in a straightforward manner. Nevertheless, the 10-K reports give lit-

SECURITIES AND EXCHANGE COMMISSION
Washington, D. C. 20549

FORM 10-K

ANNUAL REPORT PURSUANT TO SECTION 13 OR 15(d) OF THE SECURITIES EXCHANGE ACT OF 1934

For the fiscal year ended December 31, 1976
Commission file number 1-6052

FIRST CHICAGO CORPORATION
(Exact name of registrant as specified in its charter)

DELAWARE	**36-2669970**
(State or other jurisdiction of incorporation or organization)	(I.R.S. Employer Identification No.)

One First National Plaza Chicago, Illinois	**60670**
(Address of principal executive offices)	(Zip Code)

(Registrant's telephone number, including area code) **312-732-4000**

Securities registered pursuant to Section 12(b) of the Act:

Title of each class	Name of each exchange on which registered
Common Stock, $5.00 par value	New York Stock Exchange
	Midwest Stock Exchange
	Pacific Stock Exchange
6¼ % Notes due 7-15-78	New York Stock Exchange
6¾ % Notes due 11-1-80	New York Stock Exchange
7¾ % Notes due 10-15-86	New York Stock Exchange

Securities registered pursuant to Section 12(g) of the Act:

None

Indicate the number of shares outstanding of each of the issuer's classes of common stock, as of the close of the period covered by this Report (applicable only to corporate issuers) 39,618,923

Indicate by check mark whether the registrant (1) has filed all reports required to be filed by Section 13 or 15(d) of the Securities Exchange Act of 1934 during the preceding 12 months (or for such shorter period that the registrant was required to file such reports), and (2) has been subject to such filing requirements for the past 90 days. Yes___X___. No_____.

Figure 8

tle indication of the qualitative aspects of a bank management, which can be perceived from the language and structure of the less regimented annual report.

Item 1—Business

This item reviews the ownership, organization, and basic financial information of the bank. Most of this information duplicates information available in greater detail from several other sources. Nevertheless, this section provides a particularly succint review of this essential information.

This item also shows information for several areas of banking that may not be available elsewhere. For example, among major banks the 10-K often provides information concerning difficulties of particular classes of loans and information concerning difficulties in certain categories of securities. The amount of detail shown in a 10-K report reflects how the Securities and Exchange Commission interprets its responsibilities to shareholders.

Item 2—Summary of Operations

This section shows the basic financial information of a bank. This information is often shown elsewhere, particularly in the annual report. But, again, this section of the 10-K report provides a concise summary of the essential information.

Item 3—Properties

This section shows the location of its principal properties and whether the properties are owned or leased. Any significant mortgage on a property or other encumbrance is noted.

Item 4—Parents and Subsidiaries

This section identifies the principal owner of the bank. It also provides a review of significant subsidiaries, and if the subsidiaries are significant, it shows the ownership position of the parent.

This section is important to a bank analyst because it identifies important activities of the bank that are usually available from no other source. Moreover, many of the subsidiaries involve activities outside the mainstream of commercial banking and represent liabilities or benefits that might otherwise be overlooked.

Item 5—Pending Legal Proceedings

Banks are almost as closely involved in the legal profession as they are with financial markets. The rights, responsibilities, obligations, and penalties of countless numbers of individual transactions, as well as the much-broader new legal issues of public welfare and responsibility have made banks a lawyer's dream come true. Moreover, banks, along with insurance companies, are represented to the public as wealthy institutions. The rise of class-action suits has acted to increase the willingness of attorneys to accept cases that individually are minor in importance financially, but collectively represent cases with major sums at stake.

A review of the major pending legal proceedings of most major banks shows suits that, if plantiffs' full claims were realized, would amount to substantial funds. However, suits against banks seldom involve major damages. Banks employ considerable legal talent, are major clients of outside counsel, and are skilled at winning cases.

Item 6—Increases and Decreases in Outstanding Securities

This section shows any changes in shares or debenture securities. It shows a detailed analysis of the stock transactions from the bank's point of view, and if there are convertible securities, shows the number of shares converted, along with the value of that conversion.

Sales of commercial paper are also shown in this section. The section also shows whether the parent corporation has issued unregistered commercial paper, which it is legally entitled to do under certain conditions. Most sales of these types of securities are made by a few large bank holding companies.

Item 7—Approximate Number of Equity Security Holders

This section shows the number of holders of outstanding stock and convertible debentures.

Item 8—Executive Officers

The names, titles, and age of senior executives are shown in this section. Often brief background information is also shown. In some cases, there is a note indicating whether there are family relationships among the officers.

Item 9—Indemnification of Directors and Officers

Bankers act in a public and private capacity and transact business that exposes them to the possibility of a wide range of misunderstandings on the part of customers. To cover this risk, banks purchase liability insurance against possible losses from suits against officers who act in good faith. This section reviews the legal basis of indemnification and in some cases the extent of coverage.

Item 10—Financial Statements and Exhibits

The financial statements of the 10-K report ordinarily begin with the report of the independent public accountants. (In contrast, most annual reports of banks show the accountants' opinion at the end of the financial statements). The report of the accountants indicates whether the attached financial statements are reported consistently with those of previous years, whether they are presented "in conformity with generally accepted accounting principles," and whether they fairly show the results of operations. In fact, only in difficult circumstances are there exceptions to the accountants' opinion. Most of the original differences between a bank and the independent accountants have been reconciled prior to the issuance of the 10-K report.

The extent and detail of the tables and notes of the section covering financial statements and exhibits depend on the size and complexity of the bank. The large companies usually show 10 statements, including statements of condition and income for the corporation and parent company, statements of condition for the bank and nonbank subsidiaries, as well as other statements. Following the financial statements are notes explaining and interpreting the statements. The notes are often a valuable source of further financial information. Medium-sized and small banks, of course, show less detail because their operations are less complex. Rules of the Securities and Exchange Commission require certain disclosures and then state that there must be any other information which would be necessary to keep the statements from being misleading.

Supplemental schedules and exhibits often complete this section. Some of these schedules provide further detail to the notes appearing earlier in the financial statements section. Some banks show schedules that include loans to directors and officers and details of the dividends received from affiliates which may be helpful in analyzing the performance of nonbanking subsidiaries, as well as other information. Exhibits may include, for example, changes in contracts with employees through profit-sharing plans. Some banks omit the schedules with a comment that the information is not applicable or is shown elsewhere.

Item 11—Principal Security Holders and Security Holdings of Management

Item 12—Directors of Registrant

Item 13—Remuneration of Directors and Officers

Item 14—Options Granted to Management to Purchase Securities

Item 15—Interest of Management and Others in Certain Transactions

The items 11 through 15 are usually deleted in the 10-K report and are shown in the proxy statement.

FORM 10-Q

Form 10-Q (usually referred to as the 10-Q report) is filed with the Securities and Exchange Commission and is available to the public 45 days after the end of each of the initial three quarters of a year (Figure 9). It is a briefer version of the 10-K report. The report is usually available free from the bank. Copies are available at $0.10 per page from the Securities and Exchange Commission,

Public Reference, 500 North Capitol Street, N.W., Washington, D.C. 20549, telephone 202-523-5506.

The 10-Q report consists of consolidated statements of condition, earnings, changes in financial position, and notes to these financial statements. It also provides a management's discussion and analysis of earnings, various other financial information, and a signature of the bank's principal financial officer.

The 10-Q report is useful mainly to review developments of small-sized banks that may issue only brief quarterly reports to shareholders. Often these reports show only a balance sheet and exclude an earnings statement and

SECURITIES AND EXCHANGE COMMISSION

Washington, D.C. 20549

F O R M   1 0 - Q

Quarterly Report Under Section 13 or 15(d)
of the Securities Exchange Act of 1934

For Quarter Ended March 31, 1976 Commission file number...1-6052.......

FIRST CHICAGO CORPORATION
(Exact name of registrant as specified in its charter)

DELAWARE   36-2669970
(State or other jurisdiction of   (I.R.S. Employer
incorporation or organization)   Identification No.)

ONE FIRST NATIONAL PLAZA
CHICAGO, ILLINOIS   60670
(Address of principal executive offices)   (Zip Code)

Registrant's telephone number, including area code. 312-732-4000.........

NO CHANGE
Former name, former address and former fiscal year, if changed since last report.

Indicate by check mark whether the registrant (1) has filed all reports required to be filed by Section 13 or 15(d) of the Securities Exchange Act of 1934 during the preceding 12 months (or for such shorter period that the registrant was required to file such reports), and (2) has been subject to such filing requirements for the past 90 days.

Yes   X   No_____

Figure 9

analysis of earnings. In these cases, the 10-Q report is the only regular public source of more complete information.

CONSOLIDATED REPORT OF INCOME

The Consolidated Report of Income (often referred to as the "I and D" report, an abbreviation of the report's earlier title of Income and Dividend Report) is a report of national banks that is filed quarterly with the U.S. Administrator of National Banks, under the Office of the Comptroller of the Currency (Figures 10–14). (The two exceptions are state-chartered banks that are members of the Federal Reserve System and file with them, and state-chartered banks that are not members of the Federal Reserve System and file with the Federal Deposit Insurance Corporation.) This report shows information for the bank only. Virtually all banks do not disclose the earnings of their bank subsidiaries in either their quarterly or annual reports to shareholders. Since banks comprise the bulk of earnings of bank holding companies, this report provides an important part of information that is available from no other source. The report is usually available at no charge from the bank or at $0.10 per page, plus a small service fee from the Comptroller of the Currency, Public Disclosure Office, 490 L'Enfant Plaza, Washington, D.C. 20219, telephone 202-447-1825. It is usually available to the public about one month following the end of a quarter.

The report is divided into six sections and shows an income statement, changes in equity (which includes a line for cash dividends declared on common stock), changes in the reserve for possible loan losses, sources of both other operating income and expenses and a memoranda showing the provision for domestic and foreign income taxes and a listing of all mergers, consolidations, and purchases during the reporting period.

The Consolidated Report of Income was designed to enable the Comptroller to evaluate the earnings of all national banks on a common basis and to show whether their dividends have been excessive. The comparison of dividends and earnings is a central issue to regulators, since it indicates whether the bank's management is interested in long-term viability or possibly is interested in paying excessive dividends. The comparison also bears on the ability of the bank to generate capital internally.

CONSOLIDATED REPORT OF CONDITION

The Consolidated Report of Condition (often referred to as the "call report") is a quarter-end report of national banks that is filed with the Administrator of Banks of the U.S. Comptroller of the Currency. There are three versions of this report. All of the reports show information concerning the bank only.

Each of these reports is usually available free of charge from the bank. Copies are available at $0.10 per page, plus a small service fee from the Comptroller of the Currency, Public Disclosure Office, 490 L'Enfant Plaza, Washington, D.C. 20219, telephone 202-447-1825. The three regular call

Comptroller of the Currency
Administrator of National Banks

CONSOLIDATED REPORT OF INCOME
(Including Domestic and Foreign Subsidiaries)

> For Comptroller of the Currency Use Only

CHARTER NUMBER: ___8___

NAME OF BANK: ___The First National Bank of Chicago___

CITY: ___Chicago___

STATE: ___Illinois___   ZIP CODE: ___60670___

CALL: ___DECEMBER 31 1976___
         Month   Day Year

Thousands of dollars

THOUSANDS	Hnds	Cts

Total assets as of report date: (Including domestic and foreign subsidiaries) (Thousands of dollars) | 18,678,010 | xxx | xx |

Name, title and phone number of person to whom inquiries may be directed:

Thomas Rock

Vice President

(312) 732 - 4094

I, ___Thomas Rock___
        Name

___Vice President___
        Title

of the above-named bank do hereby declare that this Report of Income is true and correct to the best of my knowledge and belief.

Thomas Rock
Signature

1/31/77
Date

SECTION A—SOURCES AND DISPOSITION OF INCOME (Indicate losses in parentheses)

	Current Quarter Thousands of dollars			Year To Date Thousands of dollars			
	THOUSANDS	Hnds.	Cts.	THOUSANDS	Hnds.	Cts.	
1. Operating income:							
a. Interest and fees on loans	210,879	XXX	XX	853,878	XXX	XX	1a
b. Interest on balances with banks	32,670	XXX	XX	122,530	XXX	XX	b
c. Income on Federal funds sold and securities purchased under agreements to resell in domestic offices	4,761	XXX	XX	21,349	XXX	XX	c
d. Interest on U.S. Treasury securities	23,415	XXX	XX	97,345	XXX	XX	d
e. Interest on obligations of other U.S. Government agencies and corporations	3,672	XXX	XX	8,831	XXX	XX	e
f. Interest on obligations of States and political subdivisions of the U.S.	10,382	XXX	XX	43,501	XXX	XX	f
g. Interest on other bonds, notes, and debentures	2,462	XXX	XX	9,360	XXX	XX	g
h. Dividends on stock	490	XXX	XX	1,845	XXX	XX	h
i. Income from direct lease financing	1,578	XXX	XX	3,879	XXX	XX	i
j. Income from fiduciary activities	8,027	XXX	XX	30,288	XXX	XX	j
k. Service charges on deposit accounts in domestic offices	1,833	XXX	XX	7,131	XXX	XX	k
l. Other service charges, commissions, and fees	11,277	XXX	XX	41,143	XXX	XX	l
m. Other income (Section D, Item 4)	13,323	XXX	XX	40,381	XXX	XX	m
n. Total operating income (sum of Items 1a thru 1m)	324,769	XXX	XX	1,281,461	XXX	XX	n
2. Operating expenses:							
a. Salaries and employee benefits	31,217	XXX	XX	122,074	XXX	XX	2a
b. Interest on time certificates of deposit of $100,000 or more issued by domestic offices	50,556	XXX	XX	230,861	XXX	XX	b
c. Interest on deposits in foreign offices	80,682	XXX	XX	301,648	XXX	XX	c
d. Interest on other deposits	27,417	XXX	XX	107,385	XXX	XX	d
e. Expense of Federal funds purchased and securities sold under agreement to repurchase in domestic offices	38,695	XXX	XX	143,947	XXX	XX	e
f. Interest on borrowed money	3,860	XXX	XX	9,099	XXX	XX	f
g. Interest on subordinated notes and debentures	NONE	XXX	XX	NONE	XXX	XX	g
h. 1. Occupancy expense of bank premises, Gross	8,621	XXX	XX	34,148	XXX	XX	h1
2. Less: Rental income	2,618	XXX	XX	10,169	XXX	XX	h2
3. Occupancy expense of bank premises, Net	6,003	XXX	XX	23,979	XXX	XX	h3
i. Furniture and equipment expense	4,034	XXX	XX	15,155	XXX	XX	i
j. Provision for possible loan losses (or actual net loan losses) (Section C, Item 4)	37,666	XXX	XX	118,932	XXX	XX	j
k. Other expenses (Section E, Item 3)	19,589	XXX	XX	75,972	XXX	XX	k
l. Total operating expenses (sum of Items 2a thru 2k)	299,719	XXX	XX	1,149,052	XXX	XX	l
3. Income before income taxes and securities gains or losses (Item 1n minus 2l)	25,050	XXX	XX	132,409	XXX	XX	3
4. Applicable income taxes (domestic and foreign)(tax credits in paren.)	7,602	XXX	XX	45,151	XXX	XX	4
5. Income before securities gains or losses (Item 3 minus 4)	17,449	XXX	XX	87,258	XXX	XX	5
6. a. Securities gains (losses), Gross	17,580	XXX	XX	25,100	XXX	XX	6a
b. Applicable income taxes (domestic and foreign)(tax credits in paren.)	8,649	XXX	XX	12,388	XXX	XX	b
c. Securities gains (losses), Net	8,931	XXX	XX	12,712	XXX	XX	c
7. Net income (Item 5 plus or minus 6c)	26,379	XXX	XX	99,970	XXX	XX	7
OR							
7. Income before extraordinary items		XXX	XX		XXX	XX	7
8. Extraordinary items, Net of tax effect (Section F, Item 2c)		XXX	XX		XXX	XX	8
9. Net income (Item 7 plus or minus 8)		XXX	XX		XXX	XX	9

NAME OF BANK: The First National Bank of Chicago   CHARTER NUMBER: ___

All Figures in Sections B through F are to be Year to Date

SECTION B—CHANGES IN EQUITY CAPITAL

(Indicate decreases and losses in parentheses)	A. Preferred stock (Par value)	B. Common stock (Par value)	C. Surplus	D. Undivided profits and capital reserves	E. Total equity capital
					Thousands of dollars
1. Balance beginning of period	NONE xxx xx	200858 xxx xx	425947 xxx xx	173427 xxx xx	800232 xxx xx
2. Net income (loss)				99970 xxx xx	99970 xxx xx
3. Sale, conversion, acquisition or retirement of capital ...	NONE xxx xx	NONE xxx xx	NONE xxx xx	NONE xxx xx	NONE xxx xx
4. Changes incident to mergers and absorptions	NONE xxx xx	NONE xxx xx	NONE xxx xx	NONE xxx xx	NONE xxx xx
5. Cash dividends declared on common stock				(34594) xxx xx	(34594) xxx xx
6. Cash dividends declared on preferred stock				(NONE) xxx xx	(NONE) xxx xx
7. Stock dividends issued	NONE xxx xx	NONE xxx xx	NONE xxx xx	NONE xxx xx	NONE xxx xx
8. Other increases (decreases) (itemize):	NONE xxx xx	NONE xxx xx	NONE xxx xx	NONE xxx xx	NONE xxx xx
....					
9. Balance end of period	NONE xxx xx	200858 xxx xx	425947 xxx xx	238803 xxx xx	865608 xxx xx

SECTION C—RESERVE FOR POSSIBLE LOAN LOSSES (Valuation Reserve)

Thousands of dollars

	THOUSANDS	Hnds	Cts	
1. Balance beginning of period	110,184	XXX	XX	1
2. Recoveries credited to reserve	7,650	XXX	XX	2
3. Changes incident to mergers and absorptions	NONE	XXX	XX	3
4. Provision for possible loan losses (must equal Item 2j of Section A)	118,932	XXX	XX	4
5. Losses charged to reserve	(141,257)	XXX	XX	5
6. Balance end of period (must equal Subitem 9b of Report of Condition)	95,509	XXX	XX	6

SECTION D—OTHER OPERATING INCOME

Other income

	Thousands of dollars
1. Trading account income, Net	12,794 xxx xx
2. Equity in net income (loss) of unconsolidated subsidiaries and associated companies	3,760 xxx xx
3. All other: (itemize amounts over 25% of Item 4 below)	
Foreign Exchange $8,881	23,827 xxx xx
4. Total (must equal Section A, Item 1m)	40,381 xxx xx

SECTION E—OTHER OPERATING EXPENSES

Other expenses

	Thousands of dollars
1. Minority interest in consolidated subsidiaries	NONE xxx xx
2. All other: (itemize amounts over 25% of item 3 below) ....NONE..............	75,972 xxx xx
3. Total (must equal Section A, Item 2k)	75,972 xxx xx

Figure 12

NAME OF BANK: __The First National Bank of Chicago__ ___CHARTER NUMBER: _

SECTION F—MEMORANDA (Year to date)

	Thousands of dollars			
	THOUSANDS	Hnds.	Cts.	
1. Provision for income taxes for current period: (tax credits in paren.)				
a. Provision for Federal income taxes	36,385	XXX	XX	1a
b. Provision for State and local income taxes	2,522	XXX	XX	b
c. Provision for foreign income taxes	18,632	XXX	XX	c
d. Total (must equal Section A, Items 4 and 6b and Section F, Item 2b)	57,539	XXX	XX	d
2. Extraordinary items (itemize):				
a. Extraordinary Items, Gross	NONE	XXX	XX	2a
b. Less: Applicable income taxes (domestic and foreign) (tax credits in paren.)	NONE	XXX	XX	b
c. Extraordinary Items, Net (must equal Section A, Item 8)	NONE	XXX	XX	c
3. Number of employees on payroll at end of period	7,836			3
a. Number of full time equivalent employees on payroll at end of period	7,575			3a
4. Number of subsidiaries consolidated .....(Direct)..	14			4
5. List all mergers, consolidations and purchases during reporting period:				
Name and location	Date			
....				5
....				
....				

Figure 13

reports are usually available one month following the end of the quarter. The large bank supplement to the call report is available six weeks after the end of a quarter.

Report of Condition—Consolidating Domestic and Foreign Subsidiaries

This report is a one-page balance sheet, along with selected memoranda items of the bank that consolidates domestic and foreign subsidiaries (Figures 15, 16). This balance sheet is printed in legal, business, and other publications and is the financial table that probably receives the greatest exposure to the public. Often, the names of the bank's directors are printed along with the balance sheet.

Report of Condition—Consolidating Domestic Subsidiaries (Short Form)

This report of condition includes the balance sheet of the domestic bank and domestic bank subsidiaries only. It is useful when compared with the domestic and foreign consolidated report, since by subtraction it is possible to obtain an estimate of the foreign balance sheet of a bank. (In accordance with the Comptroller of the Currency's instructions, Edge Act subsidiaries are considered to be foreign.) There is no report available to the public showing foreign items on a line-by-line basis of the balance sheet. Although the step of consolidation presents an added unknown step to the bank analyst, a simple subtraction serves as an approximation of a foreign balance sheet.

Report of Condition—Consolidating Domestic Subsidiaries (Long Form)

The long form of the domestic report of condition shows the balance sheet and selected memoranda noted before. In addition, on the reverse side of this report, there are nine schedules (Figures 17–21). These schedules provide useful information about the bank.

Schedule A shows seven general classifications of loans, as well as numerous subclassifications. Schedule B shows the maturity distribution of four classifications of securities. Other schedules show details of the balance sheet lines of cash and due from banks, federal funds sold, federal funds bought, deposits, other assets, and other liabilities.

NAME OF BANK: __The First National Bank of Chicago__   CHARTER NUMBER: ___8___

CITY & STATE: __Chicago__   __Illinois__

SPECIAL SUPPLEMENT TO SECTION B, REPORT OF INCOME FOR THE YEAR ENDED DECEMBER 31, 1976

COMPONENTS OF "OTHER INCREASES AND DECREASES" IN UNDIVIDED PROFITS AND CAPITAL RESERVES

A. Definitional adjustments

   1. Contingency portion of IRS Reserve for Bad Debts .... [THOUSANDS | XXX | XX]   A.1

   2. Less interest collected not earned included in undivided profits as of December 31, 1975 .... [| XXX | XX]   A.2

   3. Net definitional adjustments (A.1 minus A.2) .... [THOUSANDS NONE | XXX | XX] A.3

B. Non-definitional adjustments

   1. Accretion of discount through December 31, 1975 (net of deferred taxes) for banks not accreting prior to 1976 .... [| XXX | XX]   B.1
     (see note below)

   2. Plus other increases (itemize below)* .... [| XXX | XX]   B.2

   3. Less other decreases (itemize below)** .... [| XXX | XX]   B.3

   4. Net non-definitional adjustments (B.1 plus B.2 minus B.3) .... [NONE | XXX | XX] B.4

C. Total of A.3 & B.4. Report in Section B, line 8, column D of the Report of Income .... [NONE | XXX | XX] C

*Increases   **Decreases

NOTE: For Item B.1, Accretion of discount, an amount should be entered only by those banks that began accreting for the first time in 1976. No amount should be entered either by those banks that accreted prior to 1976 or by those banks below $25 million in assets that have elected not to accrete.

THIS FORM MUST BE ATTACHED TO YOUR 1976 REPORT OF INCOME FOLLOWING PAGE

SHOULD ASSISTANCE BE REQUIRED IN COMPLETING THIS FORM, PLEASE CALL (202) 447-1825

COMPTROLLER OF THE CURRENCY COPY

(ORIGINAL)

Comptroller of the Currency
Administrator of National Banks

CONSOLIDATED REPORT OF CONDITION

(Including Domestic and Foreign Subsidiaries)

CHARTER NUMBER: __8__

NAME OF BANK: ___The First National Bank of Chicago___

CITY: ___Chicago___

STATE: ___Illinois___   ZIP CODE: ___60670___

CALL: ___DECEMBER   31   1976___
           Month   Day   Year

I, ___Thomas Rock___
          Name
___Vice President___
          Title

NOTE: This report must be signed by an authorized officer, attested to by not less than three directors other than the officer signing the report and forwarded within ten days after receipt of request for Report of Condition. The Comptroller of the Currency must be promptly notified if publication has not been made within the time specified.

of the above-named bank do hereby declare that this Report of Condition is true and correct to the best of my knowledge and belief.

Thomas Rock
          Signature
          1/31/77
          Date

We, the undersigned directors attest to the correctness of the Report of Condition. The Report of Condition includes the statement of resources and liabilities, supporting schedules and applicable supplements. We declare that it has been examined by us, to the best of our knowledge and belief is true and correct, and that it has been or will be published in the manner prescribed by 12 U.S.C. 161, within twenty days from the date of the request for Report of Condition, or as otherwise prescribed by the Comptroller of the Currency.

William Wood Prince
Thomas G. Ayers   Directors
Frederick D. Jacob

Name, title and phone number of person to whom inquiries may be directed:

___Thomas Rock___

___Vice President___

___(312) 732 - 4094___

NAME OF BANK: __The First National Bank of Chicago__   CHARTER NUMBER: ____

BALANCE SHEET at the close of business on ___12___ ___31___ ___76___
Statement of Resources and Liabilities

		THOUSANDS	Hnds.	Cts.	
ASSETS	1. Cash and due from banks	4,032,366	XXX	XX	1
	2. U.S. Treasury securities	1,276,328	XXX	XX	2
	3. Obligations of other U.S. Gov't. agencies and corps.	245,460	XXX	XX	3
	4. Obligations of States and political subdivisions	790,138	XXX	XX	4
	5. Other bonds, notes, and debentures	107,986	XXX	XX	5
	6. Federal Reserve stock and corporate stock	33,471	XXX	XX	6
	7. Trading account securities	146,698	XXX	XX	7
	8. Federal funds sold and securities purchased under agreements to resell	333,163	XXX	XX	8
	9. a. Loans, Total (excluding unearned income) 11077079 XXX XX				9a
	b. Less: Reserve for possible loan losses 95509 XXX XX				b
	c. Loans, Net	10,981,570	XXX	XX	c
	10. Direct lease financing	52,313	XXX	XX	10
	11. Bank premises, furniture and fixtures, and other assets representing bank premises	227,010	XXX	XX	11
	12. Real estate owned other than bank premises	37,204	XXX	XX	12
	13. Investments in unconsolidated subsidiaries and associated companies	73,532	XXX	XX	13
	14. Customers' liability to this bank on acceptances outstanding	110,245	XXX	XX	14
	15. Other assets	230,526	XXX	XX	15
	16. TOTAL ASSETS (sum of Items 1 thru 15)	18,678,010	XXX	XX	16
LIABILITIES	17. Demand deposits of individuals, prtnshps., and corps.	2,092,003	XXX	XX	17
	18. Time and savings deposits of individuals, prtnshps., and corps.	4,485,156	XXX	XX	18
	19. Deposits of United States Government	25,634	XXX	XX	19
	20. Deposits of States and political subdivisions	187,008	XXX	XX	20
	21. Deposits of foreign govts. and official institutions	590,373	XXX	XX	21
	22. Deposits of commercial banks	888,421	XXX	XX	22
	23. Certified and officers' checks	51,849	XXX	XX	23
	24. TOTAL DOMESTIC DEPOSITS (sum of Items 17 thru 23)	8,320,444	XXX	XX	24
	a. Total demand deposits 2,714,756 XXX XX				a
	b. Total time and savings deposits 5,605,688 XXX XX				b
	c. Total deposits in foreign offices	5,758,842	XXX	XX	c
	d. TOTAL DEPOSITS IN DOMESTIC AND FOREIGN OFFICES	14,079,286	XXX	XX	d
	25. Federal funds purchased and securities sold under agreements to repurchase	3,029,048	XXX	XX	25
	26. Liabilities for borrowed money	223,023	XXX	XX	26
	27. Mortgage indebtedness	202	XXX	XX	27
	28. Acceptances executed by or for account of this bank and outstanding	110,255	XXX	XX	28
	29. Other liabilities	370,588	XXX	XX	29
	30. TOTAL LIABILITIES (excluding subordinated notes and debentures)	17,812,402	XXX	XX	30
	31. Subordinated notes and debentures	NONE	XXX	XX	31
EQUITY CAPITAL	32. Preferred stock No. shares outstanding NONE (par value)	NONE	XXX	XX	32
	33. Common stock a. No. shares authorized 10,042,910				
	b. No. shares outstanding 10,042,910 (par value)	200,858	XXX	XX	33
	34. Surplus	425,947	XXX	XX	34
	35. Undivided profits	238,803	XXX	XX	35
	36. Reserve for contingencies and other capital reserves	NONE	XXX	XX	36
	37. TOTAL EQUITY CAPITAL (sum of Items 32 thru 36)	865,608	XXX	XX	37
	38. TOTAL LIABILITIES AND EQUITY CAPITAL (sum of Items 30, 31, and 37)	18,678,010	XXX	XX	38
MEMORANDA	1. Average for 15 or 30 calendar days ending with call date:				
	a. Cash and due from banks (corresponds to Item 1 above)	3,163,979	XXX	XX	1a
	b. Fed. funds sold and securities purchased under agreements to resell (corresponds to Item 8 above)	410,054	XXX	XX	b
	c. Total loans (corresponds to subitem 9a above)	10,930,557	XXX	XX	c
	d. Time deposits of $100,000 or more in domestic offices (corr. to memoranda 3a plus 3b below)	3,593,841	XXX	XX	d
	e. Total deposits (corresponds to Item 24 d above)	13,031,048	XXX	XX	e
	f. Fed. funds purchased and securities sold under agreements to repurchase (corr. to Item 25 above)	3,162,453	XXX	XX	f
	g. Liabilities for borrowed money (corresponds to Item 26 above)	189,514	XXX	XX	g
	2. Standby letters of credit (outstanding as of report date)	364,891	XXX	XX	2
	3. Time deposits of $100,000 or more (outstanding as of report date)				
	a. Time certificates of deposit in denominations of $100,000 or more	3,560,266	XXX	XX	3a
	b. Other time deposits in amounts of $100,000 or more	217,428	XXX	XX	b

DF-2

COMPTROLLER OF THE CURRENCY COPY
(ORIGINAL)

Form CC-6022-18

Figure 16

43

Comptroller of the Currency
Administrator of National Banks

CONSOLIDATED REPORT OF CONDITION

(Including Domestic Subsidiaries)

```
00008-6    CHIEF EXECUTIVE OFFICER
THE FIRST NATIONAL BANK OF CHICAGO
1 FIRST NATIONAL PLAZA
CHICAGO, ILLINOIS            60670
```

CHARTER NUMBER: _____8_____

NAME OF BANK: _____The First National Bank of Chicago_____

CITY: _____Chicago_____

STATE: _____Illinois_____ ZIP CODE: __60670__

CALL: _____DECEMBER 31 1976_____
              Month Day Year

I, _____Thomas Rock_____
              Name
_____Vice President_____
              Title

NOTE: This report must be signed by an authorized officer, attested to by not less than three directors other than the officer signing the report and forwarded within ten days after receipt of request for Report of Condition. The Comptroller of the Currency must be promptly notified if publication has not been made within the time specified.

of the above-named bank do hereby declare that this Report of Condition is true and correct to the best of my knowledge and belief.

_____Thomas Rock_____
             Signature
_____1/31/77_____
             Date

We, the undersigned directors attest to the correctness of the Report of Condition. The Report of Condition includes the statement of resources and liabilities, supporting schedules and applicable supplements. We declare that it has been examined by us, to the best of our knowledge and belief is true and correct, and that it has been or will be published in the manner prescribed by 12 U.S.C. 161, within twenty days from the date of the request for Report of Condition, or as otherwise prescribed by the Comptroller of the Currency.

Directors

Name, title and phone number of person to whom inquiries may be directed:

_____Thomas Rock_____

_____Vice President_____

_____(312) 732 - 4094_____

Figure 17

44

NAME OF BANK: The First National Bank of Chicago CHARTER NUMBER: –

BALANCE SHEET at the close of business on 12 (month) 31 (day) 76 (year)

Statement of Resources and Liabilities

	Item	Sch.	Item	Col.				Thousands of dollars (THOUSANDS)		Cts.	
ASSETS	1. Cash and due from banks	C	7					1,339,651	XXX	XX	1
	2. U.S. Treasury securities	B	1	E				1,276,328	XXX	XX	2
	3. Obligations of other U.S. Gov't. agencies and corps	B	2	E				245,460	XXX	XX	3
	4. Obligations of States and political subdivisions	B	3	E				790,138	XXX	XX	4
	5. Other bonds, notes, and debentures	B	4	E				43,868	XXX	XX	5
	6. Federal Reserve stock and corporate stock							31,219	XXX	XX	6
	7. Trading account securities							135,108	XXX	XX	7
	8. Federal funds sold and securities purchased under agreements to resell	D	4					332,964	XXX	XX	8
	9. a. Loans, Total (excluding unearned income)	A	10		7,581,195	XXX	XX				9a
	b. Less: Reserve for possible loan losses				88,233	XXX	XX				b
	c. Loans, Net							7,492,962	XXX	XX	c
	10. Direct lease financing							28,147	XXX	XX	10
	11. Bank premises, furniture and fixtures, and other assets representing bank premises							212,507	XXX	XX	11
	12. Real estate owned other than bank premises							35,862	XXX	XX	12
	13. Investments in unconsolidated subsidiaries and associated companies							106,090	XXX	XX	13
	14. Customers' liability to this bank on acceptances outstanding							26,525	XXX	XX	14
	15. Other assets	G	7					470,331	XXX	XX	15
	16. TOTAL ASSETS (sum of Items 1 thru 15)							12,567,160	XXX	XX	16
LIABILITIES	17. Demand deposits of individuals, prtnshps., and corps.	F	1f	A				2,093,542	XXX	XX	17
	18. Time and savings deposits of individuals, prtnshps., and corps.	F	1f	B+C				4,485,156	XXX	XX	18
	19. Deposits of United States Government	F	2	A+B+C				25,634	XXX	XX	19
	20. Deposits of States and political subdivisions	F	3	A+B+C				187,008	XXX	XX	20
	21. Deposits of foreign govts. and official institutions	F	4	A+B+C				590,373	XXX	XX	21
	22. Deposits of commercial banks	F	5+6	A+B+C				927,341	XXX	XX	22
	23. Certified and officers' checks	F	7	A				51,849	XXX	XX	23
	24. TOTAL DEPOSITS (sum of Items 17 thru 23)							8,360,903	XXX	XX	24
	a. Total demand deposits	F	8	A	2,755,215	XXX	XX				a
	b. Total time and savings deposits	F	8	B+C	5,605,688	XXX	XX				b
	25. Federal funds purchased and securities sold under agreements to repurchase	E	4					3,025,178	XXX	XX	25
	26. Liabilities for borrowed money							NONE	XXX	XX	26
	27. Mortgage indebtedness							NONE	XXX	XX	27
	28. Acceptances executed by or for account of this bank and outstanding							26,525	XXX	XX	28
	29. Other liabilities	H	9					288,946	XXX	XX	29
	30. TOTAL LIABILITIES (sum of Items 24 thru 29 excluding Items 24a & b)							11,701,552	XXX	XX	30
EQUITY CAPITAL	31. Subordinated notes and debentures							NONE	XXX	XX	31
	32. Preferred stock No. shares outstanding None (par value)							NONE	XXX	XX	32
	33. Common stock a. No. shares authorized 10,042,910										
	b. No. shares outstanding 10,042,910 (par value)							200,858	XXX	XX	33
	34. Surplus							425,947	XXX	XX	34
	35. Undivided profits							238,803	XXX	XX	35
	36. Reserve for contingencies and other capital reserves							NONE	XXX	XX	36
	37. TOTAL EQUITY CAPITAL (sum of Items 32 thru 36)							865,608	XXX	XX	37
	38. TOTAL LIABILITIES AND EQUITY CAPITAL (sum of Items 30, 31, and 37)							12,567,160	XXX	XX	38
MEMORANDA	1. Average for 15 or 30 calendar days ending with call date:										
	a. Cash and due from banks (corresponds to Item 1 above)							1,114,892	XXX	XX	1a
	b. Fed. funds sold and securities purchased under agreements to resell (corresponds to Item 8 above)							401,692	XXX	XX	b
	c. Total loans (corresponds to subitem 9a above)							7,517,257	XXX	XX	c
	d. Time deposits of $100,000 or more (corresponds to memoranda subitems 3a plus 3b below)							3,593,841	XXX	XX	d
	e. Total deposits (corresponds to Item 24 above)							8,073,114	XXX	XX	e
	f. Fed. funds purchased and securities sold under agreements to repurchase (corr. to Item 25 above)							3,160,551	XXX	XX	f
	g. Liabilities for borrowed money (corresponds to Item 26 above)							15	XXX	XX	g
	2. Standby letters of credit (outstanding as of report date)							290,165	XXX	XX	2
	3. Time deposits of $100,000 or more (outstanding as of report date)										
	a. Time certificates of deposit in denominations of $100,000 or more							3,560,266	XXX	XX	3a
	b. Other time deposits in amounts of $100,000 or more							217,428	XXX	XX	b

COMPTROLLER OF THE CURRENCY COPY (ORIGINAL) C-2

Figure 18

SCHEDULE A—LOANS
(Including rediscounts and overdrafts)

Thousands of dollars

	THOUSANDS	Hnds	Cts	
1. Real estate loans (include only loans secured primarily by real estate):				
a. Construction and land development	179,266	xxx	xx	1a
b. Secured by farmland (including farm residential and other improvements)	10,159	xxx	xx	b
c. Secured by 1-4 family residential properties:				
(1) Insured by FHA or guaranteed by VA	20,064	xxx	xx	c1
(2) Conventional	214,352	xxx	xx	c2
d. Secured by multi-family (5 or more) residential properties:				
(1) Insured by FHA	7,427	xxx	xx	d1
(2) Conventional	37,926	xxx	xx	d2
e. Secured by nonfarm nonresidential properties	221,870	xxx	xx	e
2. Loans to financial institutions:				
a. To real estate investment trusts and mortgage companies	632,326	xxx	xx	2a
b. To domestic commercial banks	18,492	xxx	xx	b
c. To banks in foreign countries	24,364	xxx	xx	c
d. To other depository institutions (Mutual Savings Banks, Savings and Loan Associations, Credit Unions)	5,000	xxx	xx	d
e. To other financial institutions	827,863	xxx	xx	e
3. Loans for purchasing or carrying securities (secured or unsecured):				
a. To brokers and dealers in securities	469,996	xxx	xx	3a
b. Other loans for purchasing or carrying securities	78,241	xxx	xx	b
4. Loans to farmers (except loans secured primarily by real estate; include loans for household and personal expenditures)	38,724	xxx	xx	4
5. Commercial and industrial loans (except those secured primarily by real estate)	4,026,314	xxx	xx	5
6. Loans to individuals for household, family, and other personal expenditures (include purchased paper):				
a. To purchase private passenger automobiles on installment basis	8,187	xxx	xx	6a
b. Credit cards and related plans:				
(1) Retail (charge account) credit card plans	373,612	xxx	xx	b1
(2) Check credit and revolving credit plans	810	xxx	xx	b2
c. To purchase other retail consumer goods on installment basis:				
(1) Mobile homes (exclude travel trailers)	NONE	xxx	xx	c1
(2) Other retail consumer goods (exclude credit cards and related plans)	10,640	xxx	xx	c2
d. Installment loans to repair and modernize residential property	8,909	xxx	xx	d
e. Other installment loans for household, family, and other personal expenditures	33,856	xxx	xx	e
f. Single-payment loans for household, family, and other personal expenditures	120,300	xxx	xx	f
7. All other loans	227,845	xxx	xx	7
8. Total loans, Gross (sum of Items 1 thru 7)	7,596,543	xxx	xx	8
9. Less: Unearned income on loans	15,348	xxx	xx	9
10. Total loans (excluding unearned income) (must equal Asset subitem 9a)	7,581,195	xxx	xx	10

SCHEDULE B—SECURITIES—DISTRIBUTION BY REMAINING MATURITY (Book Value)

Investment Securities (Items correspond to Asset, Items 2, 3, 4, and 5)	A. 1 year and less	B. Over 1 thru 5 years	C. Over 5 thru 10 years	D. Over 10 years	E. Total	
1. U.S. Treasury securities	943,686 xxx xx	195,725 xxx xx	136,917 xxx xx	NONE xxx xx	1 276 328 xxx xx	1
2. Obligations of other U.S. Government agencies and corporations	58 xxx xx	51,142 xxx xx	90 xxx xx	194,170 xxx xx	245,460 xxx xx	2
3. Obligations of States and political subdivisions	42,902 xxx xx	179,386 xxx xx	200,346 xxx xx	367,504 xxx xx	790,138 xxx xx	3
4. Other bonds, notes, and debentures	NONE xxx xx	41,533 xxx xx	35 xxx xx	2,300 xxx xx	43,868 xxx xx	4
5. Total	986,646 xxx xx	467,786 xxx xx	337,388 xxx xx	563,974 xxx xx	2 355 794 xxx xx	5

Thousands of dollars

Figure 19

SCHEDULE C—CASH AND DUE FROM BANKS

Thousands of dollars

	THOUSANDS	Hnds	Cts	
1. Cash items in process of collection and unposted debits (unposted debits from Schd. I)	469,646	XXX	XX	1
2. Demand balances with banks in the United States	68,484	XXX	XX	2
3. Other balances with banks in the United States	10,542	XXX	XX	3
a. Including interest bearing balances	10,542 XXX XX			a
4. Balances with banks in foreign countries	4,270	XXX	XX	4
a. Including interest bearing balances	NONE XXX XX			a
5. Currency and coin	97,167	XXX	XX	5
6. Reserve with Federal Reserve Bank	689,542	XXX	XX	6
7. Total (must equal Asset, Item 1)	1,339,651	XXX	XX	7

SCHEDULE D—FEDERAL FUNDS SOLD AND SECURITIES PURCHASED UNDER AGREEMENTS TO RESELL

Thousands of dollars

	THOUSANDS	Hnds	Cts
1. With domestic commercial banks	207,830	XXX	XX
2. With brokers and dealers in securities and funds	58,029	XXX	XX
3. With others	67,105	XXX	XX
4. Total (must equal Asset, Item 8)	332,964	XXX	XX

SCHEDULE E—FEDERAL FUNDS PURCHASED AND SECURITIES SOLD UNDER AGREEMENTS TO REPURCHASE

Thousands of dollars

	THOUSANDS	Hnds	Cts
1. With domestic commercial banks	2,657,342	XXX	XX
2. With brokers and dealers in securities and funds	25,625	XXX	XX
3. With others	342,211	XXX	XX
4. Total (must equal Liability, Item 25)	3,025,178	XXX	XX

SCHEDULE F—DEPOSITS

Thousands of dollars

Deposits	A. Demand	B. Savings	C. Time	
1. Deposits of individuals, partnerships, corporations:				
a. Individuals and nonprofit organizations		987,641 XXX XX		1a
b. Corporations and other profit organizations		19,244 XXX XX		b
c. Total (sum of 1a and 1b)	2,092,312 XXX XX	1,006,885 XXX XX	3,472,971 XXX XX	c
d. Mutual savings banks	1,230 XXX XX	NONE XXX XX	5,300 XXX XX	d
e. Deposits accumulated for payment of personal loans			NONE XXX XX	e
f. Total (sum of 1c, 1d and 1e) (Col. A must equal Liability, Item 17 and Cols. B and C must equal Liability, Item 18)	2,093,542 XXX XX	1,006,885 XXX XX	3,478,271 XXX XX	f
2. Deposits of United States Government	12,690 XXX XX	12,944 XXX XX	NONE XXX XX	2
3. Deposits of States and political subdivisions	51,821 XXX XX	9,214 XXX XX	125,973 XXX XX	3
4. Deposits of foreign governments and official institutions, central banks, and international institutions	4,426 XXX XX	NONE XXX XX	585,947 XXX XX	4
5. Deposits of commercial banks in the United States	457,817 XXX XX	NONE XXX XX	336,154 XXX XX	5
6. Deposits of banks in foreign countries (including balances of foreign branches of other American banks)	83,070 XXX XX	NONE XXX XX	50,300 XXX XX	6
7. Certified and officers' checks, travelers' checks, letters of credit (must equal Liability, Item 23)	51,849 XXX XX			7
8. Total deposits	2,755,215 XXX XX	1,029,043 XXX XX	4,576,645 XXX XX	8

Figure 20

NAME OF BANK: _____The First National Bank of Chicago_____ CHARTER NUMBER: ___8___

SCHEDULE G—OTHER ASSETS

	Thousands of dollars		
	THOUSANDS	Hnds	Cts
1. Securities borrowed	NONE	xxx	xx
2. Due from foreign branches, Net	354,914	xxx	xx
3. Income earned or accrued but not collected	76,912	xxx	xx
4. Prepaid expenses	2,544	xxx	xx
5. Cash items not in process of collection	NONE	xxx	xx
6. All other (itemize): a. Balances with savings and loan associations	NONE	xxx	xx

(Itemize amounts over 25% of Item 7 below)

NONE ....
....
....
....

....	35,961	xxx	xx
7. Total (must equal Asset, Item 15)	470,331	xxx	xx

SCHEDULE H—OTHER LIABILITIES

	Thousands of dollars		
	THOUSANDS	Hnds	Cts
1. Securities borrowed	NONE	xxx	xx
2. Due to foreign branches, Net	NONE	xxx	xx
3. Dividends declared but not yet payable	NONE	xxx	xx
4. Expenses accrued and unpaid	76,806	xxx	xx
5. Amounts in transit to banks ...	NONE	xxx	xx
6. Minority interest in consolidated subsidiaries ...	NONE	xxx	xx
7. Deferred income taxes: a. IRS bad debt reserve	33,027	xxx	xx
b. Other	18,222	xxx	xx
8. All other (Itemize amounts over 25% of Item 9 below)			

Liab. for Bonds Sold
Not Owned $88,290
....

....	160,891	xxx	xx
9. Total (must equal Liability, Item 29)	288,946	xxx	xx

SCHEDULE I—OTHER DATA FOR DEPOSIT INSURANCE ASSESSMENTS

	Thousands of dollars			
	THOUSANDS	Hnds	Cts	
1. Unposted debits (see instructions): a. Actual amount of all unposted debits or single factor ____% of Item 24	NONE	xxx	xx	1a
or: b. Separate amount of unposted debits or separate factors: 1. Actual amount for demand deposits or ____% of subitem 24a	NONE	xxx	xx	b1
2. Actual amount for time and savings deposits or ____% of subitem 24b	NONE	xxx	xx	b2
2. Unposted credits (see instructions): a. Actual amount of all unposted credits or single factor ____% of Item 24	NONE	xxx	xx	2a
or: b. Separate amount of unposted credits or separate factors: 1. Actual amount for demand deposits or ____% of subitem 24a	NONE	xxx	xx	b1
2. Actual amount for time and savings deposits or ____% of subitem 24b	NONE	xxx	xx	b2
3. Uninvested trust funds (cash) held in bank's own trust department not included in Item 24	NONE	xxx	xx	3

Figure 21

Large Bank Supplement to the Call Report

In addition to the regular call report, there is a supplemental report prepared by banks with total assets of $300 million or more (Figures 22–26). This report provides information concerning the maturities of major selected domestic deposits and domestic and international loans, as well as loan losses and recoveries of loans according to five classifications.

This supplement is usually available from the bank or is available from the Comptroller of the Currency, Public Disclosure Office, 490 L'Enfant Plaza, Washington, D.C. 20219, telephone 202-447-1825.

FORM 8-K

In addition to the requirements to file regular reports with the Securities and Exchange Commission, there is an additional requirement to file an 8-K report if there is any significant change in the nature of the business of a bank

Comptroller of the Currency
Administrator of National Banks

LARGE-BANK SUPPLEMENTS
TO THE CALL REPORT

CHARTER NUMBER: ___8_____

NAME OF BANK: ___The First National Bank of Chicago_____

CITY: _____Chicago_____

STATE: _____Illinois_____ ZIP CODE: ___60670_____

CALL: _____DECEMBER___31___1976_____
           Month   Day   Year

GENERAL INSTRUCTIONS

Forwarding date

The supplements should be forwarded to the Comptroller of the Currency together with the reports of condition and income.

Large Bank

$300 million or more in total assets as of the previous December 31 fully consolidated foreign-and-domestic Report of Condition.

Disclosure

The Large-bank Supplements will be subject to public disclosure.

Foreign offices

Includes foreign branches, foreign subsidiaries, Edge Act and Agreement Corporations and branches in Puerto Rico and U. S. territories and possessions.

Reporting

Do not amend the captions of any item appearing in the supplements. An amount or the word "none" must be entered at every item in the supplements.

Rounding

All dollar amounts should be rounded to the nearest thousand.

Comments

A comments section has been provided in each supplement to allow banks, at their discretion, to include brief comments relating to the supplement.

Abbreviations

Col.:	Column	R/I:	Report of Income
LBS:	Large-bank Supplements	Sch.:	Schedule
R/C:	Report of Condition	Sec.:	Section

COMPTROLLER OF THE CURRENCY COPY
(ORIGINAL)

LS-1

Figure 22

LARGE BANK SUPPLEMENT A—REMAINING MATURITIES OF SELECTED LOANS
(Dollar amounts in thousands)

Type of loan	A. One year or less			B. Over one thru 5 years			C. Over 5 years			D. Total (Book Value)			
	THOUSANDS	Hnds.	Cts.	THOUSANDS	Hnds.	Cts.	THOUSANDS	Hnds.	Cts.	THOUSANDS	Hnds.	Cts.	
1. Loans in domestic offices:													
a. Construction and land development loans secured primarily by real estate (R/C, Sch. A, Item 1a)	115,960	xxx	xx	49,621	xxx	xx	13,685	XXX	XX	179,266	xxx	xx	1a
b. Other loans secured primarily by real estate (excluding loans secured by 1-4 family residential properties) (R/C, Sch. A, Items 1b+1d+1e)	132,275	xxx	xx	112,149	xxx	xx	32,958		xxx	xx	277,382	xxx	xx	b
c. Commercial and industrial loans (R/C, Sch. A, Item 5	2,147,520	xxx	xx	1,492,731	xxx	xx	386,063		xxx	xx	4,026,314	xxx	xx	c
d. Other loans (excluding loans to individuals *and* loans secured by 1-4 family residential properties) (R/C, Sch. A, Items 2+3+4+7)	1,629,092	xxx	xx	569,592	xxx	xx	121,567		xxx	xx	2,320,251	xxx	xx	d
2. Loans in foreign offices	1,528,551	xxx	xx	1,593,871	xxx	xx	385,155		xxx	xx	3,507,577	xxx	xx	2
3. Total (sum of Items 1 thru 2	5,553,398	xxx	xx	3,817,964	xxx	xx	939,428		xxx	xx	10,310,790	xxx	xx	3
4. Loans in Item 3:[2]													
a. With predetermined interest rate	1,300,980	xxx	xx	497,212	xxx	xx	201,351		xxx	xx	1,999,543	xxx	xx	4a
b. With floating interest rate	4,252,418	xxx	xx	3,320,752	xxx	xx	738,077		xxx	xx	8,311,247	xxx	xx	b

Remaining Maturity[1]

[1] Scheduled repayments of principal should be reported in the appropriate maturity period or periods. Demand loans, loans having no stated schedule of repayments and no stated maturity, past due loans, and overdrafts should be reported in Col. A, one year or less.
[2] Item 4a plus 4b, Col. A thru D must equal Item 3, Col. A thru D, respectively.

Comments:

COMPTROLLER OF THE CURRENCY COPY
(ORIGINAL)

LS-2

Figure 23

NAME OF BANK:___The First___National Bank of Chicago___CHARTER NUMBER:__8___
CITY & STATE:___Chicago, Illinois_____ REPORT DATE:___DECEMBER 31, 1976___

LARGE BANK SUPPLEMENT B—MATURITY DISTRIBUTION OF DEPOSITS
(Dollars amounts in thousands)

Remaining Maturity	A. Time certificates of deposits of $100,000 or more issued by domestic offices[1]			B. Total interest-bearing deposits in foreign offices			
	THOUSANDS	Hnds	Cts	THOUSANDS	Hnds	Cts	
1. 3 months or less	2,214,047	XXX	XX	4,712,240	XXX	XX	1
2. Over 3 thru 6 months	639,487	XXX	XX	371,880	XXX	XX	2
3. Over 6 thru 12 months	570,888	XXX	XX	192,645	XXX	XX	3
4. Over 12 months	135,844	XXX	XX	88,369	XXX	XX	4
5. Total (sum of Items 1 thru 4)	3,560,266	XXX	XX	5,365,134	XXX	XX	5

[1]Item 5, Col. A must equal R/C, Memoranda, Item 3a for corresponding date.

Comments:

Figure 24

(Figures 27 and 28). The 8-K report is filed 10 days after the end of the month in which a reportable event occurs. The 8-K report is usually available from the secretary of the bank at no charge. A copy is also available at $0.10 per page from the Securities and Exchange Commission, Public Reference, 500 North Capitol Street, N.W., Washington, D.C. 20549, telephone 202-523-5506.

The Securities and Exchange Commission lists 14 items covering the areas of disclosure pertaining to an 8-K report, including changes in control, a significant acquisition or disposition of assets, legal proceedings, various enumerated changes in securities, revaluation of assets or a restatement of capital accounts, submission of matters to a vote of security holders, other materially important events, and financial statements and exhibits. This is a broad coverage of possible events and provides a source of information about events that a bank may not wish widespread publicity.

The problem of using 8-K reports is not knowing when they are released. A bank may not release an 8-K for many months because a reportable event did not occur and then do so when such an event occurs. One of the simplest methods of keeping abreast of an 8-K release is to scan the *SEC News Digest*, which shows at least once a week a summary of all 8-K filings. Bank analysts may find this digest in larger libraries, or subscriptions may be placed for the

NAME OF BANK:_The First National Bank of Chicago___ CHARTER NUMBER:__8___
CITY & STATE:__Chicago, Illinois_____ REPORT DATE:___DECEMBER 31, 1976___

LARGE BANK SUPPLEMENT C—SECURITIES HELD IN TRADING ACCOUNTS IN DOMESTIC OFFICES
(Dollar amounts in thousands)

Type of security	A. Amount as of current date[1]			B. Daily average for current quarter			
1. U.S. Treasury securities	86,687	XXX	XX	74,434	XXX	XX	1
2. Obligations of other U.S. Government agencies and corporations	11,183	XXX	XX	21,073	XXX	XX	2
3. Obligations of States and political subdivisions	37,238	XXX	XX	47,635	XXX	XX	3
4. Other bonds, notes, and debentures	NONE	XXX	XX	NONE	XXX	XX	4
5. Total (sum of Items 1 thru 4)	135,108	XXX	XX	143,142	XXX	XX	5

[1]Item 5, Col. A must equal R/C, Assets, Item 7 for corresponding date.

Comments:

Figure 25

LARGE BANK SUPPLEMENT D—SUMMARY LOAN LOSS EXPERIENCE AND RESERVE FOR POSSIBLE LOAN LOSSES
(Dollar amounts in thousands)

Summary Loan Loss Experience

		Thousands of dollars		
		THOUSANDS	Hnds	Cts.
1. Balance of reserve, beginning of period (R/I, Sec. C, Item 1)		110,184	xxx	xx	1
2. Changes incident to mergers and absorptions (R/I, Sec. C, Item 3)		NONE	xxx	xx	2
3. Provision for possible loan losses (R/I, Sec. C, Item 4)		118,932	xxx	xx	3

4. Charge-offs and recoveries during period:	A. Charge-offs (R/I, Sec. C, Item 5)			B. Recoveries (R/I, Sec. C, Item 2)			
	THOUSANDS	Hnds	Cts.	THOUSANDS	Hnds	Cts.	
a. Loans in domestic offices:							
1. Loans secured primarily by 1-4 family residential properties (corresponds to R/C, Sch. A, Item 1c)	NONE	xxx	xx	NONE	xxx	xx	4a1
2. Other loans secured primarily by real estate (including construction loans) (corresponds to R/C, Sch. A, Items 1a, 1b, 1d, and 1e)	38,075	xxx	xx	1,276	xxx	xx	a2
3. Commercial and industrial loans (corresponds to R/C, Sch. A, Item 5)	39,806	xxx	xx	3,504	xxx	xx	a3
4. Loans to individuals (corresponds to R/C, Sch. A, Item 6)	9,186	xxx	xx	2,502	xxx	xx	a4
5. All other loans (corresponds to R/C, Sch. A, Items 2, 3, 4, and 7)	41,707	xxx	xx	233	xxx	xx	a5
b. Loans in foreign offices	12,483	xxx	xx	135	xxx	xx	b
c. Total	141,257	xxx	xx	7,650	xxx	xx	c

5. Less net charge-offs during period (Item 4c, Col. A minus Col. B)	(133,607)	xxx	xx	5
6. Balance of reserve, end of period (R/Sec. C, Item 6)	95,509	xxx	xx	6

MEMORANDA

1. Total loans in domestic and foreign offices before deduction of valuation reserves (corresponds to R/C, Assets, Item 9a)	Daily average for current period			
	10,793,653	xxx	xx	1

Comments:

Figure 26

Figure 27

Item 13. Other Materially Important Events

(a) On June 1, 1972, Citizens State Bank, Lyndonville, New York ("Lyndonville"), a unit bank with total resources of $5,552,000 at March 31, 1972, was merged into The Citizens Central Bank, Arcade, New York, a wholly-owned subsidiary of Charter New York Corporation ("Charter"). Pursuant to the Plan of Merger, Charter, on that date, issued an aggregate of 20,000 shares of its Common Stock to the shareholders of Lyndonville.

(b) Charter New York Corporation ("Charter") and The Hayes National Bank of Clinton ("Hayes") entered into an agreement dated as of June 6, 1972 under which Charter or a subsidiary of Hayes (excluding directors' qualifying shares of capital stock of Hayes (excluding directors' qualifying shares), on the basis of 6.75 shares of Charter's Common Stock, par value $10 per share, for each of the 9,000 shares of Hayes' Capital Stock, par value $25 per share, presently outstanding. The acquisition is subject, among other factors, to the approval of State and Federal regulatory authorities and to acceptance by stockholders of Hayes. On March 31, 1972, resources of Hayes totaled $16,313,434.

(c) On June 28, 1972, The First National Bank of Painted Post, Painted Post, New York ("Painted Post"), a unit bank with total resources of $10,798,000 at March 31, 1972, was merged into Central Trust Company Rochester N.Y., a wholly owned subsidiary of Charter. Pursuant to the Plan of Merger, Charter, on that date, issued an aggregate of 29,998 shares of its Common Stock to the shareholders of Painted Post.

The issuance of the shares described in (a) and (c) above was exempt from registration under the Securities Act of 1933, as amended, becuase no sale was involved within the meaning of Section 5 of that Act and Rule 133 thereunder.

SIGNATURE

Pursuant to the requirements of the Securities Exchange Act of 1934, the registrant has duly caused this report to be signed on its behalf by the undersigned hereunto duly authorized.

CHARTER NEW YORK CORPORATION

By S/ Stephen A. Swartz

Stephen A. Swartz,
Assistant Secretary

Dated: July 7, 1972

Figure 28

53

digest through the Superintendent of Documents, Government Printing Office, Washington, D.C. 20402.

PROSPECTUS

From time to time most banks sell securities to the public and prepare a S-7 registration statement, "red herring," and a prospectus, which is sometimes called an offering circular (Figure 29). The S-7 is a report which is filed with the Securities and Exchange Commission. The red herring is a preliminary prospectus used for information purposes in obtaining indications of interest from prospective buyers of the securities and does not include the price of the proposed equities or debentures. Although the illustration showing the offering circular for Chase was filed with the Comptroller of the Currency because it referred to a bank issue, the format and content are similar to the offering circulars of the Securities and Exchange Commission.

Usually the S-7 statement, red herring, and prospectus show identical information. Nevertheless, on occasion, the Securities and Exchange Commission has requested that the prospectus should show additional information from what is shown in the red herring. Such a request, when it has occurred, has created a stir in securities markets and made an offering more difficult or impossible to execute.

The red herring and prospectus are available from the underwriting group. This group usually announces that these documents are available free of charge in an advertisement in major business newspapers. The S-7 is available at $0.10 per page from the Securities and Exchange Commission, Public Reference, 500 North Capitol Street, N.W., Washington, D.C. 20549, telephone 202-523-5506.

The prospectus provides much of the same basic information concerning the bank that is shown in the 10-K report. The special value of a prospectus is that it often is issued at a time other than the end of the year and usually includes more detailed information than is found in a 10-K report. Moreover, in a prospectus a bank analyst obtains the current thinking of management and a review of that thinking by the Securities and Exchange Commission at some time during the course of the year, rather than only at year-end.

Although the Securities and Exchange Commission indicates on the face of every prospectus that it does not pass on the accuracy or adequacy of a prospectus (and it is written on the front cover of a prospectus that it is a criminal offense to imply otherwise), in certain cases, this regulatory agency has indicated minimum disclosure requirements in its guides 61 and 3, as amended in 1976. Moreover, the agency sometimes acts to set standards without discussion. For example, in the spring of 1975, Chemical New York Corporation issued a red herring that failed to disclose its real estate investment trust losses, and the Securities and Exchange Commission, according to press reports, requested that the prospectus should include this information. The information was shown in the final prospectus. The offering was subsequently withdrawn by Chemical and not marketed.

$200,000,000

The Chase Manhattan Bank
(National Association)

8¾% Capital Notes Due 1986

Interest payable May 15 and November 15.

The Capital Notes are subordinated in right of payment to the claims of depositors and certain other creditors to the extent set forth under "Description of Capital Notes".

The Capital Notes are not redeemable prior to November 15, 1983.

Application will be made to list the Capital Notes on the New York Stock Exchange.

THE CAPITAL NOTES ARE NOT DEPOSITS AND ARE NOT INSURED BY THE FEDERAL DEPOSIT INSURANCE CORPORATION OR ANY OTHER GOVERNMENT AGENCY AND ARE INELIGIBLE AS COLLATERAL FOR A LOAN BY THE CHASE MANHATTAN BANK (NATIONAL ASSOCIATION).

	Price to Public(1)	Underwriting Discounts and Commissions	Proceeds to the Bank(1)(2)
Per Capital Note	99.67%	.80%	98.87%
Total	$199,340,000	$1,600,000	$197,740,000

(1) Plus accrued interest from May 15, 1976, if any.

(2) Before deduction of estimated expenses of $500,000.

THESE SECURITIES HAVE NOT BEEN APPROVED OR DISAPPROVED BY THE COMPTROLLER OF THE CURRENCY NOR HAS THE COMPTROLLER PASSED UPON THE ACCURACY OR ADEQUACY OF THIS OFFERING CIRCULAR.

The Capital Notes are offered subject to prior sale, to withdrawal, cancellation or modification of the offer without notice, to delivery to and acceptance by the Underwriters, and to certain further conditions. It is expected that delivery of the Capital Notes will be made at the office of Lehman Brothers Incorporated, New York, New York, on or about May 25, 1976, against payment therefor in New York funds.

Lehman Brothers
Incorporated

Lazard Frères & Co.

Merrill Lynch, Pierce, Fenner & Smith
Incorporated

The date of this Offering Circular is May 18, 1976.

Figure 29

55

PROXY

Banks with publicly traded shares issue proxy statements prior to their annual meetings (Figure 30). The proxy statements explain the issues on which management asks shareholders to vote. These issues involve the election of the board of directors for the ensuing year, the appointment of the independent auditors, and often involve financial issues. In addition, some bank managements show proposals that have been initiated by shareholders in the

CHEMICAL
NEWYORK CORPORATION
20 Pine Street
New York, New York 10005

Notice of Annual Meeting of Stockholders To Be Held Wednesday, April 21, 1976

The Annual Meeting of Stockholders of Chemical New York Corporation (the Corporation) will be held in the Chemical Bank Auditorium, 13th Floor, 55 Water Street, New York, New York, on Wednesday, April 21, 1976, at 10:00 a.m., New York Time, to consider the following matters:

(1) the election of directors;

(2) the ratification of the appointment of independent accountants for the current year;

(3) the approval of the 1976 Employee Stock Purchase and Savings Plan of Chemical New York Corporation; and

(4) the transaction of such other business as may properly be brought before the Meeting, including, if introduced at the Meeting, taking action upon the resolutions which are quoted under the heading "Stockholder Proposals" in the accompanying Proxy Statement.

Pursuant to the By-laws of the Corporation, the Board of Directors has fixed the close of business on March 16, 1976 as the time for determining stockholders of record entitled to notice of, and to vote at, the Meeting.

                                                              JOHN B. WYNNE
                                                              Secretary

March 22, 1976

You are invited to attend the Meeting,

but if you do not expect to be present at the Meeting,

please date and sign the enclosed form

of proxy and mail it promptly

in the enclosed return envelope.

Figure 30

proxy, along with a supporting statement, even if the bank's management urges shareholders to vote against the proposal. The proxy is mailed to all shareholders of record and is usually available to others on request to the secretary of the bank.

Proxy statements of major banks usually show five items of the 10-K requirement that are often omitted from the 10-K report, although these items are not specifically identified. As the first item, the proxy usually shows how senior management is compensated. This information shows the direct remuneration as well as possible stock option plans, options granted to senior management, stock bonus plans, stock purchase plans, other incentive plans, and various retirement plans and estimates of the retirement benefits of the principal officers. This information is valuable in understanding how the bank provides financial incentives to its senior officers. Financial incentives are one of the principal motivations to senior managers. How these incentives are determined and the basis of their award may be an important clue to the dynamics of a bank.

The proxy usually shows the equity securities holdings of management and the directors. It also indicates whether there are any holders of record with ownership of 10 percent or more of the stock. With major banks few shareholders hold one or two percent of the total outstanding shares, although small banks often have 10 percent or more of their shares concentrated in one individual.

The proxy usually includes a statement and information concerning loans from the bank to the directors and principal officers. Loans from banks to directors or to the firms of the directors involve the closest banking relationships, and this is a delicate issue with banking managements. This part of the proxy usually indicates whether the loans have been made on the same basis as loans with ordinary customers and whether the terms of the loans are being fulfilled.

SECONDARY SOURCES

There are numerous secondary sources of bank information that provide financial information in a standardized and often succinct format. This service is valuable to bank analysts who need to survey many banks and who otherwise would need to assemble information from many different sources.

There are three problems with the use of data from secondary sources. First, information from secondary sources is never as timely as data from the banks themselves. The secondary sources must record each piece of new information before it can be transmitted and this step always involves some delay. Timeliness is often critical to the analysis of banks, and secondary sources are never as current as the banks themselves. Moreover, the secondary sources do not always provide restatements of earlier data. In many cases, the banks restate historical data in supplementary tables and charts in special reports or in special sections of regular reports that are not recorded by the secondary sources.

The information from many secondary sources is restricted to financial data.

This type of secondary information includes all of the computer tapes and data sheet printouts. The information does not include notes, which are essential to an evaluation of the financial data. Moreover, the nonfinancial information is also absent. The convenience of the use of secondary sources may be a useful substitute for the original documents, but it is often helpful for primary sources to be close by as support documents.

Several suppliers of data also provide special information services for security analysts and investors. The following list includes several of the major firms that supply this information, but it is by no means a complete list.

Compustat

Compustat is a major source of data. This company prepares 165 quarterly series and 232 annual series showing information that may be obtained most easily with a computer terminal. All of the quarterly series are restated for changes of year earlier data, and 55 items of the annual series are restated for the previous five years. All other data are not restated. Printouts of data are also available from Financial Dynamics, which, like Compustat, is a name of a product of Investors Management Sciences, Inc. In turn, Investors Management Sciences is a subsidiary of Standard & Poor's Corporation.

> Compustat
> Investors Management Sciences, Inc.
> 7400 South Alton Court
> Englewood, Colorado 80110
> 800-525-8640

Cates, Lyons & Co., Inc.

Cates, Lyons & Co. provides a service called Bancompare that reviews balance sheet and income statement information for about 247 banks. The reports provide an interesting analysis of bank holding company information, as well as 180 ratios that are ranked in deciles.

> Cates, Lyons & Co., Inc.
> 20 Exchange Place
> New York, New York 10005
> 212-269-8785

Robinson Humphrey Co., Inc.

The Robinson Humphrey data base provides income and average balance sheet data for 145 banks on an annual basis and for 30 banks on a quarterly basis. The service restates data for earlier years and the year earlier quarters. This service also provides data for a number of peer group and composite banks, as well as state-by-state ratios. There is also a computer program through the Service Bureau Company (a division of Control Data Corporation). In addition, Robinson Humphrey displays data in an easily used booklet. Robinson Humphrey Co., Inc., is a regional brokerage firm.

> The Robinson Humphrey Co., Inc.
> Bank Securities Department
> Two Peachtree Street, N.W.
> Atlanta, Georgia 30303
> 404-581-7176

Keefe Management Services

Keefe Management Services provides 41 lines of income statement and 45 lines of balance sheet data, as well as special reports that analyze banks from various points of view. Data are shown for 14,000 banks in the United States. Keefe Management Services is a subsidiary of Keefe, Bruyette & Woods, Inc., which is a brokerage and securities underwriting firm that specializes in banks.

> Keefe, Bruyette & Woods, Inc.
> One Liberty Plaza
> New York, New York 10006
> 212-349-4321

Reports of Security Analysts

Many major brokerage and underwriting firms include security analysts on their staffs. These analysts, taken as a group, provide a perspective to the banking industry that may be useful to bank analysts. Often their comments provide insights into the strategies and goals of banks. Security analysts are mainly in business to give earnings forecasts and to offer opinions concerning the attractiveness of holding stock of a bank. Although this is a narrow objective, much of the information they provide has application for other purposes, and their conclusions have broader application than stock price decisions.

Most security analysts are not as independent as their position might first indicate, and taken as a group, their opinions should always be interpreted in light of the needs of the firms that employ them. These firms primarily obtain commissions from the sale or trade of securities, the underwriting of securities, and the specialty service fees from the merger of firms. Thus the direct source of income for most security analysts is some service of their firm other than the analysts' opinions. Nevertheless, a few firms provide only their security analysts' opinions.

Most security analysts of banks tend to develop their opinions and write reports for only a few banks. They tend to specialize in banks having a large trading volume of stock or they specialize in a few banks with situations where they believe that share prices are undervalued compared with likely future prices. Thus bank analysts will find relatively little information and virtually no written analysis concerning most other banks. Perhaps 95 percent of all security analysis effort is directed to 25 or 30 banks. Thus bank analysts who wish to obtain information concerning the other approximately 14,000 banks in the United States most likely will not find the work of security analysts to be of much help.

Among each of the major banks, bank analysts often will find different opinions concerning both the approach to analysis and to the conclusions. It is worthwhile for bank analysts to secure several different opinions in order to gain perspective. However, uniformity of opinion concerning a bank should not be construed as certainty of the correctness of an opinion. Security analysts, like everybody else, have been known to be collectively wrong.

Bank analysts will find some difficulty in obtaining the writings of security analysts or have difficulty in obtaining access to their time, unless they are associated with a major financial institution or with a major corporation that normally conducts business with a bank, or are a customer of a brokerage or investment banking house. Nevertheless, the reports and time of most security analysts are available on a fee basis.

The principal security analysts of banks who have been recognized for superior performance by the *Institutional Investor Magazine* in the October 1975 issue follow. These analysts work for New York City firms that primarily trade securities among institutional holders, an important segment of the securities business. There are many outstanding bank security analysts employed outside New York City, employed by fund managers and others that are not shown here.

Mr. Mark C. Biderman
Oppenheimer & Co.
One New York Plaza
New York, New York 10004

Mr. James G. Ehlen Jr.
Goldman, Sachs & Co.
55 Broad Street
New York, New York 10004

Mr. William R. Fisher
Donaldson, Lufkin & Jenrette
  Securities Corporation
140 Broadway
New York, New York 10005

Mr. Irving M. Geszel
Bear, Stearns & Co.
55 Water Street
New York, New York 10041

The Keefe Bruyette Woods Team
One Liberty Plaza
91 Liberty Street
New York, New York 10006

Mr. Warren R. Marcus
Salomon Brothers
One New York Plaza
New York, New York 10004

Mr. David L. Rothgabor
Dean Witter & Co., Inc.
130 Liberty Street
New York, New York 10006

Mr. George M. Salem
Reynolds Securities, Inc.
One Battery Park Plaza
New York, New York 10004

Mr. William M. Weiant
The First Boston Corporation
20 Exchange Place
New York, New York 10005

Mr. James H. Wooden
Merrill Lynch, Pierce, Fenner &
  Smith, Inc.
One Liberty Plaza
New York, New York 10006

In addition to secondary sources of financial information, in recent years the financial press has provided an increasingly broad coverage of the banking industry. Articles on the banking industry and individual banks appear in such widely known periodicals as *Fortune, Business Week, Forbes, Economist, Time, Newsweek,* the *New York Times,* and the *Los Angeles Times.*

CHAPTER 3

A TOUR THROUGH ONE BANK'S FINANCIAL STATEMENTS

Numbers are the principal language used by banks to show their performance. An initial step in evaluating a bank is understanding the significance of the most important of those numbers.

This chapter provides a description of the financial statements of J. P. Morgan & Co., Incorporated. This bank is used as an example because overall its financial statements are among the most complete and its notes are among the clearest in the banking industry.

The core financial statements are reviewed here. They include the tables in the financial statements and notes of the 1976 annual report, which precede the accountants' opinion. This information has been audited and may be regarded as representing the hardest data available concerning a bank. Other data, which are presented elsewhere, often are useful to outside participants, since the data may be specially presented and arranged. Nevertheless, the other data usually are unaudited and based on this core data.

There are 11 financial tables, 15 notes to the tables, and the accountants' opinion to Morgan's core financial statements. The bank analyst should consider all of them as a unified whole. When viewed collectively, these tables and notes provide an indication of the bank's philosophy, which is available from no other source with such precision and clarity. The information presented provides an insight into how a bank keeps its numbers. An understanding of this philosophy through the financial statements is particularly crucial in a bank, since money is its business, and how the money is counted lies at the heart of its guiding policies. A look at the core financial statements is as close as an outside bank analyst can come to being present

63

during an internal financial discussion of its senior management (Figures 31–50).

The difference between a bank holding company and a commercial bank is a fundamental point. The broad scope of a bank holding company encompasses a wide variety of financial services and may include several commercial banks as subsidiaries. In contrast, a commercial bank mainly provides a safe haven for deposits and is a source of loans to borrowers. What we today call banks are, in many cases, bank holding companies that own as their principal subsidiary a commercial bank.

The initial two tables show J. P. Morgan & Co.'s financial position. These tables are essential in viewing the Morgan organization as a whole and may be regarded as being the most important financial tables in the annual report.

Financial data   *Financial statements*

Other financial data

Figure 31

A

Consolidated statement of income

J. P. Morgan & Co. Incorporated

In thousands, except per share

		1976	1975
	Interest income from:		
1	Loans	$ 989 775	$1 169 164
2	Federal funds sold and securities purchased under agreements to resell	10 014	18 141
3	U.S. Treasury securities	116 519	94 687
4	Obligations of states and political subdivisions	60 616	55 466
5	Other investment securities	50 108	49 379
6	Trading account securities		
	Obligations of states and political subdivisions	3 154	6 467
	Other securities	31 814	35 455
7	Other sources	297 681	323 253
8	Total interest income	1 559 681	1 752 012
	Interest expense due to:		
9	Deposits	792 839	983 467
10	Federal funds purchased and securities sold under agreements to repurchase	149 689	140 178
11	Other borrowed money	71 395	82 525
12	Notes and debentures	29 205	19 820
13	Total interest expense	1 043 128	1 225 990
14	Interest income net of interest expense	516 553	526 022
	Noninterest operating income		
15	Trading account profits and commissions	29 437	2 865
16	Corporate trust, other trust, and agency income	101 480	91 811
17	Foreign exchange trading income	33 844	32 459
18	Other operating income, mainly fees and commissions	87 682	81 792
19	Total noninterest operating income	252 443	208 927
	Total operating income net of interest expense	768 996	734 949
	Noninterest operating expenses		
20	Salaries	142 043	126 817
21	Deferred profit sharing	14 185	13 332
22	Additional compensation Note 12	5 170	4 475
23	Other employee benefits Note 12	42 686	37 426
24	Provision for possible loan losses Note 5	68 208	96 645
25	Net occupancy expense Note 11	37 591	33 780
26	Equipment rentals, depreciation, and maintenance	16 071	14 448
27	Other operating expenses	67 115	52 619
28	Total noninterest operating expenses	393 069	379 542
29	Income before income taxes and securities gains (losses)	375 927	355 407
30	Applicable income taxes Note 8	173 169	163 514
31	Income before securities gains (losses)	$ 202 758	$ 191 893
32	Per share Note 9	$5.04	$4.96
33	Net securities losses	$ (2 955)	$ (13 697)
34	Income tax benefit Note 8	2 880	5 629
35	Net income	$ 202 683	$ 183 825
36	Per share Note 9	$5.04	$4.76
37	Dividends declared per common share	$1.85	$1.80

See notes to financial statements on pages 36–44

Figure 32

B

Consolidated balance sheet

J. P. Morgan & Co. Incorporated

	December 31 1976	December 31 1975
Assets		
(1) Cash and due from banks	$ 3 635 357	$ 3 315 159
(2) Interest-bearing deposits at banks	5 525 455	4 185 074
(3) U.S. Treasury securities *Note 3*	1 796 351	1 468 326
(4) Obligations of U.S. government agencies *Note 3*	196 917	127 099
(5) Obligations of states and political subdivisions *Note 3*	1 109 077	829 776
(6) Other investment securities *Note 3*	503 551	399 325
(7) Trading account securities, net *Note 3*	331 032	405 547
(8) Federal funds sold and securities purchased under agreements to resell	249 682	382 348
(9) Loans	13 883 174	13 223 196
(10) Real estate	76 783	46 715
(11) Total loans and real estate	13 959 957	13 269 911
(12) Less: reserve for possible loan losses *Note 5*	150 160	134 892
(13) Net loans and real estate	13 809 797	13 135 019
(14) Premises and equipment, net of accumulated depreciation and amortization of $77 230 000 in 1976 and $70 236 000 in 1975 *Note 7*	123 102	114 363
(15) Customers' acceptance liability	801 635	706 106
(16) Other assets	683 554	763 043
(17) Total assets	$28 765 510	$25 831 185
Liabilities		
(18) Demand deposits	$ 6 756 408	$ 5 805 714
(19) Time deposits	3 014 193	3 603 649
(20) Deposits in foreign offices	11 703 657	10 528 308
(21) Total deposits	21 474 258	19 937 671
(22) Federal funds purchased and securities sold under agreements to repurchase *Note 6*	2 534 244	1 560 560
(23) Commercial paper *Note 6*	194 396	338 570
(24) Other liabilities for borrowed money	1 057 898	855 986
(25) Accrued taxes and expenses *Note 8*	405 798	435 706
(26) Liability on acceptances	806 688	708 333
(27) Dividend payable	19 348	16 519
(28) Long-term debt *Note 7*	544 001	389 188
(29) Other liabilities	273 331	368 099
(30) Total liabilities	$27 309 962	$24 610 632
Stockholders' equity		
(31) Preferred stock, no par value (1 000 000 shares authorized; none issued)	—	—
(32) Common stock, $2.50 par value (authorized: 50 000 000 shares; issued: 38 818 538 in 1976 and 36 814 638 in 1975) *Notes 7, 13*	$ 97 046	$ 92 037
(33) Capital surplus	485 057	386 050
(34) Retained earnings	879 578	747 594
	1 461 681	1 225 681
(35) Less: treasury stock (122 530 shares in 1976 and 106 468 shares in 1975) at cost	6 133	5 128
(36) Total stockholders' equity	1 455 548	1 220 553
(37) Total liabilities and stockholders' equity	$28 765 510	$25 831 185

See notes to financial statements on pages 36–44

Figure 33

C

Consolidated statement of condition

Morgan Guaranty Trust Company of New York

		In thousands	
		December 31 1976	December 31 1975
Assets			
Cash and due from banks		$ 3 630 353	$ 3 310 083
Interest-bearing deposits at banks		5 500 455	4 155 079
U.S. Treasury securities *Note 3*		1 723 041	1 430 640
Obligations of U.S. government agencies *Note 3*		191 928	127 099
Obligations of states and political subdivisions *Note 3*		1 109 077	829 776
Other investment securities *Note 3*		499 904	390 797
Trading account securities, net *Note 3*		331 032	405 547
Federal funds sold and securities purchased under agreements to resell		283 482	352 608
Loans		13 579 264	12 999 128
Real estate		74 287	44 364
Total loans and real estate		13 653 551	13 043 492
Less: reserve for possible loan losses *Note 5*		147 573	133 522
Net loans and real estate		13 505 978	12 909 970
Premises and equipment, net of accumulated depreciation and amortization of $77 204 000 in 1976 and $70 218 000 in 1975 *Note 7*		123 038	114 301
Customers' acceptance liability		801 635	706 106
Other assets		653 485	744 854
Total assets		$28 353 408	$25 476 860
Liabilities			
Demand deposits		$ 6 766 641	$ 5 817 641
Time deposits		3 014 193	3 618 649
Deposits in foreign offices		11 703 675	10 528 326
Total deposits		21 484 509	19 964 616
Federal funds purchased and securities sold under agreements to repurchase *Note 6*		2 534 244	1 560 560
Commercial paper of a subsidiary *Note 6*		92 484	83 935
Other liabilities for borrowed money		1 057 685	855 667
Accrued taxes and expenses *Note 8*		398 042	429 828
Liability on acceptances		806 688	708 333
Dividend payable		25 000	23 750
Convertible debentures of a subsidiary (4¾%, due 1987) *Note 7*		50 000	50 000
Capital notes (6¾%, due 1978) *Note 7*		100 000	100 000
Capital notes (5%, due 1992) *Note 7*		80 718	84 191
Mortgage payable *Note 7*		14 590	15 130
Other liabilities		271 438	367 751
Total liabilities		$26 915 398	$24 243 761
Stockholder's equity			
Capital stock, $25 par value (authorized and outstanding: 10 000 000 shares in 1976 and 9 500 000 shares in 1975)		$ 250 000	$ 237 500
Surplus		518 385	427 085
Undivided profits		669 625	568 514
Total stockholder's equity		1 438 010	1 233 099
Total liabilities and stockholder's equity		$28 353 408	$25 476 860

Member of Federal Reserve System and Federal Deposit Insurance Corporation
See notes to financial statements on pages 36–44

Figure 34

D

Statement of changes in stockholders' equity

J. P. Morgan & Co.
Incorporated
(consolidated) and
J. P. Morgan & Co.
Incorporated
(parent)

	In thousands	
	1976	*1975*
Common stock		
Balance, January 1	$ 92 037	$ 91 739
① Sale of 2 000 000 shares	5 000	—
② Conversion of debentures *Note 7*	—	292
③ Stock options exercised *Note 13*	9	6
Balance, December 31	97 046	92 037
Capital surplus		
Balance, January 1	386 050	380 268
④ Sale of common stock, 2 000 000 shares	98 800	—
⑤ Conversion of debentures *Note 7*	—	5 666
Stock options exercised *Note 13*	207	116
Balance, December 31	485 057	386 050
Retained earnings		
Balance, January 1	747 594	629 754
Net income	202 683	183 825
Cash dividends declared	(70 699)	(65 985)
Balance, December 31	879 578	747 594
Less: treasury stock		
Balance, January 1	5 128	3 970
Purchases	1 078	1 184
Distribution of shares under terms of additional compensation plan *Note 12*	(73)	(26)
Balance, December 31	6 133	5 128
Total stockholders' equity, December 31	$1 455 548	$1 220 553

See notes to financial statements on pages 36–44

Figure 35

The remaining tables show parts of the consolidated totals. These tables review the four principal legal parts of Morgan—the consolidated corporation, the holding company (parent only), the bank only, and the nonbank subsidiaries.

A. CONSOLIDATED STATEMENT OF INCOME—J. P. MORGAN & CO., INCORPORATED

A major responsibility of banks is to provide a profit for their legal owners, who are the shareholders. There is an established method of using earnings to evaluate how well banks accomplish this task. The concept of earnings has been given such a degree of refinement in recent years that many bank analysts consider earnings as representing a precise figure, much as though bank earnings were literally a sum of cash which remains after all of a bank's bills were paid. The difficulties of evaluating banks on the basis of earnings alone will be examined in a later section that reviews profitability. Nevertheless, the current widely held emphasis on earnings as a basis of evaluating banks underscores the importance of an earnings statement to bank analysts.

There is one important overall observation concerning a bank's earnings statement. It is an estimate of earnings. Despite the widespread use of generally accepted accounting practices, there are many areas of legitimate

E

Consolidated statement of changes in financial position

J. P. Morgan & Co. Incorporated

In thousands

	1976	1975
Financial resources were provided by:		
Net income	$ 202 683	$ 183 825
Noncash charges included in net income		
Depreciation and amortization	10 382	9 256
Provision for possible loan losses	68 208	96 645
① Deferred income taxes	14 432	7 708
Financial resources provided by operations	295 705	297 434
Increases in:		
Borrowed funds	1 175 596	127 916
Commercial paper	—	46 485
② Deposits	1 536 587	154 279
③ Decrease in loans and real estate	—	530 871
Sale of $150 000 000 8% notes, due 1986 . . .	147 375	—
Issuance of promissory note	10 000	—
Sale of common stock	103 800	—
Issuance of common stock upon conversion of debentures and		
exercise of stock options	216	6 080
	3 269 279	1 163 065
Financial resources were used for:		
Increases in:		
Cash and due from banks	1 660 579	587 192
Securities	706 855	459 318
④ Loans and real estate	610 321	—
Decrease in commercial paper	144 174	—
Expenditures for premises and equipment	21 786	19 795
Cash dividends paid	67 870	65 940
Acquisition of treasury stock	1 078	1 184
Acquisition of capital notes and conversion of debentures . .	2 657	8 200
Other uses, net	53 959	21 436
	$3 269 279	$1 163 065

See notes to financial statements on pages 36–44

Figure 36

F

Statement of income

J. P. Morgan & Co. Incorporated (parent)

In thousands

	1976	1975
Income		
Dividends from Morgan Guaranty Trust Company of New York . .	$ 98 750	$ 95 000
Interest, including $14 578 000 in 1976 and $14 387 000 in 1975		
on advances to subsidiaries	29 448	30 257
Total income	128 198	125 257
Expenses		
Interest	27 587	29 082
Other	2 403	2 215
Total expenses	29 990	31 297
Income before income tax benefit and undistributed income of		
subsidiaries	98 208	93 960
Income tax benefit *Note 8*	857	798
Income before undistributed income of subsidiaries	99 065	94 758
Equity in undistributed income of subsidiaries		
Morgan Guaranty Trust Company of New York	101 110	86 927
Other subsidiaries	2 508	2 140
Total equity in undistributed income of subsidiaries . . .	103 618	89 067
Net income	$202 683	$183 825

See notes to financial statements on pages 36–44

Figure 37

G

Balance sheet

J. P. Morgan & Co.
Incorporated
(parent)

		In thousands	
		December 31 1976	December 31 1975
Assets			
Cash ($6 977 000 in 1976 and $8 265 000 in 1975 on deposit at Morgan Guaranty Trust Company of New York)		$ 11 980	$ 13 339
Time deposits at banks ($18 000 in 1976 and $15 018 000 in 1975 on deposit at Morgan Guaranty Trust Company of New York)		25 018	45 013
Marketable securities (market value: $83 666 000 in 1976 and $45 348 000 in 1975)		80 727	44 918
Loans .		74 659	1 144
Dividend receivable from Morgan Guaranty Trust Company of New York		25 000	23 750
(1) Advances to nonbank subsidiaries *Note 10*		221 922	212 532
Investments in subsidiaries			
Morgan Guaranty Trust Company of New York		1 438 010	1 233 099
Other subsidiaries *Note 10*		26 026	22 782
Securities purchased under agreements to resell		—	49 550
Other assets		22 876	18 640
(2) Total assets		$1 926 218	$1 664 767
Liabilities			
(3) Commercial paper *Note 6*		$ 101 911	$ 254 635
Secured borrowings from Morgan Guaranty Trust Company of New York		33 800	19 810
Dividend payable		19 348	16 519
(4) Long-term debt *Note 7*		308 826	150 000
Other liabilities		6 785	3 250
Total liabilities		$470 670	$ 444 214
Stockholders' equity			
Preferred stock, no par value (1 000 000 shares authorized, none issued)		—	—
Common stock, $2.50 par value (authorized: 50 000 000 shares; issued: 38 818 538 in 1976 and 36 814 638 in 1975) *Notes 7, 13* .		$ 97 046	$ 92 037
Capital surplus		485 057	386 050
Retained earnings		879 578	747 594
		1 461 681	1 225 681
Less: treasury stock (122 530 shares in 1976 and 106 468 shares in 1975) at cost		6 133	5 128
(5) Total stockholders' equity		1 455 548	1 220 553
Total liabilities and stockholders' equity		$1 926 218	$1 664 767

See notes to financial statements on pages 36–44

Figure 38

differences about how to present earnings. For this reason, the earnings statements should be read with a bank analyst's perception of the philosophy of the bank in the background. For example, is the bank aggressive? Is it evenhanded in explaining issues? Is the bank quiet with its accomplishments? The bank analyst should keep these types of questions in mind when reviewing financial statements.

The format of the income statement of most banks adds all income (that is, all revenues), subtracts all business expenses and taxes, and shows a profit if there is a surplus of income over expenses or a loss if there is a deficit. "Sources of income" refer to commercial transactions of the bank that

H

Statement of changes in financial position

J. P. Morgan & Co. Incorporated (parent)

	In thousands	
	1976	1975
Financial resources were provided by:		
Net income	$202 683	$183 825
Noncash charges (credits) included in net income		
Deferred income taxes	781	479
Equity in undistributed income of subsidiaries	(103 618)	(89 067)
Increase in dividend receivable from Morgan Guaranty Trust Company of New York	(1 250)	—
Financial resources provided by operations	98 596	95 237
Increase in borrowed funds	—	26 015
Decreases in:		
Cash and time deposits at banks	21 354	45 983
Securities purchased under agreements to resell	49 550	—
Sale of $150 000 000 8% notes, due 1986	147 375	—
Issuance of promissory note	10 000	—
Sale of common stock	103 800	—
Issuance of common stock upon conversion of debentures and exercise of stock options	216	6 080
Other sources, net	42	—
	430 933	173 315
Financial resources were used for:		
Cash dividends paid	67 870	65 940
Increases in:		
Loans	73 515	266
Marketable securities	35 809	27 230
Securities purchased under agreements to resell	—	42 562
Decrease in borrowed funds	138 734	—
Additional investment in and advances to subsidiaries	113 927	27 247
Acquisition of treasury stock	1 078	1 184
Other uses, net	—	8 886
	$430 933	$173 315

See notes to financial statements on pages 36–44

Figure 39

increase its net worth, and "expenses" refer to transactions that decrease its net worth.

However, in 1976 Morgan changed this format to show earnings on the basis of net interest income and other income and expense. The change focuses attention on the central importance of intermediation for a bank. It is the service of being a money middleman that is banking's business, and the new organization of the income table indicates the importance of this concept in the thinking of Morgan's financial management.

Interest Income

A-1 Loans. This line includes interest and fees pertaining to loans that are shown in the balance sheet. Interest and fees on loans usually account for one-half or more of all income for banks, underscoring the importance of loans.

Interest and fees on loans include regular bank loans, interest on acceptances, interest on commercial paper purchased in the open market, interest on drafts for which a bank has given deposit credit to customers, interest on loan paper that has been rediscounted with the Federal Reserve and other banks, and paper purchased under resale agreements or pledged as collateral for bills payable. Profit or losses from the sale of loans, acceptances, and commercial paper are also included in interest on loans. Interest rebated to customers on loans paid before maturity is deducted from interest on loans.

A-2 Federal Funds Sold and Securities Purchased Under Agreements to Resell. This line includes income from U.S. government securities that is loaned to other banks for the purpose of enabling the banks to meet their reserve requirements with the Federal Reserve Bank. The federal funds sold

I

Combined statement of income and retained earnings

Nonbank subsidiaries of J. P. Morgan & Co. Incorporated

	In thousands	
	1976	*1975*
Operating income		
Interest on loans	$21 824	$20 948
Other operating income	1 755	752
Total operating income	23 579	21 700
Operating expenses		
Interest on advances *Note 10*	14 578	14 387
Salaries and other employee expenses	648	513
Provision for possible loan losses *Note 5*	1 567	1 090
Other operating expenses	660	681
Total operating expenses	17 453	16 671
Income before income taxes	6 126	5 029
Applicable income taxes	3 618	2 889
① Net income	2 508	2 140
Retained earnings (deficit), January 1	(3 956)	(6 096)
Retained earnings (deficit), December 31	$ (1 448)	$ (3 956)

J

Combined statement of changes in financial position

Nonbank subsidiaries of J. P. Morgan & Co. Incorporated

	1976	*1975*
Financial resources were provided by:		
Net income	$ 2 508	$ 2 140
Noncash charges (credits) included in net income		
Depreciation	5	4
Provision for possible loan losses	1 567	1 090
Deferred income taxes	607	(2)
Financial resources provided by operations	4 687	3 232
Increase in advances		
from J. P. Morgan & Co. Incorporated (parent)	9 390	26 397
Decreases in:		
Cash	407	—
Investment securities	77	—
Income tax benefit receivable		
from J. P. Morgan & Co. Incorporated (parent)	192	936
Additional investment		
by J. P. Morgan & Co. Incorporated (parent)	736	850
Other sources, net	—	3 371
	15 489	34 786
Financial resources were used for:		
Increases in:		
Cash	—	3 118
Investment securities	—	750
Loans and real estate	6 820	27 602
Direct lease financing	6 562	3 316
Other uses, net	2 107	—
	$15 489	$34 786

See notes to financial statements on pages 36–44

Figure 40

K

Combined balance sheet

Nonbank subsidiaries of J. P. Morgan & Co. Incorporated

	In thousands	
Assets	December 31 1976	December 31 1975
Cash (substantially all on deposit at Morgan Guaranty		
Trust Company of New York)	$ 3 257	$ 3 664
Investment securities	1 219	1 296
Loans	229 250	222 925
Real estate	2 496	2 351
Less: reserve for possible loan losses *Note 5*	2 587	1 370
Net loans and real estate	229 159	223 906
Direct lease financing	13 702	7 140
Income tax benefit receivable from J. P. Morgan & Co.		
Incorporated (parent)	234	426
Other assets	4 549	4 361
Total assets	252 120	240 793
Liabilities		
Advances from J. P. Morgan & Co. Incorporated (parent)		
Note 10	$221 922	$212 532
Accrued taxes and expenses	3 127	4 806
Other liabilities	1 045	673
Total liabilities	$226 094	$218 011
Stockholder's equity		
Common stock and capital surplus	$ 27 474	$ 26 738
Retained earnings (deficit)	(1 448)	(3 956)
Total stockholder's equity	26 026	22 782
Total liabilities and stockholder's equity	$252 120	$240 793

See notes to financial statements on pages 36–44

Figure 41

represent Morgan's excess reserves that were sold to other banks. Morgan sells these reserves to earn interest on the funds.

The securities purchased under agreements to resell are not reserves. In this case, Morgan sold its temporarily idle cash funds to dealers or other banks to earn interest on the funds.

A-3 U.S. Treasure Securities. This category includes revenues from U.S. treasury bills, notes, and debentures. This source of income expanded for Morgan from 1975 to 1976 and—when read with the gain in U.S. treasury securities noted in the bank's balance sheet—indicated a growing importance of the bank's position in treasuries. This line in the Morgan table also includes income from securities of U.S. government agencies that are widely regarded as being as risk-free as treasuries. Many other banks show agency income as a separate line. As discussed in a later chapter, this shift in assets of Morgan increased the liquidity of the bank.

A-4 Obligations of States and Political Subdivisions. This line shows the bank's income from state and municipal securities, which are exempt from federal taxation. In some states, securities of governmental units in the state are also exempt from certain state taxes. This exemption means that the income of state and municipal securities is carried through to earnings without a deduction for taxes. Income from state and municipal securities is approximately twice as valuable as the figures would indicate and cannot be properly considered on the same basis as most other sources of income. The income is twice as valuable because most taxable income of banks is taxed at approximately a 50 percent rate.

The income from state and municipal securities of Morgan was reduced in 1976 because of the financial difficulties of New York City, as is outlined in

L

Notes to financial statements

1. Accounting policies

The accounting and reporting policies and practices of J. P. Morgan & Co. Incorporated, Morgan Guaranty Trust Company of New York, and other subsidiaries conform with generally accepted accounting principles and general practice within the banking industry.

Certain 1975 amounts have been reclassified to conform with 1976 classifications.

The following is a description of the more significant policies and practices.

Consolidation

The consolidated financial statements include the accounts of J. P. Morgan & Co. and all subsidiaries (companies in which its percentage of ownership exceeds 50%). The equity method of accounting is generally utilized in determining the carrying values of investments in companies in which the percentage of ownership is 20% or more but not more than 50%. Investments of J. P. Morgan & Co. Incorporated (parent) in subsidiaries are carried at equity in their underlying net assets.

The results of operations of foreign branches and subsidiaries included in the consolidated statement of income are for the 12 months ended November 30, and the financial position of foreign branches and certain subsidiaries included in the consolidated balance sheet is as of December 31.

Securities

Securities are held for both investment and trading purposes. Debt securities held for investment are carried at cost, adjusted for amortization of premiums and discounts. Equity securities held for investment are carried at the lower of aggregate cost or market value, except for investments in securities of companies in which the percentage of ownership is 20% or more but not more than 50%, which are carried generally at underlying equity value. Net gains or losses on the sale of investment securities other than U.S. Treasury bills are shown separately in the consolidated statement of income. The excess over cost of the proceeds upon sale or maturity of U.S. Treasury bills held for investment is included in interest on U.S. Treasury securities.

Trading account securities are carried at market value. Interest earned on trading account securities is shown in the consolidated statement of income separately from interest earned on investment securities. Gains and losses on trading account securities are considered to be a normal part of operations and are recorded in the caption "trading account profits and commissions." (*See Note 3.*)

Reserve for possible loan losses

The provision for possible loan losses is the amount which in the judgment of management is required to bring the reserve for possible loan losses to an appropriate level, based on a continuing evaluation of the potential losses in the loan portfolio.

Premises and equipment

Premises and equipment are stated generally at cost, less accumulated depreciation and amortization. Depreciation is computed generally by the straight-line method over the estimated useful lives of the related assets. Leasehold improvements are amortized over the lives of the respective leases or the estimated useful lives of the improvements, whichever are the shorter periods. Expenditures for repairs and maintenance are charged to operating expenses as incurred. Amounts expended for improvements which extend the life of an asset are capitalized and depreciated over the life of the asset.

Income taxes

In the financial statements the tax effects of transactions are recognized in the same fiscal periods as the related items of income and expense, regardless of when they are recognized for tax purposes. The accumulated provisions for deferred taxes required as a result of such timing differences are included in "accrued taxes and expenses" in the consolidated balance sheet.

Investment tax credits pertaining to direct lease financing are amortized to income over the terms of the leases. Other investment tax credits are amortized over the estimated useful lives of the related assets.

Other

J. P. Morgan & Co. and its subsidiaries are on an accrual basis of accounting except for fiduciary fees and certain minor sources of income, which are recorded in the year in which payment is received. These exceptions have not had a material effect on the financial statements.

Morgan Guaranty follows the general practice of valuing its foreign exchange trading position monthly and recording the profit or loss resulting from the valuation. This valuation includes pricing all spot and forward positions generally to market rates at the time of valuation. Income or loss from foreign exchange trading, including that resulting from such monthly valuations, is shown separately in the consolidated statement of income.

Real estate and related assets which have been acquired in connection with loans are shown as "real estate" on the consolidated balance sheet. Charge-offs and recoveries relating to these assets are reflected in the reserve for possible loan losses.

Figure 42

2. Foreign currency translation gains and losses

The aggregate foreign currency translation gains
(losses) included in "other operating income" were
$694,000 in 1976 and $(631,000) in 1975.

3. Securities

A comparison of the book value and market or appraised value of all securities at December 31, 1976
and 1975 follows. Appraised values are used for securities without market quotations. The market values of
obligations of states and political subdivisions are
established with the assistance of an independent

pricing service and are based on available market data,
which often reflect transactions of relatively small
size and are not necessarily indicative of the prices at
which large amounts of particular issues could readily
be sold or purchased.

	1976, in thousands		1975, in thousands	
Investment securities	Book value	Market or appraised value	Book value	Market or appraised value
U.S. Treasury securities	$1 796 351	$1 860 199	$1 468 326	$1 483 186
Obligations of U.S. government agencies	196 917	207 000	127 099	125 874
Obligations of states and political subdivisions	1 109 077	1 112 105	829 776	671 110
Other investment securities	503 551	519 245	399 325	409 589
Trading account securities, net	331 032	331 032	405 547	405 547
Total securities	$3 936 928	$4 029 581	$3 230 073	$3 095 306

Investment securities at December 31, 1976 included the following:

	In thousands	
	Book value	Market or appraised value
Obligations of the City of New York	$ 83 844	$ 62 883
Obligations of New York City agencies	12 600	10 053
Obligations of Municipal Assistance Corporation for the City of New York	102 323	86 053
Obligations of New York State	56 725	56 921
Obligations of New York State agencies	175 790	173 776
Obligations of other municipal borrowers in New York State	11 853	12 006
	$443 135	$401 692

Obligations of the City of New York included in the
above table were notes originally scheduled to mature
one year after issuance. They were subject to a moratorium enacted by New York State in 1975 and were
also, pursuant to the terms of a November 1975 agreement among various banks, the Municipal Assistance
Corporation for the City of New York, and others,
subject to a reduction in interest rate to 6% and to ex-
tensions of maturity to February 1986. Interest income
on these securities amounted to $5,564,000 in 1976,
which was $1,579,000 less than it would have been if
interest rates on them had remained unchanged from
those originally established. Because the moratorium
was declared unconstitutional by the New York Court
of Appeals in November 1976, the continuing opera-
tiveness of provisions of the November 1975 agreement applicable to these securities is being questioned
by various parties including Morgan Guaranty, and
discussions with public officials who assert that the
provisions remain applicable are in progress.

Certain of the Municipal Assistance Corporation
obligations included in the above table were received
during 1976, pursuant to the November 1975 agreement, in exchange for obligations of the same obligor

having a shorter maturity or a higher interest rate.
Interest income from Municipal Assistance Corporation obligations during 1976 was $6,357,000, which
was $2,066,000 less than it would have been had the
exchanges not taken place. The overall effective
yield on Municipal Assistance Corporation obligations
was 6.03% at December 31, 1976. If they bear interest
throughout 1977 at the rates in effect at the end of
1976, interest income from such obligations will be
$6,170,000. Negotiations are presently going on con-
cerning a possible further extension of the maturity
of certain of such obligations.

The above table is limited to all those obligations of
New York City, New York State, and related political
subdivisions included in investment securities and
does not include trading account securities, which
were carried at market values, or loans, which were
not material in relation to the total loan portfolio.

Net gains on sales of U.S. Treasury bills in the trading account have been reclassified from interest income to "trading account profits and commissions."
The amounts reclassified were $4,136,000 and
$8,394,000 for 1976 and 1975, respectively.

Figure 43

Note 3 of Morgan's financial statements. This note also discusses the effect of
changes in the payment schedule for 1976 and shows the bank analyst how
the problems of New York City are related to Morgan. It also provides a basis
of calculating the effect of possible further changes of New York City securities on the bank.

A-5 Other Investment Securities. This line shows the income from all stocks, notes, and debentures that do not fit into the forementioned categories of investment securities. If the bank is a member of the Federal Reserve System, as is Morgan, dividends from its stock in the system would appear here. As will be discussed in the balance sheet, this line would typically include only minor dividends from corporate equities.

A-6 Trading Account. These two lines show interest earned on trading account securities. The trading account information reflects its historical importance in bank examination. In the 1920s many banks took speculative positions in their trading accounts, often as part of an underwriting function

Notes to financial statements
(continued)

4. Pledged assets

Assets carried at $2,476,752,000 and $1,622,140,000 in the consolidated balance sheet at December 31, 1976 and 1975, respectively, were pledged as collateral for borrowings, to qualify for fiduciary powers, to secure public monies as required by law, and for other purposes.

5. Reserve for possible loan losses

An analysis of the reserve for possible loan losses follows:

	1976, in thousands			1975, in thousands		
	Morgan Guaranty	Nonbank subsidiaries	J. P. Morgan & Co. (consolidated)	Morgan Guaranty	Nonbank subsidiaries	J. P. Morgan & Co. (consolidated)
Balance, January 1 . . .	$133 522	$1 370	$134 892	$120 858	$ 280	$121 138
Recoveries	754	—	754	1 487	—	1 487
Charge-offs	(52 757)	(350)	(53 107)	(84 378)	—	(84 378)
Net charge-offs.	(52 003)	(350)	(52 353)	(82 891)	—	(82 891)
Provision	67 086	1 567	68 653	95 653	1 090	96 743
Translation adjustment .	(445)	—	(445)	(98)	—	(98)
Sale of subsidiary . . .	(587)	—	(587)	—	—	—
	66 054	1 567	67 621	95 555	1 090	96 645
Balance, December 31	$147 573	$2 587	$150 160	$133 522	$1 370	$134 892

6. Federal funds, repurchase agreements, and commercial paper

Data on Federal funds purchased on a day-to-day basis, securities sold under agreements to repurchase, and commercial paper are shown in the following table:

	J. P. Morgan & Co. Incorporated (consolidated); dollars in thousands		J. P. Morgan & Co. Incorporated (parent); dollars in thousands	
	1976	1975	1976	1975
Federal funds purchased				
Average balance	$1 408 000	$1 264 000	—	—
Maximum balance	2 571 000	2 527 000	—	—
Average interest rate				
During year	5.03%	5.82%	—	—
At year-end	4.23	4.55	—	—
Securities sold under agreements to repurchase				
Average balance	$1 556 000	$1 137 000	$ 31 000	$ 17 000
Maximum balance	2 579 000	1 780 000	101 000	55 000
Average interest rate				
During year	5.05%	5.87%	5.15%	6.19%
At year-end	4.44	5.18	4.47	5.75
Commercial paper				
Average balance	$ 258 000	$ 388 000	$ 169 000	$ 303 000
Maximum balance	430 000	456 000	344 000	358 000
Average interest rate				
During year	6.87%	7.21%	5.48%	6.91%
At year-end	6.97	6.85	4.62	6.16

Average interest rates during each year are computed by dividing total interest expense by the average amount borrowed. Original maturities for sales of securities under agreements to repurchase and for commercial paper are not in excess of six and nine months, respectively.

Figure 44

7. Long-term debt

Long-term debt of J. P. Morgan & Co. at December 31, 1976 and 1975 consisted of:

J. P. Morgan & Co. Incorporated (parent)	*In thousands*	
	1976	1975
6¾% note, due 1979	$ 10 000	—
8% notes, due 1986	150 000	—
4¾% convertible debentures, due		
1998	150 000	$150 000
	310 000	150 000
Less unamortized discount on		
8% notes	1 174	—
	308 826	150 000
Morgan Guaranty Trust Company of New York		
Capital notes		
6¾%, due 1978	100 000	100 000
5%, due 1992	81 458	85 000
4¼% convertible debentures, due		
1987	39 867	39 867
Mortgage payable	14 590	15 130
	235 915	239 997
Less unamortized discount		
on 5% capital notes	740	809
	235 175	239 188
Total long-term debt	$544 001	$389 188

The 5% capital notes are subordinated and junior in right of payment to obligations to depositors and other creditors. The indenture requires a sinking fund, which began in 1972, to retire $3,000,000 principal amount of such notes annually. Subject to the approval of the Superintendent of Banks of the State of New York, the notes are redeemable in whole or in part at 101.925% through January 31, 1977 and at prices declining annually thereafter to 100% after January 31, 1987.

The 6¾% capital notes are not redeemable prior to maturity. They are subordinated and junior in right of payment to obligations to depositors and other creditors.

The 4¼% convertible debentures sold by J. P. Morgan Overseas Capital Corporation, an indirect subsidiary of Morgan Guaranty, are convertible into J. P. Morgan & Co. common stock at $52.25 a share. Payment of principal and interest is uncondi-

tionally guaranteed by J. P. Morgan & Co. The debentures are redeemable in whole or in part at 103.50% through June 14, 1977 and at prices declining annually thereafter to 100% after June 14, 1982, provided, with respect to any redemption occurring prior to June 15, 1977, that the closing market price of the common stock on the New York Stock Exchange shall not have been less than 150% of the conversion price on any day during the period from the 45th through the 16th days preceding the date of the notice of redemption. At December 31, 1976, $10,133,000 principal amount of debentures had been converted into 193,876 shares of common stock and 763,004 shares of common stock remained reserved for issuance upon conversion of the remaining debentures.

The 4¾% convertible debentures are convertible into J. P. Morgan & Co. common stock at $80 a share and are redeemable in whole or in part at 104.04% through October 31, 1977 and at prices declining annually thereafter to 100% after October 31, 1993. At December 31, 1976 there had been no conversion of the debentures and 1,875,000 shares of common stock remained reserved for issuance upon conversion of these debentures.

In 1976, J. P. Morgan & Co. sold $150,000,000 of 8% notes due in 1986 and a 6¾% note due in 1979 in the amount of $10,000,000.

The building at 15 Broad Street, utilized by Morgan Guaranty as part of its main office, and the land on which it stands are subject to a mortgage outstanding in the amount of $14,590,000 at December 31, 1976, payable in level installments amounting to $1,062,500 annually (covering interest at 3½% and principal) to 1995. The land and building had a net book value of approximately $41,023,000 at December 31, 1976.

The aggregate amounts of long-term debt maturities and remaining sinking fund requirements for the five years subsequent to December 31, 1976 are $3,017,000 (1977), $103,579,000 (1978), $13,599,000 (1979), $3,621,000 (1980), and $3,643,000 (1981).

Figure 45

for new securities of governments and corporations. When the difficulties of the 1930 depression spread, trading accounts of many banks included worthless securities. The bank examiners and shareholders once burned were twice shy and subsequently have closely reviewed the activities of trading accounts.

A-7 Other Sources.   This is the second most important source of income for Morgan. It declined from 1975 to 1976, but is still of major proportions. Other interest income for Morgan mainly includes interest on deposits held overseas. This interest is largely paid on deposits of Morgan in other banks, primarily from other major banks engaged in Eurocurrency deposit and lending activities.

A-8 Total Interest Income.   This line shows the total of the above lines. It shows the sum of interest revenues from all sources.

Interest Expense

A-9 Deposits.   Interest paid on deposits is the largest individual expense item of most banks, including Morgan.

A-10 Federal Funds Purchased and Securities Sold Under Agreements to Repurchase. The federal funds purchased represent other banks' excess reserves purchased by Morgan. Morgan buys these reserves to meet its reserve requirement with the Federal Reserve Bank. The securities sold under repurchase agreements represent the purchase of customers' temporarily idle funds.

Notes to financial statements (*continued*)

8. Income taxes

J. P. Morgan & Co. and its domestic subsidiaries file consolidated federal income tax returns. The current and deferred portions of the income tax provisions included in the consolidated statement of income, including the income tax benefit of net securities losses, are as follows:

	1976, in thousands			1975, in thousands		
	Current	Deferred	Total	Current	Deferred	Total
Federal	$ 54 602	$ 5 542	$ 60 144	$ 31 060	$4 565	$ 35 625
State and local .	55 814	7 519	63 333	51 491	1 158	52 649
Foreign	45 441	1 371	46 812	67 626	1 985	69 611
	$155 857	$14 432	$170 289	$150 177	$7 708	$157 885

Deferred tax provisions resulted from:

	In thousands	
	1976	1975
Direct lease financing transactions recorded in the accounts using the financing method	$12 997	$15 331
Difference between provision for possible loan losses charged as an operating expense and current deduction under applicable tax laws	(3 352)	(13 963)
Other, net	4 787	6 340
	$14 432	$ 7 708

The total provisions for income taxes of $170,289,000 for 1976 and $157,885,000 for 1975 reflect effective rates of 45.7% and 46.2%, respectively. The reasons for the differences between the United States statutory income tax rate and the effective rates are shown in the following table:

	1976		1975	
	Amount in thousands	% of pretax income	Amount in thousands	% of pretax income
Tax at statutory rate.	$179 027	48.0	$164 021	48.0
Decrease due to tax-exempt income from loans and investments	(41 606)	(11.1)	(41 327)	(12.1)
Increase due to state and local taxes, net of federal income tax effects . .	32 933	8.8	27 377	8.0
Increase (decrease) due to miscellaneous items, each less than 5% of tax at statutory rate, net	(65)	—	7 814	2.3
	$170 289	45.7	$157 885	46.2

The amounts of investment tax credits relating to direct lease financing that were included in "other operating income" were $1,928,000 in 1976 and $2,028,000 in 1975. Other investment tax credits, amortized to income as a reduction of the provision for income taxes, amounted to $384,000 in 1976 and $247,000 in 1975. The amount of investment tax credits to be utilized in the 1976 income tax return is estimated to be $4,919,000. The amount utilized in the 1975 return was $743,200.

The approximate cumulative amounts of deferred income taxes included in the caption "accrued taxes and expenses" are as follows:

	In thousands	
	1976	1975
Deferred income taxes	$105 277	$91 069
Deferred investment tax credits	1 576	1 352
	$106 853	$92 421

Morgan Guaranty follows the policy of providing additions to the reserve for possible loan losses in the maximum amounts allowed under the applicable tax laws. At December 31, 1976 and 1975, the reserve for possible loan losses for federal income tax purposes exceeded the amount reported for financial statement purposes by $75,586,000 and $82,763,000, respectively. Deferred income taxes applicable thereto, amounting to $35,735,000 and $39,087,000 at December 31, 1976 and 1975, respectively, are included in "accrued taxes and expenses" in the consolidated balance sheet.

Figure 46

9. Earnings per share

Earnings per share (common and common equivalent) are computed by dividing adjusted income before securities gains (losses) of $206,177,000 in 1976 and $195,357,000 in 1975 and adjusted net income of $206,102,000 in 1976 and $187,288,000 in 1975 by the weighted average number of common and common equivalent shares outstanding during each year (40,933,157 shares in 1976 and 39,370,616 shares in 1975). Common and common equivalent shares include the average number of shares of common stock outstanding, the average number of shares issuable upon conversion of the 4¼% and 4¾% convertible debentures, and, under the treasury stock method, the average number of shares attributable to employee stock options which have a dilutive effect. Income before securities gains (losses) and net income are adjusted by adding thereto the interest on the debentures, less the related income tax effect.

10. Combined financial statements of nonbank subsidiaries

J. P. Morgan & Co. Incorporated (parent) makes interest-bearing advances to its nonbank subsidiaries which are funded by the proceeds of the parent's issuance of commercial paper and debt securities, including the 8% notes due in 1986 and the 6¾% note due in 1979. The interest rates on advances are substantially the same as those on the commercial paper and debt securities through which funds for the advances are obtained.

Changes in common stock and capital surplus of nonbank subsidiaries result solely from additional investments by J. P. Morgan & Co. Incorporated (parent).

Investments in and advances to nonbank subsidiaries for 1976 and 1975 were as follows:

	In thousands	
Investments	1976	1975
Balance, January 1	$ 22 782	$ 19 792
Additional investments	736	850
Net income of nonbank subsidiaries	2 508	2 140
Balance, December 31	$ 26 026	$ 22 782
Advances		
Balance, January 1	$212 532	$186 135
Net increase during year	9 390	26 397
Balance, December 31	$221 922	$212 532

11. Commitments and contingent liabilities

In the normal course of business, various commitments and contingent liabilities are outstanding, such as commitments to extend credit, forward foreign exchange contracts, guarantees, "standby" letters of credit, etc., which are not reflected in the financial statements. The management of J. P. Morgan & Co. does not anticipate any material losses as a result of these transactions.

At December 31, 1976 outstanding guarantees and "standby" letters of credit issued by Morgan Guaranty and its subsidiaries amounted to $1,194,448,000.

Operating expenses include net rentals of $20,479,000 in 1976 and $17,363,000 in 1975. Future minimum rental commitments on all noncancellable leases for premises (reduced by sublease rentals, which are not material) are as follows:

1977	. . . .	$11 068 000	1982–86.	. . .	$49 606 000
1978	. . . .	10 839 000	1987–91.	. . .	35 940 000
1979	. . . .	10 847 000	1992–96.	. . .	25 404 000
1980	. . . .	10 720 000	1997–2030	. .	20 976 000
1981	. . . .	10 613 000			

Certain leases contain renewal options and escalation clauses.

12. Employee benefits

Noncontributory retirement plans are in effect for substantially all full-time employees of Morgan Guaranty over 25 years of age. Morgan Guaranty's policy is to fund the accrued cost of the retirement plans. The actuarially determined contributions under the plans charged to income for the years 1976 and 1975 were $10,010,000 and $8,995,000, respectively.

The plan for United States employees, covering a

Figure 47

Morgan, like many banks, is both a buyer and a seller of federal funds, as well as of repurchase agreements, to maintain steady access to both sides of this market. The subtraction of purchased funds from funds sold is not shown on the balance sheet. This is done to give an indication of the participation in these markets. This calculation would show Morgan's net position in these funds.

A-11 Other Borrowed Money. Interest on other borrowed money was paid for commercial paper issued by the holding company and other liabilities for borrowed money.

A-12 Notes and Debentures. Interest on capital notes and debentures is paid on these types of long-term debt.

A-13 Total Interest Expense. This line shows the sum of all interest expenses and is the total of all above-interest expense lines.

Notes to financial statements
(continued)

large majority of all employees, provides for normal retirement at age 65. Under specified conditions the plan also permits early retirement and payment of spouse's and eligible children's benefits and provides for payment of vested benefits to terminated employees. Effective July 1, 1976 certain changes were made in the plan to comply with the Employee Retirement Income Security Act. Pursuant to such changes, an employee with ten years of service after age 22 is vested as to 100% of the benefit due, and gains and losses, including changes in market value of the plan's assets, are recognized on the basis of a five-year moving average in the determination of the annual contribution to the plan. Prior service liabilities under the plan are fully funded. At December 31, 1976 tne market value of the plan's assets exceeded the actuarially computed value of the vested benefits by approximately $23,600,000.

J. P. Morgan & Co. has an additional compensation plan designed to promote the success of that company and participating subsidiaries, including Morgan Guaranty, by providing additional compensation for services rendered during any year by senior or junior executives who have made important contributions during that year. Under the plan, the Board of Directors of J. P. Morgan & Co. determines the individual awards as well as the aggregate amount awarded, subject to a maximum specified in the plan.

13. Stock options

Under the stock option plan, approved by the stockholders of J. P. Morgan & Co. on March 20, 1974, 800,000 shares of common stock were reserved for issuance to key employees. At the discretion of a committee of the Board of Directors of J. P. Morgan & Co. administering the plan, the options may be qualified or nonqualified as defined in the United States Internal Revenue Code.

Options may be granted at a price not less than the market price on the date of the grant and are exercisable commencing at least one year following the date of the grant, and in no event later than ten years from the date of the grant. Options have been granted each year since 1974 but may not be granted under the plan after March 20, 1979.

The following is a summary of transactions during 1976 and 1975 under the plan:

	Shares under option	*Option price*		*Market value**	
		Per share	*Aggregate in thousands*	*Per share*	*Aggregate in thousands*
Granted					
1976	164 600	$61¼	$10 082	$61¼	$10 082
1975	157 100	66¾	10 486	66¾	10 486
Exercised					
1976	3 900	52⅛	203	52⅛ to 63⅛	227
1975	2 200	52⅛	115	56½ to 67 1/16	130
Canceled					
1976	8 400				
1975	5 800				
Balance, December 31					
1976	455 500**	52⅛ to 66¾	27 422		
1975	303 200	52⅛ to 66¾	18 066		
Became exercisable					
1976	154 600	66¾	10 320	61¼	9 469
1975	154 100	52⅛	8 032	66¾	10 286

* *At dates options were granted, were exercised, or became exercisable, as applicable*
** *Including nonqualified options for 327,300 shares*

On December 31, 1976 and 1975, 338,400 and 494,600 shares, respectively, were available for future grant.

At the time an option is exercised, the par value of the shares issued is credited to common stock and the excess of the proceeds over the par value is credited to capital surplus. For nonqualified stock options, an additional credit is made to capital surplus to record the tax benefit resulting from applying the applicable tax rate, at the date of exercise, to the difference between the option price and the market value at the date of exercise. There are no charges or credits to income in connection with the options.

Figure 48

14. Selected quarterly financial data

Listed below are financial data showing results for each quarter in the two years ended December 31, 1976. These results are unaudited; however, in the opinion of management all adjustments (consisting only of normal recurring accruals) necessary for a fair presentation have been included.

	In millions, except per share, three months ended:							
	March 31		June 30		September 30		December 31	
	1976	1975	1976	1975	1976	1975	1976	1975
Interest income net of interest expense	$130.3	$137.0	$128.3	$135.9	$128.0	$126.4	$130.0	$126.7
Noninterest operating income	53.0	55.7	55.6	44.9	61.3	51.7	82.5	56.6
Noninterest operating expenses	98.4	103.3	99.6	91.5	97.9	91.2	97.2	93.5
Income before income taxes and securities gains (losses)	84.9	89.4	84.3	89.3	91.4	86.9	115.3	89.8
Applicable income taxes	40.0	40.5	39.2	45.7	41.3	37.4	52.7	39.9
Income before securities gains (losses)	$ 44.9	$ 48.9	$ 45.1	$ 43.6	$ 50.1	$ 49.5	$ 62.6	$ 49.9
Per share	$1.15	$1.26	$1.11	$1.13	$1.24	$1.28	$1.54	$1.29
Net securities gains (losses)	$(0.3)	$(5.5)	$(1.0)	$(3.3)	$ 1.8	$(4.4)	$(3.4)	$(0.5)
Income tax benefit (expense)	0.6	2.7	0.9	2.0	(0.2)	2.7	1.6	(1.8)
Net income	$ 45.2	$ 46.1	$ 45.0	$ 42.3	$ 51.7	$ 47.8	$ 60.8	$ 47.6
Per share	$1.16	$1.19	$1.11	$1.10	$1.27	$1.24	$1.50	$ 1.23

15. Legal proceedings

Various actions and proceedings are pending against or involve J. P. Morgan & Co. and its subsidiaries. Among these are:

(1) actions and proceedings which are related to the bankruptcy of Penn Central Transportation Company, including one which seeks to invalidate or subordinate, or to invalidate the pledge of collateral for, certain loans in which Morgan Guaranty has a participation of $25,000,000 ($12,500,000 of which was charged to the reserve for possible loan losses in 1970 and $6,250,000 of which was charged to the reserve in 1974);

(2) actions under the securities and other laws against various defendants, including Morgan Guaranty, on behalf of purported classes of persons who purchased large amounts of securities issued by New York City and by certain New York State agencies in which plaintiffs allege fraud and misrepresentation in connection with such sales and claim compensatory damages. In the cases in which Morgan Guaranty is named as a defendant, the amounts of the damages claimed are unspecified. In a case filed against various institutions (other than Morgan Guaranty) as representatives of a class, it may be claimed that Morgan Guaranty was a member of the class of defendants from which plaintiffs claim damages of approximately $4 billion;

(3) proceedings and actions which are related to the bankruptcy of W. T. Grant Company and which have been brought against numerous defendants including Morgan Guaranty and certain other banks which had extended credit to Grant. In the bankruptcy proceeding itself, the Trustee in Bankruptcy of Grant has as-

serted claims against Grant's lending banks for the return of alleged preferential transfers and for unspecified damages for injury purportedly inflicted on Grant's business and assets through the banks' alleged domination and control of Grant. In addition, there are actions brought outside the bankruptcy proceeding, including (i) an action brought under the federal securities laws and other laws on behalf of a purported class of purchasers of Grant securities from about 1973 through 1975, against Grant, certain of its former officers and directors, its former outside accountants and Morgan Guaranty (both individually and as agent for Grant's lending banks), which seeks an unspecified amount of damages resulting from an alleged scheme to conceal Grant's deteriorating financial condition from the investing public; (ii) an action brought on common law principles on behalf of a purported class of holders of Grant securities, against Morgan Guaranty and two other banks, which seeks $1 billion in damages for losses allegedly stemming from the banks' alleged conspiracy to prevent the rehabilitation of Grant; (iii) an action brought under the federal securities laws and other laws on behalf of a purported class of purchasers of Grant common stock during 1973, against J. P. Morgan & Co., Morgan Guaranty, and a former common director of Grant, J. P. Morgan & Co., and Morgan Guaranty, which seeks an unspecified amount of damages allegedly caused when the Trust and Investment Division of Morgan Guaranty sold approximately 1 million shares of Grant stock allegedly on the basis of material adverse inside information concerning Grant's financial condition; and (iv) an action brought on common law principles on

Figure 49

A-14 Interest Income Net of Interest Expense. This line is the net interest income for Morgan and shows the gross interest spread in dollars. This spread declined slightly from $526,022,000 in 1975 to $516,553,000 in 1976. As details of these lines show, the smaller spread reflected a more rapid reduction in interest income than in interest expense.

Noninterest Operating Income

A-15 Trading Account Profits and Commissions. Profits and commissions from Morgan's short-term purchase and sale of securities and underwriting activities on behalf of various municipal securities are shown here.

A-16 Corporate Trust, Other Trust, and Agency Income. This line includes income from any fiduciary services of the bank. Trust department services represent business that is different from that of a financial intermediary, and trust departments of banks may be regarded as being an independent profit center. Morgan's trust department manages one of the largest trust assets of any bank and issues a separate report on these activities.

A-17 Foreign Exchange Trading Income. Large international banks have become major traders in the currencies of the world. To a large extent, this business may be considered both as an ancillary service for customers of other services of the bank and also as a separate specialty business that generates its own customers.

The management of international currency positions represents one of the most important new issues for the management of banks. The debacle of the Herstatt Bank in 1974 left many banks with a loss or a claim that was frozen in bankruptcy proceedings. The income of Morgan from this line indicates

Notes to financial statements *(continued)*

behalf of a purported class of former employees of Grant, against J. P. Morgan & Co., Morgan Guaranty, certain former officers and directors of Grant and former auditors of Grant, which seeks $1.4 billion in damages for the alleged loss to the plaintiff class of employment and related benefits as a result of the defendants' alleged conspiracy to destroy the business

of Grant by preventing its rehabilitation under the Bankruptcy Act.

Management, after reviewing with counsel all actions and proceedings pending against or involving J. P. Morgan & Co. and its subsidiaries, considers that the aggregate liability or loss, if any, resulting from them will not be material.

M

Accountants' opinion

To the Directors and Stockholders of J. P. Morgan & Co. Incorporated:

We have examined the consolidated balance sheet of J. P. Morgan & Co. Incorporated and subsidiaries, the balance sheet of J. P. Morgan & Co. Incorporated (parent), and the combined balance sheet of the nonbank subsidiaries of J. P. Morgan & Co. Incorporated as of December 31, 1976 and 1975, the related statements of income (combined statement of income and retained earnings for the nonbank subsidiaries), changes in stockholders' equity, and changes in financial position for the two years ended December 31, 1976, and the consolidated statement of condition of Morgan Guaranty Trust Company of New York and its subsidiaries as of December 31, 1976 and 1975. Our examination was made in accordance with generally accepted auditing standards, and accordingly included such tests of the accounting records and such other

auditing procedures as we considered necessary in the circumstances.

In our opinion, such financial statements present fairly the financial position of J. P. Morgan & Co. Incorporated and subsidiaries, J. P. Morgan & Co. Incorporated (parent), and the nonbank subsidiaries of J. P. Morgan & Co. Incorporated at December 31, 1976 and 1975, the results of their operations and the changes in their financial position for the two years ended December 31, 1976, and the financial position of Morgan Guaranty Trust Company of New York and subsidiaries at December 31, 1976 and 1975, in conformity with generally accepted accounting principles consistently applied.

New York, N.Y.
January 12, 1977   Haskins & Sells

Figure 50

substantial income from this business. Profits may be large for banks having major positions in foreign exchange, since modest funds are required and expenses largely comprise only the expenses of traders.

A-18 Other Operating Income, Mainly Fees and Commissions. This line includes all sources of income not covered in the forementioned items. In the example of Morgan, the line includes translation gains, international commissions, and domestic banking commissions. Equity earnings of subsidiary operations are also shown here, where 20 percent to 50 percent of the equity is held by a bank.

A-19 Total Noninterest Operating Income. The line shows all sources of income not related to interest spread.

Noninterest Operating Expenses

A-20 Salaries. The compensation of employees is the most important controllable expense of banks. Banking is a service business that relies on the efforts and skills of employees working with customers. The success of a bank largely reflects how its employees perform their work and how compensation is handled can be a major part of an explanation of a bank's earnings performance. Salaries represent the largest item of the total compensation package of banks.

A-21 Deferred Profit Sharing. A second type of compensation for Morgan is titled "deferred profit sharing." It would have been useful for Morgan to have given further information about this line in the financial statements.

A-22 Additional Compensation, Note 12. This line includes the expenses related to the contributions to the additional compensation plan. The line includes a special bonus program, outlined in the fourth paragraph of Note 12. This program of compensation represents a carrot for selected employees and is probably the most potent type of compensation of all. The note indicates that junior, as well as senior, executives may be eligible for these benefits, indicating that Morgan's personnel policies may involve detailed monitoring to many levels of management.

A-23 Other Employee Benefits. This line primarily includes contributions to the pension program.

A-24 Provision for Possible Loan Losses, Note 5. This line shows the provision for the loan loss expense and is not the actual loan charge-offs. The actual loan losses are charged to earnings in a roundabout manner, shown in Note 5 of the financial statements. The procedure of charging actual loan loss to earnings follows the sequence of lines in the table: An ongoing reserve for losses is transferred from the expense line of the income statement and added to that reserve (this is the line shown in the income statement). Any recoveries on loans that have been charged off are also added to the reserve; loan charge-offs are deducted from the reserve, and the loan loss reserve is shown with a new total. Note 5 for Morgan also shows that virtually all of the loan loss reserve pertains to the bank only.

The decision to charge loan losses to earnings through a reserve is a fairly recent development. Prior to 1969, loan losses were charged against shareholders' equity. This earlier approach reflected a conservative view that loan losses were bad, and well run banks avoided as much as possible their stigma. Banks were viewed as places where depositors needed protection, and each loan should be repaid according to original terms. If there were a doubt about the repayment possibilities of a loan, the conventional wisdom was that it should not be made. Since shareholders' equity is the heart of the capital structure of a bank, loan loss charges had the effect of touching the chief financial officer's feet to fire every year. Many observers believed that this painful process was beneficial because bank managements were annually reminded of the need to use caution and prudence in making loans, and it emphasized the importance of expanding shareholders' equity in relation to loan expansion.

The effect of the changes in accounting in 1969 was to reduce much of the pain associated with loan losses. In fact, many observers began to consider some part of loan losses as a public benefit, since they were interpreted as indicating an expansive character of bank management, which promoted the development of commerce. Banks were viewed, according to this approach, as risk takers, and if banks were run well, they were risk managers. Small depositors were assumed to be protected by the Federal Deposit Insurance Corporation. Large depositors had an implied protection by the Federal Reserve Board, which would come to the rescue of errant banks.

To assure that an adequate amount would be charged to earnings to replenish the loan loss reserve, and as an alternative to making the provision equal to actual losses, a formula was developed by the Comptroller of the Currency. The required minimum charge to expenses was to be at least equivalent to the average ratio of losses computed on the basis of net charge-offs to total loans over the previous five years. Of course, a bank's loan loss provision could exceed the number shown by the five-year average ratio. Following the sharp growth of loan losses of most banks in recent years, this formula has been dropped from active coverage by regulatory agencies.

A-25 Net Occupancy Expense, Note 11.   Despite their strong service orientation, banks still must transact their business from a location. Moreover, specialized facilities to protect funds and records are a necessary part of banking. The expenses associated with these facilities, including rents, are shown on this line. The term "net" is used because banks reduce their occupancy expenses by the amount of income earned from subleasing their properties.

Banks may own or lease their facilities. The third paragraph of Note 11 gives details of the future rental commitments of Morgan.

A-26 Equipment Rentals, Depreciation, and Maintenance.   This line includes depreciation charges, rental costs of office machines and data processing equipment, computers, and repairs and servicing costs for the furniture and equipment. Expenses for furniture and equipment and sales taxes are also included here.

A-27 Other Operating Expenses.   This line includes all other miscellaneous expenses. It covers such items as fees paid to directors, the cost of temporary employees, contracted guard services, office supplies purchased, bank automobile expenses, losses from counterfeit money and forged checks, net cash shortages in tellers' till boxes, and the cost of supervisory examinations, to name only a few.

A-28 Total Noninterest Operating Expenses.   This line shows the sum of the noninterest operating expenses, from salaries to other operating expenses.

A-29 Income Before Income Taxes and Securities Gains (Losses).   This is the first line of earnings and is the difference between operating income and operating expense. Along with securities gains, it is the sum available for the payment of income taxes and shareholders.

A-30 Applicable Income Taxes, Note 8.   This line shows an estimate of gross income taxes based on book income before income taxes and securities transactions. Deductions are made for tax-exempt income, such as municipal securities and adjustments for any nondeductible expenses. The estimate shows the tax provision for the current year. The provision does not necessarily indicate the actual amount of income taxes paid. The provision is based on book income, while the tax liability is the actual tax payable; and the difference between the two is deferred taxes, which is shown as a liability in the balance sheet.

Note 8 shows details of the tax provision. Banks receive numerous tax benefits from tax exempt loans and investments, lease financing, and the difference between loan loss provisions and allowable deductions under tax laws, to name a few items. Many banks gloss over these benefits in their annual reports because they believe that to call attention to them gives the public the impression that banks receive special tax privileges. Banks do receive tax privileges, but less than some other industries—such as insurance—and probably no more than many basic manufacturing industries.

Banks that provide straightforward notes concerning their taxes are usually straightforward in other areas as well. Thus the tax notes serve as a useful test of the guiding policies of disclosure of a bank.

Note 8 of Morgan is one of the most complete in the banking industry. It is easy to follow and shows clear details of the tax deferrals and a step-by-step sequence from the statutory tax rate to the actual tax rate. In working through the numbers, the bank analyst adds or subtracts the income tax effect of net securities losses or gains of the income statement (line A-33) to the applicable income taxes (line A-30). This figure shows the total tax provision, and it compares directly with the total shown in Note 8. It would have been helpful if Morgan had performed this step in its note.

A-31 Income Before Securities Gains (Losses).   This line shows the subtraction of applicable income taxes from income before income taxes and securities gains or losses. This line if often referred to as operating income and is the figure for the profits of a bank which is most often quoted in the press. It has become the accepted profit figure by many bank analysts because it is usually the easiest figure to obtain from most secondary sources.

The concept of operating income was also introduced into bank accounting in 1969 and is intended to show the earnings of a bank from those resources over which it was considered to have direct control. Changes in the value of investment securities are excluded because they are regarded as reflecting changes in long-term interest rates, over which banks have no control. The more traditional view of profits continues to be shown in the net income figure.

Despite its current widespread use, the use of operating income as the final measure of profits of a bank is not entirely satisfactory. Banks can control the magnitude and the maturity of their investment securities portfolio. By so doing, they have considerable discretion in the market risk of their securities and may be regarded as being accountable for this aspect of their management as much as any other.

A-32 Per Share, Note 9.   This line shows the result of a division of adjusted income before securities losses by the average number of common and common equivalent shares outstanding. The adjustments to income for Morgan assume that all convertible debentures have been converted, and earnings have been recalculated eliminating the interest expenses associated with the convertible debentures, adjusting again for taxes. Note 9 gives further details. These steps give the equivalent of fully diluted earnings per share. This is a sound approach at reporting earnings per share. It leaves no room for surprises, nor the need for further adjustments to common shares outstanding.

A-33 Net Securities Losses.   This line shows the net result of all securities profits and losses that the bank realized by buying and selling investment securities above or below book value. In the case of Morgan during 1975 and 1976, the line shows losses. In other instances, banks may show net securities gains in the line.

A bank's securities portfolio is divided into two parts. The first part includes trading account securities, and its income is shown as part of the regular income statement (noted previously). The second part is its portfolio account, which includes the largest portion of the bank's securities.

Securities designated as portfolio or long-term holdings are given special treatment. Losses or gains are shown below the operating profit line. The designation of the securities between the two accounts is determined by the bank's chief financial officer.

The change in accounting that permitted this handling of investment securities transactions occurred in 1969, during one of the sharpest bear markets in bonds on record. At the same time, the demand for loans from banks accelerated in response to stepped-up inflation. It was a difficult time for banks to accommodate loan customers, sell bonds, and not hurt earnings.

The development of the line for securities transactions and the widespread use of operating income in addition to net income added a subtlety and complexity to income statements of banking companies, since banks continue to show net income. The use of two measures for profit and an emphasis on the less inclusive measure may not be in the best long-term interests of the banking industry.

A-34 Income Tax Benefit, Note 8.   The tax benefits resulting from securities transactions are shown on this line. In instances in which there were securities gains, banks would show tax charges on the line.

A-35 Net Income.   This line is the total of all previous lines (excluding subtotals) and shows the earnings of the bank that would not be subject to further adjustment. It is sometimes referred to as the "bottom line."

Sometimes when a bank suffers a major loss due to an extraordinary and nonrecurring event, there is an additional line which is titled "extraordinary loss." This line would appear above net income.

A-36 Per Share, Note 9.   This line shows net earnings per share, and its calculation involves the same adjustments to earnings and shares that were just discussed with the line for income before securities transactions.

A-37 Dividends Declared Per Common Share.   All dividends declared during the year (but not necessarily paid) are shown in this line. This is a memo line, and it is useful to bank analysts in noting the comparison of dividends per share that were declared and the net income per share. The comparison provides a rough guide of how liberally surplus earnings cushion the dividend and how strongly the bank is reinvesting its net earnings into its capital structure. In the instance of Morgan, the dividends declared represented slightly more than one-third of net earnings in 1976, leaving a large cushion for the dividend; and a significant proportion of net earnings was transferred to capital.

B. CONSOLIDATED STATEMENT OF CONDITION—J. P. MORGAN & CO., INCORPORATED

The "consolidated statement of condition" is a term banks use for what most other industries describe as a "balance sheet," and the two terms are used here interchangeably. The balance sheet includes the standard broad categories of assets, liabilities, and shareholders' equity. Traditionally, the balance sheet has been presented in annual reports of banks as the initial table. Morgan and many other banks now place the income statement first as a way of emphasizing the importance of earnings.

Assets

The two most important assets of banks are loans and securities. These two uses of funds ordinarily account for about two-thirds to three-quarters of total assets of a bank.

B-1 Cash and Due from Banks. This line includes all cash in the bank's vaults and tellers' boxes, funds on account with other domestic banks' checks, and other items that it has credited to customers that are drawn on other banks, but have not yet been paid by those banks. The latter transactions are often referred to as float or items in collection, and they typically comprise the bulk of this line.

Cash is still an essential part of the banking business, since it is the ultimate instrument of liquidity. Nevertheless, for most purposes, it represents an anachronism for major banks like Morgan; and cash is not widely used by most other banks. The disadvantages of cash are that it earns no interest, is bulky, and can be stolen and reused without any record. Most transactions of major banks involve checks, letters of credit, lines of credit, and other methods of payment and promises for payment. The willingness of the 12 district Federal Reserve Banks to buy U.S. government securities has eliminated the need for money center banks to hold more than token amounts of cash for liquidity purposes.

B-2 Interest-Bearing Deposits at Banks. This line includes overseas deposits made to other banks, which for Morgan are principally to banks engaged in Eurodollar transactions. The table shows that Morgan's deposits increased from 1975 to 1976. These deposits are reciprocated, in most instances, by other banks that hold deposits with Morgan. The major Eurodollar banks typically have a net position of deposits placed with them, and they have used these deposits to fund their loans. Morgan's balance sheet does not show details in deposit liabilities of banks to review this point.

This deposit category often is not shown separately in the balance sheet of many banks, especially among banks carrying on activities entirely within the United States. In these instances, the information is usually a part of the balance sheet item of cash and due from banks. Morgan is unusual in showing this key information.

Many U.S. banks regard their international operations as one area of their business that lies outside close regulatory supervision. These banks may not be interested in voluntarily giving regulators, much less shareholders, information that might lead to closer regulation and monitoring. Nevertheless, it is possible to obtain an approximate estimate of this item in banks not showing a line for overseas deposits by subtracting the line showing cash and due from banks on the domestic only call report from the same line from the domestic and foreign call report.

B-3 U.S. Treasury Securities, Note 3. U.S. treasury securities are regarded as the safest and most marketable of all U.S. securities. They are obligations involving the full faith and credit of the U.S. government.

These securities, as well as other securities, appear on the balance sheet at book value, which is the cost of purchase, plus an adjustment for any difference between the purchase price and par value at redemption. Note 3 shows details of differences between book value and year-end market value.

B-4 Obligations of U.S. Government Agencies, Note 3. The obligations of the U.S. government agencies technically do not have the backing of full faith and credit of the U.S. government, although they are regarded by most observers as being equal in creditworthiness as U.S. treasuries because of the implied obligation of the federal government to sustain them. Moreover, the Federal Reserve System permits banks to offer either treasuries or agencies as regular collateral at its discount window, indicating their equal status in the eyes of the Federal Reserve. There are numerous agencies of the U.S. government that issue notes and debentures. These agencies include the Federal Home Loan Bank, Federal Land Bank, Farmers Home Administration, Federal National Mortgage Association, and the United States Postal Service, to name a few examples.

In addition, banks may hold the securities of international agencies of which the U.S. government is a participant, including the International Bank for Reconstruction and Development (World Bank), InterAmerican Development Bank, and Asian Development Bank. The latter agencies provide a moderately higher yield than U.S. treasuries and also provide beneficial tax treatment of income to banks. Their risk is regarded as being greater than treasuries.

B-5 Obligations of States and Political Subdivisions, Note 3. State and local securities (sometimes referred to as "munis") are obligations of all other government units located in the United States and mainly include debts of states, counties, and cities and agencies of these governments, such as public housing agencies. Note 3 shows further details of the valuation of the bank's holdings of obligations of New York City, New York State, and other related New York government agencies. These holdings showed a market value significantly less than book value at year-end 1976. Nevertheless, total obligations of states and political subdivisions showed a market value that was slightly above book value, indicating that Morgan held a number of municipal securities that were at a market premium compared with their book value.

Details of other individual holdings of state and municipal securities are not shown in Morgan's note, nor are they shown in the financial statements of other banks. The financial difficulties of certain cities have raised questions concerning the valuation of those securities and raise questions of the quality of the securities portfolio of banks that hold those securities. There is no public source that outside bank analysts may use to obtain this information.

B-6 Other Investment Securities, Note 3. Other securities include the amount of all investment stocks, notes, and debentures not shown in any of the above securities categories. In the United States, banks are generally not permitted to invest in securities of commercial corporations, to prevent them from gaining control of these corporations as has occurred in many European countries. Nevertheless, there are certain exceptions to this general rule. Member banks of the Federal Reserve System own stock in their district Federal Reserve Bank, and this stock is reported in the other securities category. Minority interests, which include corporate holdings that are retained under grandfather clause exceptions, are included in this account. Banks may make equity investments through small business investment corporations, which technically are subsidiaries of bank holding companies. Also, in certain cases, banks are permitted to convert loans into equity of a borrower, if such a conversion would prevent the bankruptcy of the borrower and meet certain other tests.

B-7 Trading Account Securities Net, Note 3   Banks divide their securities into investment securities (noted earlier) and trading account securities. Trading account securities include those held for the purpose of dealing in securities. These securities are held for the business purpose of providing a market for municipal or government securities to accommodate the bank's customers, or they are held for the speculative purpose of anticipating capital gains. They are shown on a net basis, indicating all trading positions (long or short) have been included.

There is an important accounting difference between investment and trading account securities. The valuation of trading account securities is the value at market on the date of the balance sheet. Thus banks cannot shield their trading account securities from changes in prices of securities as they can with investment securities.

B-8 Federal Funds Sold and Securities Purchased Under Agreement to Resell.   Banks seldom precisely match their reserve requirements with cash and unpledged U.S. government securities that fulfill these requirements. Many large money center banks show a deficit, while many country banks show a surplus of federal funds. Banks are permitted to buy and sell these funds, and the price where these funds trade is regarded as one of the key barometers of interest rates.

Federal funds sold are a type of short-term loan. They may be of various maturities, although many are short-term, such as the maturity of one day. Federal funds sold and securities purchased under agreement to resell are shown in this account.

Some banks are simultaneously a buyer and seller of federal funds, for the purpose of attempting to make profit in their arbitrage (where there is an important difference between quotes on the buy and sell side of the market) or as a means of expanding both sides of their balance sheet to increase their total assets. Federal funds sold are not permitted to be netted against federal funds purchased. The requirement to show both sides of these transactions separately in a bank's balance sheet provides an opportunity to see the magnitude of a bank's market making activity in federal funds.

B-9 Loans.   The business of providing loans is one of the principal purposes of banking. Loans represent the largest category of assets of banks and have increased their proportion to assets over the past four decades. Loans have been a more profitable use of funds than securities, and in the postwar years banks sought earnings more than the safety of securities.

Beginning in 1975, total loans of all banks have been shown net of unearned discount, which is the difference between the face value of a discounted loan and the actual funds received by the borrower. Previously, some banks showed gross loans on this line.

Most banks provide no detail concerning the types of loans on their balance sheet. The line for loans in Morgan's balance sheet shows only a total. This one line accounts for more than one half of Morgan's total assets. The bank analyst often requires more information concerning this line. Banks provide additional detail about their loans in other parts of their annual report and in their call report. Because of the importance of knowing where a bank makes its loans, a brief look outside the core financial statements may be useful. For example, there are seven broad classifications of loans available from Schedule A of the Consolidated Domestic Call Report. Since this report gives information for domestic loans only, and Morgan has major international loans, the figures for each category do not include an important part of Morgan's loans. (A sample of Schedule A is shown in Chapter 2.)

Real Estate Loans. Included in this category are a wide variety of loans, all of which are secured by real property. Almost all bank loans for real estate are in the form of mortgages, which are long-term loans. Most banks hold fairly large proportions of real estate loans for residential properties of one to four family units. Most of these loans may be considered to be a type of consumer loan, since most residential mortgages are made to individuals. The use of amortization schedules has made these loans a predictable source of funds, and they are attractive to banks for this reason. Moreover, in the past four decades, the price of nearly all residential real estate has risen steadily. In this period banks have seldom suffered loan losses from this category of loans, since the market value of the properties has usually exceeded the amount of the mortgage.

Loans to Financial Institutions. Banks are the primary source of funds to independent smaller-sized lenders and financial intermediaries, such as sales finance companies, personal finance companies, and factoring companies. In addition, banks make loans to other banks, savings and loan associations, mutual savings banks and credit unions, providing these organizations with short-term financing.

Loans for Securities. Brokerage houses and investment bankers have a long tradition of being two highly leveraged businesses, and they rely heavily on bank credit. Securities firms use bank loans to finance securities purchased on margin by customers, as well as a source of funds for their own operations. In addition, many individuals borrow directly from banks for the purchase of securities.

In addition to brokerage loans, banks are major suppliers of funds to investment bankers. These firms are principally located in New York City and often require major short-term financing between the time that securities are purchased by investment banking firms and the sales of the new securities to final customers.

Loans to Farmers.   This category of loans includes all loans to farmers except mortgages. These loans include farm equipment (which otherwise would be considered commercial loans), as well as loans for autos and home appliances (which otherwise would be considered consumer loans). Thus this category of loans is a special measure of the farm industry's credit and largely reflects the special interest of government regulatory agencies in the well-being of farmers. In banks in rural areas, this is an important category of loans. It may also be a significant portion of loans for many banks in states allowing statewide branching.

Commercial and Industrial Loans.   Commercial and industrial loans (often referred to as "C & I" loans) comprise the major category of loans for many larger banks. These loans cover a wide range of purposes, from inventory loans for large corporations to startup loans for independent shopkeepers. The payback period of an outstanding balance is often indefinite. For example, large corporations often build up their bank borrowings and then refinance their bank debt with an offering of long-term debentures or equity. In other instances the repayment of some of the commercial and industrial loans is tied to the cash flow of the borrower, especially smaller-sized borrowers.

Commercial and Industrial loans show a lower average interest rate than other loans, but they are not necessarily less profitable than loans with higher interest rates. These loans usually require compensating balances and often contigency fees (a fee for the privilege of having an open-ended line of credit up to a specified amount), as well as other fees.

Another category of commercial and industrial loans in recent years has been interim construction loans to developers and builders. Often large apartment or office buildings or shopping centers are financed in this manner. These loans usually are for an 18-month duration and provide financing between the time a project is designed on paper and the time the final bricks and mortar are in place. Construction loans are usually made only by banks when final takeout financing has been arranged, often with an insurance company. This arrangement insures that the bank will not be forced into a long-term financing of a major real estate project. Even so, construction financing has involved considerable risks, since contractors may not perform according to contract, and developers have sometimes not completed their projects according to original specifications. Most banks take considerable effort to administer these loans in order to attempt to control risks. Interest rates and fees for these loans are considerably above those for permanent mortgages. This category also includes loans to real estate investment trusts, many of which have faced serious difficulties in recent years.

Loans to individuals.   Loans for personal expenditures include automobile, installment, mobile home, home repair, as well as other personal loans. Most of these loans involve fixed repayments, and banks can count on fairly steady inflows of funds from these loans. Nevertheless, a growing proportion of consumer loans are for revolving credit and credit card loans, which do not require any specific change in outstanding balance over a period of time. Thus from the point of view of a bank's management of its funds, consumer loans are becoming more like commercial and industrial loans.

Interest rates on consumer loans are higher than interest rates for most other categories of loans. An important factor in the higher rates is the considerably greater administrative expense for consumer loans, especially revolving credit and credit card loans. In a few states, usury laws place limits on interest rates and tend to constrain the use of these loans.

All Other Domestic Loans. All other loans, which is the miscellaneous category of Schedule A, include loans to churches, educational institutions, and hospitals, as well as overdrafts. This category of loans is usually comparatively small.

Overseas Loans. There is no source of detail for overseas loans comparable to the domestic loans shown in Schedule A. Nevertheless, for Morgan, overseas loans are important. A table showing net interest earnings in management's discussion and analysis of the consolidated statement of income section of the annual report shows that Morgan's loans at foreign offices averaged $5988 million in 1976 and averaged $6929 for loans at domestic offices. Even though the distinction between a domestic and foreign loan is not precise, these numbers indicate sizeable overseas credits.

B-10 Real Estate. This line shows primarily swaps and foreclosures of Morgan. *Swaps* are an exchange of real estate for loans that were not working out. This line for real estate includes swaps for former loans to real estate investment trusts.

B-11 Total Loans and Real Estate. This line shows the total of the two forementioned lines and indicates the total funds of the bank committed to loans and loan-type assets.

B-12 Less: Reserve for Possible Loan Losses, Note 5. Banks now show their valuation reserve for possible loan losses as a contra-asset, indicating that a proportion of loans may not be recovered. The amount of this reserve reflects the bank's assessment of its loan portfolio, recent loan loss experience, and possible pressure from the Federal Reserve System. On the whole, the Federal Reserve System frowns on reserves for possible loan losses which are less than 0.80 percent of loans prior to adjustment for the reserve. The ratio for Morgan at year-end 1976 was 1.08 percent, significantly above that minimum ratio.

B-13 Net Loans and Real Estate. This line shows the total funds of Morgan in loans and loan-type assets, after adjustment for the possibility of losses. The line attempts to show an assessment of loans and loan-type assets that might approximate their market price under favorable conditions.

B-14 Premises and Equipment, Net of Accumulated Depreciation and Amortization of $77,230,000 in 1976 and $70,236,000 in 1975, Note 7. This item includes bank buildings, land, furniture and fixtures, such as vaults and automatic coin counters, and represents book value less accumulated depreciation. Among large banks, this item represents a relatively small proportion of total assets. Bank premises and equipment comprise a larger portion of the total assets of small new banks.

B-15 Customers' Acceptance Liability. Acceptances may be considered as a specialized type of loan. They are the liability to the bank of its customers on drafts and bills of exchange, that, in turn, have been accepted by the bank (or by other banks) for its account. An acceptance is usually secured by goods. Acceptances involve a short-term credit arrangement that enables businesses to obtain funds to finance the shipment of goods between the producer and purchaser or wholesaler and purchaser, when a transit time involves weeks or months. Overseas shipments of bulk cargos are often financed in this manner. The accepting bank, in effect, considers the goods as collateral for the loan while the goods are not in the possession of the principals of the transaction.

B-16 Other Assets. This item includes all miscellaneous assets. This category includes income earned but uncollected, principally interest, and current accruals of insurance and other prepaid expenses. The amount of direct leveraged lease financing is also included in this category, if it is not shown as a separate line.

B-17 Total Assets. This line shows the total of all assets, which includes all individual lines from B-1 to B-16.

Liabilities

Liabilities represent sources of funds of a bank. Demand deposits and consumer passbook savings are major sources of funds, and money center banks also obtain funds directly from money markets by issuing certificates of deposit, sales of commercial paper, and issuing long-term debt. Shareholder's equity represents a small part of the sources of funds of all established banks.

The sequence of the lines in the liabilities section of the balance sheet reflects a traditional approach to bank analysis that stresses shortness of maturity. The items at the top of this category are usually (but not always) the shortest term liabilities.

B-18 Demand Deposits. These deposits are also called checking account deposits. Funds held in these accounts may be withdrawn on demand by the depositor. The checking account depositor does not need to give any advance notice of his wish to issue a check, and he is under no obligation to keep his funds on deposit for any period.

Checking accounts represent a service that has traditionally differentiated banks from other financial organizations, and it is still generally true that only banks can provide checking account services. Nevertheless, other types of financial service organizations have sought and in some cases obtained this privilege. Checking accounts are a highly valuable specialty service of banks, since they provide a way of enabling a depositor to have the full command of his funds without carrying a penny in his pocket. Recent changes in legislation have enabled mutual savings banks in certain states of the Northeast to offer a type of service similar (and indistinguishable in ordinary transactions) to bank checking accounts. Moreover, legislation before Congress would, if enacted, further extend checking account powers to other mutual savings banks and to savings and loan associations.

Banks are prohibited by Regulation Q of the Federal Reserve System from paying interest on demand deposits in the United States. In most other countries banks pay a low rate of interest on these deposits. The prohibition against the payment of interest on demand deposits began in the depression of the 1930s when the Federal Reserve wanted to eliminate interest rate competition among banks and thereby provide a surer base for bank earnings and bank solvency. Thus by not having to pay interest, demand deposits represent a low cost of funds to a bank.

The figures shown for demand deposits in Morgan's balance sheet are gross domestic deposits. Demand deposits include "float," deposits that are currently in the process of collection. For example, if a deposit is made to Morgan of a check drawn on another bank, several days often elapse until the funds are transferred to Morgan. Moreover, as is the case with Morgan, many large banks receive deposits from correspondent banks that are earmarked for certain customers and which are a type of compensation to the larger bank for other banking services to the corresponding bank.

The Federal Reserve permits banks to subtract float and correspondent bank deposits from gross demand deposits in the calculation of reserve requirements. The reserve requirements on these net demand deposits represent an important cost to a bank, since they reduce the investable portion of demand deposits. Member banks of the Federal Reserve System are required to hold cash balances with one of the 12 regional Federal Reserve banks. As an alternative to those deposits with the Federal Reserve bank, member banks may hold vault cash.

Demand deposits are important to banks because they have been a stable source of funds. The stability partially reflects the unique position of banks in offering checking accounts. In addition, banks give special attention to customers with demand deposit accounts, especially corporate accounts. Banking relationships with these customers are maintained on a close, personal basis at the highest levels between the bank's officers and the company's officers. Often these business associations reflect only one part of a broader scope of friendship. In some banks, this friendship has been handed from generation to generation. Thus most established corporate banking relationships have tended to be stable throughout the years.

Banks also give attention to the demand deposits of small businesses and individuals. The link between a bank and these businesses and persons is often not so well established. Nevertheless, checking accounts are given to businesses and individuals who pass certain credit standards. Banks regard checking accounts as key relationship accounts and value them as a link that can lead to other banking services.

B-18 Time Deposits. This category includes consumer savings deposits and certificates of deposit, two different categories of deposits. *Consumer savings deposits* mainly consist of passbook savings accounts and are usually used by depositors who prefer to forego check-writing privileges for interest on the balances. The passbook savings deposit of most banks may be withdrawn at any time at the wish of the depositor, although banks continue to include a clause in the terms of a savings account that permits the bank to require a waiting period. It is doubtful whether a bank would ever enforce such a clause, since a delay in payment of funds would likely damage confidence of other depositors who might hear of the action.

Unlike demand deposits, banks compete for savings deposits with many other types of institutions. Savings and loan associations have been major competitors for these deposits, and mutual savings banks, company-sponsored credit unions, as well as other consumer credit organizations, offer similar savings deposit services.

Banks compete for savings deposits while offering lower interest rates than are offered by other institutions. As noted, interest rate ceilings for banks are regulated by the Federal Reserve System under Regulation Q. One-quarter of one percent difference in interest rate commonly separates rates on savings accounts between banks and savings and loan associations. It is maintained to provide a minimum, but noticeable advantage to savings and loan associations. These institutions are regarded by regulators as being slightly less well established as banks and require an inducement to attract deposits. Moreover, regulators support a public policy of encouraging the development of institutions that are lenders to home buyers. Deposits in both types of institutions are insured by a government agency currently up to $40 thousand per depositor's passbook. As a practical matter, the difference in interest rates between banks and savings and loan associations is usually small enough so that other considerations such as convenience of location and the availability of other services have a bearing on the choice of a consumer's savings deposit institution.

The interest rates paid by many other deposit institutions, such as credit unions and consumer thrift organizations, are often significantly higher than rates paid by banks. These higher interest rates reflect the less well-established positions of many of these institutions in the eyes of depositors and greater concern of depositors concerning the safety of their funds. Some of these institutions are not insured by a government agency. Their higher rates are compensation for greater risk.

In contrast to passbook savings deposits, the deposits classified as other time deposits have fixed maturities, and depositors can obtain their funds prior to maturity only by the payment of penalty fees. These other deposits are often referred to as certificates of deposit or simply as CDs. In turn, CDs are often divided into large CDs with amounts of $100,000 or more and small CDs for amounts of less than $100,000. Their maturities typically range from 30 days to many years. In return for the assurance of a fixed period of deposit, as well as for a larger unit of deposit (and lower transactions costs), banks usually offer higher interest rates on other time deposits. In denominations less than $100,000, the interest rate is regulated by the Federal Reserve System under Regulation Q. In denominations of $100,000 or more, there are no interest rate ceilings. During the 1974 credit crunch, large CDs were an important source of funds for major banks.

Proposed legislation based on the Hunt Commission's recommendations would eliminate Regulation Q and open all deposits to competitive rates. There is currently much debate as to the effect of this change in bank regulation. It appears that the abolition of Regulation Q would increase competitive pressures for deposits and would sharpen the distinction between stronger and weaker banks.

B-20 Deposits in Foreign Offices. This line includes all deposits held in international offices of the bank. These offices include all of the bank's consolidated foreign branches. Morgan obtained more than one half of its deposits from these sources. Most banks show a much smaller proportion of deposits from foreign offices or do not show a separate line for this account.

Overseas deposits consist of Eurocurrency and indigenous deposits. Technically, *Eurocurrency deposits* are the deposit of funds of one country in a bank of another country, although most of these deposits consist of offshore-dollar deposits. The practice was developed by the Russians who, for political reasons, did not want to keep dollar balances in the United States. Eurocurrency deposits became widespread as a way around the squeeze on deposits of U.S. banks during the 1967 credit crunch. At that time interest rate ceilings in this country encouraged depositors to shunt their funds to Europe, where deposits could be placed in branches of U.S. banks at higher interest rates. Once trained in this practice, U.S. banks found a new reason for the development of their foreign branches.

Today, the term "Eurocurrency" is a misnomer, since there are deposits of currencies in banks of many countries located outside Europe. A better term would be "international currency deposits," but the term Eurocurrency has become a generic one.

There are important differences between Eurocurrency deposits and indigenous deposits. *Indigenous deposits* are those of a local currency in the country of the currency. Currency transfer risks are involved with these deposits for U.S. banks. For example, a dollar deposit from an OPEC country would be assessed by an analyst of a bank in a completely different way if a deposit of the same sum comprised a large number of individual depositors and businesses of an unindustrialized country. Unfortunately for bank analysts, there is no detail of this type of information in Morgan's core financial statements or elsewhere, nor is this information available in financial reports of other banks. The information is confidential to banks.

B-21 Total Deposits. This line shows the total of the three previous deposit categories.

B-22 Federal Funds Purchased and Securities Sold Under Agreements to Repurchase, Note 6. These funds are often called "federal funds borrowings." They are funds needed to fulfill deficiencies of a bank's reserve requirement. (These funds represent the other side to federal funds sold shown in line A-2). Federal funds borrowings are usually extended for a period of one or a few days.

B-23 Commercial Paper. This line shows the amount of commercial paper outstanding, which is a short-term, unsecured obligation of J. P. Morgan & Co., Inc. (the parent), and a subsidiary of the bank, J. P. Morgan of Canada. Only the largest, most recognized bank holding companies are able to sell commercial paper on a regular basis.

B-24 Other Liabilities for Borrowed Money. This category includes all other short-term borrowings. It may include short-term loans from other banks and from the Federal Reserve Bank, and term federal funds.

B-25 Accrued Taxes and Expenses, Note 8. This accrued taxes category includes unpaid tax liabilities. This line includes tax liabilities to federal, state, and local governments, as well as tax liabilities to overseas governments. The line for accrued taxes and expenses, which mainly consists of deferred taxes, represents a substantial sum for Morgan, as well as for most banks. However, many banks do not show this line. Note 8 shows some of the sources of deferred taxes.

The line points up the importance of tax accounting and the tax law to banks. Deferred taxes appear to represent a temporary, if not a long-term infusion of funds into banks on the part of governments, which require no interest payment or dividends.

B-26 Liability on Acceptances. This line represents the other side to the asset line of customers' liabilities on acceptances (line B-15). The liability on acceptances represents the funds to a bank to support customers' acceptances and are usually the funds from the sale of customers' acceptances. A quick look shows that these two lines of acceptances are usually nearly in balance, as they are in Morgan's balance sheet. They may not be perfectly in balance on any particular day because of some new customers' liabilities not having been sold and prepayments of interest.

B-27 Dividend Payable. This line shows the funds earmarked for dividend payment.

B-28 Long-Term Debt, Note 7. This line shows all long-term debt of Morgan and its subsidiaries. *Long-term debt* usually includes debt that matures in a period longer than one year from the date of the financial statements. Note 7 gives details, which include two issues of convertible debentures, two issues of capital notes, two issues of notes and a mortgage.

B-29 Other Liabilities. This line includes all other liabilities not included before this, such as interest expense incurred but not paid and expenses accrued and unpaid. The amount shown on the line is usually relatively small, as it is with Morgan.

Stockholders' Equity

Stockholders' equity includes the portion of Morgan's sources of funds for which there is no contractual obligation for repayment. Stockholders' and shareholders' equity are two terms that have the same meaning and are used interchangeably. All other sources of funds, including all liabilities, require either repayment at some future date or a possibility of repayment. Stockholders' equity is the center of the capital structure of a bank.

Stockholders' equity is usually divided into five parts. By presenting this amount of detail on a summary balance sheet, bank financial statements give recognition to the importance of each of their sources of capital funds. Nevertheless, it is the total shareholders' equity that is most meaningful to bank analysts.

B-31 Preferred Stock. Most banks have not issued preferred stock, even though many have authorized its issuance. Banks show a line for preferred stock in their balance sheet, because it is required in Call Reports to the U.S. Comptroller of the Currency. Moreover, banks may like to remind shareholders of this category of equity, even if it is not used.

Preferred stock has a preference over common stock in dividend payment. But in no case is a bank required to pay dividends to preferred stockholders. Preferred stockholders also usually enjoy a position ahead of common shareholders if there were a distribution of assets on the dissolution of a bank.

B-32 Common Stock $2.50 Par Value, Notes 7, 13. The dollar figure for this line shows par value times the number of shares outstanding. In the case of Morgan it also shows an assigned or "par" value of each share of stock, the number of shares authorized for issuance, and the number of shares actually issued on the date of the balance sheet.

There may be other reasons for showing par value. When a bank is originally incorporated, many state laws prohibit the issuance of stock at a price less than par value. Some states also require that dividends cannot be paid if funds from the par value of common stock are required to do so.

Banks often show details of their stock option plan in footnotes to this line, if they have one. In many instances, as is shown in Note 13 for Morgan, stock options are made from authorized but not issued shares.

B-33 Capital Surplus. Banks receive funds from sales of stock that are in excess of the par value of the stock. The difference is a surplus, shown in the line for capital surplus. Banks may also transfer funds from retained earnings to the capital surplus line, which has the effect of reducing the amount which would be available for the payment of dividends. This line is sometimes designated as paid-in surplus stock.

B-34 Retained Earnings. Retained earnings represent a broad measure of the cumulated profits of a bank from all sources since the bank first opened its doors, less dividends that have been paid. Retained earnings are sometimes titled earned surplus or undivided profits. This is the account from which dividends are paid.

B-35 Less: Treasury Stock at Cost. This line includes stock that has been held by the public and has been purchased by the bank. It is held in the bank's treasury and represents issued, but no longer outstanding stock. It is carried at its repurchased cost. The line for treasury stock usually includes the number of shares the bank holds in its treasury. The dollar value of treasury stock is subtracted from other categories of stockholders' equity, because the bank has given back funds to the public to acquire these shares. Treasury stock may be used for corporate acquisitions which are termed "pooling of interest" and thus has special value in those circumstances.

B-36 Total Stockholders' Equity. This line represents the sum of the five previous lines and includes preferred stock, common stock par value, capital surplus, retained earnings, and a deduction of any treasury stock. It is the total of all sources of owners' funds from the owners themselves and the combined success and failure of the bank's operations since it began its business.

B-37 Total Liabilities and Stockholders Equity. This line shows the total of all individual lines from B-18 to B-36.

C. CONSOLIDATED STATEMENT OF CONDITION—MORGAN GUARANTY TRUST COMPANY OF NEW YORK

This is the consolidated statement of condition of the bank only, which is Morgan Guaranty Trust. The bank represents almost all of the resources of the consolidated corporate balance sheet. Thus virtually all of the figures shown in the comparable lines of the two balance sheets are identical. For many years, the balance sheet of the bank was the only financial information that was provided to the public. It is the same information shown in the Domestic and Foreign Consolidated Bank Call Report, which in the instance of Morgan is filed with the Federal Reserve.

D. STATEMENT OF CHANGES IN STOCKHOLDERS' EQUITY—J. P. MORGAN & CO., INCORPORATED (CONSOLIDATED) AND J. P. MORGAN & CO., INCORPORATED (PARENT)

This section shows details of changes that have occurred in each of the stockholders' equity accounts during the recent year. Many of the lines in this table are from the balance sheet or income statement. For example, the line for common stock, balance, January 1, 1976, corresponds to the line for common stock, $2.50 par value, December 31, 1975, in the balance sheet. The line for net income is similar to the same line in the income statement. Most other lines are self-descriptive, such as the lines showing changes in treasury stock and cash dividends declared. Nevertheless, a few lines are noted here.

D-1 Sale of 2,000,000 Shares.   On March 9, 1976, Morgan sold 2,000,000 shares of common stock at $54 per share. After underwriters' discounts and commissions of about $2 per share and other fees, Morgan realized $103.8 million. This sum was distributed in shareholders' equity in two lines. Under the heading common stock (D-1) $5.0 million is shown and under the heading of capital surplus (D-4) $98.8 million is shown. The $5.0 million was shown under common stock to preserve the $2.50 par value, and the remainder was placed in capital surplus.

D-2 Conversion of Debentures, Note 7.   These lines D-2 and D-5, which appear under headings for common stock and capital surplus, show that Morgan received no addition to stockholders' equity through the conversion of debt into equity in 1976. There were small additions in 1975. Note 7 gives details.

D-3 Stock Options Exercised, Note 13.   The award of stock options to senior management in banks has grown in recent years. The lines under headings for common stock and capital surplus show that Morgan's employees exercised comparatively few options in 1975 or 1976. Nevertheless, the bank's stock option plan is still in its infancy, as is described in Note 13.

D-5 Conversion of Debentures, Note 7.   The line shows that there were no conversions of convertible debentures to equity in 1976. Since Morgan shows earnings per share only on a fully diluted basis, this line is of technical interest.

E. CONSOLIDATED STATEMENT OF CHANGES IN FINANCIAL POSITION—J. P. MORGAN & CO., INCORPORATED

This table provides an insight into the changes in the flow of funds into and out of Morgan. The table is sometimes referred to as the table of sources and uses of funds. It shows how the balance sheet and the income statement interact.

Many of the lines represent year-end 1975 to year-end 1976 changes from lines on the income statement and the balance sheet. For example, the financial resources provided by increases in deposits (E-2), represents the difference between total deposits at year-end 1975 and year-end 1976. Most of the lines are not difficult to compare with the income statement and balance sheet. However, the decrease in loans and real estate (E-3) and increases in loans and real estate (E-4) include not only changes in loans (net of valuation reserve) shown in the balance sheet, but also add changes in federal funds sold and subtract the provision for loan losses. It would have been helpful if these steps were separately identified in this table.

The major value of this table is that the bank analyst can quickly see which changes in the bank's business were important. A review of the columns for 1975 and 1976 shows that there were major shifts in Morgan's business. For example, in 1975 loans and real estate decreased (E-3), but this category increased during the following year.

F, G, H. FINANCIAL STATEMENTS OF HOLDING COMPANY—J. P. MORGAN & CO., INCORPORATED (PARENT)

Statement of Income

The first of the three tables showing the holding company financial statements is a statement of earnings and is designated Table F. Again, the unity of the consolidated statements and the holding company statements is shown by net income per share, which appears as the same figure in the bottom lines of both tables. The lines showing revenues, expenses, and other items transform operating results into information which fulfills the obligations of bank holding company law.

Balance Sheet

Table G shows the total assets of the parent corporation (G-2) as a small fraction of the consolidated assets (B-17). The table shows that the parent holding company is largely a financial shell, with the principal assets elsewhere. Nevertheless, total stockholder's equity of the holding company (G-5) is the same as total stockholders' equity of the consolidated corporation (B-36) indicating the common ownership between the holding company and the consolidated corporation figures.

Holding companies are permitted to issue commercial paper and thereby finance their nonbank activities with a low cost of funds. (Banks only can issue certificates of deposit.) Morgan showed an amount in commercial paper outstanding (G-3) which was about one-half of the amount of advances to nonbank subsidiaries (G-1) at year-end 1976; and the two lines were about equal at year-end 1975. Most nonbank activities of holding companies involve short-term lending, and funding these credits with low-cost, short-term borrowing is customary. By any comparison, these amounts are small for Morgan, which indicates that Morgan has not moved into nonbank financial activities with the zeal of a few other banking companies. Thus this balance sheet gives one indication that Morgan is still structured principally as a bank and not as a financial conglomerate.

A second major liability of the holding company is the total of $308.8 million in long-term debt, which includes convertible debentures and notes (G-4), which are discussed in Note 7. The convertible debentures may be regarded as frozen shareholders' equity, which could thaw over a period of time. These debentures have been largely put to use in money market instruments, shown in the assets part of the balance sheet. If interest rates should moderate over a period of years, Morgan would lose money on this transaction, since the borrowings are long and the investments are short. But these transactions provide considerable liquidity to the holding company, and liquidity has value.

The convertible debentures have not been transferred into the equity of the bank only, (which would be permitted), adding an indication of the restrained way these securities have been handled in the financial statements. In contrast, many banks have made borrowings at the holding company level and then transferred (or downstreamed) these funds into the equity of the subsidiary bank. The transfer is practiced by many banks primarily because the Federal Reserve System prefers to use bank balance sheet information in calculating capital ratios. Despite the approval granted this practice, it must strain the credibility of even diffident bank analysts. Morgan has high capital ratios and does not need this practice.

Statement of Changes in Financial Position

This table, designated as Table H, shows the holding company's financial statements. Again, the table includes information that mainly reflects the special legal needs of bank holding company requirements.

I, J, K. FINANCIAL STATEMENTS OF NONBANK SUBSIDIARIES—J. P. MORGAN & CO., INCORPORATED (PARENT)

The final group of financial statements shows the balance sheet, income statement, and changes in financial position of the nonbank subsidiaries. The nonbank subsidiaries of Morgan include J. P. Morgan Interfunding Corporation and The 23-Six Corporation. This information is indicated in the final section of the annual report, which is a directory of officers and organizations. The J. P. Morgan Interfunding Corporation is a domestic and international leasing subsidiary. The 23-Six Corporation is a limited partnership, which participates with other organizations in government assisted housing for families with low or moderate income.

Taken together, these two activities of Morgan are small in comparison with Morgan's banking activities. This small proportion indicates that the bank has chosen to tread lightly in nonbank activities. Moreover, the turnaround in earnings from 1974 to 1975 of Morgan's nonbank subsidiaries carried through to 1976 (I-1) and could indicate that even these small parts of Morgan's business may not have been immune from pressures to seek profits. In contrast, many banks have treated their nonbank subsidiaries with benign indulgence.

L. NOTES TO FINANCIAL STATEMENTS

There are 15 notes to Morgan's financial statements. These notes explain the numbers of the tables and give additional background information. they also provide an interpretation of the importance of the numbers. To a large extent the disclosures shown in the notes are required by regulatory agencies.

The notes also provide a deeper insight into the reasoning process of the bank's financial management than is available from any other source. The notes have passed a review by lawyers and accountants and thus are worded in a more formal manner than other parts of the annual report. They also often explain what at first glance may appear to be an obscure part of a bank's activities. The notes, usually not a pleasure to read, are working papers, and this is what makes them valuable.

The notes convey whether a bank's own working papers are logical, clear, and incisive. The test in reading notes is whether they meet these tests. Banks do not reveal all activities through financial statements. In fact, important useful information is not shown. For example, the magnitude of various categories of problem loans, the concentration of holders of the bank's certificates of deposit, and profits by branch or type of financial service are not shown in Morgan's financial statements or in any other bank's financial statements. Nevertheless, the notes are the tip of an iceberg of information and represent a step that is less than full disclosure, but better than no information.

Many of Morgan's notes are referenced in the financial tables. Several are not, including Note 1, which discusses accounting policies and Note 15, which discusses legal proceedings.

M. ACCOUNTANTS' OPINION

The final part of the financial statements is the accountants' opinion. This opinion represents as much assurance as is available to bank analysts that the financial statements are reasonably stated. It is simply this and no more. the accountants' opinion only indicates whether a bank's financial statements fairly show its financial condition. The accountants' opinion for Morgan gives the bank an unqualified opinion and is typical of most opinions.

Occasionally, the accountants' opinion indicates that part or all of the financial statements of a bank are qualified. The qualification is not necessarily a condemnation. It usually indicates that the magnitude of some difficulty cannot be assessed with confidence and that analysts should use more caution than usual in making conclusions based on the financial statements.

Bank analysts should not rely on the accountants' opinion as a guide to the future soundness of a bank. They need to use the information provided in the financial statements, as well as other information, and form their own conclusions.

CHAPTER 4

PATTERNS OF DATA

The previous two chapters reviewed information of a bank as it existed at one point in time. Nevertheless, banks change, and the way that they change has major importance in evaluating their operations. This chapter looks at the patterns of the data over time.

All time series may be divided into four patterns—long-term trends, cyclical fluctuations, seasonal variations, and the remaining irregular factors. The task of the bank analyst is to determine whether a change of one quarter or the change of one year represents a continuation of past patterns or indicates that a new pattern is emerging. The task appears simple, but like so many fundamental issues, there often is considerable difficulty in separating the wheat from the chaff. The results are worth the effort, since the ability to show patterns in time series provides important indicators of the direction of banks' activities.

TREND

The long-term trend of a bank's operations covers the longest sweep of time. The term "secular trend" was used for many years in describing the long-term character of trends. The word *secular* refers to the original Latin meaning of a long-term or enduring nature. Today, the term often is also used to describe shorter periods where data have shown a consistent pattern. In this work, trend will be used in its original, technical long-term meaning.

There are no established minimum time limits for trends, although it is reasonable to assume that a trend should cover at least two complete swings of the business cycle. By taking two cycles as a minimum period, trends can be more clearly separated from cycles. The typical business cycle lasts from four to six years, thus the minimum period of a trend is probably about ten years.

The chart showing earnings per share before securities transactions of Citicorp illustrates a typical trend series (Figure 51). The chart shows that earn-

105

Figure 51 Citicorp earnings before securities transactions. *Source:* Investors Management Sciences, Inc., Citicorp 1975 Annual Report.

ings before securities transactions have increased regularly each year from 1959 to 1975, except for 1961. Even without this information, the eye can quickly survey the series and determine that there has been a pervasive, fairly steady upward direction in the series for 16 years, a period that may be regarded as being sufficiently long to indicate a trend.

The chart is displayed on a semi-log scale to better identify rates of change of the series. A *semi-log scale* depicts a series so that equal slopes show similar rates of change. For example, the scale that shows the dollar amounts in the Citicorp chart shows the same distance from $50 million to $100 million as is shown from $100 million to $200 million. In both instances, there is an identical 100 percent gain. The use of a semi-log scale enables a bank analyst to quickly determine whether there has been a change in the rate of expansion or contraction of the series. Ordinary arithmetic scales do not show similar slopes for the same rate of change, and when looking for trends (and cycles), arithmetic scales are less satisfactory than semi-log scales. For most other uses, arithmetic scales are well suited to show information in a simple manner.

Earnings before securities transactions are used in the examples of this chapter because they provide a good measure of a series that reflects the impacts of trend, cyclical, and seasonal factors. Citicorp's earnings before securities transactions increased from $68.0 million in 1959 to $348.2 million in 1975. There is some difference in the accounting basis of the figures over the period, but these differences do not significantly distort the overall trend. This gain represented more than a fourfold increase in the 16-year period.

Many bank analysts, nevertheless, would find that this approach requires refinements. The first would be a trend line of average relationship, which evens out unusually large gains or declines in various years. One approach in drawing a line of average relationship would be for the observer to visually move a transparent plastic ruler over the series so that the edge of the ruler balanced as much area on one side of the line as the other. This line would show the average rate of expansion in earnings. While this method of showing an average rate of gain lacks technical precision, it is satisfactory in many instances that require only general observations.

A further refinement would be to show the average annual rate of change in the trend. This is often referred to as a "compound growth rate" and shows a constant factor, which, when multiplied by the original number, will yield the final number in a line of average relationship in as many years as separate the two points. An annual rate of change is the common unit of measure in making virtually all comparisons of data.

Many bank analysts show growth rates by taking the initial and the final year of a series and calculate an annual rate of change. This method has been used for years, but it is not satisfactory when a series is not smooth. In these cases, there is always the possibility that an unusually large gain or decline for the initial or final year would distort the growth rate.

The complete method of showing a growth rate is to calculate the average annual growth rate together with the coordinates for charting. Several advanced hand calculators include this feature and are available from most computer program packages. In the chart for Citicorp, for example, the average annual growth rate for the 16-year period was 10.6 percent, and the chart shows plots of that growth rate with a dashed line.

The proper selection of years of a series is of greater importance than the use of a method to develop a growth rate. For example, the bank analyst may ask whether it is more appropriate to show a trend for Citicorp's earnings that begins in 1959, 1961, or 1963. The year 1959 was selected in this example because the year preceded the 1960 recession, and a series from 1959 to 1975 covers two full business cycles. The year 1961 could be used as the initial year of the trend because that year marked the last year when earnings per share declined. Taking a different point of view, the year 1963 could mark the first year of the trend series because that year represented a dividing point between a period of moderate expansion in earnings per share from 1959 to 1963 and a period of rapid gains in earnings that followed.

There is no formula that could determine which years should be used in a trend. The bank analyst must rely on his judgment as he examines a series. As a practical matter, nevertheless, there is a general rule that the longer the period of the trend, the smaller the difference in growth rates. Thus, for example, the trend of Citicorp's earnings during the 14-year period from 1961 to 1975 was 11.9 percent, which represents a relatively small difference from the 10.6 percent of the 16 years from 1959 to 1975.

One purpose of determining a trend line is to see whether the bank appears to be following a program of attempting to provide a steady direction in its earnings progression. Some chief executive officers of banks have indicated that they would like to provide steady earnings expansion. Most managements are reluctant to discuss this point in much detail, because it might imply that the bank can manage its earnings and that implication could suggest that each year's financial information does not completely reflect the business developments of that year. Regardless of the indications of management, a bank analyst often wants to know if a bank has demonstrated a capability to expand earnings steadily.

The chart for Crocker National Corporation shows earnings before securities transactions from 1959 to 1975 and illustrates some of the difficulties in selecting the appropriate years for a trend (Figure 52). The series for Crocker shows a fairly steady upward progression from 1959 to 1971. Earnings increased during each of those twelve years. However, during the three subsequent years, from 1972 to 1974, earnings declined. In 1975, earnings bounded upward to reach a new high for the sixteen-year period.

A single trend line from 1959 to 1975 for Crocker could be drawn in a similar manner to Citicorp's trend line, showing a line of average relationship for all of the annual earnings points. Nevertheless, a careful look at the chart shows the three periods described earlier. A bank analyst might consider that the 1959 to 1971 expansion reflected a period where management sought steady earnings gains. The 1972 to 1974 period might have reflected a completely different period, when management may have striven to maintain an earlier policy of showing regular annual gains, but fell increasingly short of its objectives.

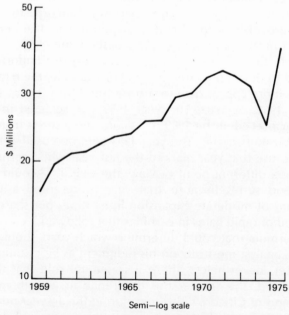

Figure 52 Crocker National Corporation earnings before securities transactions. *Source:* Investors Management Sciences, Inc., Crocker National Corporation 1975 Annual Report.

The bank analyst might note that the sharp drop in earnings in 1974 might indicate extreme efforts to come to grips with the earnings shortfall that began in 1972. In this case, the rebound of earnings in 1975 could reflect a correction of the difficulties of the previous three years and could represent the return of the bank to its historical growth pattern of the 1960s. In this interpretation, the period from 1972 to 1974 could be regarded as an aberration of a longer trend. The earnings performance in 1975 would then appear to be about on target.

In another interpretation, the rebound in 1975 could reflect heroic, but unsustainable efforts to push earnings as high as possible. In this interpretation, part of the sharp increase in 1975 may have been borrowed from the depressed earnings results in 1974. This view would indicate that Crocker's earnings have been moving along a trend from 1971 to 1975, which is significantly lower than the trend from 1959 to 1971. If this interpretation is used, the management of this bank might have abandoned its earlier strategy of seeking a regular steady earnings expansion for a strategy that emphasized temporary short-term measures. Of course, there is no way of determining this view on the basis of the earnings figures alone.

The illustration of Crocker shows the benefits, as well as the limitations, of using any type of data to develop opinions of long-term programs. Patterns of performance may be regarded as indicators of a program of a bank. Nevertheless, in many instances, the patterns of data are difficult to determine; and it is usually not entirely certain, using only a data series, exactly which program may have been undertaken to cause or correct a situation.

The latter point also illustrates again that there are benefits and limitations to the extent that statistical and mathematical techniques can be helpful. The use of these techniques adds precision. Moreover, in making comparisons among several banks, the use of standard measures, such as the average annual rate of gain, provides yardsticks that put comparisons on a common objective basis. The selection of time periods that bracket the trend lines is always arbitrary, but hopefully, is reasonable. There are qualitative limits to the use of mathematics that a bank analyst can hope to mitigate, but can never eliminate.

CYCLE

Business cycles are perhaps the most common experience of economics to most persons. Almost everybody is familiar with periods of expansion in business activity. In these periods, employment is strong, profits tend to rise, and the business climate is optimistic. Similarly, it is difficult to imagine anyone who is not familiar with the difficulties of a recession, which include higher levels of unemployment, weak profits, and concern over the business outlook. The swings from expansion to contraction in business activity over two centuries of recorded economic data have lead bank analysts to believe that there is an inherent rhythm to business conditions. There is a strong disagreement among many economists about whether the swings of business conditions must occur or whether the swings are responsive to other, more basic, controllable forces. Nevertheless, most observers of the business scene regard these alternations as part of a cycle or pattern that is almost certain to repeat.

Business cycles are a major consideration to banks, and how banks respond to them provides a further insight into their operations. Some banks, like Citicorp prior to 1977, have shown little effect of these cycles on their earnings or other series. The ability to adjust banking operations so that they are apparently always in balance with the changes in business conditions would indicate a program of considerable flexibility in coping with short-term changes in business conditions. This capability would tend to support the view that a program of steady upward progression of earnings could be maintained.

Most banks have not handled business cycles so adroitly. These banks show interruptions to their overall direction in earnings that coincide regularly with certain changes in business conditions. These interruptions may reflect programs of a management that lacks concern over the downside of a business cycle or an interest in programs which mainly look to the expansion phase and stress activities mostly effective at that time.

The chart shows earnings before securities transactions for Chase Manhattan Corporation from 1959 to 1975 (Figure 53). Earnings of Chase have risen on an overall basis throughout the sixteen-year period. Nevertheless, there have been three interruptions to this trend. Earnings declined in 1961, in 1969, and again in 1975. With the exception of 1969, these years were periods of recession or early recovery in general business conditions. In contrast, earnings of Chase showed almost steady, regular gains during the bulk of the periods of expansion in general business conditions. There also appears to have been a pattern of two weak years in earnings following the periods of expansion. Thus Chase appears to be a classic example of a bank whose earnings were sensitive to the business cycle.

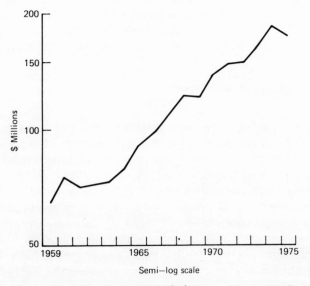

Semi—log scale

Figure 53 Chase Manhattan Corporation earnings before securities transactions. *Source:* Investors Management Sciences, Inc., Chase Manhattan Corporation 1975 Annual Report.

The chart showing earnings before securities transactions for Western Bancorporation shows a pattern similar to Chase (Figure 54). Earnings of Western Bancorporation declined in 1961, in 1971, and in 1975. These periods of decline were of similar magnitude, indicating that the effects of the recessions and early recoveries on this bank were about the same. Moreover, the periods of expansion in earnings, which occurred from 1961 to 1970 and from 1971 to 1974, were at about the same pace. Thus Western Bancorporation also appears to be a bank holding company whose earnings were sensitive to the business cycle.

The chart showing earnings before securities transactions, which have been adjusted to common periods of recession in general business activity for Western Bancorporation, illustrates the earnings sensitivity more explicitly (Figure 55). The shaded bar represents the principal year of recession. The space to the left of the recession bar represents the period of late expansion. The chart shows that the immediate impact of recessions has been beneficial to Western Bancorporation's earnings. Nevertheless, following the recession, the earnings of Western Bancorporation have regularly declined. In the subsequent year, earnings have expanded.

The examples of Chase and Western Bankcorporation show earnings patterns that would encourage bank analysts to look into policies, programs and the management of banks that were linked closely to economic conditions.

SEASONAL VARIATION

Seasonal variations are a part of everybody's daily life. There are seasonal variations in many financial series as well. These variations may reflect the weather or they may reflect patterns in behavior that do not relate to calendar changes, but rather reflect business patterns that have been continued so long as to be regarded as having regular periodic character. In either case, there is sometimes considerable seasonal variation of financial information of banks.

For many years, seasonal variation was not considered to be an issue of much importance. Most bank analysts looked only at annual data. Where quarterly data were reviewed, the analysts made adjustments on a rough and informal basis to arrive at annual forecasts, since the calendar year was a basic reference point.

Now, there is a growing importance of quarterly data. The importance of these data reflects the growing interest of investors and large depositors in the condition of banks on a more frequent basis. It also reflects the use of computers among banks, which makes the compilation of quarterly data a manageable task.

Now that quarterly data are available, bank analysts are given four reviews of a bank's performance. Although quarterly data are often not as detailed as annual data, they still provide a more timely way of enabling bank analysts to note changes of direction among banks. Nevertheless, quarterly data cannot be used in a simple fashion and must be adjusted for recurring variations.

The chart shows quarterly plots of earnings per share before securities transactions for Continental Illinois Corporation (Figure 56). The chart shows

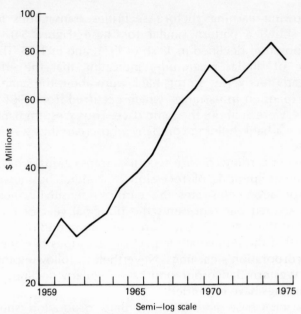

Figure 54 Western Bancorporation earnings before securities transactions. *Source:* Investors Management Sciences, Inc., Western Bancorporation 1975 Annual Report.

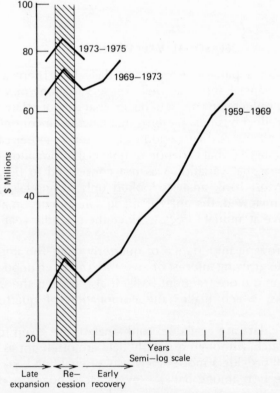

Figure 55 Western Bancorporation earnings before securities transactions adjusted to common periods of recession in general business activity. *Source:* Investors Management Sciences, Inc., Western Bancorporation 1975 Annual Report.

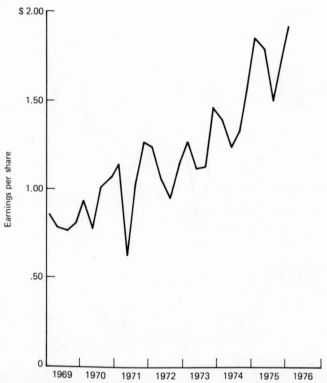

Figure 56 Continental Illinois Corporation earnings per share before securities transactions quarterly plots. *Source:* Continental Illinois Corporation Quarterly Reports.

that earnings per share have expanded on an overall basis from 1969 through 1976. Nevertheless, a close look at the data shows that about one third of the quarter-to-quarter movements of earnings per share have been downward. Moreover, within the span of a year, the movement of the series appears irregular and haphazard. The bank analyst may wonder whether a small decline of one quarter's earnings per share is an indication of a significant drop in earnings or whether one or two quarters of small gains in earnings per share represent a strengthening of the bank's earnings position.

The next chart shows exactly the same data points of the series, but the data points of the quarters of the same year are linked as a group (Figure 57). The scale of this chart has been multiplied by four to show the quarterly earnings per share results at an annual rate. This change of scale has no effect on the pattern of the data series.

The chart shows a pattern of "V" or "U" configuratious that are regularly repeated. The earnings per share for the first quarter are usually at a compara-tively high level for the year. The earnings for the second and third quarters are at relatively lower levels, and the final quarter is usually at the highest level of all four quarters. The chart indicates the visual pattern of one bank's seasonal variation. A bank analyst needs some method that adjusts the data so the eye alone is not required to determine whether a quarterly change represents an advance or a decline.

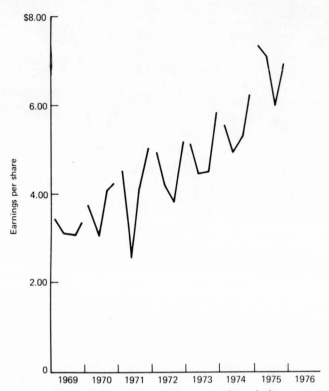

Figure 57 Continental Illinois Corporation earnings per share before securities transactions quarterly series at annual rate. *Source:* Continental Illinois Corporation Quarterly Reports.

Four Quarters Trailing Method

The first method of adjusting for seasonal variation is "four quarters trailing" and is shown in the chart as the dashed series for earnings per share for Continental Illinois Corporation (Figure 58). The four quarters trailing method of seasonal adjustment is widely used among banks. Its attraction reflects its simplicity of calculation, the visual smoothness of results, and the use of only hard data in its calculation.

The *four quarters trailing series* is the addition of four quarters of data. As each more recent quarter's data is added, the oldest data point is dropped. Thus the series shows the increment or decline of each new quarter's results over the year-ago quarter's results. The addition of the intermediate quarters weights the results to an annual total.

The chart also shows the typical smoothness of a four quarters trailing series. A comparison of the earlier charts, which show the actual quarterly data, with the chart showing the four quarter trailing series points up the significant smoothing effect of the four quarter trailing series. Smooth running series are intuitively appealing to almost everyone, and probably this characteristic has been a major factor in the acceptance of the four quarters trailing method of seasonal adjustment.

A final consideration is the use only of what many bank analysts regard as

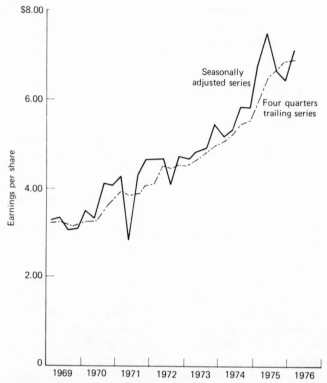

Figure 58 Continental Illinois Corporation earnings per share before securities transactions quarterly series at annual rate shown according to four quarters trailing and census X-11 seasonal adjustment. *Source:* Continental Illinois Corporation, Interactive Data Corporation.

"hard data." This term refers to the use of numbers that are added together, without complicated formulas which introduce intermediate steps.

Seasonal Adjustment

Despite the appealing advantages of the four quarters trailing method, it is challenged successfully by the seasonal adjustment method on one issue. Seasonally adjusted data are quicker to respond to changes in cycle and trend. The greater responsiveness of seasonally adjusted data is a critical advantage, since the principal reason for the interest in examining quarterly data is to detect changes in the direction of a bank's activities or results.

The chart showing both the four quarters trailing series and the seasonally adjusted series illustrates this advantage. The seasonally adjusted series shows that earnings per share of Continental Illinois Corporation reached a high in the second quarter of 1975 and fell during subsequent quarters. The decline in the seasonally adjusted series contrasts the continued gain of the four quarter trailing series.

The two series told different stories during this period. The seasonally adjusted series indicated that during the third and fourth quarters of 1975 earnings per share were under downward pressure. The four quarter trailing series did not convey this message. This series indicated that the upward pace of earnings per share merely slackened.

The seasonally adjusted series has a second advantage, which is less critical, but still significant. The annual rate of the data pertains only to the quarter that is measured. In contrast, the four quarter trailing series includes three quarters of data that do not pertain to the measured quarter. Thus when a series is rising, the advance of the four quarter trailing series tends not only to lag, but also shows a lower value for the annual rate than the seasonally adjusted series. With a declining series, the four quarter trailing series also tends to lag and shows a higher value for the annual rate than the seasonally adjusted series. This is a technical issue and does not much affect the practical use of the data, unless there are sharp swings in the series. In these circumstances, the bank analyst does not require seasonal adjustment techniques to perceive that major changes have taken place.

A characteristic of seasonally adjusted data is its volatility, and this characteristic may be a disadvantage. There are, on occasion, serious drawbacks to greater volatility. For example, in the second quarter of 1971 and in the third quarter of 1972, the earnings per share of Continental Illinois Corporation dropped sharply (Table 2). A bank analyst could have concluded that a major shock to earnings had occurred. Nevertheless, both of these declines represented temporary, special circumstances. Using only the data of the series, the bank analyst might not have arrived at these conclusions.

A major disadvantage of the use of seasonally adjusted data is the complexity of calculation. Even the most simple methods of calculation involve effort. One simple method is shown in Table 2, shown here for explanatory purposes only. A more complicated, superior type of seasonal adjustment that requires use of a computer will be discussed later.

The table's left-hand column shows quarterly earnings per share from the fourth quarter of 1971 to the fourth quarter of 1975. The second column shows the percent change from one quarter to the next for the period. These percent changes include all four factors of trend, cyclical, seasonal, and irregular variations. Some way has to be devised to eliminate the trend and cyclical factors, or the seasonal factors will be obscured. The next column represents an effort to remove the trend and cyclical effects of the quarter-to-quarter changes. The total year's quarter-to-quarter change (as distinct from each quarterly change) may be regarded as reflecting the combined trend and cyclical factors. This total yearly change is subtracted if the annual change is positive (and added if the annual change is negative) to eliminate the trend and cyclical factors. The third column shows this annual adjustment divided by four. On occasion, when the total annual change leaves a fraction, the adjustment for one or two quarters is a bit higher or lower. The fourth column is the result of the arithmetic of the second and third columns. This column represents the seasonal change expressed as a percent for each of the running quarters for the four-year period. The fifth and final columns show the seasonal changes expressed as a factor rather than as a percentage. The conversion from the fourth to the fifth column is simply arithmetic. The decimal of the percent seasonal change is moved two spaces to the left, and this number is added to 1.000. Seasonal factors are the conventional way that

Table 2 Continental Illinois Corporation
A Simple Method of Calculating Seasonal Factors

Year	Quarter	Earnings per Share	Quarter-to-Quarter Change	Elimination of Trend and Cycle	Seasonal Change	Seasonal Factors
1971	4	$1.14	—	—	—	—
1972	1	1.24	+ 8.8%	− 5.2%	+ 3.6%	1.036
	2	1.05	−15.3	− 5.2	−20.5	0.795
	3	0.95	− 9.5	− 5.2	−14.7	0.853
	4	1.30	+36.8	− 5.2	+31.6	1.316
Total			+20.8%	−20.8%	0%	4.000
1973	1	1.27	− 2.3%	− 4.4%	− 6.7%	0.933
	2	1.12	−11.8	− 4.4	−16.2	0.838
	3	1.13	+ 0.9	− 4.5	− 3.6	0.964
	4	1.48	+31.0	− 4.5	+26.5	1.265
Total			+17.8%	−17.8%	0%	4.000
1974	1	1.39	− 5.4%	− 2.3%	− 7.7%	.923
	2	1.24	−10.8	− 2.3	−13.1	.869
	3	1.33	+ 7.3	− 2.3	+ 5.0	1.050
	4	1.57	+18.0	− 2.2	+15.8	1.158
Total			+ 9.1%	− 9.1%	0%	4.000
1975	1	1.84	+17.2%	− 3.4%	+13.8%	1.138
	2	1.77	− 3.8	− 3.4	− 7.2	.928
	3	1.50	−15.3	− 3.3	−18.6	.814
	4	1.73	+15.3	− 3.3	+12.0	1.120
Total			+13.4%	−13.4%	0%	4.000

Source: Continental Illinois Corporation Quarterly Reports.

seasonal variation is described. A quick review shows that there is considerable fluctuation of the seasonal factors for any individual quarter.

Seasonal factors may also be derived using the Census X-11 seasonal adjustment program (Table 3). This seasonal adjustment program requires the use of a computer and is regarded among statisticians as the most advanced technique for making seasonal adjustments. It was developed by the Bureau of Census of the U.S. Department of Commerce and has undergone numerous refinements. The Census X-11 computer program is available from many software suppliers, including Tymshare, Inc., 20705 Valley Green Drive, Cupertino, California, telephone 408-257-6550, and from Interactive Data Corporation (a subsidiary of Chase Manhattan Bank), 486 Totten Pond Road, Waltham, Massachusetts, telephone 617-290-1234.

A comparison between the simple method and the Census X-11 method of seasonally adjusting earnings per share of Continental Illinois shows a broad similarity. Both methods indicate that earnings per share show strong seasonal variation among the four quarters. Both methods indicate that during the fourth quarter earnings per share may be expected to be the strongest, during the second quarter earnings are likely to be less strong, and that during the middle two quarters of the year, earnings may be expected to be least strong. Those broad similarities should be expected among different methods of seasonal adjustment.

Nevertheless, there are also important differences between many of the individual seasonal factors, and these differences could involve major differences in evaluating a series. For example, the average seasonal factor for the fourth quarter of Continental Illinois Corporation's earnings per share was 1.213 for the simple method shown here and 1.082 for the Census X-11 method. The difference is a factor of 0.131 or approximately 12 percent. This difference could be significant in interpreting whether earnings advanced or declined for the quarter. There are statistical techniques to determine the appropriateness of methods to adjust for seasonal variation, and the Census X-11 method is a superior technique compared with the simple method shown here.

The earnings per share of Continental Illinois provide an example of simplicity in explaining the procedure of seasonal adjustment, since there were no pronounced cyclical swings in the period covered by the series. A more typical example of a bank series is shown in the chart for Manufacturers Hanover Corporation. This chart shows quarterly earnings per share from 1969 through the first quarter of 1976 (Figure 59). During this period, there were two complete cycles. The seasonally adjusted series showed considerably greater volatility than the four quarters trailing series. Nevertheless, the seasonally adjusted series caught the winds of cyclical change more quickly. For example, in the third quarter of 1970, the seasonally adjusted series turned down and continued to decline in the fourth quarter of that year. The series shows that two consecutive quarters of decline strongly indicate a beginning of a cyclical decline. Furthermore, the seasonally adjusted earnings weakness continued in the first quarter of 1971. Throughout this period, the four quarter trailing series continued to climb or held steady. It was in the second quarter of 1971 that the four quarter trailing series declined.

Table 3 Continental Illinois Corporation
Calculation of Four Quarters Trailing Series and Seasonally Adjusted Series Using the Census X-11 Method

Year	Quarter	Earnings Per Share Before Securities Transactions	Four Quarters Trailing Series	Quarterly Series Times Four	Census X-11 Seasonal Factor	Seasonally Adjusted Earnings Per Share Before Securities Transactions
1968	1	$0.72		$2.88	1.059	$2.72
	2	0.73		2.92	0.900	3.25
	3	0.88		3.52	1.015	3.47
	4	0.75	$3.08	3.00	1.027	2.92
1969	1	0.85	3.21	3.40	1.060	3.21
	2	0.78	3.26	3.12	0.900	3.47
	3	0.76	3.14	3.04	1.005	3.03
	4	0.79	3.18	3.16	1.037	3.05
1970	1	0.93	3.26	3.72	1.064	3.50
	2	0.76	3.24	3.04	0.900	3.38
	3	1.01	3.49	4.04	0.983	4.11
	4	1.09	3.79	4.36	1.058	4.12

Table 3 *(Continued)*

Year	Quarter	Earnings Per Share Before Securities Transactions	Four Quarters Trailing Series	Quarterly Series Times Four	Census X-11 Seasonal Factor	Seasonally Adjusted Earnings Per Share Before Securities Transactions
1971	1	1.14	4.00	4.56	1.067	4.28
	2	0.63	3.87	2.52	0.899	2.80
	3	1.04	3.90	4.16	0.961	4.33
	4	1.27	4.08	5.08	1.076	4.72
1972	1	1.24	4.18	4.96	1.067	4.65
	2	1.05	4.60	4.20	0.906	4.64
	3	0.95	4.51	3.80	0.939	4.05
	4	1.30	4.54	5.20	1.086	4.79
1973	1	1.27	4.57	5.08	1.068	4.76
	2	1.12	4.64	4.48	0.918	4.88
	3	1.13	4.82	4.52	0.923	4.90
	4	1.47	4.99	5.88	1.085	5.42
1974	1	1.39	5.11	5.56	1.071	5.19
	2	1.24	5.23	4.96	0.933	5.32
	3	1.33	5.43	5.32	0.909	5.85
	4	1.57	5.53	6.28	1.079	5.82
1975	1	1.84	5.98	7.36	1.079	6.82
	2	1.77	6.51	7.08	0.938	7.55
	3	1.50	6.68	6.00	0.904	6.64
	4	1.73	6.84	6.92	1.076	6.43
1976	1	1.92	6.92	7.68	1.084	7.09

Source: Continental Illinois Corporation, Interactive Data Corporation.

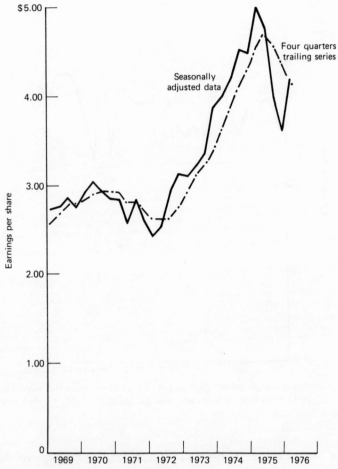

Figure 59 Manufacturers Hanover Corporation earnings per share before securities transactions. *Source:* Manufacturers Hanover Corporation, Interactive Data Corporation.

Thus bank analysts would have received a clear indication of earnings weakness one-half year earlier by the use of the seasonally adjusted series.

IRREGULAR VARIATION

The patterns to the variations of series that have been reviewed thus far include trend, cycle, and seasonal fluctuations. All of these patterns indicate common characteristics. For example, the cycle of one series of a bank bears a recognizeable likeness to the cycle of another bank.

However, there are variations that do not appear to fit into any of these three regular patterns and are usually referred to as irregular variations. These irregular fluctuations are a residual, which cannot be explained by any of the three principal patterns. The fact that there are irregular fluctuations indicates that despite efforts to distill a bank's earnings per share into neat components of trend, cycle, and seasonal variation, there are still many forces that bear on

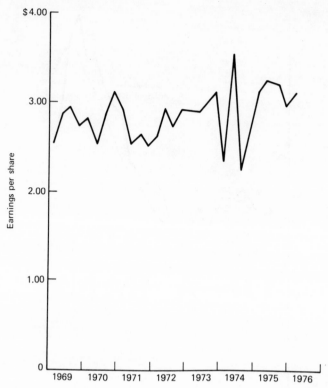

Figure 60   Security Pacific Corporation earnings per share before securities transactions quarterly data, seasonally adjusted shown at annual rate. *Source:* Security Pacific Corporation, Interactive Data Corporation.

earnings that are fortuitous. These random factors are a part of the life of a banking organization and include such well-known developments as a windfall loan at superb pricing or a sudden loss from a venture that had once been regarded as having assured success.

The chart shows quarterly earnings per share of Security Pacific Corporation on a seasonally adjusted basis from the first quarter of 1969 to the first quarter of 1976 (Figure 60). The chart shows neither an indication of upward or downward trend nor a clear indication of a cycle. The seasonal variation is barely measureable. The fluctuations that remain may be regarded as being irregular, reflecting the alternating random favorable and unfavorable developments of the bank.

There is sometimes a tendency to reject the possibility that the series of some banks do not fit into regular categories. But in fact, the series of some banks appear to be in a kind of long-term equilibrium and principally reflect a variety of happenings that are largely fortuitous.

PART TWO
PERCEIVING
THE POLICIES
OF A BANK

CHAPTER 5
LIQUIDITY POLICY

Liquidity represents the closeness of assets to cash. Banks with liquidity have numerous strengths. A nearness to cash indicates an assurance to depositors that they would be able to obtain funds for their deposits under almost all circumstances. It also indicates assurances to other bank analysts, including investors, borrowers and directors.

IMPORTANCE

One of the remarkable achievements of Western civilization is the widespread trust of banks. This belief is shared throughout the United States, England, Germany, Japan, as well as in other Western countries. The trust is felt at all levels of society—the poor, the rich, liberals, conservatives—all share the belief that banks are safe places to deposit funds. Perhaps this trust reflects a deep-seated confidence in the ability of Western society to control its destiny.

Most of the world's population do not use banks. These individuals and organizations keep their funds in hiding places, precious metals, jewels, tangible investments, and real properties. The threat of confiscation of funds placed on deposit by governments, either through taxation or inflation, or an uncertainty over the prospects of local banks pervades in the thinking of many potential depositors in these countries. Banks do not hold major portions of wealth in such countries as India, Chile, or the Central African countries. There appears to be a lack of confidence on the part of most persons in these countries that the reins of the future are firmly in grasp, and events could overwhelm them.

The trust of U.S. banks is based on a simple belief. Depositors of these banks believe that they will obtain their funds if desired, without question. These depositors believe that there is no doubt that this trust would be fulfilled. Thus there would be no benefit (other than complete confidentiality) and disadvantages of a lack of safety in keeping funds in personal vaults or secret hiding places.

The logic of this trust is simple. The benefits to individuals, society, and the economy are enormous. By channeling excess funds into banks, large sums can be loaned to persons and organizations that want to expand. Without the middleman role of banks, funds could not be easily concentrated or channeled to users in greatest need.

The bank failures of the past generation have been minor and have not penalized depositors. Many depositors are aware of the Federal Deposit Insurance Corporation and the commitment of the Federal Reserve to protect the U.S. banking industry. But even here, the strength of the public's faith that deposits are safe probably lies deeper than the presence of these organizations. It is a simple confidence that the U.S. society and government will support whatever measures are needed to enable banks to fulfill their deposit obligations.

All faith must ultimately be based on performance, and the ability of banks to honor their deposit obligations rests on their liquidity. Liquidity is not a particularly popular subject among banks. To raise the question of whether the bank's liquidity is in good shape almost represents an admission that there might be reason for less than complete confidence in the ability of the bank to fulfill its deposit obligations. The fact that questions of liquidity can be awkward indicates the seriousness of the issue.

Liquidity is important to banks because they are so illiquid, if they were ever pressed by a large proportion of their depositors. Confidence of depositors sustains banks. It is a crucial point. It is also a point where banks differ most clearly from virtually every other type of business organization—manufacturing, utilities, finance, and loan companies. These organizations do not expose the source of their funds to the whims and emotions of depositors. The only other comparable organizations to banks are mutual savings banks and savings and loan associations.

The liquidity policy of a bank is a strategy for dealing with uncertainties and emergencies. These would not be business as usual circumstances. Liquidity represents a defense against the effect of extreme pressures on a bank that would represent a loss of confidence by depositors and could lead to a "run" on the bank, that is, when depositors collectively attempt to withdraw deposits. Such a development is the worst problem a bank can face.

Most banks, of course, have either the resources of the Federal Reserve or rely on a line of a credit with a bank that is a member as a supplementary source of liquidity. One of the original purposes of creating the Federal Reserve System was to provide this type of backup to banks that were basically sound, but for whatever reason, had temporarily lost the confidence of depositors. The Federal Reserve System represents the lender of last resort, since it can buy any of the assets of a bank at face value for cash. Such purchases have the effect of providing full and complete liquidity to the assets of a bank. Of course, the total assets of the bank would shrink to the extent that the Federal Reserve monetized an asset, and funds were paid to depositors.

There are three types of circumstances when the commitment of the Federal Reserve could be called to defend a bank's liquidity. The first instance would be when a single bank had run into difficulty and depositors and short-term lenders withdraw their funds, although the banking system in general would be in good condition. This is a situation where rumors would have raised questions concerning the future viability of a bank, largely because of concern over the company's specific banking practices. The attempt to rescue Franklin National Corporation represents an example of this type of situation.

The second instance is where depositors and short-term lenders would be worried about the banking system in general. This type of situation would reflect extreme duress in the economy, such as might occur during a severe recession or depression. Depositors would be concerned that the assets of banks would be worth much less than their face value. The loans of banks would have been made to many bankrupt companies and individuals and thus their worth would be only a fraction of their original value. The United States faced this situation in 1933.

The third instance would be when depositors and investors would flee from a paper currency and seek refuge for funds in nonmonetary assets, such as commodities and real property. This situation could occur during a period of super inflation when prices advance daily. Banks would find that, despite a write-up in the value of assets, an equivalent write-up in the value of deposits might not occur, because all funds that would not be needed for immediate transaction purposes would be drained from the banking system. The Federal Reserve would be required to monetize the assets of the banking system. There has not been an inflation in the United States of this magnitude in living memory, although it has occurred in other countries, such as Germany in 1923. Nevertheless, the United States approached this situation during the Revolutionary War and the Civil War.

Investors and depositors look on the liquidity of a bank as being important when it is threatened. Nevertheless, during most periods—in fact during virtually all of the life span of most of the population—liquidity has been an overlooked consideration. For nearly all banks liquidity has represented protection against an adversity that has not occurred.

Liquidity is important during periods when banks appear to have no problems, because when liquidity is most needed, it is usually difficult to obtain. For example, when a bank faces a crisis of confidence, such as occurred at Franklin National Corporation in 1974, the bank usually finds that many depositors and holders of the bank's short-term debt take their funds to other banks. Moreover, customers who remain with the distressed bank usually do so only with the attraction of sharply higher interest rates, adding to the burden on earnings. Building liquidity from public sources under these circumstances would be virtually impossible. Moreover, if the banking system as a whole is under duress, it would be still more difficult for a bank to bolster its liquidity.

HOW LIQUIDITY IS MANAGED

Banks have five ways of managing liquidity. They can attempt to manage their liquidity through any one method or a combination of these methods. Nevertheless, the most certain approach includes the initial two methods, the self-liquidating assets approach and the asset saleability approach. The earnings flow approach and the new funds approach involve greater uncertainty. The final approach, using the discount window of a Federal Reserve Bank, may involve an element of uncertainty, if the bank has a record of too much independence in attempting to move against policies of the Federal Reserve System.

Self-Liquidating Asset Approach

The self-liquidating asset approach to liquidity looks to the repayment of funds to the bank as a source of liquidity. These funds are repaid to the bank in line with the terms of loan agreements or the maturity of securities. Liquidity is acquired through the automatic self-liquidation of the obligations due the bank. This approach to liquidity was sometimes referred to as the "real bills doctrine" in England during the eighteenth century and later as the "commercial loan theory" of banking in the United States during the nineteenth century.

It is an approach to liquidity that is particularly well suited to a mercantilist economy, where the principal users of bank credit are merchants, shippers, and traders. For example, a cotton trader may use bank credit to finance the ownership of cotton during shipment from Calcutta to London. The bank loan is secured at the time the cotton is acquired, and the loan is paid off perhaps two months later. The bank would receive its funds and the bank's liquidity, so far as this transaction is concerned, would be completely restored when the loan would be extinguished. The cotton trader might secure another loan to ship manufactured cotton cloth from London to Boston, and the bank would prepare a separate new loan for this purpose.

This approach to liquidity stresses loans that are secured by tangible property, such as cotton, automobiles, or grain, and which are for short periods, always less than six months and preferably not longer than three months. The loans are for working capital purposes, and the borrower regularly goes through the motions of completing loan arrangements, returning funds to the bank and taking out new loans. Acceptances are an example. Currently, banks make a large proportion of term, mortgage, or revolving credit arrangements with customers that last for several years and may involve only the good faith of the borrower as collateral. Nevertheless, even today, there is an important proportion of short-term loans that come due on a monthly basis, and the self-liquidating asset approach to liquidity continues to affect banking practices.

The spirit of the self-liquidating asset approach to lending and to liquidity continues to thrive to the present in some of the merchant banks of England. Many of these specialty banks continue to specialize in short-term specialty lending, although they seldom require collateral from their well-known customers. These merchant banks represent a kind of living fossil, from an institutional point of view, of the way banking was conducted at the turn of the nineteenth century.

Asset Saleability

The ability of a bank to sell its assets represents another approach to liquidity. This approach is sometimes described as the "shiftability" approach to liquidity. It refers to the ability of a bank to sell its loans and securities to other banks and to the open market. This approach to liquidity looks at the current market value of total assets, and as long as the book value of the bank's assets is reasonably close to the immediate market value of those assets, the bank is regarded as having liquidity.

This approach to liquidity developed a following in the early part of the twentieth century. During this period, banks expanded their lending of term loans to large industrial corporations and individuals for home mortgages. Both of these types of loans were for a longer duration than loans to traders and merchants, and banks sought a new way to protect their liquidity. The development of a national market for securities and quick communication among correspondendent banks concerning loans enabled many major banks to attempt to manage their liquidity from the point of view of asset saleability for most of the past half century.

Nevertheless, there have been important periods when banks have not been able to sell their assets near their purchase price. When the banking system as a whole is in a state of shock, the sale of assets becomes difficult. During the sharp price declines in securities value in 1907, 1920, 1931–1933, and 1938, most banks were unable to sell their securities without loss. Moreover, during these periods, the sale of other assets, including loans, also was difficult, because other banks, which were potential purchasers of loans, were reluctant to purchase loans and thereby reduce their liquidity without a substantial discount. Thus when liquidity is most needed, it may involve pro-hibitively high costs. The periods of difficulty for the banking system have been infrequent, and they have not left scars which have affected the widespread belief that the normal condition of the banking system is one with sufficient liquidity to satisfy all requests for depositors' funds.

New Funds

Throughout the past two centuries, most discussion of liquidity has focused on the closeness of assets to cash. The assets have implicitly been existing assets—the loans and securities already on the books of a bank. Nevertheless, in the late 1960s, a new approach to liquidity developed that looked at the ability of a bank to attract new funds.

Banks face stiff competition for savings deposits from other financial institu-tions such as savings and loan associations. They also are regulated concerning the maximum rate that they can pay for these funds. Consequently, there is relatively little opportunity to attract new savings deposit funds quickly. However, banks are permitted to seek funds in large amounts with no restric-tions in rates in the United States and abroad. This source has become the principal source of the new funds approach to liquidity. There have been many refinements to the approach. For example, funds may be obtained from financial markets in such a way as to always be an insignificant part of those markets. In this manner the funds would not disrupt the markets. Moreover, funds may be obtained from a variety of markets so that no one source of funds would be able to use its position to extract premium rates or specially advantageous terms during periods of stress.

This approach to liquidity rests on the reputation of a bank. Reputations are largely determined by the way banks fulfill the expectations of the financial community. Thus this approach to liquidity is probably limited to a small number of banks with international reputations.

A major problem with liquidity managed by the new funds approach is that new funds are usually difficult to obtain when liquidity is most needed. If investor expectations are not fulfilled and large depositors and sources of funds become disappointed, this source of liquidity can evaporate. Of course, it is always possible that a bank could hope to develop an overall program that would be designed to keep investors' expectations always fulfilled. Such a program would need to be unusually subtle and complete. The future is likely to continue to be full of surprises, and a program that would always enable a bank to appear favorably in the eyes of the investment community certainly would be an extraordinary program.

Borrowers' Earnings Flow

The earnings flow approach to liquidity suggests that loans are not inherently self-liquidating, but rather that they are paid off from the earnings of the borrower. This approach is sometimes referred to as the "doctrine of anticipated income" and looks at the financial health of a bank's customers. As long as these borrowers are profitable enough to cover the interest cost and possibly the sinking fund requirements of their bank loans, as well as their other obligations, there would be sufficient liquidity for the bank. Often sinking fund requirements are viewed in the broad context of gains in implicit reserves of the borrowers. The borrowers' earnings flow approach to liquidity is sometimes supported using interest costs alone as the test for meeting liquidity requirements.

A close analysis of the borrower's earnings flow approach indicates that it does not represent a direct approach to liquidity. It rests on assumptions of the conditions of a bank's borrowers, not on the assets of the bank itself. It says nothing about the other assets of a bank, including securities, because in recent years securities have become a relatively minor proportion of total assets of banks. This shift in emphasis to the borrower's condition appears almost as a rationale of current practice. It is an approach that is widely believed. Perhaps in the short run, what is believed is all that is important in liquidity, since at any specific time liquidity relies much on confidence.

Yet to be sustained, liquidity involves more than confidence. It requires that the assets of a bank are in fact close to cash. The two older approaches to liquidity, the self-liquidating asset approach and the asset saleability approach, are concerned specifically with this key aspect of liquidity. Stated in different terms, if the assets of a bank are close to cash, it has the structural basis of providing liquidity on a short run and most probably on a long-run basis.

All of the previous approaches to liquidity assume that the assets of a bank are fairly valued on its balance sheet. This requirement, of course, would require significant adjustments to the value of the loans shown on the balance sheet if there were any interruption in the agreed-on flow of interest income to the bank. Thus the value of all problem loans would be reduced to some measure of their market value. For example, during a recession, there would likely be a rise in the number of borrowers who would miss or renegotiate interest payments, including some municipalities. The value of the loans and securities would be diminished. These markdowns could be offset to the extent that there were reserves, including loan-loss reserves and reserves for securities. Beyond that, the markdowns could involve a reduction in shareholders' equity.

If these steps should bring about a loss of confidence on the part of depositors and holders of short-term paper of a bank, as happened in the minds of customers of Franklin National Corporation and Beverly Hills Bancorp, they could then take funds out of the bank. It is precisely at this point that the critical issues are joined. The question of where funds could be obtained to pay these customers is the issue of liquidity.

Federal Reserve Discount Window

The discount window of the one of the twelve Federal Reserve Banks is another source of liquidity to member commercial banks. A Federal Reserve Bank has been given authority by Congress to lend on any of the assets of a member bank and thereby provide a bank with a way of monetizing its assets.

The use of the window often involves little more than a procedural detail. There is actually a window, much like an old-fashioned teller's cage, in many Federal Reserve Banks for this purpose, almost always on the first floor. The discount window can be used to provide relatively minor funding of assets, enabling a bank to meet its reserve requirements. This use involves little ceremony.

However, if the basic liquidity of a bank is an issue, there will be a discussion of the proper use of the Federal Reserve discount window. Usually, the president of the Federal Reserve Bank invites the president of the member bank into his office to impress the gravity of the situation. The offices of presidents of most Federal Reserve Banks are paneled in dark wood, and the furniture is made of solid hardwood. The president and often the first vice president discuss the importance of sound banking practices and the need for a bank to build its own liquidity. The lesson is administered by Federal Reserve officials who are business and often social friends of bank presidents, and the message is made clear in the superficially pleasant, but underlying serious tone of important discussions in banking.

The Federal Reserve regards the word-of-mouth discussions among member banks about the way a discount window should be used as part of its educational service to banking. Virtually all actions taken by one of the district Federal Reserve Banks are discussed with the staff of the Board of Governors. Usually, this discussion merely involves mutual advisories. Nevertheless, if the issue of liquidity involves more serious implications from the point of view of the Federal Reserve Board of Governors, one of the governors of that board may be involved in the discussions.

The Federal Reserve System is regarded as the lender of last resort. Nevertheless, there is discretion in the use of the discount window, and in recent years, this discretionary power has emerged as an important issue.

The Bank of the Commonwealth represented a landmark case in the use of the discount window. In the late 1960s this bank attempted to avoid the restrictions of interstate branch banking by acquiring banks on a partnership basis rather than on the usual corporate basis. Moreover, in order to improve its earnings, the Bank of the Commonwealth lengthened the maturity of its municipal securities. As a consequence, it moved against the Federal Reserve System on two issues. It appeared to be a maverick bank that had found a way around a half century of restrictive legislation to prevent interstate banking. Moreover, the program of lengthening the maturity and reducing the quality of municipal securities to boost earnings was done against the expressed wishes of the Federal Reserve System. The program had the effect of challenging the Federal Reserve Board, since the Board was concurrently engaged in a program of draining liquidity from the banking system to control inflation. To meet the growing tightness in credit markets, the Board wanted banks to build their internal liquidity. The stage was set for a major confrontation.

The Bank of the Commonwealth had applied to the Federal Reserve Board for permission to open a branch in the Bahama Islands, which was turned down. The request was fairly routine, and under more ordinary circumstances, probably would have been granted. The Board took what had been previously regarded as being an unusual step of using this occasion to give a public opinion concerning its view of the bank. The *Wall Street Journal* published part of the Board's letter to the bank which stated that the Board "militated against the action of the Bank of the Commonwealth." Governor J. L. Robertson was named as an interested party. The Federal Reserve System seldom uses words like "militate," which convey overtones of a fighting spirit. It was clear that the bank did not have a friend on the part of Governor Robertson.

The credit crunch of the summer of 1970 caught up with the Bank of the Commonwealth in the fall of the year. The bank was unable to show sufficient cash and U.S. government securities to meet its reserve requirement from market sources and was forced to apply to the discount window of the Federal Reserve Bank of Chicago. The window was closed. The Federal Reserve Bank indicated that it would open the discount window only after the management of the bank resigned, which it did quickly. Subsequently, with new management, the Federal Reserve Bank supported the bank.

The decision of the Board not to support a major bank in need of the use of the discount window indicates that it may not always be the liquidity source of last resort. The Bank of the Commonwealth represented an extreme example of a bank that clearly moved against the principles that the Federal Reserve System was promoting and clearly was not a typical bank. Yet support was refused. From that point forward, there would be a question concerning the extent that differences would be permitted between member banks and the Federal Reserve System without a withdrawal of support by the central bank.

IMPLICATIONS OF LIQUIDITY

Implications for Earnings

In the past two decades the liquidity of most banks has declined, which has provided support to gains in earnings. Virtually all actions which increase liquidity also hamper earnings. Although there are a number of exceptions to this general rule, it holds for most cases.

The most direct type of liquidity is where assets of a bank are self-liquidating. The bank does not need to take action to obtain funds, which are payable on the maturity of the asset. Thus a short maturity of an asset indicates a liquid asset.

The chart indicates the yields of various maturities of U.S. treasury securities on June 30, 1976 (Figure 61). It shows regular fixed coupon and callable issues. This type of chart is often referred to as a yield curve. During most periods of the business and credit cycle it is positive sloping, or the line of average relationship moves upward in yield as the maturity lengthens. The chart shows that at midyear 1976 a bank which might hold an average maturity of roughly six months would have received approximately a 6 percent yield from its U.S. treasury portfolio. If the bank had chosen a portfolio with an average maturity of 20 years, it would have received a yield of about 8 percent, representing income that would have been one-third larger. The chart shows that on the date of the quotations a bank which chose liquidity would have penalized

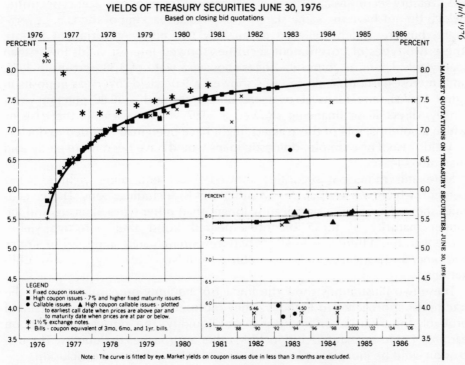

Figure 61

Source: Treasury Bulletin, July 1976.

earnings; or stated the other way, earnings could have been augmented through a reduction of liquidity by lengthening maturities.

Yield curves vary throughout the course of the business cycle. During periods of considerable credit ease, they show a more pronounced positive slope. In contrast, during periods of a credit crunch, when funds are difficult to locate, the yield curve shows a negative slope, indicating that borrowers, including banks, are eagerly seeking short-term funds—some may be seeking them desperately. Except for a credit crunch, yield curves usually show a positive slope.

The ease by which assets could be sold affects their liquidity. U.S. government securities are the most easily sold assets of a bank because there is a broad market for these securities, and they are regarded by the public as being almost equivalent to cash. High-quality municipal securities are also highly liquid, since there is also a broadly based market for most of these securities. High-quality loans rank next in liquidity. The market for these assets is much narrower than for securities, since they are principally traded among banks and major financial companies. Finally, the other loans of a bank are at a lower level of liquidity, because potential purchasers may question whether they have sufficient background to assess all elements of risk. On the whole, securities are more liquid than loans, largely because the market for securities is much better developed.

Banks usually receive a lower interest rate from their more liquid assets. For example, Chase Manhattan Corporation averaged a 7.03 percent yield from U.S. treasury securities in 1975, and 7.50 percent from federal agency securities (which do not have the same stated unequivocal backing of the U.S. government, but are widely believed to be fully backed by government intent). These two types of government securities showed interest yields lower than loan yields. Loans at domestic offices showed a yield of 8.38 percent in 1975, and interest earning bank deposits showed a 9.07 yield (overseas deposits in other banks), and loans at overseas offices showed a 10.06 percent yield. Finally, direct lease financing showed a 10.97 yield. As a rule, the ease by which a potential sale of these assets might have been made tended to decline as yields rose. For example, domestic loans would have been more easily sold than direct leases.

State and municipal securities showed a tax equivalent yield of 12.61 percent, which was well above all other yields, including loans. These securities showed a maturity significantly longer than other types of assets, and the longer maturity of these securities helped boost their effective yields. Moreover, the differences in yields between Chase's state and local securities and other assets included adjusted returns from New York City and MAC obligations.

These two illustrations show the impact of liquidity on earnings, using the traditional approaches to liquidity. They represent the most fundamental and probably the most important measures of liquidity. The impact of liquidity on earnings could be extended to include other approaches to liquidity. The discussion wold be more complicated, but would show the same conclusion.

It is no surprise that during the past decade, when there has been a major emphasis given to bank earnings, that liquidity has declined for almost all banks. Most bank analysts gave higher marks to a major earnings expansion than to the maintenance of liquidity. In fact, a strong liquidity position came to be regarded as an indication of underused capacity. Thus the gains in earnings of many banks can be regarded, in part, as the reduction of liquidity. To this extent, earnings received a special boost that could not likely be sustained on a long-term basis. In fact, if the conditions of the past one or two decades should reverse and liquidity should again be emphasized, the long-term trend of earnings of banks could be hindered.

Implications for Bank Analysts

A bank analyst who would be a depositor would select the way he approaches the liquidity of a bank according to his concern over present and future financial developments. If he felt that there were no major worries and that the bank in which he placed a deposit possessed extraordinary powers of money management, he might measure liquidity using the new funds approach. He would be content that even if an emergency should arise, the Federal Reserve Bank would provide whatever temporary liquidity would be needed to tide the bank over the difficulties.

An investor with a similarly sanguine view of present and future financial developments might also come to the same conclusion in an evaluation of the importance of liquidity. This investor would regard the ability of a bank to obtain additional funds as an advantage which could aid earnings and would seek banks that had developed the practice of purchasing liquidity.

Bank directors might look on liquidity with more concern, even if they were convinced that the future for credit markets looked bright. Their concern would reflect their special responsibilities. Unlike an investor or even a depositor, a bank director cannot easily sidestep his responsibilities, if difficulties arise. His commitment is more durable, and his requirements for liquidity could be more stringent.

For example, a director might require more specific information concerning management's assurances that liquidity could be purchased through the use of new funds. The director might ask to be informed of the details and specifics of the operation, together with the experience of the bank during past credit crunches. He might request background information concerning the bank's relationship with the discount window of the Federal Reserve Bank. Of course, much of this information usually is discussed at board meetings over the course of a year, yet it might not be organized in a way that could be easily evaluated in light of the banking company's liquidity policy.

It is also possible that bank analysts might hold a more conservative outlook for credit markets and the future of business conditions. Their approach to liquidity could then be considerably different.

For example, a major depositor who believed that future credit conditions were likely to be difficult might review banks from the point of view of their liquidity as shown by self-liquidating assets or saleable assets. This depositor would not benefit from making a deposit in banks with less liquid positions using these approaches to liquidity. If there were to be a temporary interruption in the access to funds for any reason, the loss could be considerable. Thus a depositor might wish to avoid liquidity risks as a simple matter of policy. His approach to liquidity would be that of a fundamentalist, and he would have a skeptical attitude toward liquidity policies which required major optimistic assumptions about markets or the likely way people holding discretionary power would act.

An investor who believed that credit markets might likely face a difficult future would also view liquidity from a conservative point of view. Nevertheless, in recent years, many investors have not regarded liquidity as an issue of importance and have not given much attention to the liquidity policies that banks use. It would probably require major financial difficulties in credit markets for these investors to become concerned over the liquidity policies of banks.

Bank directors might be expected to show considerable concern over the manner in which liquidity would be approached, if they believed that storm warnings were flying in credit markets. They might look for programs to meet even remote contingencies and might wish to review personally certain of these programs to assess their credibility.

MEASURING LIQUIDITY

Three of the five approaches to liquidity can be measured. These measures are only approximations of what could be described as the actual liquidity of a bank. A bank analyst can never know precisely what the real liquidity might be, because he does not have access to the full information of the bank's financial accounts. Nevertheless, the measures available to bank analysts provide, in most instances, reliable indications of a bank's liquidity policy. And it is this perception that is important to bank analysts in making judgments about banks.

Average Maturity of Securities

Table 4 shows the maturity distribution of the securities portfolio of Charter New York Corporation for year-end 1974 and 1975. This table provides a measure for the first approach to liquidity—the self-liquidating approach—which was discussed earlier.

The most simple measure is the average maturity for each of the categories of securities. The U.S. government securities averaged 1.7 years at year-end 1975, down from 2.4 years one year earlier. Charter did not make this information publicly available for year-end 1976. This reduction in average maturity of U.S. government securities during the previous two years indicated that the liquidity of this important part of Charter's securities portfolio increased. In contrast, the average maturity of Charter's securities of state and political subsidivisions increased from 5.0 years to 5.9 years from year-end 1974 to year-end 1975. Again, data for 1976 were not available. This increase in average maturity indicated that this part of Charter's securities portfolio declined. The other securities portion of the portfolio remained steady. The total of all secu-

Table 4
Statistical Summary 1971-1975 (Continued)

Charter New York Corporation

Maturity Distribution of Securities Portfolio

	December 31, 1975				December 31, 1974			
	U.S. Govts.	States and Political Subdivisions	Other	Total	U.S. Govts.	States and Political Subdivisions	Other	Total
Within 1 Year . . .	61.1%	25.0%	17.0%	37.8%	35.6%	45.0%	14.1%	37.3%
1 to 5 Years	33.1	32.0	69.6	38.3	50.1	23.8	62.6	37.9
5 to 10 Years	4.7	20.1	5.3	11.8	13.0	13.5	17.1	13.9
Over 10 Years . . .	1.1	22.9	8.1	12.1	1.3	17.7	6.2	10.9
Average Maturity (In Years)	1.7	5.9	3.7	3.9	2.4	5.0	3.7	4.0

Note: The statistical summary includes the accounts of Charter New York Corporation and all of its subsidiaries. Banks acquired and accounted for under the pooling of interests method are included for all periods presented.

Source: 1975 Annual Report

rities showed a small decline in average maturity from 4.0 years to 3.9 years in the period, indicating liquidity edged upward.

The upper portion of Table 5 shows that of Charter's total securities, at year-end 1976, 25.7 percent would turn into cash within one year. Total securities of Charter New York Corporation amounted to $956 million at year-end 1976. Thus Charter would be expected to receive $246 million in cash from the self-liquidation of its securities portfolio. This figure represents 2.8 percent of its $8699 million in deposits at year-end 1976. The figures show that one year earlier Charter's ratio was higher, indicating that this measure of liquidity had declined.

Citicorp showed a different approach of liquidity in its policy. Table 6 shows the average maturity of U.S. treasury and agency securities and state and municipal securities.

Even though the categories of Citicorp's securities portfolio are not entirely comparable with Charter New York Corporation's categories, the figures show a broad outline of much longer maturities for Citicorp. At year-end 1976 the average maturity of U.S. treasury and federal agencies securities was 4.7 years (56 months) and 11 years for state and municipal securities. The latter securities were shown after the maturities of New York City had been lengthened. A review of the average maturities for comparable earlier years shows that the maturities at year-end 1976 were longer for governments and shorter for municipals than earlier years, suggesting that in recent years on an overall basis Citicorp may have maintained a long-term decision concerning its liquidity policy.

Table 7 shows the ratio of estimated funds from securities to deposits for Citicorp reflects the same strategy of less liquidity. This table represents an

**Table 5   Charter New York Corporation
Securities Liquidity to Deposit Ratio
($ Millions)**

	December 31, 1975	December 31, 1976
Percent of securities which will mature within one year	37.3%	25.7%
Total securities	1171	956
Cash funds from securities due within one year	437	246
Total deposits	9835	8699
Ratio of cash funds from securities due within one year to total deposits	4.4%	2.8%

Source: 1976 Annual Report.

estimate based upon incomplete information concerning the maturity of trading account securities, but shows one way of making an estimate for the total. At year-end 1976, U.S. treasury, agency, state, municipal, and other securities due within one year totalled $3543, and the ratio of these securities to the total of all maturities of this group of securities was 19.4 percent. This ratio may be applied to the total securities of Citicorp, amounting to $4637, to obtain an estimate of $900 million in funds from securities which could be due within one year. A comparison of these funds with $49,136 million in total deposits shows an estimated ratio of 1.8 percent of cash funds from securities due within one year.

Loan-Deposit Ratio

The loan-deposit ratio provides a measure of the asset saleability approach to liquidity. It shows how fully a bank is "loaned up." A high loan-deposit ratio indicates that a bank has a large proportion of its interest earning assets in loans and a small proportion in securities. Because loans are not as easily sold as securities, a high loan-deposit ratio would indicate that a bank would have comparatively low liquidity. Similarly, a low loan-deposit ratio would indicate high liquidity.

The expansion in the use of large certificates of deposit and other types of purchased funds such as commercial paper has not diminished the usefulness of the loan deposit ratio as an indicator of liquidity. A large portion of these purchased funds have been in the form of certificates of deposit, which are included in the calculation of this ratio. The amount of funds that might escape being included in this measure of liquidity is small in proportion to total deposits for all but a few major banks that regularly use purchased funds. In measuring liquidity for these banks a ratio showing cash and due from banks, total securities, and net federal funds divided by total liabilities is useful.

Table 8 shows that the total loan deposit ratio for Charter New York Corporation was 59.2 percent in 1976. This ratio indicated that less than one-half

Table 6

Investment Securities

Maturity and Yield** at December 31, 1976

Carrying Value (In Millions)	U.S. Treasury	Federal Agencies	State and Municipal	Other (Principally in Overseas Offices)
Due within 1 year	$ 69	$ 2	$ 185	$ 430
Yield	5.05%	7.27%	6.72%	*
After 1 but within 5 years	782	137	205	666
Yield	6.19%	7.15%	5.62%	*
After 5 but within 10 years	61	17	246	108
Yield	7.52%	7.52%	5.65%	*
After 10 years	13	52	365	205
Yield	7.72%	8.10%	4.20%	*
Total	$ 925	$ 208	$1,001	$1,409
Yield	6.23%	7.43%	5.31%	*

*Information not readily obtainable.
**Computed by dividing annual interest (net of amortization of premium or accretion of discount) by the carrying value of the respective investment securities at December 31, 1976.

State and Municipal Investment Securities

Maturity Distribution at December 31, 1976

Carrying Value (In Millions)	Due Within 1 Year	2-5 Years	6-10 Years	Over 10 Years	Total
Obligations of					
New York City*	$ 13	$ 53	$ 52	$ 15	$ 133
New York State					
General	134	31	20	–	185
Municipal Assistance Corporation*	14	65	105	9	193
Other New York State Agencies	8	19	28	105	160
All Other State and Municipal	16	37	41	236	330
	$185	$205	$246	$365	$1,001

*Discussions among New York City and MAC officials and representatives of Citibank and certain other holders of New York City Notes, which commenced following the issuance by the New York Court of Appeals of its opinion that the moratorium covering New York City Notes was unconstitutional, may affect the terms of the New York City Notes and certain Municipal Assistance Corporation obligations held by Citicorp. See Note 2 of Notes to the Financial Statements for additional information concerning market values and New York obligations.

Investment Securities

Average Maturity at Year-End

Year	U.S. Treasury and Federal Agencies	State and Municipal
1976	56 months	11 years
1975	31 months	14 years
1974	43 months	14 years
1973	33 months	13 years
1972	22 months	17 years
1971	24 months	19 years

Source: Citicorp 1976 Annual Report

Table 7   Citicorp
Securities Liquidity to Deposit Ratio ($ Millions)

Securities Due Within One Year—Carrying Value	December 31, 1975	December 31, 1976
U.S. Treasury securities	517	69
Federal agency securities	35	2
State and municipal securities	44	185
Other	361[a]	430
Total cash funds from above securities due within one year	957	686
Total treasury, agency, and municipal securities	4,282	3,543
Percent treasury, agency, and municipal securities due in one year	22.3%	19.4%
Total securities of Citicorp (including trading account)	5,127	4,637
Estimated cash funds from securities due within one year, 22.3% and 19.4% of total securities	1,143	900
Total deposits	44,681	49,136
Ratio of estimated cash funds from securities due within one year to total deposits	2.6%	1.8%

[a] Based on same percent as year-end 1976.
Source: 1976 Annual Report.

of Charter's interest earning assets were in securities. This ratio has remained in a range from 49.5 percent to 59.2 percent during the 1971–1976 period. The international loan-deposit ratio for Charter New York Corporation was much lower than the total ratio. This ratio was 35.8 percent in 1976 and has tended to rise in recent years, indicating considerable liquidity, from the point of view of saleability of assets for this bank's international interest earning assets. The domestic loan-deposit ratio was 71.7 percent in 1976, rising during the 1971–1976 period.

Again, Citicorp showed a loan-deposit ratio that reflected a different liquidity policy (Table 9). The total loan-deposit ratio for Citicorp was 81.8 percent in 1976 and showed an upward trend in recent years. The overseas loan-deposit ratio was 79.9 percent in 1976, also higher than it was during earlier years. The domestic ratio was 84.8 percent in 1976.

Volatile Domestic Liabilities Ratio

The ability of a bank to attract new funds represents a third approach to liquidity. Nevertheless, it is difficult to measure the ability of a bank to attract these funds. In fact, it is probably impossible to measure the full potential ability of a bank to draw in such resources, since the measure lies in the minds of the persons who make lending decisions; and there is no public indicator of these evaluations.

Table 8   Charter New York Corporation
Loan—Deposit Ratio
($ Millions, Average Balances)

	1971	1972	1973	1974	1975	1976
Domestic						
Loans[a]	2550	2924	3717	4280	4163	4049
Deposits	4545	4479	5477	6243	6249	5651
Loan-deposit ratio	56.1%	65.3%	67.9%	68.6%	66.6%	71.7%
Foreign						
Loans[a]	195	235	396	630	838	990
Deposits	919	1074	1794	2433	2536	2763
Loan-deposit ratio	21.2%	21.9%	22.1%	25.9%	33.0%	35.8%
Total						
Loans[b]	2703	3118	4068	4857	4940	4978
Deposits	5464	5553	7271	8676	8785	8414
Loan-deposit ratio	49.5%	56.2%	55.9%	56.0%	56.2%	59.2%

[a] Domestic and foreign loans are shown before adjustment for reserve for possible loan losses.
[b] Adjusted for reserve for possible loan losses.
Source: 1975, 1976 Annual Report.

Table 9   Citicorp
Loan—Deposit Ratio ($ Millions, Average Balances)

	1971	1972	1973	1974	1975	1976
Domestic						
Loans	9,810	10,873	13,428	16,546	16,940	14,974
Deposits	12,363	13,041	15,232	18,578	19,363	17,664
Loan-deposit ratio	79.4%	83.4%	88.2%	89.1%	87.5%	84.8%
Overseas						
Loans	6,483	8,198	10,237	14,006	18,728	21,966
Deposits	9,632	11,477	14,729	20,277	24,930	27,500
Loan-deposit ratio	67.3%	71.4%	69.5%	69.1%	75.1%	79.9%
Total						
Loans	16,293	19,071	23,665	30,552	35,668	36,940
Deposits	21,995	24,518	29,961	38,855	44,293	45,164
Loan-deposit ratio	74.1%	77.8%	79.0%	78.6%	80.5%	81.8%

Source: 1975, 1976 Annual Report.

The management of a bank that proposes the new funds approach to liquidity believes that it can evaluate its ability to seek additional funds. This management should be in hourly communication with many of its sources of funds, and through this close rapport, it believes that it knows when the limits to its new funds capacity are distant, near, or perhaps even have been exceeded. The outside bank analyst, of course, is not aware of this information. Moreover, even if the information should be made available to a director, or even to an outside analyst, there is no way that these bank analysts can be certain whether the information reflects the opinion of the bank's suppliers of funds or the hopes of management. Thus for all practical purposes, there is probably no way for bank analysts to measure the capacity of a bank to obtain new funds.

Nevertheless, it is possible to gain an indication of the extent that a bank has used purchased funds in the past. While this measure does not fit the needs of an indicator of new funds capacity, it does indicate whether a bank has established a basic competence in obtaining funds from money markets. Purchased funds are regarded as being important to the ability to attract new funds because they are a link between a bank and major money markets. It is the major money markets—which include insurance companies, pension fund managers, other banks on a worldwide basis, governments, and individuals—that respond to a bank's bid for funds. The responsiveness of these sources of funds is all an outside bank analyst can measure. Since these funds are usually provided strictly on a financial basis, they can appear and disappear quickly, reflecting the current opinions of the sources of funds concerning a bank. The funds are not usually closely tied with long-term business and social relationships.

Table 10 shows the volatile domestic liabilities ratio of Charter New York Corporation in 1975 and 1976. The three important sources of purchased funds included in the table are commercial paper, domestic certificates of deposit (CDs), and net borrowed federal funds. This measure refers to a domestic capability of obtaining purchased funds, because there is no source of information for international certificates of deposit. Despite this limitation, the measure can serve as an indication of the possible broader liquidity policies of a bank overseas.

Total commercial paper averaged $4 million for Charter New York Corporation (parent) in 1975, and domestic certificates of deposit amounted to $377 million of the Irving Trust Company, the principal bank, at year-end 1976. Each of these borrowing sources is a different legal entity, and unfortunately most banks do not show details of their borrowings on a consolidated basis. In adding these two sources of funds together, it is assumed that the commercial paper of the parent holding company has not been used to purchase a large amount of certificates of deposit of the principal bank. (If this transfer should have occurred, there would be a double counting of funds.) Finally, federal funds sold and purchased and other borrowed funds are added, giving total domestic purchased funds of $1251 million in 1976. The total domestic bank liabilities averaged $5669 million, and the ratio of volatile domestic liabilities to total domestic liabilities was 22 percent. This figure was up from 17 percent one year earlier. This percent represented the extent to which Charter was

**Table 10   Charter New York Corporation
Volatile Domestic Liabilities
($ Millions, Averages)**

	1975	1976	Source
Commercial paper	15	4	Annual Report
Domestic CDs	498[a]	377[b]	Schedule B, Large Bank Supplement to Call Report—Irving Only
Federal funds sold	(133)	(102)	Annual Report
Federal funds purchased	706	927	Annual Report
Other borrowed funds	62	45	
Net borrowed funds	635	870	
Total	1,148	1,251	
Total domestic bank liabilities 12/31/74	7,179		Call Report
Total domestic bank liabilities 12/31/75	5,734	5,734	Call Report
Total domestic bank liabilities 12/31/76		5,604	Call Report
Total domestic bank liabilities average	6,457	5,669	
Ratio of volatile domestic liabilities to total domestic bank liabilities	17%	22%	

[a] 6/30/76.
[b] 12/31/76.

relying on sources of funds that could be withdrawn quickly if money markets grew tight or an important change occurred in the way money market managers evaluated the bank. The ratio also served as an indicator of the limited use of this market as a source of funds for Charter. This measure gives indications of a liquidity policy for Charter similar to the other measures noted earlier.

The comparable ratio for Citicorp in 1976 was 40 percent, which was considerably higher than that for Charter (Table 11). The higher ratio for Citicorp and the large volume of $9393 million in purchased funds indicated that this bank actively participated in markets for purchased funds. It also indicated that this bank tended to rely on this approach to liquidity, rather than the more traditional approaches of self-liquidating assets and saleability of assets. Thus all measures of liquidity for Citicorp gave similar indications of the liquidity policy of the bank.

Measuring Other Approaches to Liquidity

The two remaining approaches to liquidity, the borrower's anticipated income approach and the Federal Reserve as lender of last resort, either cannot be measured using historical information or cannot be measured without considerable difficulty, if at all.

The borrower's anticipated income approach requires a forecast of interest income of a bank's loan customers and other government securities. The problem with this approach is that it is not appropriate to develop a liquidity policy from a forecast. Forecasts provide an evaluation of how a bank could

Table 11   Citicorp
Volatile Domestic Liabilities
($ Millions, Averages)

	1975	1976	Source
Commercial paper	1,276	1,213	Annual Report
Domestic CDs	7,049	4,969	Schedule B, Large Bank Supplement to Call Report
Federal funds sold	(228)	(377)	Annual Report
Federal funds borrowed	2,139	2,614	Annual Report
Other borrowed funds	1,267	1,491	
Net borrowed funds	3,178	3,728	
Total	11,503	9,393	
Total domestic bank liabilities 12/31/74	26,365		Call Report
Total domestic bank liabilities 12/31/75	23,786	23,786	Call Report
Total domestic bank liabilities 12/31/76		24,014	Call Report
Total domestic bank liabilities average	23,075	23,900	
Ratio of domestic volatile liabilities to total domestic bank liabilities	46%	40%	

fare under future business and credit conditions. They require an understanding of the policies of a bank before they are made. This approach puts the cart before the horse.

The availability of the Federal Reserve discount window involves an evaluation of the past decisions of the Federal Reserve System and some knowledge of the record of a bank's rapport with the Federal Reserve System, as well as some forecast of future policies of the System. Unfortunately for bank analysts, it is virtually impossible to obtain specific information on the subject, since the relation between the Federal Reserve System and a member bank is usually regarded by both parties as a private matter.

Nevertheless on occasion, there are bits of information concerning aspects of the relationship between the Federal Reserve System and a member bank that can be used to shed some light on the general relationship between the parties. These shreds of information, which are sometimes released to the press, are infrequent. This is, at best, tenuous information on which to base a hard conclusion covering a broad subject. It is true that under normal circumstances, the Federal Reserve System's discount window is open to member banks, and normal circumstances account for virtually 99 out of 100 instances. Yet the severe loss that shareholders and some lenders could sustain if liquidity difficulties were to arise and the discount window were not open gives importance to even a remote possibility of the event. An open Federal Reserve discount window is not a certainty, and there is no certain way that a bank analyst can know whether it might be open to a bank in the future.

CHAPTER 6
CREDIT RISK POLICY

The hallmark of a market economy is uncertainty. There is always a possibility that plans will not be fulfilled and that events will bring surprises. If future events prove to be better than expected, lenders, such as banks, are paid promptly. However, there are often unexpected difficulties. Credit risk is the possibility that difficulties could develop that would either delay or prevent the payment of interest or bring about losses.

IMPORTANCE OF RISK TAKING

The taking of credit risks is a principal function of banks. How a bank approaches credit risks represents one of its most important policies. The willingness of banks to take credit risks has provided a major service to market economies throughout banking history. For example, in the fourteenth-century city-states of Italy, the development of banking and money lending provided an impetus to the commercial energies of a people who had spent literally a millennium in the dark ages. The benefits were an expansion of trade, wealth, and art that was truly impressive. The balance sheets and letters of merchants and bankers indicate that the aspirations of bankers of this period were little different from today. Banking was then, and still is, an engine of business expansion.

The nemesis of this expansion in banking was a loss from a loan. The correspondence of merchants of this period or any period shows their considerable concern over losses. Losses occurred often in ways that surprised both merchants and bankers. Wars erupted and devastated caravans, storms sank ships, and revolutions in government changed the basis of obligations to repay debts. Even the supremely successful sixteenth-century German banker Jacob Fugger was brought to his knees when the King of England repudiated England's debt to him. Little has changed in credit risk, except the names.

The heart of the banking business is assessing credit risks—not necessarily taking risks, but assessing them. The distinction is important, because the ability to assess risks is a skill, and whether credit risks are taken or not taken is a management decision. The other functions of a bank rest on the public's confidence that this work is done properly. If a bank does not assess risks accurately or acts unwisely on its assessment of risks, virtually every other aspect of the bank's operations will likely show difficulties. Under these circumstances, deposits will become more difficult to obtain, borrowers who have a choice will seek alternative sources of funds, and investors will be reluctant to buy the bank's equities or debt. The effect is as if the keystone of an arch were pulled askew, and the whole structure were under stress.

The assessment of risk involves the most time-honored traditions of banking, as well as new adaptations. It is a difficult problem, and despite considerable effort and research, it is not entirely clear that today there are better answers than there were a century ago. Bankers have more information today, but it is not certain that they make better credit decisions.

Recently, there have been four principal types of assets of a bank that have experienced difficulties that can be traced to credit risk decisions—loans, securities, foreign exchange transactions and minority investments. Actually, virtually all assets involve some degree of credit risk, although the four mentioned here include the bulk of the assets of a bank.

The credit risk of loans had been considered to be a minor issue for virtually a quarter century from the end of the Second World War to 1970. Loan losses had been negligible throughout the period. However, from 1970 to 1976, loan losses for many banks rose from that earlier period. Dollar totals of loan losses exceeded hundreds of millions of dollars for some major banks and even though banking assets expanded rapidly in recent years, these reports of losses created an awareness of credit risks for everyone who reads newspapers.

A similar pattern was shown by credit risks of the securities portfolios of banks. Throughout the past quarter century, the securities portfolio of most banks had been regarded as being close to cash, and was largely beyond question. The occasional difficulties that occurred were regarded as special or unusual cases. Nevertheless, the financial difficulties of New York City in 1974 and 1975 dimmed that earlier confidence. The value of New York City securities declined, and the creditworthiness of other municipalities facing financing difficulties became an issue.

Foreign exchange trading had long been considered as a routine service of banks. During the decades of the 1950s and 1960s foreign remittances were closely controlled by most foreign governments. There were agreements to honor fixed rates of exchange, and the daily intervention of central banks usually kept exchange rates steady. However, in the early 1970s the rapid growth of Eurodollar and Eurocurrency pools, the shift to floating exchange rates, and the loosening of exchange controls of many major industrial countries changed the foreign exchange environment. The change occurred rapidly.

Banks committed large proportions of their assets to these transactions. When these commitments were not matched and the risks of commitments to buy and sell currencies were not in balance, the door was open for banks to reap handsome profits or face large losses. The Herstatt Bank pursued such a program. The failure of the Herstatt Bank in 1974 to pay obligations sent a shock wave throughout the international banking community. Another new issue of credit risk had emerged.

Throughout the decade of the 1950s and the early part of the 1960s, most banks expanded their overseas operations at a slow pace and preferred the more conservative approach of expanding no faster than could be achieved by opening a branch or taking other steps that assured the bank full control over the overseas operation. As a part of the effort of U.S. banks to expand internationally, many banks sought representation abroad through equity positions in foreign banks, finance companies, as well as other financially related companies, such as mortgage banking and real estate developments.

Although minority interests represent equity interests rather than debt, they are noted here because the decision to make them is similar to credit risk decisions. The recent difficulties of these minority interests have not been given as widespread publicity as other credit difficulties. Yet there have been major losses from these equity investments; and in certain cases, the losses have even exceeded the amount of the original investment. These losses have resulted from the effort of banks to protect customers as well as their own reputations, when the other parties of the minority interest have abandoned their position.

HOW CREDIT RISK IS MANAGED

Banks manage their credit risks according to two general policies—one to minimize risk and the other to price risk. Both approaches require an ability to assess credit risks. The difference between the two policies is the way assessments of risk are used by banks.

Minimal Risk Approach

The minimal risk approach to credit risk management attempts to separate loans, securities, and other assets into two groups. The first group includes credits in which there is no reasonable doubt that the asset will be redeemed at face value, or in the case of equity investments, no reasonable doubt that the investments will provide a significant return over a period of years. The other group includes all assessments of credit risks where it appears that a credit might not be redeemed or an equity investment might not provide a good return.

The minimal risk approach has been the traditional policy of banks during the past 40 years. This approach reflects the deep concern of many bankers who spent their formative years during the depression of the early 1930s. At this time, loan losses were cascading on all banks, and many firms and customers who were insolvent were kept in operation by their bankers' benign oversight. The experience was traumatic. It touched the lives of bankers who lost their jobs, as well as bankers who kept their jobs (at reduced salaries). Many young bankers of the time told themselves that they would do whatever was needed to prevent the experience from happening again.

One preventive measure was to look carefully at the quality of new loan applications. Little could be done about past loans. Many of them were either on a workout basis or unsalvageable. But new loans and some renewed loans were the type of business over which a banker had some discretion. Bankers did not feel confident about drawing fine lines of various degrees of risk and creditworthiness. Loans which were not likely to be repaid, beyond reasonable doubt, simply were not made. The same attitude pertained to securities, especially municipal securities.

The minimal risk approach relies on the classic three "Cs" of credit—character, capacity, and capital. It is significant that these three tests of a credit risk usually begin with "character." Perhaps the story is apocryphal, but J. P. Morgan is reported to have said that he would not lend a penny to a man who did not have character, even if he had full collateral. The story illustrates the importance that bankers place on this component of risk evaluation.

Good character is not a subjective evaluation from a banker's point of view. It is the record of whether a person or the management of a corporation or a government have regularly paid their commitments without difficulty. There may be mitigating circumstances, but these almost always have to be because of extraordinary conditions beyond the borrower's control, such as an earthquake, flood, or untimely death. Even then, character is shown if an effort is made to fulfill the terms of the original agreement.

Another apocryphal story is that the U.S. ambassador to France during the First World War had borrowed funds in his youth from a midwest bank for an investment that unexpectedly turned into a failure. The bank directors voted to write-off the loan as a loss. The future ambassador, who was then a young man of ordinary income was relieved and told his wife of the news, but she insisted on repaying the principal of the loan in full and living on reduced personal income. One of the directors of the bank was looking for a man of "character," found his man that day, and subsequently backed him on a successful political career. This is a romantic story of another era. But most bankers still think in these terms. Obviously, anyone who tries to hide behind legal technicalities or use clever stratagems to turn the terms of a bank loan to his favor is not regarded as possessing good character.

The second test of creditworthiness is the capacity to repay a loan or other debt or the capacity of an equity investment to show a good future return. The capacity to show a return of funds to the lending or investing bank is largely based on the record of business success, as measured by income or profits. The financial record includes the standard balance sheet and income statements. This information gives a historical perspective to the question of whether a borrower or an investment is based on sound business practice and will be able to repay the borrowing or will show a reasonable return. It looks at the business aspects of credit risk, cash flow projections, and seeks such information as whether there is a sufficient market for a product, whether the operations of the borrower are efficiently run, or whether a municipality has a stable tax base.

The ability to repay a debt involves an irony of banking. It is frequently said that if a borrower needs a loan he can't get one, but if he doesn't need one, it is available to him. The adage illustrates the importance of a borrower's sound position prior to a loan. Nevertheless, sometimes a borrower's financial position deteriorates after a loan has been made, and banks face workout situations. These cases may require considerable advisory services of a bank, reduction or postponement in interest income, or a write-off of the loan if the borrower becomes bankrupt.

The third test of creditworthiness is capital, which refers to shareholders' equity of a business concern, and sometimes long-term debt. Capital does not apply to government credits, although the unencumbered tax revenue can be used in the same context. Capital represents funds that are kept on a long-term basis in an organization, and in the truest meaning of the term, capital represents funds placed at risk for the benefit of an organization. These funds support an organization, and if it fails, the holders of equity capital are last to be compensated, if at all. Banks are interested in lending to organizations that have a large proportion of their funds in capital. The capital represents an ongoing commitment to the future of the organization that will not quickly erode, even in the event of adversity. This commitment is important to banks.

There is an additional factor that should be given special attention. The servicing of a loan or an investment is important in making the minimal risk approach work successfully. The presence of a banker who is concerned about the success of a borrower's organization adds an element of financial discipline that otherwise might be lacking. The effect of bankers on an organization can be similar to that of a board member. In many cases the effect of a banker may be even more pronounced than a board member, because many board members have no significant investments in the organizations that they oversee, but bankers often have large sums loaned or invested in organizations.

The minimal risk approach to credit risk requires that bankers act as a helpful friend, a consultant, and an advisor who uses firm persuasion when necessary. This informal relationship adds a subtle, but strong, pressure to the management of any organization to keep its affairs in good shape. Moreover, if a banker approaches credit risk from the minimal risk approach, his effort is directed to prevent any losses from occurring. There is no place in his thinking for losses, and he makes extraordinary efforts to fulfill this outlook. To a banker with this credit risk approach and with dedication to his customers, there is often a feeling of personal failure if a loss occurs. This psychological incentive to prevent losses provides an important part of the attitude of bankers with a strategy that strives to minimize risk.

The effect of the minimal risk approach is that it tends to keep activities restricted to areas that are already well known to a bank. New areas of banking involve greater uncertainties than areas that are part of daily banking activity. A step outside this circle of knowledge and friends reduces the value of years of banking acquaintances in other established areas of business or government. Although the minimal risk approach has this important limitation built into its philosophy, many banks have been very successful for many years following this policy of credit risk.

Price for Risk Approach

Risk pricing recently has developed as an alternative approach to credit risk. Risk pricing attempts to make the graduations of risk a part of the cost of a loan. The interest rate charged for a loan where there was little risk would be lower than an interest rate for a loan of greater risk. In recent years, this approach also has relied on the basic methods of credit analysis noted with the minimal risk approach, but carries the conclusions much farther.

The risk pricing approach looks at all degrees of risk as a normal part of the banking business. In effect, it views the assets of the bank—loans, securities, and investments—in various shades of white and gray and accepts all of them as legitimate, worthwhile assets. Assets of greater credit risk involve greater risk of loss, but these assets are expected to be priced to earn enough more interest income to offset their credit risk, with a profit for the bank. Assets of little credit risk involve low risks of loss. These assets are expected to earn lower interest rates and also earn a profit for a bank. If risk pricing is done properly, assets of all types of credit risk should show approximately the same profit to a bank.

The risk pricing approach reflects two trends in banking during the past decade. First, there has been a growing assurance among many banks that they possess the technical capabilities of assessing risk to a greater extent than did an earlier generation of bankers. New techniques have been applied to banking that did not exist a generation ago. Computers have enabled banks to handle much greater quantities of information. Operations research and systems research have opened new ways of analyzing information. A new generation of thinking has risen which believes that it can make more accurate conclusions based on factual experience than on the rule-of-thumb guides and the personal judgments of credit officers, loan officers, and securities traders. Many bankers have been emboldened by these greater technical resources in much the same way and at about the same time that many economists developed their confidence in being able to "fine tune" the economy and many psychologists developed their confidence about "motivating" people. All of these approaches to knowledge rest on a supreme confidence that there are highly refined ways of conducting operations that will bring superior results.

The second trend that underlies the growth of risk pricing is the recent emphasis for banks to show strong earnings gains. Risk pricing opens the door to a major expansion in the banking business. A large proportion of business that would be turned down on the basis of the minimal risk approach becomes choice bankable business. The added volume of business could expand earnings almost immediately. There would be no immediate requirement to increase loan loss reserves to offset the higher risk assets. Thus earnings of a bank could be raised for a long period, perhaps many years, before the problems and costs associated with the higher risk assets might come due.

To work successfully over a long period, the risk pricing approach requires three conditions. The first requirement is a need for a large number of assets in the bank's asset portfolio. The basis of risk pricing is that a banker does not know which loan, security, or investment will require emergency efforts, reduced terms, or fail, but he should have a good idea of the likelihood that these difficulties could occur in a large portfolio. For example, a bank might hold five thousand commercial loans in its portfolio in a medium-risk category. The bank would expect, perhaps, that one and a half percent of the loans in this category would be in some type of difficulty. However, if there were only three dozen loans in the portfolio, there would be some additional risk beyond the one and a half percent probability of difficulty. If one of these loans were in difficulty, the risk category would be at three percent (one bad loan in thirty-six loans). A thin loan portfolio makes risk pricing difficult to administer, although this is not an insurmountable difficulty if there are several similar risk categories.

The second requirement is that the bank needs a staff with considerable analytical skills. The process of assessing various degrees of risk is not a task that a one- or two-man credit department can easily handle. The development of a risk pricing format for a bank involves a major statistical operation. Moreover, the risk pricing format of one bank would not necessarily be appropriate for another bank. A risk pricing format provides specific guidelines showing the way a particular bank will price a loan, security, or investment and reflects the franchise of a particular bank, its personnel, and its ongoing business relationships with customers.

The third requirement is that a bank needs to possess an outstanding forecasting capability. Risk pricing is concerned about the future and must make much more complete and accurate assumptions concerning the future conditions of credit markets, business activity, attitudes of debtors, and even the likelihood of war or peace. For example, if a bank were to hold major assets in a country that could be ravaged by a local, but devastating war, the risk pricing of loans, securities, and investments would require a substantial risk premium. In another instance, an outlook of easy money market conditions, full employment, and high levels of business profits would involve a lower risk premium than an outlook that would be similar to that of financial conditions in 1970 or 1975.

There are many methods of forecasting, some of which are discussed in a later chapter. Although some banks have shown a better record than others, no one appears to have developed a simple, reliable method. Yet a mistake on the ability of an insurgent group to wage a war or the timing and depth of a recession could turn out to be a matter of serious concern to a bank that fully used risk pricing.

As a practical matter, there is considerable doubt whether many banks use risk pricing in a thoroughgoing manner. Most banks that have developed risk pricing techniques probably still temper the conclusions with other standards, including that anathema of statisticians, the judgment and intuition of senior management.

Diversity of Risk

Credit risk management often diversifies a portfolio of loans, securities, and investments as a simple yet effective way of keeping problems of credit risk under control. However, the approach is sometimes mistakenly used to justify taking greater individual credit risks or slimmer risk price premiums than otherwise would be justified, which is a mistake.

In fact, diversity can only partially control risk, and it is not an approach to credit risk that can stand independently of other approaches. For example, if the credit department of a bank is cowered by other departments, or is not well managed, and low-quality assets are acquired with no appreciable risk premium, a program to diversify these assets would not eliminate their risk. It would mean that the bank would hold a wide variety of low quality assets. Diversity permits the more fundamental approaches to credit risk—minimal risk and risk pricing—to be fulfilled in truer colors. It reduces the likelihood that a random or accidental occurrence will have an appreciable effect on one of these fundamental policies.

A major practical problem in diversifying credit risk is determining what constitutes diversity. There are literally thousands of ways of classifying assets, and a case could be made that many of the categories represent diversity on logical grounds. Yet to be effective, risk diversity requires relevant categories, and the determination of relevant categories is not an easy matter.

Risk categories that are relevant to one bank are not relevant to another. For example, real estate loans include loans for single dwelling homes, loans for small and medium-sized owner-operated apartments, loans for large apartment houses, loans for the development of commercial properties, as well as many other classifications. One bank may make most of its real estate loans to owners of single dwelling homes, and another bank may make most of its real estate loans to the developers of real estate properties. The category of real estate loans means two entirely different types of loans as it is applied to the two banks. From the position of a bank analyst, it is sometimes not entirely clear what diversity of assets means, since detail is often not available.

IMPLICATIONS OF CREDIT RISK APPROACHES

Implications for Earnings

The minimal risk approach to credit risk can have the effect of keeping banking activities confined to the areas where a bank has developed competence, and it can tend to restrict major expansions in earnings. Of course, a bank could expand new areas of its business to a limited extent and still maintain a minimal risk approach to credits. For example, Morgan Guaranty Trust has practiced a minimal risk strategy in regard to its specialty lending area to major corporate customers. Nevertheless, the bank has gradually expanded its banking services to individuals in recent years. The development of the individual accounts represented a relatively small expansion in Morgan Guaranty's scope of business and did not involve a basic change in approach to credit risk.

The risk pricing approach could provide a temporary impetus to earnings. If a bank shifts from a minimal credit risk approach to a risk pricing approach, there would likely be a period of a few years when additional credit risk has been added to a bank's portfolio, yet losses from the portfolio would not yet have occurred. Current earnings may benefit temporarily from the lag that usually occurs between the time when a loan, security, or investment is booked and the time that difficulties occur. Thus a bank could significantly boost its earings for many years if it increased the proportion of its portfolio from minimal risk to risk pricing throughout the period. Eventually, the boost to earnings would diminish, as the asset portfolio became largely risk priced, and losses reached a higher level. At this time, the provision for loan losses, which represents a charge on earnings, would be increased.

Implications for Liquidity

Banks that follow a minimal risk strategy may be expected to have less difficulty in managing their liquidity. Many depositors and suppliers of funds would likely continue to believe that risk pricing could increase negative surprises. The minimal risk strategy is a credit risk policy that most depositors accept without difficulty. A bank that departs from this standard may find liquidity management involves more difficulties than otherwise. The exceptions would be those few banks that have established credentials of significantly superior credit assessing capabilities.

An important watershed in credit strategy occurred in 1969. Prior to that year, the loan loss provision was considered as a subtraction from shareholders' equity. From 1969 forward, the loan loss provision has been considered as a business expense. The change was significant. It meant that the initial impact of a loss was shifted from shareholders to all borrowers. Shareholders, of course, bear the final cost of loan losses, and this responsibility remains, regardless how the initial impact is distributed.

By taking higher loan losses from earnings, banks have strong incentives to attempt to recoup the cost of higher loan loss provisions from loan pricing, exactly as risk pricing would indicate. The difficulty that many banks may face is that it is not easy to increase interest rates selectively on loans that are higher risk. These loans might be expected to be most affected by a need to increase the pricing structure of higher risk loans. A much easier alternative is to raise the entire pricing structure so that the spread between the cost of funds and net interest income expands. If this occurs, risk pricing could turn out in practice to require that good customers would cover bad ones. High-quality borrowers could be penalized and could find their banking interests better served with banks using the minimal risk strategy.

Implications for Shareholders

Shareholders may be attracted to either approach of credit risk. Shareholders with a long-term outlook would look for banks that could regularly provide earnings to support dividends. These shareholders would look for banks that are not likely to show surprises from loan losses.

Shareholders with a short-term outlook would find that a bank that uses a risk pricing policy might suit their needs. These shareholders look for securities with the prospect of major earnings gains within one or a few years and would seek banks that recently announced plans to adopt the risk pricing strategy. Such a change in credit risk management could raise possibilities of a gain in earnings that might be unexpected by many investors.

Not all shareholders might hold the view the risk pricing is entirely manageable by most banks. Some of these skeptics might wish to take a short position in shares of banks that had embraced the risk pricing strategy when there might be indications that a recession was beginning. At that time, loan losses might be expected to rise particularly sharply for banks that had adopted a risk pricing policy. Even investors who were acquainted with the full implications of risk pricing—and the possibility that higher earnings could cover all likely loan losses, securities losses, and equity investment—might be disturbed by the higher losses. These investors might not be prepared to support the stock of such a bank under stress.

Implications for Depositors

Depositors would be most concerned that any credit risk strategy would maintain the confidence of all suppliers of funds to the bank. A credit risk approach that raised doubts and uncertainties would represent an element of risk to these suppliers of funds. Many depositors would want to hold funds only in those banks which held assets with quality standards that were considered beyond question. Other depositors might consider holding funds in banks that had adopted risk pricing policies that had come under question, if there were a significant interest rate premium.

MEASURING CREDIT RISKS

The task of measuring credit risk policies involves several tests. These tests are often informative even if a bank should present its credit risk strategies in an annual report or other special reports. A bank analyst can never be certain that these comments are entirely accurate. A bank might present one credit risk policy in a report and actually practice another approach. The effort is not necessarily intended to mislead the public. Some banks might like to employ one policy, especially risk pricing, but are unable to do so because the personnel who are needed for its successful practice may not yet be experienced in the policy.

Minimal Risk Policy

The Ratio of Loan Losses to Average Loans. The ratio of net loan losses to average loans serves as the most basic measure of a bank's credit risk policy. Net loan losses are loan losses adjusted for recoveries from loans that had been previously charged off. A ratio of net loan losses to average loans shows an indication of the quality of a bank's loan portfolio. Since loans account for about two-thirds of a typical bank's assets, a measure of the quality of loans can represent a proxy for broad credit policies and the bank's credit strategy.

A ratio which is low (approximately 1/4 to 1/3 of one percent or less) or declining over a period of years would indicate a minimal risk strategy. A high or rising ratio could indicate a low-quality loan portfolio, or it could reflect a risk pricing policy.

Table 12 shows the ratio of loan losses to loans outstanding at year-end of Rainier Bancorporation declined on an overall basis from 1972 to 1976. The ratio was 0.38 percent in 1972 and declined to 0.03 percent in 1974. It rose to 0.20 percent in 1976, which was a year that followed a major recession. Nevertheless, the ratio was approximately one-half the level of 1972. The downward direction of the ratio for this bank could suggest that new and more stringent credit risk policies may have been adopted during the period. However, the bank ascribes the improvement to an improving local economy and, more importantly, large recoveries of loans previously charged off earlier in the decade.

Risk Adjusted Margin.   The risk adjusted margin represents a measure of whether a bank has successfully practiced a risk adjusted policy. Its calculation begins with a bank's net interest margin and subtracts the ratio of net loan losses to assets. The remainder is risk adjusted margin, which represents the net interest margin on loans and securities after losses have been taken into account. If the bank holds securities that involve major discounts because of questions about whether they might be redeemed, an adjustment would also be made for these securities.

If a bank successfully practices credit risk pricing, risk adjusted margin should remain fairly steady, since an increase in the net loan loss ratio would be accompanied or soon followed by an increase in net interest margin. This development would indicate that the bank was booking higher risk loans and was sustaining higher loan losses. Similarly, a drop in the loan loss ratio would be accompanied or soon followed by a decline in the net interest margin. Such a development would indicate that the bank was accepting lower risk loans and was reporting lower loan losses.

Table 13 shows that the ratio of net interest margin (on a tax equivalent basis) to average total assets rose from 1972 to 1976 for Rainier. In the same period, the ratio of net loan losses to loans outstanding declined. The risk adjusted margin of Rainier rose, indicating that the bank apparently pursued a minimal risk strategy for loans and still increased its margin.

Nonperforming Loans.   Another approach in viewing credit risk policy is through "nonperforming loans." These loans include loans where the borrower is not fulfilling the terms of the original agreement. They include

Table 12   Rainier Bancorporation
Ratio of Net Loan
Losses to Average Loans (Net of Unearned Discount)

1972	0.38%
1973	0.26
1974	0.03
1975	0.10
1976	0.20

Source: 1976 Annual Report.

**Table 13   Rainier Bancorporation
Risk Adjusted Margin**

	1971	1972	1973	1974	1975	1976
Ratio of net interest margin (tax equivalent basis) to average total assets	3.08%	2.95%	3.14%	3.29%	3.90%	3.96%
Ratio of net loan losses to average total assets	0.12	0.20	0.14	0.01	0.06	0.12
Risk adjusted margin	2.96	2.75	3.00	3.28	3.84	3.84

Source: 1975, 1976 Annual Report.

nonaccrual loans, renegotiated loans, and the category of other real estate. Rainier showed that at year-end 1976, 0.88 percent of its loans were on a nonperforming basis. Compared with 20 major banks that showed an average of 5.1 percent of nonperforming loans to total loans at that year-end, the figure for Rainier appears small and tends to confirm the conclusion noted in regard to the conservative loan loss ratio.

Securities Valuation.   Securities are the second major part of the assets of a bank. As has been discussed, securities represent a major part of the liquidity of a bank. Thus securities represent a type of asset that is in the common ground of the liquidity strategy and the credit risk strategy of a bank. This common ground represents a vulnerable position for a bank. If there were to be serious question concerning the liquidity or value of these securities, the implications would affect the public's perception of the bank's liquidity strategy. This linkage between credit risk and liquidity is a major reason for the requirement that banks show their investment securities at a book value or carrying value basis. In contrast, an estimate of the market value of securities could show major fluctuations in the value of those securities. The Securities and Exchange Commission requires banks to show their securities at market value in 10-K reports.

Table 14 shows the comparison between market and book value of Rainier. The book value or carrying value of bank securities represents the cost of these securities less the amortized premium (where the securities were purchased at a price above par value) or the addition of accreted discount (where the securities were purchased at a discount from par value). These adjustments attempt to show the value of these securities assuming that they were held to maturity or call date. The figures for book value or carrying value are the same as are shown in the consolidated balance sheet.

The table shows that there was a shift toward higher market value comparisons for Rainier Bancorporation from 1974 to 1976. The shortfall between market and book value for state and local governments amounted to 6.8 percent in 1974, the shortfall was reduced to 2.9 percent in 1975, and there was a 2.0 percent gain in 1976. The shift for all U.S. government securities was from a deficit of 0.6 percent in 1974 to a surplus of 1.6 percent in 1976. These changes reflected improved market conditions.

Table 14   Rainier Bancorporation
Investment Securities

	Book Value	Market Value	Market Value Over (Under) Book Value
December 31, 1974 (Thousands)			
U.S. Government securities	$109,561	$108,917	−0.6%
State and local governments	204,685	190,829	−6.8
Other securities	3,899	5,088	+30.5
December 31, 1975 (Thousands)			
U.S. Government securities	$134,628	$135,114	+0.4%
State and local governments	216,767	210,386	−2.9
Other securities	4,922	6,296	+27.9
December 31, 1976 (Thousands)			
U.S. Government securities	$170,969	$173,653	+1.6%
State and local governments	245,252	250,067	+2.0
Other securities	6,336	8,485	+33.9

Source: 1976 10-K Report.

In addition, the group of securities titled "Other Securities" includes other stocks and was small in size compared with the portfolio of governments. Nevertheless, the market value of other securities was 30.5 percent above book value in 1974 and 33.9 percent over book value in 1976.

Risk Pricing Policy

Ratio of Loan Losses to Average Loans.   Table 15 shows the ratio of net loan losses to average net loans for Citizens and Southern National Bank of

Table 15   The Citizens and Southern National Bank (Georgia)
Ratio of Net Loan Losses
to Average Net Loans

	1972	1973	1974	1975	1976
Net loan losses (thousands)	$6,924	$15,915	$35,176	$29,616	$33,024
Average net loans (thousands)	$1,519,932	$1,964,621	$2,135,163	$1,931,000	$1,956,000
Ratio of net loan losses to average net loans	0.46%	0.81%	1.65%	1.53%	1.69%

Source: 1976 Annual Report.

Table 16
Loan losses

Loan losses in 1972 amounted to $6,717,948. We anticipated losses and had provided for them with a comfortable reserve. We call it our research and development fund. But, losses are still too high even though they improved in 1972 over 1971 as a percentage of our average outstanding loans. This percentage is important because our loans are growing very rapidly. Here is the breakdown of our losses by department and what we anticipate for 1973.

	Net Loan Losses		
	1971	**1972**	**1973 (projected)**
The C&S National Bank, Atlanta			
Branches.	$1,614,149	$1,310,744	$1,321,000
Corporate Accounts Department.	316,256	324,208	250,000
Term Loan Department.	214,628	9,296	225,000
The C&S Community Development Corporation.	46,724	703,038	184,000
Charge Account Service.	818,617	1,587,644	770,000
Sales Finance Department.	125,874	575,558	25,000
The C&S DeKalb Bank (Avondale Estates).	14,686	41,212	80,000
The C&S Bank, East Point.	57,345	51,568	20,000
The C&S Emory Bank.	29,909	17,885	30,000
Total, Atlanta banks/departments	**3,238,188**	**4,621,153**	**2,905,000**
The C&S National Bank, Athens.	23,526	41,070	108,000
The C&S National Bank, Augusta.	196,566	264,144	210,000
The C&S National Bank, Macon.	453,670	(1,072,849)	275,000
The C&S National Bank, Savannah.	615,535	538,671	374,000
The C&S National Bank, Valdosta.	106,469	102,327	120,000
The C&S Bank of Albany.	207,154	90,538	105,000
C&S Bank of Dublin	23,278	20,788	25,000
The C&S Newnan Bank.	3,960	4,793	9,000
C&S Bank of Thomaston	15,893	40,245	48,000
The C&S Bank of West Georgia.	12,898	9,905	21,000
Total, other banks	**1,658,949**	**39,632**	**1,295,000**
C&S Holding Company Group			
Factoring Department.	561,773	1,364,541	1,750,000
Real Estate Department.	(27,219)	388,900	1,700,000
The C&S Financial Corporation.	332,486	365,876	294,000
C&S Optimation Services, Inc.	186,769	(197,430)	—
The C&S Credit Service Corporation.	310,459	—	—
Total, Holding Company Group.	**1,364,268**	**1,921,887**	**3,744,000**
International Group			
International Department.	473,910	70,149	100,000
C&S International Bank, Miami.	244,074	65,127	60,000
C&S International Bank of New Orleans.	—	—	25,000
Total, International Group.	**717,984**	**135,276**	**185,000**
Total, The C&S National Bank and Subsidiaries.	**$6,979,389**	**$6,717,948**	**$8,129,000**
Net loan losses as a percentage of average outstanding loans.	.57%	.46%	.47%

Georgia. This ratio increased sharply from 0.46 percent in 1972 to 1.65 percent in 1974. The ratio of net loan losses to average net loans for 1975 declined slightly to 1.53 percent, but rose to 1.69 percent in 1976. The table indicates that apparently there was a major change in this bank's credit risk policy from 1972 to 1976. It is also possible that this bank attempted to follow a minimum risk policy, but was unsuccessful in implementation.

Table 16 is from Citizens and Southern Bank's 1972 annual report, and shows a forecast of net loan losses of $8,129,000 for 1973. Actual net loan losses in 1973 were $15,915,000, or nearly double that forecast. The year 1973 was not a recession year and represented a continuation of an ongoing economic recovery. The loan loss difficulties reflected policies of the bank, and clearly the bank's credit risk strategy had met major difficulties. For whatever reason, it would appear that the bank had abandoned a conservative credit risk policy. This comparison would have provided an early warning of future difficulties.

Nonperforming Loans. Further perspective on the credit risk policy of Citizens and Southern is shown by the performance of nonperforming loans (including other real estate) to average total loans, which rose from 0.53 percent in 1974 to 5.94 percent in 1976. This increase was substantial and reflected the sharp gains in loan losses of the bank in the interval.

Risk Adjusted Margin. Table 17 shows the risk adjusted interest margin for The Citizens and Southern National Bank. Risk adjusted interest margin was 5.17 percent in 1972 and fell to 3.70 percent in 1976. The decline in risk adjusted margin reflected both a decline in net interest margin and a rise in loan losses. The table suggests that this bank might have attempted to embody the policy of risk pricing, but only carried through the easy part and neglected the difficult aspects of the policy. It appears that the bank made higher-risk loans, but failed to charge adequately.

The intent of the management of Citizens and Southern may never be clearly known. Several reports in the press indicate that the bank's management was unaware of the risks of its loans and did not believe that premium

Table 17   The Citizens and Southern National Bank (Georgia)
Risk Adjusted Interest
Margin

	1972	1973	1974	1975	1976
Ratio of net interest margin (tax equivalent basis) to average total assets	5.47%	4.95%	5.10%	5.31%	4.76%
Ratio of net loan losses to average total assets	0.30	0.55	1.10	0.99	1.06
Risk adjusted interest margin	5.17	4.40	4.00	4.32	3.70

Source: 1976 Annual Report.

loan pricing was needed. Yet the risk pricing strategy places a special burden of accurate forecasting on the shoulders of any bank management that undertakes it. The record suggests that the bank may have followed a forecast that proved to be grossly optimistic.

The reported loan losses of a bank represent only the tip of an iceberg of problem loans. Many bank analysts have sought additional information concerning substandard loans, doubtful loans, as well as loan losses. These categories, as well as the category of other loans especially mentioned, represent the terms of the national bank examiners for various classifications of problem loans. A few major banks have provided limited information concerning problem loans. Nevertheless, at present, most of the information is fragmentary and does not cover a long enough period to be meaningful to develop information that would shed much light on credit risk policies.

There is always a problem of determining whether an unfavorable loan loss ratio reflected a turn for the worse in a few lending markets that happened to be the principal loan markets for the bank. It is useful to test if the ratio of net loan loss to loans is unusually high in only a limited area.

Most of the major loan losses for Citizens and Southern were because of difficulties in real estate. Many banks, including Citizens and Southern, show details of loan losses by type of loan. This information is useful in testing how broadly credit policies are reflected throughout a bank. The Citizens and Southern ratio of loan losses to average loans for commercial and industrial loans was 1.29 percent in 1975, on a year-end basis (not shown in table). This ratio was high enough in comparison with the overall ratio of 1.58 percent for 1975 to suggest that the high loan losses of the bank were because of widely

Table 18   The Citizens and Southern National Bank
Investment Securities

	Carrying Amount	Market Value	Market Value Over (Under) Book Value
December 31, 1974 (Thousands)			
U.S. Government securities	$22,905	$22,881	−0.1%
State and local governments	291,314	285,346	−2.0
December 31, 1975 (Thousands)			
U.S. Government securities	$131,773	$131,874	+0.1%
State and local governments	233,296	228,300	−2.1
December 31, 1976 (Thousands)			
U.S. Government securities	$218,972	$219,267	+0.1%
State and local governments	162,348	171,848	+5.9

Source: 1975, 1976 10-K Report.

Table 19   The Citizens and Southern National Bank
and Subsidiaries

4. SECURITIES

A comparison of the carrying amount and market
value of securities follows:

	Carrying Amount	Market Value
	(In thousands)	
December 31, 1975:		
Investment securities:		
U.S. Government	$131,773	$131,874
Obligations of states and political subdivisions	233,296	228,300
Other securities:		
Marketable equity securities, principally capital stocks of banks and bank holding companies	20,579	20,579
Other	17,140	17,114
Total	$402,788	$397,867
Trading account securities	$ 3,699	$ 3,703
December 31, 1974:		
Investment securities:		
U.S. Government	$ 22,905	$ 22,881
Obligations of states and political subdivisions	291,314	285,346
Other securities:		
Marketable equity securities, principally capital stocks of banks and bank holding companies	41,538	18,279
Other	11,270	12,302
Total	$367,027	$338,808
Trading account securities	$ 4,060	$ 4,060

Source: 1975 Annual Report.

practiced credit risk policies, rather than an unfortunate difficulty in one lending market.

Securities Valuation. Table 18 shows the difference between carrying
amount and market value for the major investment securities of Citizens and
Southern for year-end 1974, 1975, and 1976. At year-end 1976, the market
value of government securities was 0.1 percent above the carrying amount
and the market value of state and local governments was 5.9 percent above
the carrying amount. This assessment of a strong securities portfolio contrasts
the credit risk policy for loans.

Only one part of the securities portfolio showed a significant flaw in recent
years. In 1974, marketable equity securities, principally capital stock of banks,

and bank holding companies, showed a carrying amount of $41,538,000, and an estimated market value of $18,279,000, representing a potential markdown of 56 percent (Table 19). In 1975 the carrying amount and the market value for this line were identical, $20,579,000. In December, 1975 the Statement of Financial Accounting Standards No. 12 was issued by the Financial Accounting Standards Board, which recommended that marketable equity securities should be carried at the lower of their aggregate cost or market value. The difference in this instance was an unrealized loss, which was charged directly to Citizens and Southern's shareholders' equity. These figures are small in comparison with the government and municipal securities.

Overall, reviewing the quality of the three parts of the investment securities portfolio of Citizens and Southern, it appears as if there was a moderately conservative approach toward risk. When reviewed in light of the problem of the risk adjusted margins on loans, it appears that Citizens and Southern's overall credit risk policies was split in the early 1970s. Part of the bank's management moved in a new direction for loans that proved to be unfortunate. However, another part of the bank's management covering securities remained unchanged, a situation that may have saved the bank.

CHAPTER 7
INTEREST RATE POLICY

Banks are deeply involved in interest rates, the price for the use of money over time. Interest rates are both a cost and a price to banks. They purchase funds at one interest rate, which represents their "cost of funds," and they lend funds at another interest rate, which represents their "price." The difference is "interest rate spread."

Banks can make many choices in their handling of interest rate positions. They can match the funds they handle so that their interest rate spread remains fairly steady or they can unbalance the fundamentals of their spread in hopes of present or future gains in earnings. The latter activity places banks in the position of anticipating—or speculating—on the future course of financial markets.

IMPORTANCE OF SPREAD

The work of being a middleman of money appears to be one of the most simple businesses that one can imagine. The principal task is straightforward, and it is easy to understand. Nevertheless, making interest rate spread a major consideration in each day's banking activity is a difficult undertaking. Competitive pressures and the basic service character of the banking business tend to erode the importance of spread in daily decisions.

Consider what making the spread in interest rates a central strategy means to a banker. At its center lies the directive to look at all business associations as potential sources of profit. However, most bankers look at their work as a service skill to enable their customers to undertake programs or carry forward their activities. Most loan officers find that their advancement, in fact, is in direct proportion to their ability to obtain additional loan volume, either from adding loans to existing customers or from obtaining new customers. Loan officers in most banks could be regarded as performing the same task as salesmen in many other organizations.

163

Most of the senior management of banks is recruited from the ranks of the loan officers. It is difficult for anyone in a bank to turn down an established customer because he has received terms with another bank that are better. Seldom will a senior management take such a hard-nosed attitude. Moreover, whenever such a position has been taken it may prove embarassing to the bank. For example, Robert Abboud, chairman of First National Bank of Chicago, is reported to have attempted to raise the effective interest rate of Inland Steel Company, and probably believed that there would be a good chance of success because he was a member of Inland's board. Inland responded by boycotting First Chicago when they negotiated the next loan, and First Chicago relented. Thus there are strong competitive pressures that make stringent interest rate strategies difficult to practice.

There appear to be ways around the impasse that faced First Chicago that will be discussed in the chapters on market position and proprietary skills strategy. Yet a banking management must first recognize the importance of an interest rate policy before it will likely turn to these strategies, since they are strenuous to deploy.

HOW SPREAD IS MANAGED

Interest rate spread is managed by choosing among a variety of securities and loans and matching the interest rates of these assets with various deposits and debentures. The two key issues, which bear strongly on the management of spread, are whether the bank prices its loans on the basis of its incremental cost of funds and how the bank matches the maturities of its interest earning assets and interest bearing liabilities. These two issues are not often discussed by most banks. But they are the basis of making decisions that directly affect interest rate policy.

Incremental Pricing

Pricing on the basis of incremental costs occurs when a bank is certain that each additional loan has a sufficient spread to cover all of the interest costs of obtaining the matching funds for the loan. The price of the loan is based on this incremental cost of funds so that spread remains steady throughout changes in market interest rates. The addition of loans and securities would be at a fairly constant percent "markup" above the cost of the funds to support those bank assets. Similarly, during periods of slack loan demand, the reduction of loans and securities would be paralleled by a proportionately lower cost of funds.

Some banks look at the average cost of funds as the basis of their pricing. The components often include interest free demand deposits, which add nothing to interest costs, passbook savings, which have usually been a fairly low cost of funds, and purchased funds, which are often obtained from money markets at rates above the other sources of funds.

If banks could add to their sources of funds in about the same proportion as the average proportion of these three sources of funds, pricing on the basis of the average cost of funds would present little or no practical difference from incremental pricing. But in practice, the three sources are not available on such a basis. The major part of additional funds in recent years has been available only from the money markets at premium rates. This means that the incremental cost of funds has been well above the average cost of funds. Thus pricing that is based on the average cost of funds would be inadequate to preserve spread.

Interest Rate Sensitivities

A second issue involving the interest rate policy of a bank is the way it matches the interest rate sensitivities of its assets and liabilities. A bank holding the overall sensitivities of its assets and liabilities in balance is in a position to respond to changes in market interest rates so that the changes in these interest rates are fully passed along to customers. The position of the bank is then neutral to changes in interest rates, and the bank neither benefits nor is penalized by interest rate changes.

For example, if the interest rates for short-term funds should increase and if a bank has tied its loans to these changes in interest rates, then the spread in net interest income that the bank receives from these loans will increase to reflect the higher pricing base. The bank is, in this illustration, basically acting as a middleman. Carrying this illustration further, when the loan is due, the funds of the bank are released from that asset of the bank, and at the same time, a comparable sum of the bank's liabilities is due. The bank can either extinguish the debt or renew the loan and money market obligation.

Of course, no bank operates in such a simple manner. A bank's assets include securities, as well as many other money market instruments and loans; and there is a wide variety of liabilities. Even small-sized banks ordinarily have many loans and liability obligations that come due each day or week. Among major banks, the financing is complex, and any one person could never count the individual transactions. Nevertheless, the principle of matched interest rate sensitivities provides a basic guide to money management and interest rate policy.

Interest Rate Speculation

Most banks have not balanced the interest rate sensitivities of their assets and liabilities. They are acting on an incompletely hedged forecast of future interest rates, and like any speculation, the activity carries potential risks and rewards.

Banks, of course, do not like to be associated with the word speculation, since it conveys many unattractive associations. In fact, speculation is a legitimate part of the business world. It involves taking a position about the future course of business developments. Carried to its broadest meaning, speculation is an essential part of the capitalist system. Each expansion in plant and equipment of a manufacturer, for example, involves a forecast of the size of the market and the price of the product that will be manufactured. The unattractive part of speculation—and the part most bankers object to when the term is applied to their business—is that it does not always turn out favorably. Sometimes markets do not expand, prices do not rise, and interest rates do not always move in the direction that a bank may have forecast.

An example of interest rate speculation of a bank would be if our simple example noted above showed loans that were of fixed interest rate for one year. In turn, the liabilities would be certificates of deposit that would mature in six months. The maturities and interest rate sensitivities of the assets and liabilities in this example would be mismatched. If market interest rates should rise in the following six months, the bank would find its interest rate spread would narrow, and earnings would be impaired. The cost of funding its loan from certificates of deposit would rise, but the interest revenues from the loans would remain unchanged. Of course, if interest rates would decline in the example, interest rate spread would rise and earnings would be enhanced. In this example the bank would have engaged in an activity beyond its services as a middleman of money and positioned itself in a speculation about future interest rate behavior.

IMPLICATIONS OF INTEREST RATE POLICIES

Mismatched interest rate sensitivities are often used by banks because as long as yield curves are positive, earnings are enhanced. Banks would be borrowing funds at a lower interest rate (and shorter maturity) than they would be lending. This program of borrowing short and lending long requires that yield curves stay positive during most of the credit cycle and that there will always be adequate liquidity.

One view suggests that it is not the business of a bank to speculate in interest rates. These bank analysts look at banks as performing services to the public that are like a utility. They see definite limits to the role of banking, and any activities that go beyond this public responsibility would not be appropriate for banks.

Another view suggests that the scope of banking is too broad for the industry to be considered primarily as a utility. These bank analysts consider banks to be more than passive service organizations. They view banks as providing a positive force for change in the economy. This added responsibility of the banking industry requires that they should be prepared to take whatever position they believe is appropriate for their own growth and expansion. This view holds that if banks believe that they can forecast interest rates so that their organization will benefit, it is in the best interests of the banks' shareholders and customers, as well as the economy, to permit them to act on these forecasts.

A third view accepts the broad responsibilities of the banking industry, but does not believe that banks are superior forecasters of interest rates. This view suggests that forecasts of any kind of future business activity are futile, whether the task is selecting stocks likely to rise in price or selecting periods when interest rates will fall. Moreover, the view indicates that even if a bank could employ someone who had special powers of forecasting, there would be strong pressures within the bank to take longer-term risks for immediate profits, simply on the basis of the almost inherent optimism of most bank managements.

Bank directors are involved with interest rate policy implications. If a director is personally concerned that a possible future expansion in loan demand will strain the already fully used resources of the bank, he may be reluctant to encourage management to accept new loans that are not priced according to the marginal cost of securing comparable funds from money markets. He may also request that the bank should obtain these matching funds as a new loan is placed on the books.

In a contrasting example, a shareholder with short-term interests might wish to see a bank earn the highest level of earnings possible. It could be viewed as an emerging growth bank, and the value of shares might rise rapidly. This shareholder might expect that a recession would soon end and interest rates would likely fall. He would be interested to know if the bank's management would take steps to shorten the average maturity of its liabilities in anticipation of falling interest rates.

In another example, a large depositor might wish to see a bank eliminate all possible risks from its activities. This depositor would not be protected by the U.S. government deposit insurance, except for the relatively small amount of $40,000. He would neither receive benefits from an expansion in the bank's scope of activities nor would he ordinarily receive benefits from the bank's increased risk taking to secure possible future earnings improvement. He would believe that his interests would be best served by a steady and risk-free management of the bank's assets and liabilities.

MEASURING INTEREST RATE POLICY

A bank analyst can never know all of the discussions on interest rate policies that occur within a bank. Even if bank analysts were able to listen to these discussions, they might not always be able to discern a clear policy of the bank. Moreover, even if a policy were obtained from meetings, it would not always be certain the extent that the policy would be put into practice.

Interest Rate Spread

The best way a bank analyst can perceive the interest rate policy of a bank is to observe the results of its strategy in interest rate spread. Table 20 shows that the interest rate spread of Chase Manhattan Corporation in 1976 was 2.07 percent on a fully taxable basis (shown in the table as the average rate for net interest income). The table shows the interest rates earned on each of the major interest earning assets, on a tax equivalent basis, as well as a weighted total for all of those assets. For example, in 1976 the average interest rate earned on interest bearing deposits placed with banks, which were primarily overseas, was 7.07 percent. Farther down the table the average interest rate earned on loans was 8.15 percent. The average interest rate paid on all interest

Table 20

The Chase Manhattan Corporation
Net Interest Income—Taxable Equivalent Basis
(dollars in millions)

	1976 Average Balance	1976 Interest	1976 Average Rate
Interest-Earning Assets			
Interest-Bearing Deposits Placed with Banks	$ 4,339	$ 307	7.07%
Investment Securities:			
Domestic Offices:			
U.S. Treasury	1,326	88	6.67
Federal Agency	199	15	7.35
State and Municipal	1,213	154	12.77
Other Securities	218	18	7.87
Total Domestic Offices	2,956	275	9.31
Overseas Offices	223	21	9.40
Total Investment Securities	3,179	296	9.31
Trading Account Securities	278	22	7.95
Federal Funds Sold and Securities Purchased Under Resale Agreements	204	13	6.48
Loans, Net of Unearned Discount			
Domestic Offices	14,361	1,100	7.66
Overseas Offices	12,477	1,087	8.71
Total Loans, Net of Unearned Discount	26,838	2,187	8.15
Real Estate Properties Acquired in Satisfaction of Loans	185	–	–
Direct Lease Financing	71	9	12.17
Summary—Interest-Earning Assets			
Domestic Offices	18,305	1,435	7.84
Overseas Offices	16,789	1,399	8.34
Total Interest-Earning Assets	$35,094	$2,834	8.08%
Interest-Paying Liabilities			
Savings and Other Time Deposits:			
Domestic Offices:			
Savings Deposits	$ 1,948	$ 97	4.99%
Savings Certificates, Christmas Club and Nest Egg Account Deposits	410	26	6.25
Negotiable Certificates of Deposit	4,177	253	6.07
Other Time Deposits	1,757	79	4.48
Total Domestic Offices	8,292	455	5.49
Overseas Offices	15,226	964	6.33
Total Interest-Paying Deposits	23,518	1,419	6.03
Federal Funds Purchased and Securities Sold Under Repurchase Agreements	2,449	122	5.00
Other Borrowed Money—Principally Short-Term:			
Domestic Offices	1,467	90	6.12
Overseas Offices	443	42	9.44
Total Other Borrowed Money	1,910	132	6.89
Capital Notes and Debentures	598	37	6.15
Summary—Interest-Paying Liabilities			
Domestic Offices	12,806	704	5.50
Overseas Offices	15,669	1,006	6.42
Total Interest-Paying Liabilities	$28,475	$1,710	6.01%
Net Interest Income		$1,124	2.07%
Net Interest Income as a Percentage of Total Interest-Earning Assets			3.20%

Notes: Loan figures include non-accruing and reduced rate loans as applicable.
   Fees on loans are included with interest on loans and in average rate computations.

Source: Chase Manhattan Corporation, 1976 Annual Report.

paying liabilities or sources of funds was 6.01 percent. The difference between the total average interest rates earned and the total average interest rates paid was 2.07 percent.

A quick review of the page shows the wide variety of interest rates among various types of assets and liabilities. Chase received 6.48 percent in interest rate from its federal funds sold and securities purchased under resale agreements, while it received almost double that rate from its direct lease financing. Similarly, Chase paid 4.99 percent for its savings deposits in the United States, while it paid about twice as much for other borrowed money in overseas offices.

Table 21 shows the interest rate spread for Chase from 1969 to 1976, a period covering more than one swing of the business and credit cycle. A look at the spread over the period shows that there have been sharp fluctuations. Chase's spread increased from 0.38 percent in 1970 to 1.27 percent in 1971. Spread dropped sharply from 1.55 percent in 1972 to 0.99 percent in 1974. From 1974 to 1975 spread increased, and eased slightly in 1976.

The periods of lowest levels of spread, including 1969 and 1974, occurred during the late expansion phase in business activity, when short-term interest rates rose sharply. During these periods, the high cost of short-term funds represented a severe penalty to any bank that was required to use them to fund loans and securities. In individual cases, loans may have yielded less than the cost of their funding in short-term markets, which represented, on these individual cases, a negative spread. The table suggests that Chase may have been caught in this bind in 1969 and 1974.

A reverse situation occurred during the late recession and early recovery periods in general business activity, which occurred in 1971 and 1975. During these periods, short-term interest rates dropped, loans were funded with considerably lower-cost funds than the loans were yielding, and spreads widened. The table suggests that Chase benefited from this development during these years.

Comparing Maturities of Assets and Liabilities

A bank analyst can develop only general information that would indicate whether the sharp fluctuations in spread were because of, for example, the use of average pricing techniques or because of differences in average maturities between assets and liabilities. The difference is important, if a bank analyst believes that the management of a bank intends to make changes in its policies, since loan pricing is a different consideration than portfolio management.

If a bank has assets of $300 million or more, it is possible generally to assess the maturity structure of a bank's assets and liabilities from the 10-K report and the large bank supplement to the call report. Table 22 shows the sensitivity to changes in interest rates of the principal interest earning assets. The three time periods were selected to provide a common basis of comparing as many types of assets and liabilities as possible. The data are from the 1976 year-end large bank supplement to the Call Report, as revised. Admittedly, the periods are broad and lack much precision. But the periods do ena-

**Table 21 Chase Manhattan Corporation
Interest Rate Spread**

	1969	1970	1971	1972	1973	1974	1975	1976
Average interest rate received from interest earning assets	7.39%	7.93%	7.00%	6.60%	8.76%	10.94%	9.13%	8.08%
Average interest rate paid for interest yielding liabilities	7.05	7.55	5.73	5.05	7.75	9.95	6.98	6.01
Interest rate spread	0.34	0.38	1.27	1.55	1.01	0.99	2.15	2.07

Source: Chase Manhattan Corporation 1976 and earlier annual reports.

Table 22   Chase Manhattan Bank, N.A.
Sensitivity to Changes in Interest Rates of
Principal Interest Earning Assets (Loans and Investment Securities), December 31, 1976,
Billions

	One Year Or Less	Over One Through Five Years	Over Five Years	
Loans with floating interest rate[a]	$18.7	—	—	
Loans with predetermined interest rate	6.9	$1.9	$1.2	
U.S. Treasury securities—carrying value	0.1	1.6	0.1	
U.S. agency securities—carrying value	—	0.1	—	
State and municipal securities— carrying value	0.1	0.1	0.9	
Other bonds, notes, and debentures— carrying value	0.2	0.1	0.1	
Total interest earning assets in each category	$26.0	$3.8	$2.3	$32.1
Share of total	81%	12%	7%	100%

[a] For purposes of interest rate sensitivity, all loans with floating interest rate are considered as having a maturity of one year or less.
Source: Chase Manhattan Corporation 12/31/76 Large Bank Supplement to Call Report.

ble the bank analyst to look inside this aspect of the bank's maturity structure and obtain a rough indication of the balance of its assets and liabilities and thus an indication of the background to a bank's interest rate sensitivity. The table indicates that 81 percent of Chase's loans and securities were sensitive to changes in market interest rates within a period of one year or less. Of this total, the large bulk included loans in which changes of interest rates of a bank follow changes in market interest rates with relatively little lag. Approximately 12 percent of the loans and securities were in the period from one to five years, and 7 percent were in the period over five years.

Table 23 shows the maturity structure of the major interest paying liabilities of Chase. Again, the data are from the large bank supplement to the Call Report.

The table indicates that approximately 89 percent of the deposits and debentures responded to changes in interest rates of one year or less, 8 percent responded to changes in interest rates from one to five years, and 3 percent reflected changes in interest rates for securities that would mature

**Table 23   Chase Manhattan Bank, N.A.
Sensitivity to Changes in Interest Rates of
Principal Interest Paying Liabilities (Deposits and Debentures), December 31, 1976,
Billions**

	One Year or Less	Over One Through Five Years	Over Five Years	
Domestic savings	$1.9			
CDs over $100,000	4.4	0.8[a]		
Overseas deposits	15.3	1.2[a]		
Floating rate notes	0.1			
Capital notes				
4.60% 90s			0.1	
8³/₄ 86s			0.2	
Convertible capital notes				
4⁷/₈% 93s			0.1	
Convertible subordinated			0.2	Totals
debentures 6¹/₂% 96s				
Total interest paying liabilities in each category	$21.7	$2.0	$0.6	$24.3
Share of total	89%	8%	3%	100%

[a] The bulk of CDs and overseas deposits are assumed to have maturities in the one-to-five-year period.
Source: Chase Manhattan Corporation, 10-K Report for 1976, 12/31/76 Large Bank Supplement to Call Report.

more than five years in the future. Domestic savings are shown in the category of one year or less, because it is possible for these interest rates to change without any prearranged waiting period. In past years, these interest rates have tended to change infrequently. Nevertheless, the ability to change these rates quickly indicates that these deposits should be placed in this category. The major portion of Chase's interest sensitive liabilities are overseas time deposits, which include a portion of interest paying demand-type deposits, and these deposits are particularly sensitive to changes in market interest rates.

The next chart should be read as an approximation, not as a precise indication of Chase's balance between these two categories of the balance sheet (Table 24). It compares the conclusions of the tables and suggests that there was a mismatch in the maturity structure and thus presumably the sensitivity to interest rate changes for Chase's interest responsive assets and liabilities. The difference between the two categories explain part of the sharp swings in interest rate spread of Chase in recent years.

Spread Elasticity

Spread elasticity measures the change of interest rates on average interest earning assets to the change of interest rates on average interest paying liabilities. It is expressed as a ratio and provides a concise summary of the interest rate policy of a bank. Spread elasticity provides precision in measuring interest rate policy that is not available from interest rate spread. It summarizes the effect of all factors that affect interest rate policy.

In periods of changing interest rates, spread must also fluctuate if spread elasticity is to remain steady. In a world of changing interest rates—changes in market rates and changes in rates received and charged by banks—spread elasticity is the constant around which change can be measured. It is an indicator of the interest rate policy of a bank, and this characteristic makes it a useful tool for bank analysts.

The ratio of spread elasticity of 1.00 would indicate that the bank is in balance with its interest rate environment.

A spread elasticity ratio of less than 1.00 indicates that the bank is speculating on the future course of interest rates. The bank has positioned itself so that earnings would benfit if interest rates declined. Under this circumstance, interest rates paid for liabilities would tend to drop more rapidly than interest rates received from assets, and earnings would be enhanced. However, if interest rates should steadily rise, the earnings of the bank would be

Table 24   Chase Manhattan Bank, N. A.
Comparison of Sensitivity to Changes in Interest
Rates of Principal Interet Earning Assets and
Liabilities (December 31, 1976)

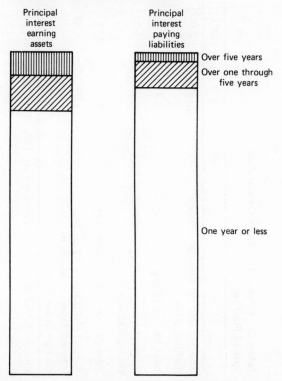

Source: Chase Manhattan Corporation, 10-K Report for 1976, 12/31/76 Large Bank Supplement to Call Report.

Table 25 Chase Manhattan Corporation Spread Elasticity

	1969	1970	1971	1972	1973	1974	1975	1976
Interest rate on average interest earning assets	7.39%	7.93%	7.00%	6.60%	8.73%	10.94%	9.13%	8.08%
Year-to-year change (percent)		+7.3	−11.7	−5.7	+32.7	+24.9	−16.5	−11.5
Interest rate on average interest paying liabilities	7.05	7.55	5.73	5.05	7.75	9.95	6.98	6.01
Year-to-year change (percent)		+7.1	−24.1	−11.9	+53.5	+28.4	−29.8	−13.9
Spread elasticity—change in interest rates on assets to change in liabilities		1.03	0.49	0.48	0.61	0.88	0.55	0.83

Source: Chase Manhattan Corporation, 1976, 1975 Annual Report.

penalized, because interest rates from assets would rise more slowly than the costs of interest rates for liabilities. A spread elasticity of more than 1.00 would reflect the opposite situation and would represent a reverse speculation on interest rates on the part of the bank.

Interest rates of a bank that are sticky in a period of declining market interest rates are often sticky when market rates subsequently ascend. Many banks feature to the public only the side of the credit cycle that they benefit. The spread elasticity measurement shows that this an an uneven interest rate policy, even when the bank is receiving the benefit.

Table 25 shows the spread elasticity of Chase from 1970 to 1976. The data on which spread elasticity is based begins with 1969, so the period covers one complete swing of the business cycle. The interest rate received on average interest earning assets for Chase rose from 7.39 percent in 1969 to 7.93 percent in 1970, representing a gain of 7.3 percent. In the same period, the interest rate costs for average interest paying liabilities rose from 7.05 percent to 7.55 percent, an increase of 7.1 percent. The spread elasticity is the change in the interest rates received compared with the change in interest rates paid, 7.3 percent divided by 7.1 percent, or a ratio of 1.03. This spread elasticity ratio is greater than 1.00, indicating that Chase's interest rate spread improved on a proportionate basis. Interest rate spread also increased for Chase from 1969 to 1970, and earnings benefited.

In contrast, the change in 1971 showed a reversal of that pattern. The interest rate from interest earning assets declined 11.7 percent, while the interest rate for interest paying liabilities dropped 24.1 percent. The interest rate spread rose, as interest rate costs dropped more rapidly than interest rate revenues. The spread elasticity of these interest rate changes declined to 0.49.

Earnings continued to benefit, but there was a significant change in the structure of those earnings. There was apparently a major shift in Chase's interest rate policy from 1970 to 1971, and this change was to have long-lasting significance. The sharp drop in the spread elasticity ratio indicated that Chase had rearranged its interest rate assets and liabilities so that earnings would benefit from declining interest rates. Following the decline in the spread elasticity ratio in 1971, Chase appeared to pursue this new interest rate policy, so that from 1972 to 1975, the ratio averaged 0.63. The management of spread for Chase from 1971 to 1975 was imbalanced. It represented the positioning of the bank for a speculation for lower-interest rates. The spread elasticity ratios for each of the years from 1971 to 1975 indicate that any pervasive upward direction in market interest rates would likely bring about lowered returns on interest earning assets. In the reverse situation, any pervasive drop in market interest rates would likely increase the return on interest earning assets.

The chart illustrates this development with Chase (Figure 62). When interest rates dropped, during 1971 and 1975, interest rate spread widened, and the spread elasticity declined to its relatively low levels of 0.49 and 0.55. When interest rates increased, during 1970 and 1974, the spread elasticity reached its comparatively high levels of 1.03 and 0.88. The average of the final five of these annual periods of change indicates that there was a tendency of Chase's earnings to be penalized by rising interest rates and aided by declining interest rates. The spread elasticity ratio quantifies that observation.

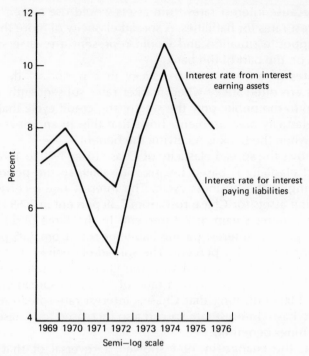

Figure 62 Chase Manhattan Corporation components of interest rate. *Source:* Chase Manhattan Corporation, 1976, 1975 Annual Report.

The period covered from 1969 to 1976 includes two years, 1970 and 1974, when interest rates reached a peak, and two subsequent years when interest rates declined, 1971 and 1975. These periods corresponded with recession and early recovery years in business conditions. A comparison of these two periods indicates that the spread elasticity of Chase may have declined slightly in the recent period. During the earlier peak year of 1970, the spread elasticity ratio was 1.03 and then dropped to 0.49 and averaged 0.76 for this turning point of the business cycle. During a comparable period of the business cycle in 1974, the ratio was 0.88 and in 1975 was 0.55, and averaged a lower ratio of 0.72 for the more recent turning point. This type of comparison attempts to adjust for possible cyclical patterns. In the case of Chase, it appears as if the decline in the ratio was marginally significant and that Chase has maintained its interest rate policy in a fairly consistent pattern in recent years.

CHAPTER 8

PROFITABILITY POLICY

This chapter reviews the policies of profitability and also serves as an introduction to the succeeding chapter, which reviews a bank's capital policies. These two policies—profitability and capital—are closely interrelated and represent two views of the same central theme of how a bank prepares for its future development.

IMPORTANCE

In simplest terms, *profitability* is a ratio of earnings to the funds used in the bank. It measures the success of a bank in its use of this investment.

The idea of profitability involves a rigorously tough standard. It is a measure of the productive ability of the resources under the control of a bank's management. Profitability serves as a common denominator of the business effectiveness of the different activities of a bank. It also is a broad gauge of the capability of a bank to increase its earnings. For these reasons, profitability is perhaps the most important single indicator of performance of banks.

Profitability is basic to the understanding of the capitalist nature of banks. It is the measure linking a bank with new investment. High or rising profitability is the only way that a bank can vigorously expand its operations on a sustained long-term basis. High profitability is an indicator that resources are being used productively and provides a base of profits from which retained earnings can be added to shareholders' equity. In addition, the strength of such a performance usually leads investors to be willing to purchase offerings of new equity.

In contrast, banks showing low profitability do not have a large base of profits from which they can add retained earnings to shareholders' equity. Unless investors believe that profitability will rise, these banks often find difficulty in attracting investors to purchase new equity. Sometimes, these banks cut their dividends in order to preserve as large a portion of earnings as possible for shareholders' equity and to keep their capital base as strong as possible.

Banks that show declining profitability and do not appear to have a viable program to offset such erosion could be on a collision course with depositors, customers, and shareholders. The profitability margin could deteriorate to a point at which the bank might not be able to absorb sudden adversities, such as major loan losses from a recession or a prolonged narrowing of overall interest spreads. In the instance of Franklin National, profitability had eroded so far that the shock of foreign exchange losses left depositors, customers, and shareholders deeply concerned, and these three groups withdrew their confidence and support from the bank.

HOW PROFITABILITY IS MANAGED

From an accounting point of view, profitability may be managed by controlling the components of earnings and assets, which serve as a measure of funds employed. The essence of managing a ratio is that it is not controlled only by attention to a single factor, but rather by an understanding of the simultaneous movement of two factors. For example, the increase of one factor—assets—lowers the ratio, while the increase in the other factor—earnings—raises the ratio. Managing for profitability is not an easy way to manage an organization. It is much simpler to pursue single goals such as increasing earnings per share or increasing the size of assets. Moreover, earnings and assets are reported to the press, while profitability is seldom reported to the press, nor is it usually discussed in much detail in the reports of banks. It requires a management with considerable inner direction or a board with special concern to keep profitability as a key goal.

Return on assets is the most basic measure of profitability because it most broadly states a bank's funds that are employed. In turn, return on assets may be segregated into the two components of return on equity and the capital ratio. The equation describing this relationship follows:

$$\text{Return on Assets} = \text{Return on Equity} \times \text{Capital Ratio}$$

$$\frac{\text{Earnings}}{\text{Assets}} = \frac{\text{Earnings}}{\text{Equity}} \times \frac{\text{Equity}}{\text{Assets}}$$

This equation represents an accounting method of putting together three key ratios. It shows that profitability of assets is equal to the profitability from equity times the capital ratio of the bank. Sometimes this equation is expressed using the return on equity divided by leverage. This variation makes no difference to the results, since leverage is the inverse of the capital ratio.

Return on Assets

Table 26 shows the most basic measure of profitability—return on assets—for First National Boston Corporation and U.S. Bancorp from 1968 to 1976. Return

Table 26 Calculation of Profitability
Return on Assets

Year	Earnings Before Securities Transactions (Millions)	Average Total Assets (Millions)	Return on Assets
First National Boston Corporation			
1968	$35.0	$3580	0.98%
1969	38.8	4210	0.92
1970	41.6	4411	0.94
1971	40.4	4796	0.84
1972	42.1	5341	0.79
1973	51.6	7202	0.72
1974	55.5	8577	0.65
1975	42.5	8225	0.52
1976	42.9	8332	0.51
U.S. Bancorp			
1968[a]	$10.7	$1566	0.68%
1969	12.5	1704	0.73
1970	12.7	1668	0.76
1971	14.5	1801	0.81
1972	16.7	2018	0.83
1973	20.1	2352	0.85
1974	23.3	2573	0.91
1975	25.3	2668	0.95
1976	29.5	2978	0.99

[a] U.S. National Bank.
Source: 1976, 1975, 1974 Annual Reports of First National Boston Corporation and U.S. Bancorp.

on assets is calculated by dividing average total assets by earnings before securities transactions.

First National Boston Corporation has shown a record of an almost steady decline in its return on assets, with a drop from 0.98 percent in 1968 to 0.51 percent in 1976. This decline in profitability occurred while First National Boston showed a substantial gain in earnings before securities transactions from $35.0 million in 1968 to $55.5 million in 1974. The decline in earnings from the level in 1974 to $42.5 million in 1975 and $42.9 million in 1976 still left earnings in 1976 well above their level in 1968. Overall, earnings advanced 23 percent from 1968 to 1976. This pattern of expansion was repeated with average total assets, which rose from $3,580 million in 1968 to $8,577 million in 1974, and then dipped to $8,225 million in 1975. There was a slight gain in 1976. The overall gain in assets from 1968 to 1976 amounted to 133 percent. The gain in assets was five times as rapid as the increase in earnings.

The decline in the return on assets of First National Boston may indicate that this bank's ability to attract profitable business was diminishing. This decline in profitability could appear as an irony. The bank had shown important gains in both earnings and assets, which are measures of performance that are widely published and regarded as being important in evaluating banks. Taken alone, these gains represented useful accomplishments. It is when the two measures are combined to show profitability that the results appear less impressive. The decline in profitability occurred as the bank sought to increase its international banking activities. The effort to expand in this highly competitive market occurred in the 1970s, when many other banks made a similar decision.

The second bank described in the table is U.S. Bancorp. This bank showed a record of a steady rise in its return on assets from 0.68 percent in 1968 to 0.99 percent in 1976. This bank also showed important gains in its earnings and assets. Earnings before securities transactions rose from $10.7 million in 1968 to $29.5 million in 1976, representing an overall gain of 176 percent. Average total assets advanced from $1,566 million in 1968 to $2,978 million in 1976,

Table 27   Calculation of Profitability
Return on Shareholders' Equity

Year	Earnings Before Securities Transactions (Millions)	Average Shareholders' Equity (Millions)	Return on Equity
First National Boston Corporation			
1968	$35.0	$316	11.1%
1969	38.8	329	11.8
1970	41.6	347	12.0
1971	40.4	374	10.8
1972	42.1	398	10.6
1973	51.6	424	12.2
1974	55.5	467	11.9
1975	42.5	496	8.6
1976	42.9	513	8.4
U.S. Bancorp			
1968[a]	$10.7	$100	9.4%
1969	12.5	107	11.7
1970	12.7	111	11.4
1971	14.5	121	12.0
1972	16.7	128	13.1
1973	20.1	140	14.4
1974	23.3	153	15.2
1975	25.3	169	15.0
1976	29.5	187	15.8

[a] U.S. National Bank.
Source: 1976, 1975, 1974 Annual Reports of First National Boston Corporation and U.S. Bancorp.

representing an overall increase of 90 percent. Here again, the gains of these two measures appeared impressive when considered separately. Yet earnings increased almost twice as rapidly as assets, and profitability for the bank rose throughout the period.

Return on Equity

In Table 27 the return on equity is shown for the two banks, as well as its components. The return on equity is calculated by dividing earnings before securities transactions by shareholders' equity.

First National Boston showed a rise in return on shareholders' equity from 11.1 percent in 1968 to 12.0 percent in 1970. The ratio dipped during the following two years and rose again to 12.2 percent in 1973. Thereafter, the ratio dropped sharply to 8.4 percent in 1976. This record shows an uneven pattern. There was not a steady drop shown by the return on assets. Nevertheless, the lack of a steady direction and the repeated attempts to increase the ratio may have indicated that this bank regarded return on equity as a principal goal of profitability and attempted to increase it, only to meet with recurring difficulties.

The overall decline in the return on equity of First National Boston reflected a slower expansion in earnings than in shareholders' equity. As noted before, earnings before securities transactions rose 23 percent from 1968 to 1976. Shareholders' equity increased from $316 million to $513 million in the same interval, a gain of 62 percent.

U.S. Bancorp showed a different pattern in its return on equity. In 1968 its return on equity was 9.4 percent, and return on equity rose almost steadily to 15.8 percent in 1976. This gain reflected almost regular increments in earnings which exceeded increases in shareholders' equity.

Capital Ratio

In Table 28 the capital ratio for the two banks is shown. The capital ratio is calculated by dividing shareholders' equity by total assets. The table shows averages for all of the figures.

The capital ratio represents the reciprocal of the leverage multiple. Both the capital ratio and the leverage multiple describe the same information. For example, First National Boston showed a capital ratio of 6.16 percent in 1976. This capital ratio was equivalent to a leverage multiple of 16×. Capital ratios are used in the tables rather than leverage multiples because the idea that a rising capital ratio indicates a growing strength in the bank's capital position appears self-evident. In contrast, a rising leverage multiple indicates a weakening capital position, not so immediately self-evident.

First National Boston showed a downward direction in its capital ratio from 1968 to 1976. The capital ratio was 8.83 percent in 1968, dropped almost steadily each year to 5.44 percent in 1974, and moved up to 6.16 percent in 1976. Overall, the capital ratio for this bank dropped nearly one-third in the seven-year period. The decline in the capital ratio reflected an overall expansion in shareholders' equity that was less rapid than the gain in total assets.

Table 28   Calculation of Profitability Capital Ratio

Year	Average Shareholders' Equity (Millions)	Average Total Assets (Millions)	Capital Ratio
First National Boston Corporation			
1968	$316	$3580	8.83%
1969	329	4210	7.81
1970	347	4411	7.87
1971	374	4796	7.80
1972	398	5341	7.45
1973	424	7202	5.89
1974	467	8577	5.44
1975	496	8225	6.03
1976	513	8332	6.16
U.S. Bancorp			
1968[a]	$100	$1566	6.39%
1969	107	1704	6.28
1970	111	1668	6.65
1971	121	1801	6.72
1972	128	2018	6.34
1973	140	2352	5.95
1974	153	2573	5.95
1975	169	2668	6.33
1976	187	2978	6.28

[a] U.S. National Bank.
Source: 1976, 1975, 1974 Annual Reports of First National Boston Corporation and U.S. Bancorp.

Shareholders' equity gained 62 percent from 1968 to 1976, while total assets rose 133 percent in the interval.

The capital ratio for U.S. Bancorp showed year-to-year fluctuations, but on the whole appeared to have held its overall position approximately level. The capital ratio was 6.39 percent in 1968 and was slightly below that position in 1976 with a ratio of 6.28 percent. Between those years, the capital ratio ranged from 5.95 percent to 6.72 percent. The overall stability in the capital ratio reflected approximately similar gains in shareholders' equity and total assets, which increased 87 percent and 90 percent, respectively, in the 1968 to 1975 period.

IMPLICATIONS OF PROFITABILITY

Implication for Risk

Profitability can affect the ability of a bank to manage credit and interest rate risks. For example, only highly profitable companies have a greater margin of safety between their level of earnings and a break-even level of operations. This higher margin might be expected to serve as a consideration in a bank's willingness to take risks that a less profitable bank might avoid.

However, the record shows that there is sometimes little relationship between profitability and risk and that higher risk does not necessarily lead to higher profitability. For example, Marine Midland showed low profitability in 1973 and 1974, with a return on average total assets of 0.35 percent and 0.30 percent, respectively. Yet this bank undertook what turned out to be a high risk approach in its lending policies. And in 1975 this bank's profitability dropped to 0.14 percent.

Implications for Bank Analysts

Profitability is not ordinarily an exciting matter to discuss. In an era where growth and expansion have assumed special importance as standards of excellence, a communication from a bank indicating that a high level of profitability had been maintained ordinarily would have little appeal to most customers and shareholders. In fact, it could be misconstrued as an indication that the bank might be stagnant. Profitability is expressed as a ratio, and ratios are often difficult to grasp. Unlike profits or assets, ratios appear obscure, without practical application. One bank analyst remarked that he could not buy or sell anything with a ratio. In a literal interpretation, this comment is entirely correct.

Yet profitability is basic to the ability of a bank to sustain or develop itself on a long-term basis. This basic measure is of importance to shareholders, debt holders, and loan customers.

Implications for Long-Term Shareholders.   Long-term shareholders have the most interest in profitability. A bank showing indications of rising profitability may pursue strategies that could provide a continued basis for an expansion in retained earnings.

A declining rate of profitability would involve questions concerning the ability of the bank to provide adequate increments of retained earnings to shareholders' equity, without reducing the capital ratio of the organization or eventually reducing the dividend. Of course, a decline in the profitability of a bank for one or two years or even several years should not necessarily be construed as a trend that would lead to difficult capital choices. Nevertheless, declining profitability, if continued, would not support liberal dividends.

Fluctuations in the profitability of a bank may be difficult to interpret. A ratio might decline for three years, then rise for two years, and decline again. This situation could reflect a neutral situation, in which the basic profitability of the bank held steady. If the profitability of the bank were already comparatively high, perhaps above 1.00 percent return on average total assets, a position of steady profitability could represent a significant accomplishment. A regularly low profitability, perhaps less than 0.40 percent return on average total assets, could indicate an acceptance of a low level of profitability without seeking ways of improving it. In the latter instance, shareholders might expect to draw as much as possible of their return from such a bank in the form of dividends because the long-term stock performance could be questionable.

Implications for Debt Holders. Holders of debentures are not directly protected by the Federal Deposit Insurance Corporation, and their position is affected by a bank's profitability. Highly profitable banks are more likely to be able to pay interest and repay principal. Banks with low profitability represent increased risk to these persons because an important cushion against unexpected adversities would be thinner. Large depositors are in much the same position as debenture holders.

Implications for Borrowers. Borrowers have usually not been concerned about the profitability of their bankers. The conventional wisdom of business relationships is that bankers are supposed to be concerned about the profitability of their customers. The profitability of a bank represents almost an unmentionable topic in business discussions between bankers and their customers. It is as if the banking source of funds is beyond the scrutiny of financial and business analysis.

The situation is not one-sided. Profitable banks should be considered the companions of profitable borrowers. Typically, profitable customers expand their operations rapidly and develop new needs for financial services. These customers are usually also attuned to the importance of maintaining a high level of profitability. A bank able to provide expanded financing represents a major consideration to these customers.

There appears to be community of thinking between highly profitable banks and their similarly situated customers. The two types of organizations can help keep each other strong. The ability to impart a spirit of profitability may be the most valuable service a bank can provide loan customers. This service is often not directly discussed in the terms of loan agreements. It is a characteristic, an emphasis that is shared. Possibly, it can not be taught, only recognized.

MEASURING PROFITABILITY

The best measure of profitability is return on average total assets. This measure has the advantage of providing the broadest coverage of all activities of a bank. There are no items that have been excluded and that can surprise the bank analyst.

There are other more specialized measures of profitability, including the return on average interest earning assets. These measures provide a sharper focus on a particular aspect of a bank's operations. Nevertheless, return on interest earning assets is a narrower measure of profitability and is less reflective of overall performance. This narrowness represents an important limitation to bank analysts who are interested in using measures of profitability as indicators of the profitability policy of a bank. The broadest scope of return on total average assets usually provides almost as much specific information, as well as an assurance that all internal factors that could affect a bank are covered.

Return on Average Total Assets

The return on total assets is calculated by dividing income before securities transactions by average total assets. Net income is sometimes used for the numerator, and it is closest to the objective of providing a final earnings figure along with a complete asset figure. Nevertheless, income before securities transactions is widely used, and in most, but not all circumstances, it is almost the same as net income. Average total assets are often shown in supplemental pages to the financial statement of annual reports. In the event average assets are not shown, an average of two year-end total assets may serve as a useful approximation. An average calculated on year-end totals is usually slightly higher than an average calculated on daily or weekly averages, because most banks engage in some degree of year-end window dressing, the practice of buying assets on a temporary basis to make the bank appear a bit larger for reporting purposes.

Components of Return on Average Total Assets

A close look at the profitability of a bank relates the principal components of an income statement to average total assets. This approach shows the contribution of various types of revenues and expenses on a profitability basis.

Table 29 shows the calculation of the principal components of the return on average total assets for First National Boston Corporation from 1970 to 1976. The line next to the bottom shows the ratio of income before securities transactions to average total assets, which is the same as the overall measure of profitability discussed earlier. As noted earlier, this measure of total profitability steadily declined from 0.94 percent in 1970 to 0.51 percent in 1976.

The table shows six major components of the overall measure of profitability for each year. These components include two components of revenues, net interest revenue on a full tax equivalent basis and other income, three components of costs, total employee expenses, provision for loan losses and other expenses, and provision for taxes. Each of these components is divided by average total assets. The ratios provide an indication of the contribution of each component to overall profitability.

The net interest revenue for First National Boston includes all interest income from loans and securities less all interest expense from deposits and borrowed funds. The interest income from municipal securities is adjusted to show revenues as if their tax exempt privilege did not apply and as if these securities yielded a higher-interest rate, which would be comparable to fully taxed securities. The net interest revenue ratio for First National Boston dropped from 3.02 percent in 1970 to 2.43 percent in 1973 and then rose to 2.91 percent in 1976. Since income from loans and securities represents the major source of income for First National Boston, this decline represented a moderate erosion in a principal factor of the bank's overall profitability.

The second component of income is the category of other income, which includes trust and agency fees, financial service fees, income from leasing operations and other income. The ratio of other income to average total assets eased moderately from 1.15 percent in 1970 to 1.07 percent in 1976. Gains in

Table 29 Calculation of Principal Components of Return on Average Total Assets
First National Boston Corporation (Tax Equivalent Basis), Millions, Except Percentages

	1970	1971	1972	1973	1974	1975	1976
Net interest revenue	$133.3	$136.6	$140.5	$174.9	$247.4	$244.6	$242.1
Ratio to average total assets	3.02%	2.85%	2.63%	2.43%	2.88%	2.97%	2.91%
Other income	$ 50.6	$ 54.5	$ 63.5	$ 91.5	$ 88.4	$ 82.0	$ 89.1
Ratio to average total assets	1.15%	1.14%	1.19%	1.27%	1.03%	1.00%	1.07%
Total employee expenses	$ 59.8	$ 62.5	$ 66.2	$ 82.0	$ 98.5	$104.6	$110.4
Ratio to average total assets	1.33%	1.30%	1.24%	1.14%	1.15%	1.27%	1.33%
Provision for loan losses	$ 4.3	$ 5.4	$ 7.0	$ 17.2	$ 35.4	$ 50.0	$ 47.0
Ratio to average total assets	0.10%	0.11%	0.13%	0.24%	0.41%	0.61%	0.56%
Other expenses	$ 33.8	$ 42.0	$ 44.6	$ 62.0	$ 81.0	$ 78.9	$ 79.8
Ratio to average total assets	0.77%	0.88%	0.84%	0.86%	0.94%	0.96%	0.96%
Income before income taxes and securities transactions	$ 87.0	$ 81.2	$ 86.2	$105.2	$111.3	$ 93.1	$ 94.0
Ratio to average total assets	1.97%	1.69%	1.61%	1.46%	1.30%	1.13%	1.13%
Tax adjusted provision for income taxes	$ 45.4	$ 40.8	$ 44.1	$ 53.6	$ 65.4	$ 50.6	$ 51.1
Ratio to average total assets	1.03%	0.85%	0.83%	0.74%	0.76%	0.62%	0.61%
Income before securities transactions	$ 41.6	$ 40.4	$ 42.1	$ 51.6	$ 55.5	$ 42.5	$ 42.9
Ratio to average total assets	0.94%	0.84%	0.79%	0.72%	0.66%	0.52%	0.51%
Memo: average total assets	$4411	$4796	$5341	$7202	$8577	$8225	$8332

Source: First National Boston Corporation, 1976, 1975 Annual Report.

trust department income and other bank services, such as leasing and the use of bankers' acceptances, were not as rapid as gains in overall assets. The total of both ratios of income dropped from 4.17 percent in 1970 to 3.98 percent in 1976.

The employee expense ratio includes salaries and all employee benefits. This ratio declined from 1.33 percent in 1970 to 1.14 percent in 1973 then rose to 1.33 percent in 1976. Overall, there was little change in this ratio in its value from 1970 to 1976. This stability could indicate that the bank had been particularly careful about granting salary increases or adding staff.

In contrast to the moderate changes in the three ratios noted above, the loan loss provision ratio increased sharply, rising from 0.10 percent in 1970 to 0.61 percent in 1975 and remained high at 0.56 percent in 1976. This increase added a major burden of expense and was the most important factor in explaining the decline in the overall profitability of First National Boston. The increase in the provision for the loan loss ratio contrasts the decline in the net interest revenue ratio. The divergent directions in the ratios indicated that the bank apparently was reducing its risk margin in loan pricing as the loan loss provision indicated an acceptance of growing risks. Risk adjusted net interest revenue, the ratio of net interest revenue less the ratio for the provision for loan losses, was 2.92 percent in 1970 and dropped to 2.35 percent in 1976 (calculations not shown in table). After adjustment for taxes, which would cut this decline in half, the after-tax effect accounted for two-thirds of the 0.42 percent decline in the overall ratio of income before securities transactions to average total assets.

The ratio of other expenses includes occupancy expense, equipment expense, and miscellaneous other expenses. This ratio rose gradually from 0.77 percent in 1970 to 0.96 percent in 1976. This gradual increase indicated that other expenses were becoming an increasing burden on the total ratio.

The subtraction of the expense ratios from the income ratios is shown in the line for income before income taxes and securities transactions. This line dropped from 1.97 percent to 1.13 percent from 1970 to 1976. The next line shows the tax adjusted provision for income taxes, which showed a parallel drop from 1.03 percent to 0.61 percent. The decline in the tax ratio mirrored the decline in pretax income. The tax rate, which represents the tax provision ratio divided by the pretax income ratio, edged upward. The tax rate was 0.52 percent in 1970 and 0.54 percent in 1976.

The final measure of profitability is the subtraction of the ratio for tax provision from pretax income, which shows the ratio of income before securities transactions to average total assets. As was noted earlier, this ratio declined almost to half of its value in the six-year span, dropping from 0.94 percent in 1970 to 0.51 percent in 1976.

Table 30 shows profitability measures for U.S. Bancorp and provides a contrasting set of developments. The overall profitability of this bank, as measured by the ratio of income before securities transactions to average total assets, rose from 0.78 percent in 1970 to 0.99 percent in 1976.

The ratio for net interest revenue rose from 3.83 percent in 1970 to 4.07 percent in 1975 and eased to 3.96 percent in 1976. Despite the drop in 1976, the increase in this ratio was fairly steady throughout the period, indicating

Table 30 Calculation of Principal Components of Return on Average Total Assets U.S. Bancorp (Tax Equivalent Basis), Millions, Except Percentages

	1970	1971	1972	1973	1974	1975	1976
Net interest revenue	$62.3	$67.2	$72.5	$87.3	$103.4	$108.5	$117.9
Ratio to average total assets	3.83%	3.73%	3.59%	3.71%	4.02%	4.07%	3.96%
Fee and other income	$15.1	$19.4	$22.9	$25.4	$ 28.2	$ 34.6	$ 41.3
Ratio to average total assets	0.93%	1.08%	1.13%	1.08%	1.10%	1.30%	1.39%
Total employee expenses	$30.2	$32.3	$35.0	$40.1	$ 46.9	$ 51.2	$ 55.3
Ratio to average total assets	1.86%	1.79%	1.73%	1.70%	1.82%	1.92%	1.86%
Provision for loan losses	$ 1.7	$ 2.4	$ 2.6	$ 3.2	$ 6.8	$ 4.4	$ 5.5
Ratio to average total assets	0.10%	0.13%	0.13%	0.14%	0.26%	0.16%	0.18%
Other expenses	$18.9	$21.1	$23.8	$27.0	$ 30.6	$ 35.9	$ 39.0
Ratio to average total assets	1.16%	1.17%	1.18%	1.15%	1.19%	1.35%	1.31%
Income before income taxes and securities transactions	$26.6	$30.8	$34.1	$42.4	$ 47.2	$ 51.7	$ 59.3
Ratio to average total assets	1.63%	1.71%	1.69%	1.80%	1.83%	1.94%	1.99%
Tax adjusted provision for income taxes	$13.9	$16.3	$17.4	$22.2	$ 23.9	$ 26.5	$ 29.8
Ratio to average total assets	0.85%	0.91%	0.86%	0.94%	0.93%	0.99%	1.00%
Income before securities transactions	$12.7	$14.5	$16.7	$20.1	$ 23.3	$ 25.3	$ 29.5
Ratio to average total assets	0.78%	0.81%	0.83%	0.85%	0.91%	0.95%	0.99%
Memo: average total assets	$1628	$1801	$2018	$2352	$2573	$2668	$2978

Source: U.S. Bancorp, 1976, 1975 Annual Report.

that apparently there was a deliberate policy of increasing the profitability from loans and securities.

The ratio for fee and other income also gained in the period. This ratio rose from 0.93 percent in 1970 to 1.39 percent in 1976. This gain reflected larger trust income, as well as increases in various other sources of income. Combined, the ratios of net interest revenues and other income rose from 4.76 percent in 1970 to 5.35 percent in 1976. Thus U.S. Bancorp strongly pushed up its total revenue ratios in the period.

The ratio for total employee expenses was fairly level in the period, rising slightly from 1.86 percent from 1970 to 1.92 percent in 1975 and returned to 1.86 percent in 1976. The relative stability of this ratio may indicate a careful monitoring of employee costs.

The ratio for the provision for loan losses rose from 0.10 percent in 1970 to 0.26 percent in 1974 and declined to 0.18 percent in 1976. This gain was moderate in proportion to the gain for First National Boston. More important, the risk adjusted net interest revenue rose in the interval, rising from 3.37 percent in 1970 to 3.78 percent in 1976. This performance indicated that U.S. Bancorp was pursuing a successful strategy of risk pricing and that this basic source of profitability was growing stronger.

The ratio for other expenses edged upward in the interval, rising from 1.16 percent in 1970 to 1.31 percent in 1976. This increase represented greater outlays for branches, electronic equipment, and other costs.

The pretax ratio, which is shown by the line for income before income taxes and security transactions, rose from 1.63 percent to 1.99 percent in the interval. As a consequence, the ratio for tax provision also gained and increased from 0.85 percent to 1.00 percent. After subtracting the tax provision ratio from the pretax ratio, the ratio of income before security transactions to average total assets rose, as was indicated earlier.

Factor Separation Analysis (FASAN)

The foregoing information concerning profitability discussed each factor alone. This information is useful in understanding the factors that were responsible for changes in the overall profitability of a bank. Nevertheless, the information developed in the profitability ratios also has application in explaining the factors affecting changes in earnings per share. Used in this manner, these components underscore the importance of profitability in trends of earnings per share.

The table shows the factor separation analysis technique (FASAN) in explaining changes in earnings. The factor separation analysis shows the contribution of equity, capital ratio, profitability ratios, tax rate, and shares outstanding to changes in earnings per share between two periods.

In the first row of Table 31 for First National Boston, there are the 1970 factors for earnings per share. Shareholders' equity of $347 million is divided by the capital ratio of 0.0787 (or 7.87 percent), multiplied by the operating ratio of 0.01972 (earnings before taxes and securities transactions divided by average total assets) times one less the tax rate of 0.4782, divided by the 12.000 million shares outstanding, all of which equals $3.46. This figure is the same as

Table 31   Factor Separation Analysis of Earnings Per Share (FASAN) First National Boston

	Equity ÷	Capital Ratio ×	Interest Income + Ratio	Other Income − Ratio	Personnel Expense Ratio
1970 factors	$347	0.0787	0.03021	0.01147	0.01333
Introduce 1976 equity	513				
Introduce 1976 capital ratio		0.0616			
Introduce 1976 interest income ratio			0.02906		
Introduce 1976 other income ratio				0.01069	
Introduce 1976 personnel expense ratio					0.01325
Introduce 1976 loan loss provision expense ratio					
Introduce 1976 other expense ratio					
Introduce 1976 1-tax rate					
Introduce 1976 number shares outstanding					
1976 factors	$513	0.0616	0.02906	0.01069	0.01325

reported earnings per share. The value of the factor separation analysis is shown in the next step, which is to repeat the same process with the substitution of shareholders' equity for 1976. This is shown in the second row, which begins with "Introduce 1976 Equity." In this row shareholders' equity of $513 million is multiplied by the same other factors for 1970 as in the first row. Thus shareholders' equity of $513 million is divided by a capital ratio of 0.0787, and so forth. The result of the factors of the second row shows a calculated earnings per share of $5.12.

The difference between the 1970 earnings per share of $3.46 and the second row, which is the calculation that holds all factors for 1970 unchanged except shareholders' equity, is $1.66. This difference indicates that the addition of shareholders' equity between the years added an estimated $1.66 to earnings per share. The greater use of leverage, shown by the decline in the capital ratio from 0.0787 in 1970 to 0.0616 in 1976, added an estimated $1.42 per share. The interest income ratio fell from 0.03021 to 0.02906 (or a drop from 3.02 percent to 2.91 percent, as was noted in the earlier table showing profitability ratios). Another major factor which reduced the earnings potential of this bank was the increase in the loan loss expense ratio from 0.00097 in 1970 to 0.00564 in 1975. This added expense reduced earnings by $1.55 per share.

Corporation Tax Equivalent Basis (Millions, Except Ratios)

Loan Loss − Provision Ratio	− Other Expense Ratio =	Total Operating Ratio)	× 1 − tax Rate	÷ No. Shares Outstanding	= Calculated Earnings Per Share	Dollar Change Attributed to Each Factor
0.00097	0.00766	0.01972	0.4782	12.000	$3.46	
					5.12	+1.66
					6.54	+1.42
					6.16	−0.38
					5.90	−0.26
					5.93	+0.03
0.00564					4.38	−1.55
	0.00958				3.74	−0.64
			0.4564		3.57	−0.17
				12.092	3.55	−0.02
0.00564	0.00958	0.01128	0.4564	12.092	$3.55	

A review of the column showing the dollar changes because of each factor provides a summary of the key factors that affected earnings per share and shows them in a way that enables the bank analyst to make comparisons of their relative impact. This column highlights the importance of changes in the various components of profitability.

The column showing dollar changes attributed to each factor also provides an indication of policies that the bank pursued during the 1970–1976 period. The expansion in shareholders' equity and leverage are both factors that could have reflected a considerable interest in expanding the size of operations of this bank. Together, the expansion in the size of operations accounted for a gain of $3.08 per share in the interval.

In contrast, possible efforts to pursue a policy of risk pricing showed opposite results. Risk adjusted interest margins reduced earnings per share by $1.93 per share in the interval. The credit department and the controllers' department of this bank may not have exerted their full impact. One overall conclusion could be that the bank pursued a policy of growth of assets, and other strategies might have been given secondary importance.

Table 32 shows the factor separation analysis for U.S. Bancorp. The same procedures apply to develop calculated earnings per share using a step-by-

Table 32 Factor Separation Analysis of Earnings Per Share (FASAN) U.S. Bancorp Tax Equivalent

	Equity ÷	Capital Ratio	× (Interest Income + Ratio	Other Income − Ratio	Personnel Expense Ratio)
1970 factors	113.121[a]	0.06949	0.03826	0.00928	0.01855
Introduce 1976 equity	187.481				
Introduce 1976 capital ratio		0.06295			
Introduce 1976 interest income ratio			0.03957		
Introduce 1976 other income ratio				0.01386	
Introduce 1976 personnel expense ratio					0.01855
Introduce 1976 loan loss provision experience ratio					
Introduce 1976 other expense ratio					
Introduce 1976 one-tax rate					
Introduce 1976 number shares outstanding					
1976 factors	187.481	0.06295	0.03957	0.01386	0.01855

[a] 1970 year-end equity was used, since earlier year figures are for bank only.
[b] Reported earnings per share in 1970 were $1.55. Calculated earnings per share

step change of each of the components. The final column of figures shows the dollar change because of each factor. It shows that an improvement in the operating ratio was responsible for a gain of $0.62 per share from 1970 to 1976. This gain represented the total of an increase of $0.23 per share for the interest income ratio, $0.80 per share for the other income ratio, less $0.15 per share for higher-loan loss provision expense, and less $0.26 per share for other expenses.

The column also shows that the major individual factor accounting for increased earnings per share from 1970 to 1976 was a gain in volume. An expansion in equity accounted for a gain of $1.02 per share and an expansion in leverage (shown by a reduction in the capital ratio) was responsible for a gain of $0.27 per share. These two factors, which represent gains in volume, together accounted for a gain of $1.29 per share in the period.

The use of the factor separation analysis method separates factors that represent volume from factors which represent profitability (shown by the operating ratio) in determining earnings per share. This distinction is basic to an understanding of the role of profitability in evaluating earnings gains.

Basis, (Millions, Except Ratios)

− Loan Loss Provision	− Other Expense Ratio	= Total Operations Ratio)	× 1 − Tax Rate	÷ No. Shares Outstanding	= Calculated Earnings Per Share	Dollar Change Attributed to Each Factor
0.00104	0.01161	0.01634	0.47744	8.1559	$1.56[b]	
					2.58	+1.02
					2.85	+0.27
					3.08	+0.23
					3.88	+0.80
					3.88	0
0.00185					3.73	−0.15
	0.01312				3.47	−0.26
			0.49696		3.61	+0.14
				8.908	3.31	−0.30
0.00185	0.01312	0.01991	0.49696	8.908	3.31	

amount to $1.557 or rounded to $1.56

Banks that hold their profitability steady or improve it may be expected to be pursuing strategies which are concerned about the quality of earnings. Changes in the factors relating to volume could reflect strategies concerned about the size of a bank's operations. Earnings gains are much more easily sustained, on a long-term basis, when profitability is steady or rising. Earnings gains that primarily reflect increased volume, but also reflect an offset of lower profitability, are not likely to be easily maintained on a long-term basis. For this reason, profitability is the central focus to an analysis of earnings.

Return on Average Interest Earning Assets

The broadest measure of profitability is the return on average total assets. Yet it is sometimes important to look at narrower, more specific measures of profitability. One of the most widely used special measures of profitability is return on average interest earning assets. The effort in measuring return on average interest earning assets is aimed at separating those assets and earnings that pertain to interest earnings of a bank from all of the other activities. The result would be the ingredients for the profitability of interest earning assets.

The practice of measuring return on interest earning assets has not yet received much interest on the part of most banks. An important difficulty is the lack of uniformity of measurement of the ratio. For example, Table 33 showing the 1976 components of earning assets for First National Boston, indicates cash and due from banks at interest (which includes cash, float, and deposits at other banks) of $1,921 million was added to securities, loans, and lease financing to total earning assets of $7,213 million. The cash and due from banks represented 27 percent of average earning assets of this bank.

In Table 34 the components of earning assets for U.S. Bancorp are shown. This table indicates loans, securities, time deposits with other banks, and a category of other earning assets, which includes lease financing, but excludes cash and due from banks. The latter category would have accounted for 12 percent of that bank's average earning assets if the definition of First National Boston had been used. The choice of where to place cash and due from banks represented a significant difference.

There is perhaps a more fundamental issue. Earnings before securities transactions represent earnings from all assets of a bank. This measure of earnings is appropriately used to measure profitability only when it is divided by total assets. Nevertheless, most measures of return on average interest earning assets use this broad measure of earnings against the narrower base of earning assets. A proper measure of the profitability of earning assets would be

Table 33

FIRST NATIONAL BOSTON CORPORATION
Consolidated Statistical Information, continued

	1976		
	Average Balance	Interest Income/ Expense	Rate
Earning Assets	(Millions)		
Cash due from banks at interest	$1,921	$114.8	6.0%
Investment securities: U.S. Government . .	376	26.7	7.1
State & municipal(1) .	296	30.1	10.2
Other(1) . . .	194	33.8	17.4
Trading account securities(1) . .	106	7.1	6.7
Loans(1)(2) . .	4,084	397.3	9.7
Federal funds sold — resale agreements . .	103	5.3	5.2
Lease financing(1) . .	133	26.5	19.9
Total . . .	$7,213	641.6	8.9

Source: 1976 Annual Report.

Table 34

U.S. Bancorp Consolidated

Year Ended December 31,			1976
In thousands	Average Balance	Income/ Expense	Average Rates Earned/ Paid
ASSETS			
Interest earning assets:			
Time deposits with other banks......	$ 40,512	$ 2,732	6.7%
Investment securities:			
U.S. Treasury obligations.........	203,582	14,001	6.9
State and municipal bonds(1)......	357,270	36,849	10.3
Other bonds and securities........	13,708	1,003	7.3
Total investment securities....	574,560	51,853	9.0
Federal funds sold etc...............	126,371	6,758	5.3
Loans:			
Commercial....................	947,301	76,548	8.1
Real estate....................	435,301	36,567	8.4
Instalment — net	284,925	34,937	12.3
Foreign branch	127,620	10,670	8.4
Total loans(2)	1,795,147	158,722	8.8
Total interest earning assets/			
interest income	2,536,590	220,065	8.7
Other earning assets...............	29,091	2,774	9.5
Total earning assets	2,565,681	$222,839	8.7%
Allowance for loan losses	(13,171)		
Cash and due from banks...........	303,914		
Other assets......................	121,768		
Total assets	$2,978,192		

Source: 1976 Annual Report.

income from these earning assets. The difficulty of separating the amount of income, which, for example, might pertain to commercial banking or to trust business from a particular branch would be a difficult task. Most banks have not attempted this feat of accounting precision for internal purposes, much less for publication to shareholders. Thus the various measures of return on interest earning assets is much less useful as a measure of profitability than return on total assets, and return on interest earning assets probably should not be used at all.

Yet the quest represented by the return on interest earning assets is clearly one of the most important issues in banking today. It represents a primitive attempt to look at a bank's profitability by divisions or departments. Carried further, this is the issue of looking at a bank as if it comprised a group of independent divisions and each of these units had a separate income statement and a comparable balance sheet. This type of analysis, no doubt, will someday be available to bank analysts and will enable them to learn which parts of banking organizations are pulling their weight and which are not. Bank analysts would then be able to judge more accurately the extent that a bank's management might be committed to a policy of profitability.

CHAPTER 9
CAPITAL POLICY

Capital represents a surplus from previous work. It represents funds that have been committed to a bank with hopes for success and without any guarantee against risk. Capital is essential for a bank to attract the other borrowed funds it needs to support its business. It represents the confidence of its owners that the bank will be able to continue to perform its banking activities into the future.

The idea that capital represents a form of surplus refers to how banks originate. It requires courage to open a new bank. A new bank represents a step into the unknown. It also needs momentum. There is no business prior to the time a new bank opens its doors. Yet the bank must open its doors to conduct business. The initial surplus or capital provides the funds that set this business process into motion.

The capital funds of a newly organized bank are entrusted to the manager of the bank without any guarantee that they will earn a penny or ever be redeemable. These funds represent the confidence of the owners of the bank that the bank will succeed. But the bank might not succeed. There are no limits to possible success or guarantees against possible business risks. Holders of a bank's capital share these opportunities and risks.

It is no accident that banks are considered the quintessence of capitalism. Banks employ relatively small amounts of capital, obtain large amounts of deposit and borrowed funds, and use these total funds in ways that affect most other business. This simple description of capitalism carries the idea that capital is closely tied with leverage and that a small amount of capital placed in a bank has an influence magnified many times. This view is entirely correct. Bank capital is the core of capitalism.

FUNCTIONS OF BANK CAPITAL

There are three principal functions of capital to a bank. Return on bank capital serves as an indication of how well a bank's programs can be sustained, and the capital sum serves as a cushion against temporary losses and as a protection to uninsured depositors and other holders of liabilities in the event of liquidation. All banks are involved in the first function as an indication of the sustainability of present policies and are judged by financial markets that act almost as a super board above a bank's own board of directors. A few banks have used their capital funds as a cushion against temporary losses. Only a very few banks are called on actually to use their total capital, which occurs when the bank ends its existence as an ongoing organization.

Link to Financial Markets

The ability of a bank to generate or attract capital determines whether the bank will be able to continue its policies over a long period. Often, several years may elapse before the full impact from financial markets reflects changes in a bank's capital position. The regulatory agencies may modify the impact of financial markets on changes in capital positions, but they cannot completely eliminate this impact. Thus capital acts as a censor to a bank, and it performs this task quietly and anonymously.

Table 35 illustrates that the level of a capital ratio is not a sure indication of strength of a bank. It shows the capital ratios, as measured by the ratio of shareholders' equity to total assets, for 15 banks at year-end 1973. Franklin National showed a comparatively low capital ratio of 3.04 percent, and Security National Bank, located in New York, showed a relatively high ratio of 6.73 percent. Within a few months, both banks were forced to merger to avoid collapse. Thirteen other banks that have continued as viable organiza-

**Table 35   Capital Ratios of Selected Banks
(Ratio of Shareholders' Equity to Total
Assets), December 31, 1973, $ Millions**

Bank	Share-holders' Equity	Total Assets	Capital Ratio
Franklin National Corporation—New York	$152.0	$5006.6	3.04%
Bancal Tri-State Corporation—California	91.5	2971.1	3.08
Crocker National Corporation—California	308.9	9820.0	3.15
Charter New York Corporation—New York	316.5	9759.6	3.24
North Carolina National Bank—North Carolina	122.3	3653.5	3.35
United California Bank—California	340.4	8974.8	3.79
First Pennsylvania Corporation—Pennsylvania	263.2	6192.6	4.25
Seattle First National Bank—Washington	195.5	3969.2	4.93
First International Bancshares, Inc.—Texas	249.4	5052.3	4.94
First National Bank of Oregon—Oregon	130.5	2514.9	5.19
Centran Bancshares Corporation—Ohio	112.3	2014.9	5.57
First Bank System, Inc.—Minnesota	386.6	6514.1	5.93
Bancohio Corporation—Ohio	186.4	3080.7	6.05
Maryland National Corporation—Maryland	118.1	1781.9	6.63
Security National Bank—New York	122.2	1815.9	6.73

Source: 1973 Annual Reports.

tions are shown with capital ratios between those two values. These banks were chosen to show organizations of approximately the same-size assets and shareholders' equity, as well to show a diversity of locations.

Capital serves as a link between financial markets and a bank's profitability. Financial markets are continuously watching the relationship between earnings, assets and capital, as bank managements respond to a tug among pressures to expand earnings, assets, and capital. At certain times, financial markets are particularly interested in the earnings benefits reflected in the return on capital. At other times they are concerned about the solvency risks from leverage. Nevertheless, it is the net result of these counterforces that financial markets are most interested in observing, and banking companies that have shown substantial earnings benefits, along with minimal solvency risks, show strong profitability. This measure of profitability, or return on assets, is measured by the return on capital divided by leverage.

Thus profitability stands at a central position in capital policy of banks. Those banks showing strong profitability have many options concerning capital policies open to them. They are regarded by financial markets as efficient organizations, and any method that such a bank chooses to raise capital is likely to be met with favor. Those banks, in effect, are being given high marks by financial markets. Usually, they may proceed with their ongoing policies and programs without interruption from concern over sources capital.

However, banks with low profitability are often regarded as inefficient organizations by financial markets, and raising capital may be difficult. Nevertheless, if a bank can show financial markets that it has changed its past policies and is successfully undertaking new programs, the negative indications of past performance can be overcome or mitigated. But the bank had better be right in its new program, because there is no greater wrath in financial markets than that from those who believe they have been misled.

Crocker provides an example of the support financial markets can provide when it is widely believed that a bank has turned a corner toward improvement. In the early 1970s this bank had one of the lowest capital ratios and had shown sluggish earnings. A new chief executive officer was installed in 1974. Earnings were strong in the first half of 1975, and on July 16, 1975, Crocker announced plans to sell new shares. The announcement had been preceded by various articles complimentary to the new chief executive and was followed on August 11 by a supportive feature article in Business Week magazine. There was a strong sense of loyalty to this venerable bank, especially among California investors. The offering was completely sold in a short time.

There is an irony in how profitability and capital are intertwined. When a bank's profitability is high, it needs little capital to attract funds, whether deposits, debentures, or equity. Financial markets are then generous, handing over funds with a smile and only an occasional question. How different are the terms with unprofitable banks. Financial markets then want their funds returned. This desire is not publicized and may not be obvious. Moreover, it is not possible for everyone to obtain funds simultaneously without creating an alarm that could endanger all holdings. The conventional wisdom is to pursue a course of attrition and shut the door to further expansion of a marginally profitable bank.

This view may appear difficult to believe in view of the erosion of profitability of nearly all banks over the past two decades. From the position of capital policy, it has appeared to have rained on the good and the bad with equal measure. Yet with important exceptions, banks showing low profitability have been denied capital. While there is no explicit documentation, the inability of these banks to raise capital has become clear only in recent years. Bank analysts never read reports of banks that have tried to raise new equity from financial markets, yet have been refused by underwriters because of unfavorable indications from securities customers.

The issue of declining capital ratios did not focus during most of the past two decades, because until 1974, leverage had been permitted to rise (capital ratios had been allowed to fall) and capital was forgotten in the minds of most bankers and suppliers of funds to banks. It had become widely believed in business and banking circles that the 1946 Employment Act should be taken seriously. This act of Congress committed the government to a policy of full employment, and presumably economic conditions during full employment would not require the use of bank capital to absorb severe operating losses. Despite the successful rescue of several weak banks in 1974 and 1975 by regulatory agencies, this earlier easy assurance has faded. Some bank analysts now question the ability of government to completely fulfill the pledge of the 1946 Employment Act.

A Cushion Against Temporary Losses

A second purpose of bank capital is to provide a cushion against temporary losses that might amount to substantial sums. Losses are a part of every bank's experience, but no bank expects sudden large losses. Nor does a bank expect that large losses will be sustained. Capital is a potential source of reserves that could tide a bank over difficulties, if its losses were severe. More important, the presence of capital provides an indication that the bank has the basis of continuity and that depositors, note holders, and shareholders have reason to look at a bank's difficulties in the broad perspective of a long time period.

There is no question that a strong upward momentum of earnings expansion provides the best defense against losses. Earnings momentum implies that a bank has a fundamentally strong earnings position. For example, in 1974, Seafirst faced a possible $22.5 million pretax loss because of the bank's involvement in the Herstatt demise. The potential loss was widely regarded as an unusual event, and Seafirst was not expected to face other similar difficulties. Moreover, the potential loss represented the upper limit of that bank's liability, and it was likely that the final settlement would involve a much lower sum. The earning power of Seafirst remained unimpaired, and there were no doubts that Seafirst could accommodate the maximum potential loss from the Herstatt difficulties from its earnings and continue as a viable organization.

Nevertheless, not all difficulties of banks are so amenable to earning power.

In some instances, there is less vitality of earnings, and earnings cannot be regarded as a completely adequate first line of defense. Moreover, a series of difficulties may have the effect of weakening the past vitality of earnings and cast doubt on future prospects of earnings. In these instances, capital represents a second line of defense of a bank against losses.

For example, when sharply higher loan losses of Marine Midland cut earnings in 1975, the problems of this bank appeared to be of a longer-term duration than that of one quarter, as was the case with Seafirst. The longer duration of the earnings difficulties and the relatively low profitability of Marine Midland were widely reviewed in the press. Total shareholders' equity of Marine Midland declined slightly from $431 million at year-end 1974 to $426 million one year later, and most depositors and liability holders assumed that the difficulties were manageable over time. The presence of that sum of capital at year-end 1975 provided some assurance that the organization could continue its presence and provided insulation against the effect of these difficulties.

Protection in the Event of Liquidation

This is the classic use of capital to stave off onrushing bankruptcy. However, there is doubt whether capital of any bank at any time could be sufficient to accommodate depositors and short-term liability holders who wanted to redeem their funds, if they became seriously concerned over the viability of a bank. The leverage of nearly all banks is so enormous that once confidence has been lost, capital can provide virtually no defense. For example, the capital of Franklin National Corporation, U.S. National Bank of San Diego, or Beverly Hills Bancorp provided no defense, once the depositors and holders of short-term liabilities believed that these banks were no longer viable. If these organizations had possessed double or triple their capital, it is doubtful whether that would have made any difference in the outcome.

How Much Capital Is Enough?

Capital adequacy is sometimes erroneously presented as an issue of paradoxes. For example, it is sometimes indicated that capital has an important role for banks, both at the time of their founding and as an ongoing liaison with financial markets, but that capital represents little protection to an organization, if confidence should turn against it. In another instance, it is suggested that highly profitable banks require little capital, because they are able to obtain additional capital whenever they might need it, while unprofitable banks needing capital are usually hard pressed to obtain it. Finally, the facilities of the Federal Reserve discount window and the deposit guarantees of the Federal Deposit Insurance Corporation act as capital substitutes, yet they are not capital themselves. These paradoxes confuse cause and effect.

Actually, the role of capital is straightforward. As has been indicated, capital is important in banks because it is the link between their operations and financial markets that provides them with an indication of how well they are performing. More importantly, these indications are usually made before serious difficulties develop, and corrective action could be taken if banking managements were alert. Banks that have an easy access to raise funds from financial markets are being told that their policies and programs are fine, and they are being given an opportunity to expand their operations. These banks, by all appearances, would have enough capital. The reverse situation would indicate that a bank should conserve its resources, examine its business policies, and reorient its business directions. The capital shortage of this bank would indicate that it should change its operating policies. Between these extremes, which includes the majority of banks, the implications of capital policy are less urgent, but not less significant.

The Federal Reserve Board acts in an important intermediary role in determining capital policy. The Federal Reserve Board has supervisory power over the capital adequacy of its member banks. Section 9 of the Federal Reserve Act and Regulation H of the Board of Governors require that the net capital and surplus of a member bank "shall be adequate in relation to the character and condition of its assets and to its deposit liabilities and other corporate responsibilities." Nonmember insured banks must agree to maintain adequate capital as a condition of deposit insurance with the Federal Deposit Insurance Corporation. Although the Comptroller of the Currency also has certain supervisory power, the Federal Reserve has been most concerned about capital adequacy and has been the regulatory agency that has most used its supervisory power. In addition to capital ratios, the Federal Reserve also evaluates a bank's liquidity, asset quality, investment concentration and risk, earnings growth, and dividend patterns, as well as managerial talents in reviewing capital adequacy.

The Federal Reserve believes that there should be as few difficulties in the banking industry as possible. The Federal Reserve is also concerned that the public's knowledge of the regulation of the banking industry could lead some members of the public to be less critical than otherwise, and that a lax attitude could lessen the effectiveness of financial markets in providing guidance and direction to banks. Thus the Federal Reserve views its intervention in capital policy as a responsibility that it cannot avoid.

In recent years the Federal Reserve has acted as a surrogate for the forces of financial markets and has moved to influence directly the capital positions of banks. The Board has indicated its concern over capital positions through its Division of Banking Supervision and Regulation. The Federal Reserve's overall concern in this area has been expressed in orders of the Board in response to applications from banks and in Congressional testimony, the texts of which are available in various Federal Reserve Bulletins. It has used its power to pass on the acceptability of bank acquisitions as a lever to force greater compliance with its interest in seeing bank capital positions improve. In some instances, the Federal Reserve reportedly has told banks to raise capital. In so doing, it has assumed the role of the financial markets, hoping to bring about compliance with its interpretation of capital positions that would reflect the best interests of the banking industry. Thus in most, but not all instances, a bank's capital position is as good as the Federal Reserve says it must be.

HOW CAPITAL POLICY IS MANAGED

Banks manage their capital using six methods, including a change in the assets of the capital ratio, a change in the dividend payment ratio, a new offering, a merger, recapitalization, or a change in profitability. The initial five methods of capital management have little or no impact on the ability of a bank to change its long-term trend in the rate of expansion of its capital base. However, the final method, a change in productivity, has an impact on the long-term capital outlook.

Capital is used here to mean shareholders' equity. This is the most basic and simple definition and the only one that does not break down on close examination. Shareholders' equity includes all funds that have been directly placed or retained by a bank without any requirements or assurances on the part of the bank. These are funds without commitments, and for this elemental reason, they are used as a basis of obtaining other funds, all having requirements and obligations of various kinds.

Change in Assets

While it is true that a capital ratio may be managed by changes in either assets or shareholders' equity, in virtually all cases assets are the major factor of change. This method of managing a bank's capital ratio represents a program of nonmanagement of capital. In recent years, assets have usually been permitted to increase, in line with efforts to increase the size of banking organizations and to increase earnings. Capital has been regarded as a separate consideration and usually overlooked in efforts to boost the expansion of assets. As a consequence, the capital ratio has dropped for most banks during the past decade.

Another approach would be to add capital in proportion to an increase in assets. The increment would come from earnings or an offering and would reflect a premium of earnings above the ordinary amount that would be expected if there were no capital "surtax." Such a program would be difficult for bankers who have grown up in an environment of strong asset expansion to accept voluntarily.

Change in Dividend Payout

This approach to capital policy involves raising more capital by keeping a greater portion of earnings and paying out a smaller proportion of dividends. The reasoning is that by retaining a higher proportion of earnings, the capital base of the bank would expand more rapidly than otherwise. This approach appears to be an attractive way of building equity capital because it does not create new shares that would dilute earnings of ongoing shareholders. Nevertheless, it is doubtful that retained earnings are a significantly less expensive way of raising capital than a new issue. The cost of retained earnings is closely linked to the cost of equity in the long run.

In adding capital, the route of retained earnings could appear cheaper than the route of higher dividends and a subsequent offering, because investors whose profits are retained for reinvestment by the bank would temporarily avoid income taxes. Nevertheless, those taxes, or a related tax, would have to be paid later, if the reinvested profits produce higher dividends and if shareholders sell their holding and presumably pay a capital gains tax on this investment. A capital gains would reduce the effective tax rate on the profits for reinvestment. Of course, there is no assurance that there will be a capital gain. Sometimes investors sell bank stocks at a loss compared with their original investment. And it is always true that current dividend is more valuable than a capital loss at any tax rate. On balance, it is not certain that a strong case can be made favoring either retained earnings or higher dividends and an offering. All of this is from an investor's point of view, because investors determine the cost of capital for a bank through their purchases or withholding of purchases of shares.

The connection between the cost of retained earnings and that of new common stock becomes more clear when bank earnings are considered as being reinvested within the organization for the benefit of shareholders. In this sense, dividends are a present distribution of these earnings. It should make little difference to investors, in the long run, whether the earnings are reinvested or paid out, because the total return to investors should be approximately the same. If dividends are high, less internally generated funds would be invested, and the bank would expand more slowly and it would be more likely to offer new stock to the market that would dilute earnings. Yet investors benefit from having dividends in hand. If dividends are low, more internally generated funds would be used by the bank, which would expand more rapidly and be less likely to float new stock. However, investors would not have received as large in-hand payments.

Of course, this overall equilibrium pertains to the long run, and most investment decisions of shareholders are made with shorter time horizons. In some instances, investors may doubt that the longer-term balance applies. Yet over the longer term of many years—which should be the basis for making observations concerning capital policy—it should make little difference to capital policy whether a dividend payment is high or low.

New Offering

Banks may raise capital by issuing new securities, including the issuance of new stock or new convertible debentures. These approaches represent approximately the same cost to a bank. Again, in the long run it is doubtful that one approach is better than the other.

On the surface, it appears as if issuing convertible bonds or convertible preferred stock would be a more inexpensive way of raising capital than issuing regular common equity. A bank may sell a convertible bond with a lower rate of interest than a straight debt issue. However, the bank has still sold a debt issue, and there is neither equity at the time of sale nor any guarantee of future new equity. Holders of the convertible bonds will convert them into stock only if the bank's stock price rises to a level above its conversion price, possible in the future. The lower cost of this type of transaction is offset by the lack of any benefit of equity capital to the bank in the present, and the possibility that there may not be any conversion in the future.

The issuance of new equity occurs in large blocks, and intervals between issues may last for many years. This pattern often gives a mistaken impression that at the time of an announcement of an offering, present shareholders face a reduction in the value of their shares as measured by book value (shareholders' equity divided by shares outstanding). Actually, the dilution of shareholders' position occurred gradually, as capital ratios weakened compared with the level that were perceived to have been necessary. Shareholders should have made a capital adjustment over the period. Of course, no one does this. But the point is valid, and in considering the long term, it is unrealistic to believe that deteriorating capital ratios represent a long-term trend that is not without a cost to shareholders.

Change in Profitability

The only effective way of managing capital ratios is through a change in profitability. Higher earnings from a more economical rise of assets has the effect of both conserving the present needs of capital and providing the basis of expansion for its future growth. A rapid growth of earnings gives the basis for a rapid expansion in shareholders' equity, and a correspondingly less rapid expansion in assets enables a bank to build its capital ratio.

Recapitalization

Recapitalization is the process of changing the fundamental ownership position of shareholders. This can take the form of a large stock offering, a merger into another bank or a withdrawal of shares to liquidate part or all of the shareholders' equity. These steps may represent drastic action by a bank.

A large stock offering is virtually impossible when confidence is in doubt. The most common way of handling difficulties of confidence is a merger with a larger, stronger organization.

If confidence in a bank has severely eroded, a partial withdrawal of capital would be difficult. Such action would indicate that some holders of equity found no market for their shares and wanted their equity funds returned because they believed that there were only doubtful prospects for the bank. Full liquidation and bankruptcy would represent a final recapitalization of a bank.

Employee Stock Ownership Plans

Employee stock ownership plans represent a special type of financing that is finding increasing use in banks. In the plan a trust is sponsored by a bank. The trust borrows funds, which it uses to buy either newly issued or existing stock of the bank for ultimate distribution to the employees, who are the beneficiaries of the trust. In this manner the bank uses debt funds to expand its equity. The bank retires the debt over one or more decades. The stock is held in trust and employees receive shares on their retirement or after a period following termination of employment.

There are numerous tax advantages to the employee stock ownership program, which reflect the interest of Congress in the objectives of the program. In reviewing these programs, a 1976 staff study for the Joint Economic Committee of Congress supported employee stock ownership programs on the basis that it should be made national policy to pursue the goal of broadened capital ownership. If stock prices of banks do not expand strongly in the future and traditional methods of raising capital prove inadequate, employee stock ownership programs may provide one of the important ways that banks may have available to raise capital.

IMPLICATIONS FOR BANK ANALYSTS

Implications for Depositors

Individual depositors with amounts up to $40,000 are not ordinarily concerned over a bank's capital policy. In virtually all banks these deposits are protected by the Federal Deposit Insurance Corporation.

Depositors with amounts exceeding $40,000 are not so protected. These depositors, including individuals and corporations, could be concerned about the safety of these deposits. The capital policy of a bank is useful to them as an indication of the certainty that their deposits may be left without unexpected and unsettling developments. A low or dropping capital ratio has the effect of raising questions whether the other policies of the bank can be sustained. Large depositors might wish to give careful consideration to long-term deposits in banks with such capital policies. Short-term deposits involve less risk. Nevertheless, some depositors may seek banks with low capital ratios, if the interest rate premium for deposits in those organizations were appropriate for the possibilities of unexpected surprises.

In contrast, a high or rising capital ratio of a bank indicates that its ongoing policies could continue. The ability of a bank to continue policies provides assurance to depositors that there will not likely be major shocks to the bank, and depositors would likely consider making deposits on a long-term basis. Interest rates would not likely be as generous as might be offered by other banks, because of the added assurance of continuity of the bank's operating policies.

Large depositors would want to be alert to major changes in capital ratios in a short period that might indicate major changes in capital policy. For example, Security National Bank of New York showed a moderately high capital ratio immediately prior to its difficulties. Yet a review of the developments of the previous two years showed that the capital ratio of this bank had fallen sharply, reflecting a major drop in overall profitability. The bank had shifted from a strategy of being a suburban bank to one of attempting to challenge the major New York City banks in wholesale banking. This change in strategy had disastrous results. The sharp declines in profitability and capital ratios were signals that the new strategy could not be sustained. Although large depositors were not harmed, because of the merger of Security National Bank into Chemical New York Corporation, these depositors most likely felt anxious moments if they were aware of developments of the bank. Part of the compensation of depositors, of course, is freedom from worry. Large depositors who are prepared to take risks often experience worried moments. They should expect to require appropriately generous compensation of high interest rates.

An opposite situation would be a bank that had shown a weakening of low capital ratio and then suddenly showed a major increase in this ratio. The gain could represent a major change in banking strategy and a change in operating policies that had improved profitability. This situation would indicate that the prospects for the bank to continue its operating policies have improved. Large depositors might be interested in considering these situations carefully. Depositors could receive a generous interest rate, because many depositors might not be aware of the significance of the improvements that had occurred. Reputations of banks often lag events, and this lag could benefit alert depositors.

Implications for Loan Customers

Borrowers might be interested in a bank's capital policy for the same reasons as large depositors. Borrowers want to be assured of the continuity of the bank to serve their needs. Banks showing a weak capital policy, as is reflected by a low or dropping capital ratio, might not be able to sustain their past lending policies. They might need to limit their expansion of loans during a future period of strong business expansion. Borrowers would then find that their ability to conduct business might be circumscribed. This situation could involve large corporate borrowers, state and local governments, as well as individuals. The large borrowers might find that their ability to expand borrowing would be limited or nonexistent, and if there were a severe credit squeeze, they might be among the first borrowers who would be asked to reduce their borrowings. Small borrowers might find that they would also find the availability of credit limited under these conditions.

Borrowers of banks with weak capital policies might be expected to seek more generous terms or lower overall borrowing costs than they might expect from most other banks. These terms would reflect the added risk that the bank might not be able to provide continuity in its lending services to loan customers on terms that had become customary.

The opposite situation could prevail for customers of banks that showed high or rising capital ratios. These banks provide considerably greater assurances of continuity of their operating policies. This assurance has value to borrowers, especially those who might need substantial new funds in coming years. Banks with strong capital positions can price their loans favorably. Loan customers receive a benefit from this capital position and may be expected to give consideration to this premium.

Other borrowers might not attach such importance to the ability of a bank to provide continuity into the future, but they, too, might benefit from this assurance. For example, an established farmer might not expect to have rapidly mounting needs for funds for many years into the future. Nevertheless, the uncertainties of weather and the fluctuations of agricultural markets represent major uncertainties to him. These uncertainties and fluctuations are not directly related to the industrial swings in business conditions. Nevertheless, he would want to avoid being caught as a customer of a bank with a weak capital position during a downswing of prices of agricultural products at a time of a severe credit squeeze stemming from overheated industrial markets. If this farmer would want to expand his farm acreage at such a time, he would want a bank that would be able to accommodate his loan request.

Implications for Shareholders

Banks with strong capital positions are more likely to be able to sustain their past growth rate in earnings per share than other banks. The strong capital position reflects a capital policy which places emphasis on operating policies that promote high profitability. It therefore provides the basis of advancing shareholders' equity in line with assets, as well as providing dividends for shareholders.

There is a second advantage of a strong capital policy to shareholders. Banks with strong capital positions are not likely to be under pressure from the Federal Reserve to raise equity capital from a new offering. New offerings of equity lower earnings per share, which has the effect of lowering the growth rate of earnings per share. Thus shareholders of banks with strong capital policies may be expected to use past trends of earnings per share with greater confidence in making projections.

Weak or declining capital positions may reflect a future need to bring about changes that could bring surprises or risks to shareholders. Changes in operating policies involve risk, and of all bank analysts, shareholders have most to lose if changes bring unexpected negative developments. A weak capital position could indicate a limited ability to raise capital internally. Policies that permit or encourage weak capital positions involve uncertainties that shareholders might want to avoid, except at an advantageous price.

For all these reasons, banks with low capital ratios often show share prices which are low compared with earnings. Capital policies of these banks do not support confidence that their earnings are as sustainable as those of many other banks and thus may not be valued so highly.

MEASURING CAPITAL ADEQUACY

There is, perhaps, no area of banking that regulators have investigated more carefully than capital ratios. Regulatory agencies recognize that they cannot direct the day-to-day activities of a bank and give such detailed instructions as which loans to accept or which areas of business to enter. Regulatory agencies also cannot direct a bank to increase its profitability. Yet regulatory authorities are empowered to require banks to maintain adequate capital. Thus the capital issue is where these agencies can impact a bank's operations.

The refinement in techniques of measuring capital adequacy reflects a desire of regulatory agencies to be as accurate as possible. This section shows a basic measure of capital ratio, as well as the six principal measures used by the Federal Reserve Board, the Comptroller of the Currency, and the Federal Deposit Insurance Corporation. The six measures were selected because they represent the approach regulatory agencies use when they conduct their business with banks. The measures are not the only ones used by these agencies. In fact, the agencies stress that they do not look at only one or two measures in making a determination of capital adequacy, but rather review a considerable number of ratios. In addition to the measures shown here, scholars and bank analysts have proposed many additional measures, but they are not discussed here because they are usually no better than the measures used by the regulatory agencies, and they do not have the weight of authority behind them.

Shareholders' Equity to Assets

The simplest measure of capital adequacy is a ratio of shareholders' equity to assets. Table 36 shows this ratio for Mellon National Corporation and Chase Manhattan Corporation. Average balances are used here to provide a broad measure for the period.

The table shows that a major difference occurred between the relative capital positions of the two banks. In 1976, Mellon showed about four-fifths more equity for each unit of assets as Chase. Both banks showed an increase in their capital ratios from 1974 to 1975, and Mellon increased its capital ratio in 1976. Mellon achieved its gain both from additions to shareholders' equity and a decline in assets.

Federal Reserve—Equity Capital Method

This capital ratio used by the Federal Reserve System attempts to compare a broad measure of equity with risk liabilities (Table 37). This measure uses data only from domestic bank operations and subsidiaries and views the bank from

Table 36 Capital Ratio
Shareholders' Equity to Total Assets of Total
Corporation ($ Millions)

	1974	1975	1976
Mellon National Corporation			
Average shareholders' equity	$ 579	$ 616	$ 649
Average total assets	9,653	9,512	9,459
Ratio	6.00%	6.48%	6.86%
Chase Manhattan Corporation			
Average shareholders' equity	$ 1,454	$ 1,587	$ 1,641
Average total assets	40,344	41,085	42,997
Ratio	3.60%	3.86%	3.82%

Source: 1976 Annual Reports.

Table 37   Capital Ratio
Federal Reserve—Equity Capital Method Bank Only—
December 31, 1976 ($ Millions)

Chase Manhattan Bank, N.A.
(Data from Consolidated Report of Condition
Including Domestic Subsidiaries)

Line 37—total equity capital	$ 1,959
Add: Line 9b—reserve for possible loan losses (valuation reserves)	237
Add: Schedule H, line 7a—domestic report, deferred income taxes: IRS bad debt reserve	79
Total numerator	2,275
Line 30—Total liabilities	23,841
Add: Line 31—subordinated notes and debentures	326
Less: Line 1—cash and due from banks	4,070
Less: Schedule A, line 9—domestic report, unearned income on loans	67
Less: Schedule H, line 7a—domestic report, deferred income taxes: IRS bad debt reserve	79
Total divisor	28,383
Ratio	8.02%

the perspective of U.S. operations alone. By using bank-only data, the Federal Reserve shows its main concern with the protection of depositors. Nevertheless, the exclusion of data for international banking activities could represent a serious   omission, since the international banking activities could create problems that might cast a shadow over a bank. The measure was developed by Vice-chairman George Mitchell of the Board and is often referred to as the Mitchell ratio within the Federal Reserve System.

Shareholders' equity is added to the valuation portion of loan loss reserves to obtain a fuller measure of equity. Total liabilities and capital notes and debentures are added, and cash and due from banks are subtracted to obtain a measure of liabilities bearing a risk of being withdrawn from a bank. Deferred income taxes and unearned income on loans are also subtracted from liabilities. The data show end-of-period totals, because call reports are the source of the data.

For many large international banks this measure of capital adequacy shows a ratio much higher than measures that include both domestic and overseas positions of equity and resources. Most equity is held in the U.S., while large international banks hold one-third or more of their resources abroad. Thus among large international banks, this measure is not an entirely appropriate measure of capital adequacy.

There is some discussion within the Federal Reserve over several fine points with the ingredients of this measure of capital adequacy. One issue is whether to include the IRS reserve for taxes, which is the deferred tax portion of the reserve for possible loan losses. The reserve presumably would be used for deferred tax liabilities in the event of liquidation and would not then be available to shareholders. Others within the System, reflecting the prevailing view, indicate that the reserve should be added to shareholders' equity.

Federal Reserve—Gross Capital Method

The second ratio used by the Federal Reserve includes a measure of capital that includes shareholders' equity, valuation reserves for loan losses, and subordinated notes and debentures (Table 38). The latter primarily include capital notes of the bank. For the notes and debentures to qualify as capital, they need to be seven or more years from maturity when they are issued, and they must specifically indicate that they are subordinated to payment of all depositors' claims in the event of liquidation. The divisor is total assets.

The inclusion of long-term subordinated debt in capital represents a major change from an earlier position of the Federal Reserve. At an earlier period, the Federal Reserve maintained that only shareholders' equity and appropriate reserves represented bank capital. The shift to include subordinated debt permitted many banks with a lower market price of their stock than book value to avoid the full impact of either selling new stock at prices that diluted the value of ongoing shareholders' positions or shrinking the size of their operations.

This measure of capital adequacy includes overseas as well as domestic positions. It provides a comparison of a bank's overall position of capital to resources, which is, perhaps, as generous as possible.

Federal Reserve—Loans to Gross Capital Method

This capital adequacy measure is a multiple of loans supported by capital (Table 39). Domestic and overseas loans are compared with the previously noted measure of gross capital.

This indication of capital adequacy has received considerable recent interest within the Federal Reserve, since it provides a composite measure of both capital adequacy and liquidity. Banks with considerable liquidity usually show

Table 38 Capital Ratio
Federal Reserve—Gross Capital Method Bank Only—
December 31, 1976 ($ Millions)

Chase Manhattan Bank, N.A.
(Data from Consolidated Report of Condition,
Including Domestic and Foreign Subsidiaries)

Line 37—total equity capital	$ 1,959
Add: Line 31—subordinated notes and debentures	326
Add: Line 9b—reserve for possible loan losses (valuation reserves)	255
Add: Schedule H, line 7a—domestic report, deferred income taxes: IRS bad debt reserve	79
Total numerator	2,619
Line 16—total assets	44,755
Add: Line 9b—reserve for possible loan losses (valuation reserves)	255
Total divisor	45,010
Ratio	5.82%

Table 39   Capital Multiple
Federal Reserve—Loans to Gross Capital Multiple Bank
Only—December 31, 1976 ($ Millions)

Chase Manhattan Bank, N.A.
(Data from Consolidated Report of Condition, Including
Domestic and Foreign Subsidiaries)

Line 9a—Total loans	
Total numerator	$30,219
Line 37—Total equity capital	1,959
Add: Line 31—subordinated notes and debentures	326
Add: Line 9b—reserve for possible loan losses (valuation reserves)	255
Add: Schedule H, line 7a—domestic report, deferred income taxes: IRS bad debt reserve	79
Total divisor	2,619
Multiple	11.5X

a relatively lower proportion of loans to securities and other assets. Thus a bank can achieve a high measure of capital adequacy, using this multiple, either by building up capital or by building up liquidity by reducing its proportion of loans to assets.

Comptroller of the Currency—Capital to Assets Method

Table 40 shows the basic measure of capital adequacy used by the U.S. Comptroller of the Currency. This measure uses data of the total bank. It adds shareholders' equity and long-term subordinated debentures and capital notes to obtain a numerator of total capital. The Comptroller uses only the valuation portion of loan loss reserves, indicating that the deferred tax portion would represent an offset to possible tax liabilities in the event of liquidation. The Comptroller views the valuation portion of the loan loss reserve as a part of capital and not as a contra-asset, as is indicated by the method of presentation on balance sheets. Total assets form the divisor.

At year-end 1976, the table shows that this measure of capital adequacy for Mellon National Corporation was more than one-third higher than the measure for Chase Manhattan Corporation. The measure of calculating capital ratios points up the practical difficulty that it is not always as possible to make a quick determination whether a note or debenture qualifies as a subordinated debt. For example, Mellon shows $125 million in long-term debt as part of liabilities in its consolidated corporate balance sheet. The debentures are part of Mellon's parent company debt and not part of the bank's debt. The bank analyst sometimes must review the prospectus of the debentures to be sure they are not subordinated, which is the situation in this case.

The Comptroller's method gives special emphasis to the total consolidated corporate figures, reflecting a concern over the overall bank. This method of calculating capital adequacy provides broad coverage of all activities of a bank, as well as a broad measure for capital.

FDIC—Total Ratio Method

The Federal Deposit Insurance Corporation (FDIC) method of calculating capital adequacy uses bank and bank subsidiary data for domestic and international operations (Table 41). As was noted with the Federal Reserve measures, the use of bank only data reflects a principal concern with the interests of depositors, and the bank is the only part of a bank holding company accepting deposits. The Federal Deposit Insurance Corporation measure adds shareholders' equity and valuation reserves of the loan loss reserve to obtain a measure of capital, which is the numerator of the ratio. Total assets are added to valuation reserves to form the divisor. Valuation reserves are added both to the numerator and to the divisor to add a contra-asset to both parts of the ratio.

The table shows that this measure of capital adequacy was about double for Mellon than for Chase. Both banks showed a gain in the ratios from 1974 to 1975 and declines the following year.

COMPARISON OF METHODS

Table 42 shows the six measures of capital adequacy for Chase which are described in this section. There is a wide variety of ratios ranging from 3.82 percent to 8.70 percent. The table demonstrates that there is no value for capital adequacy which can stand by itself as an indication of either sufficient

Table 40   Capital Ratio
Comptroller of the Currency—Ratio of Capital to Assets
Method Consolidated Corporation—December 31 ($ Millions)

	1974	1975	1976
Mellon National Corporation			
Shareholders' equity	$ 596	$ 632	$ 670
Add: Long-term subordinated debentures and capital notes	0	0	0
Total numerator	596	632	670
Total assets—total divisor	9,859	9,018	9,353
Ratio	6.05%	7.01%	7.16%
Chase Manhattan Corporation			
Shareholders' equity	$ 1,518	$ 1,621	$ 1,667
Add: Long-term subordinated debentures and capital notes	484	480	675
Total numerator	2,002	2,101	2,342
Total assets—total divisor	42,233	41,414	45,638
Ratio	4.74%	5.07%	5.13%

Source: 1976, 1975 Annual Reports.

Table 41   Capital Ratio
Federal Deposit Insurance Corporation—
Total Ratio Method Bank and Domestic Subsidiaries Only (December 31, $ Millions)

	1974	1975	1976
Mellon Bank, N.A.			
Shareholders' equity	$ 554	$ 568	$ 622
Add: Valuation reserves	59	49	55
Numerator	613	617	677
Total assets	7,389	6,672	7,341
Add: Valuation reserves	59	49	55
Denominator	7,448	6,721	7,396
Ratio	8.23%	9.18%	9.15%
Chase Manhattan Bank, N.A.			
Shareholders' equity	$ 1,776	$ 1,882	$ 1,959
Add: Valuation reserves	217	253	255
Numerator	1,993	2,135	2,214
Total assets	41,423	40,324	44,719
Add: Valuation reserves	217	253	255
Denominator	41,640	40,577	44,974
Ratio	2.38%	5.26%	4.92%

Source: 1976, 1975 Annual Reports.

or insufficient capital. Much depends on the definition of the capital measure used, and as the table indicates, there are many different ways of approaching the measurement of capital adequacy.

Which method is best? Earlier in this chapter, it was pointed out that bank analysts should be acquainted with the measures used by the regulatory agencies, since these agencies were the principal source of pressure on banks to increase capital. This view is particularly true in regard to the Federal Reserve Board. One method of approaching the measurement of capital adequacy would be to take an average of five of the principal measures used by the regulatory agencies and consider this average as being representative of the composite opinion of the regulatory agencies. Such an average would be heavily weighted to the Federal Reserve, as it should be, since this agency has acted with greatest interest on the issue of capital adequacy. This average could then be compared with other banks in the peer group of a bank under review.

The problem with this method is that it is difficult and cumbersome to calculate all of these measures of capital adequacy without a computer program. A complete set of reports of condition for a large group of banks is not readily available in most libraries or even in most reference files of research organizations. Reports of condition are not regularly mailed to bank analysts of most banks, and some banks decline to provide them even when they are individually requested. Bank analysts obtain them from regulatory agencies, and this procedure is usually not particularly prompt.

Another solution is to use a simple measure of shareholders' equity to total assets as a proxy for the more prolix measures of the regulatory agencies. This measure tracks fairly closely the relative changes of most of the measures used by regulatory agencies, because its two principal elements, shareholders' equity and assets, account for the bulk of resources that comprise the other measures. Nevertheless, the ratio of shareholders' equity to assets tends to be more conservative than most of the other measures used by regulatory agencies, since most other measures add capital notes to shareholders' equity to obtain a numerator. In recent years, the addition of capital notes by some banks would tend to make most measures used by regulatory agencies show progressively more generous capital ratios than would be shown by the basic ratio of shareholders' equity to assets. Yet this difference would not likely be critical, since the trend in these ratios is the issue of interest to bank analysts.

A second difference would be the addition of part or all of loan loss reserves to shareholders' equity. The absence of these reserves would not introduce a major distortion in the relative changes of capital ratios for most banks, and in total they usually account for only 10 percent to 15 percent of shareholders' equity. There is a more fundamental reason why these reserves should not be added to shareholders' equity. Valuation reserves for loan losses represent an appraisal of a bank of an appropriate markdown in its loan portfolio on a long-term basis. The markdown purports to show a true value for collectable loans. Thus the addition of this reserve to shareholders' equity distorts the value for shareholders' equity.

Why have debentures, notes, and reserves that would not be available to

Table 42   Comparison of Capital Adequacy Measures
Chase Manhattan Bank and
Chase Manhattan Corporation

	1976
1. Shareholders' equity to total assets (consolidated corporation)	3.82%
2. Equity capital method—Federal Reserve (domestic bank only)	8.02%
3. Gross capital method—Federal Reserve (domestic and foreign bank only)	5.82%
4. Loans to gross capital multiple (domestic and foreign bank only)	11.5X (Equal to Reciprocal of 8.70%)
5. Capital to assets method—Comptroller (consolidated corporation)	5.13%
6. Total ratio method—Federal Deposit Insurance Corporation	4.92%

shareholders when they would need them been permitted to be added to shareholders' equity? More broadly, why have measures of capital adequacy become complicated when the basic issue of measurement is fundamentally simple? There are two possible answers.

Despite the lengthy analysis of research departments, which are usually well intentioned, regulatory agencies have probably responded to the practical requests of their constituency, largely consisting of banks. The financial officers of banks instinctively dislike low numbers for their capital positions and have persistently sought methods of measurement that show large numbers. The table showing a comparison of the various capital measures indicates that the number for the basic capital adequacy measure is substantially lower than the measures used by regulatory agencies. The equity capital measure of the Federal Reserve, which was 8.02 percent for Chase in 1975 appears to indicate a much better capital position than the ratio of shareholders' equity to total assets, which was 3.86 percent for that year. The stronger appearance of a larger number is often important to banks. Actually, both measures describe the same organization, but do so from different vantage points.

A second reason that the more inclusive measures of capital are used reflects the inability of many banks to raise new equity funds from capital markets. These markets have closed the door to a large number of marginally profitable banks. Yet many of these banks, in their own evaluation, believe that they are blameless and that the capital markets are at fault. They often defend their positions with explanations showing that inflation, weak price earnings multiples, and the low market value to book value of their stock is because of government policies and conditions beyond their control. They contend that they should not be penalized for capital conditions for which they are not responsible. They then request that they should be permitted to sell debt instruments and add reserves to their capital, at least until capital markets improve. The regulatory agencies have not been deaf to this logic.

Yet capital markets represent a court of largely impersonal judges. If times are difficult, and equity capital resources are limited, many banks would be expected to live within their own capital means or reduce their operations. The kindness of regulatory agencies to grant exemptions to that austerity or to look benignly to organizations that have not performed well on the basis of profitability may not be in the best long-term interests of banks, regulatory agencies, or the public. These mitigations may not have prompted banks in recent years to have tightened their operations as quickly and effectively as otherwise they might have. All of this is, of course, conjecture. But bank analysts who would wish to see capital adequacy in a more Spartan, and perhaps more accurate view, will look at the simple ratio of shareholders' equity to assets. In the long run, this measure will probably provide fewer surprises to shareholders, depositors, borrowers, and perhaps regulators.

PART THREE
THE IMPACT
OF ENVIRONMENT

CHAPTER 10

BANKING COMPARISONS

Comparisons provide a basis of determining rank and showing the relative importance among banks. More broadly, they also show how a bank fits into its competitive environment. By making comparisons, bank analysts are able to view a bank in light of its peers, and thereby give realistic perspective to the performance of a bank.

There are two broad cautions in using comparisons. Comparisons need to be appropriate. Many banks thrive under conditions in one locality that would be difficult barely one hundred miles distant. A second caution is that a bank might rank high comparatively, but in fact, could be weak. In this instance, other banks of a particular area or group might be weaker still, and the whole group could be in difficulty.

STRUCTURE OF U.S. BANKING

The structure of U.S. banking areas rests on three basic issues. The first issue reflects the belief that any reputable person should be allowed to open a bank, if he can obtain equity capital, depositors, and loan customers. The philosophy places special emphasis on an individual person or a small group of persons being able to start a bank. In major states, such as California, about $3 million in equity capital is required to start a bank, with the sum being smaller in many other states. This sum is not particularly large, in view of the capital required to open many businesses or franchises. Second, there is a belief that an abundance of banks represents a source of commercial energy to an area's economy. Most banks promote the development of business. They promote the expansion of their customers because their expansion provides the basis of the bank's own expansion. Finally, it is widely believed that a large number of banks promote a competitive attitude on the part of the banking industry, and competition helps keep bankers more alert and more humble to their customers. The latter point is probably more important to U.S. banking structure than most bankers realize. These issues are widely held, and as long as they are believed, there will be a large number of banks in the U.S.

In contrast, the European approach to banking concentrates on the close control of banks and looks to them as a vehicle to further the broad aims of a central government. This approach also stresses the efficiency of banking operations, which a greater control over the number and location of banking offices provides. It views the presence of a handful of major banks as sufficient competition to prevent monopoly practices, and as long as banking operations are closely monitored by the government, it sees little difficulty with banks being engaged in the business of corporate securities underwriting.

In practice, U.S. banking has been able to avoid the full impact of a highly fragmented banking structure through the use of correspondent banking. This is a practice where large banks seek deposits from small regional banks. There are many other arrangements among correspondent banks, including participations in loans, as well as special services and programs. The large wholesale banks in cities have tended to obtain loans more easily than deposits, while the country or regional banks have tended to obtain deposits more easily than loans. The correspondent arrangement enables both to share in a collective interest.

Yet there are limits to the benefits of correspondent banking. These shared arrangements are never without question of their value or permanence. Neither party is usually prepared to take steps that would involve major investments over a long period of time.

GUIDELINES FOR COMPARISONS

Comparisons may be used to point out relative differences and similarities between a bank and a group of other banks. Nevertheless, comparisons are no more appropriate than the group used to contrast a bank. The selection of this reference group thus becomes a matter of considerable importance, because it, as much as a bank under review, determines the conclusions of a comparison.

This observation underscores the issue of appropriateness. An appropriate comparison is one carefully selected to reflect a group with predominately similar characteristics as the bank being compared. The purpose of making comparisons is to determine how well a particular bank performs. If the basic characteristics of a group of banks is broadly similar, then a comparison between one member of this group and other members will show that performance.

The two widely used bases for comparisons are size of operations and geographic area. In addition, there are differences of structure among banks, and there are important variations among groups of banks within each of these measures. A bank analyst needs to choose the right degree of detail—the right appropriateness—for comparisons.

National Comparisons

The broadest comparison involves a bank and all U.S. banks. This comparison provides a reference group of more than 14,000 banks and includes banks with assets ranging from a few million dollars to tens of billions of dollars. Some banks reflect their agricultural environment, others a wealthy suburban environment, and others an industrial community. The wide variety of these banks provides a kind of a composite U.S. bank for a reference group.

There are occasions when it is appropriate to make comparisons of a bank with a broad cross section of U.S. banking. If a bank were proportioned in its activities to reflect the average of all U.S. banking, a comparison with the U.S. composite would be appropriate. Such a bank is rare. Nevertheless, it is sometimes useful to make comparisons with national averages even when a bank does not reflect the typical character of U.S. banking. These comparisons may be made because it is the broadest measure possible or because a bank is interested in learning of the changes it would need to make to bring its performance into line with the U.S. average.

Comparisons with Similar-Sized Banks

There are important differences among banks according to the size of their assets, deposits, or earnings. The most common measure is deposits, which are regarded as being a basic measure of presence of a bank.

Small- and large-sized banks tend to perform differently. Table 43 illustrates this point and divides 887 banks into six categories of deposit size. The table shows that large banks tend to earn considerably less on assets than small banks. Banks of $5 billion or more in deposits showed a return on assets of 0.50 percent while banks from $100 to $150 million in deposits showed a return of 0.80 percent in 1975. The large banks also showed significantly lower capital ratios, lower net interest margins on a tax equivalent basis, and more than twice the ratio of net charge-offs to total loans than the small banks. The table also indicates that, within broad limits, banks of somewhat similar size have common characteristics among themselves. These banks reflect similar types of customers and shareholders.

Comparisons with Banks in Similar Geographic Areas

Geography is another important consideration in making comparisons among banks (Table 44). The table shows three measures of performance of all banks in three major East Coast and three West Coast states in 1975. The first column shows a capital ratio (total capital divided by total assets) of 5.5 percent for California, 7.0 percent for Oregon, and 7.3 percent for Washington. These capital ratios were considerably lower than those of three East Coast states that showed 10.3 percent for New York, 9.4 percent for Connecticut, and 9.7

**Table 43 Peer Group Averages
Based on Deposits for 1975—U.S. Banks**

Peer Group	Earned on Assets	Equity Capital to Total Assets	Net Interest Margin —Tax Equivalent Basis	Net Charge-Offs to Total Loans
$5000 million and above (18 banks)	0.50%	4.22%	3.77%	−0.95%
$1000 to $5000 million (73 banks)	0.63	5.78	4.40	−0.61
$500 to $1000 million (96 banks)	0.75	6.51	4.66	−0.63
$250 to $500 million (175 banks)	0.69	6.70	4.73	−0.59
$150 to $250 million (212 banks)	0.76	6.91	4.75	−0.48
$100 to $150 million (313 banks)	0.80	6.95	4.67	−0.45

Source: Keefe Management Services, Inc.

**Table 44 Comparison of Three Measures of Performance of All Insured Commercial Banks
Three East Coast and Three West Coast States 1975**

State	Total Capital Accounts to Total Assets	Total Loans to Total Assets	Cash and Balances with Other Banks to Total Assets
West Coast States			
California	5.5%	56.4%	15.0%
Oregon	7.0	57.8	15.4
Washington	7.3	61.6	14.4
East Coast States			
New York	10.3%	57.2%	17.6%
Connecticut	9.4	56.9	17.0
Massachusetts	9.7	55.8	14.6

Source: Assets and Liabilities, Commercial and Mutual Savings Banks, FDIC, 1975.

percent for Massachusetts. Nevertheless, in many categories there were only minimal differences among the states. For example, the ratio of total loans to total assets for California, Oregon, New York, Connecticut, and Massachusetts ranged in a narrow band from 55.6 percent to 57.8 percent.

Table 45 shows the average size of deposits for each of the same six coastal states together with capital ratios. It illustrates the variety of contrasts and similarities among the states that cuts across regions. The average size of deposits for banks in Massachusetts, Connecticut, and Washington were almost similar, ranging from $103.0 million to $106.3 million. Nevertheless, capital ratios for banks in the two East Coast states—9.7 percent for Massachusetts and 9.4 percent for Connecticut—were considerably higher than the capital ratio of 7.3 percent for Washington. In another comparison illustrating the same point, the average size of deposits among banks in California and New York were not too different, yet the average capital ratio for New York banks was nearly double that of California banks.

SOURCES OF INFORMATION FOR DOMESTIC COMPARISONS

The primary sources of information for data used in making comparisons of banks are the Federal Reserve Board, the Comptroller of the Currency, and the Federal Deposit Insurance Corporation. In most instances, the three

Table 45   Comparison of Average Size of Deposits with Capital Ratios of All Insured Commercial Banks Three East Coast and Three West Coast States 1975

State	Average Size of Deposits (Millions)	Total Capital Accounts to Total Assets
Massachusetts (145 banks)	$103.0	9.7%
Connecticut (71 banks)	104.1	9.4
Washington (91 banks)	106.3	7.3
Oregon (45 banks)	133.7	7.0
California (200 banks)	426.6	5.5
New York (267 banks)	473.5	10.3

Source: Assets and Liabilities, Commercial and Mutual Savings Banks, FDIC, 1975.

government agencies represent the only practical sources of this information, since there is considerable difficulty in separately obtaining hundreds or thousands of financial reports for individual banks and totaling the information into various groups.

Primary Sources

Annual Report of the Federal Reserve Board. The *Annual Report of the Federal Reserve Board* provides tables showing composite balance sheets of all U.S. banks. The report is usually available in July of the year following the year of the annual report. It may be obtained from the Board of Governors, Federal Reserve System, Washington, D.C. 20551, telephone 202–452–3000.

Bulletin of the Federal Reserve Board. The monthly *Bulletin of the Federal Reserve Board* shows the principal assets and liabilities of all banks and member banks of the Federal Reserve System, a detailed balance sheet of banks according to major cities on a quarterly basis, a balance sheet of large commercial banks on a weekly basis, various industry categories of loans on a monthly and a weekly basis, as well as various categories of deposits on a monthly and a quarterly basis. There is also a table showing assets and liabilities of foreign branches of U.S. banks on a monthly basis. The bulletin is distributed from the Board of Governors, Federal Reserve System, Washington, D.C. 20551, and is usually available within the week following the month of report, telephone 202–452–3000.

Operating Ratios of Member Banks in Federal Reserve Districts. This report shows annual averages of approximately sixty ratios for a majority of banks in each of the twelve Federal Reserve districts. In addition, there are separate classifications for each of the principal states, as well as subclassifications of ratios according to deposit size in some states and groups of states. The ratios include profitability measures, the return on securities and loans, a distribution of assets, as well as capital ratios and loan to deposit ratios.

The report for each of the twelve Federal Reserve districts is available from each of the district banks. A list of these banks, with their addresses, is shown in the *Annual Report of the Federal Reserve Board of Governors.* The report for most districts is usually available within four months following the end of the year on which the information is based.

Functional Cost Analysis—Federal Reserve Board. This report shows average earnings and assets for the major activities or functions of banks. For example, one function is checking accounts, and the tables show average sources of income, expenses, and earnings for this function, as well as other information. Each of the functional centers is consolidated, and average income and assets are shown. All information is shown for various classifications of deposit size for the banks.

This information should be used with care, since the data are based on assumptions, often inappropriate for a particular bank. For example, indirect overhead is allocated on the basis of "experience factors" of expense data, and this report uses a "pool of funds" concept in which the same portfolio yield is used in calculating income for each source of funds, and the same "cost of money" is charged to the functions that use funds. These assumptions can lead to erroneous conclusions. Differences in indirect allocations can be a major factor in explaining the differences in the overall performance among banks, and differences in cost of funds among units of a bank have a major impact on each unit's profits. There are other practical problems with the use of this information, including bias from a small sample size.

The report may be obtained from the Federal Reserve Board of Governors, Washington, D.C. 20551, telephone 202–452–3000. It is usually available seven months following the end of the year on which the data are based.

Annual Report of the Comptroller of the Currency. This report provides extensive annual data concerning applications for new banks, bank mergers, and the opening and closing of branches. It also shows the principal assets, liabilities, and capital of national banks in each state, categories of loans by state, outstanding balances of credit cards, direct lease financing totals, as well as detailed tables showing income and expenses of national banks by state and by deposit size. There are also tables showing composite data of foreign activities of national banks.

The report may be obtained from the Comptroller of the Currency, Administration of National Banks, Washington, D.C. 20219, telephone 202–566–2000. It is usually available only after considerable delay, usually five quarters following the eeven months fond of the year on which the data are based.

The National Bank Surveillance System. This program represents an effort to provide basic information on all banks and provides comparisons of key ratios with national peer groups. Now in its early stages of development, certain parts of the program are expected to be available to the public. Information may be obtained from the Comptroller of the Currency, Administration of National Banks, Washington D.C., telephone 202–566–2000.

Assets and Liabilities, Commercial and Mutual Savings Banks. This is a joint report among the Federal Reserve Board of Governors, the Comptroller of the Currency, and the Federal Deposit Insurance Corporation. It provides a composite of all year-end reports of condition (call reports) and reports of income data. The information is shown for banks according to states and to ten sizes of deposits. Banks are shown according to several categories, including all commercial banks, all insured banks that are members of the Federal Reserve System, national banks, and other categories.

The report is distributed by the Federal Deposit Insurance Corporation, 550 17th Street, N.W., Washington D.C. 20429, telephone 202–393–8400. It is usually available within nine months following the end of the year on which data are based.

Bank Operating Statistics. This report of the Federal Deposit Insurance Corporation shows balance sheet and income information for insured commercial banks (a category not shown in the previously mentioned publication). The data are from the year-end report of condition and report of income. The information is shown for banks in various size categories. Information for each state is shown according to geographic regions and in states that restrict statewide branch banking, the data are grouped according to counties.

The report may be obtained from the Federal Deposit Insurance Corporation, 550 17th Street, N.W., Washington, D.C. 20429, telephone 202–393–8400. It is usually available within eight months following the end of the year of the data.

Annual Report of the Federal Deposit Insurance Corporation. This report shows much of the same information shown in the reports titled "Bank Operating Statistics" and "Assets and Liabilities, Commercial and Mutual Savings Banks." The report may be obtained from the Federal Deposit Insurance Corporation, 550 17th Street, N.W., Washington, D.C. 20429, telephone 202–393–8400. It is available approximately one year following the year of the data.

Special Reports in Federal Reserve Bulletins and Economic Reviews. Sometimes the economics staff of the Board of Governors or one of the 12 regional banks issues a report on a special topic that provides additional data. For example, the November/December issue of the *Economic Review of the Federal Reserve Bank of Richmond* prepared a report titled "Performance Characteristics of High-Earning Minority Banks." This article provides considerable data concerning the income and balance sheets and a financial explanation of the reasons for success (or lack of it) in minority banks.

Secondary Sources

Most of the secondary sources noted in Chapter 2, which describes sources of information, also provide aggregates and totals. These aggregates and totals provide an important and convenient method of making comparisons among banks.

Keefe Bruyette & Woods, Inc. This organization specializes in trading bank securities and providing other special services for securities customers. The firm produces a weekly index of bank stock prices composed of price trends for 24 major banks. In addition, Keefe Bruyette & Woods prepares special studies that provide composite information on an occasional basis. These studies cover such topics as capital adequacy and loan losses. The home office is located at One Liberty Plaza, New York, New York 10006, telephone 212–349–4321.

Keefe Management Services, Inc. This group is a subsidiary of Keefe Bruyette & Woods, Inc., and specializes in supplying data concerning banks throughout the U.S. The data cover basic income statement and balance sheet information for all insured U.S. banks. As part of this service, the firm also prepares aggregates according to size and region. These aggregates provide the broadest coverage of any service and are based on reports of condition, reports of income, as well as special reports from the banks for international information. The group is located at One Liberty Plaza, New York, New York 10006, telephone 212–349–4321.

M. A. Shapiro & Co., Inc. This firm also specializes in the brokerage of bank securities and provides a quarterly report, which shows aggregate financial information for investors for 25 major banks, including such data as earnings, price earnings multiples, and dividends. The firm is located at One Chase Manhattan Plaza, New York, New York 10005, telephone 212–425–6600.

Sheshunoff & Co., Inc. This firm provides rankings of key measures of performance for approximately all U.S. commercial banks. The rankings provide basic averages of ratios and percentage changes, as well as other aggregate data. The rankings are shown in percentiles and are shown according to city and state, as well as size groups. The firm's address is P. O. Box 13203, Capitol Station, Austin, Texas 78711, telephone 512–444–7722.

Cates, Lyons & Co., Inc. This organization shows income statement and balance sheet information, as well as key ratios according to year-to-year changes. These changes are ranked according to deciles, which serve as the basis of making comparisons. The coverage includes the principal banks in the United States. The firm is located at 20 Exchange Place, New York, New York 10005, telephone 212–269–8785.

Standard and Poor's, Inc. This is primarily a securities information firm, and it provides selected aggregates for a sample of 16 banks. These aggregates include a price index, price earnings multiples, yields, and dividends. Data are available on a quarterly and an annual basis and are shown in a booklet titled "Analysts Handbook Supplement." The firm is located at 345 Hudson Street, New York, New York 10014, telephone 212–924–6400.

Bank Administration Institute. This is a nonprofit organization that provides an index of bank performance to its members, which mainly include banks. This report uses the Federal Deposit Insurance Corporation report of income and report of condition as its data source. Key ratios and year-to-year changes in operating measures are shown according to upper and lower deciles, upper and lower quartiles, and the median for banks according to the size of assets. Rankings of banks are also shown for each state. The organization is located at 303 South Northwest Highway, Park Ridge, Illinois 60068, telephone 312–693–7300.

The Robinson Humphrey Co., Inc. This brokerage firm ranks major banks according to key ratios and other measures of performance. Averages, deciles, and other statistical measures are also shown. There are also composites for 50 major banks, as well as a money center composite and a regional bank composite. The firm is located at Two Peachtree Street N.W., Atlanta, Georgia 30303, telephone 404–581–7176.

SAMPLE DOMESTIC COMPARISONS

To show various types of comparisons that may be made with some of the data from the forementioned sources, several examples of comparisons are shown here. Tables 46–48 show comparisons of the Exchange Bank, the San Diego Trust & Savings Bank, and United California Bank. These three banks are shown here to represent typical small-, medium-, and large-sized banks. Each is located in California.

Deposit Market Share

Three measures of market share are shown for each bank. The first measure shows each bank's market share of deposits compared with banks of similar size in California. The second measure compares the deposits of each bank with total deposits of California banks. The third measure compares the deposits of each bank with all U.S. banks having deposits over $100 million.

In the first example (Table 46), from 1974 to 1975 the Exchange Bank showed a major gain in market share among its peer group of banks and had small gains among its market share among all banks in California and for U.S. banks. The table illustrates the importance of reviewing carefully the market used for comparison. The major gain in market share in the California peer group principally reflected a decline in the deposits in this group from 1974 to 1975. Nevertheless, the gain in deposits for the bank was greater than the gain in deposits for California or for U.S. banks. The overall conclusion would be that

Table 46   Exchange Bank
Deposit Market Share ($ Thousands)

	December 31, 1974	December 31, 1975
California peer group—banks with deposits of $100–$150 million		
Exchange Bank—total deposits	$ 114,465	$ 127,003
California peer group—total deposits	1,986,435	1,747,068
Market share	5.76%	7.27%
California		
Exchange Bank—total deposits	$ 114,465	$ 127,003
California—total deposits	107,911,796	114,063,530
Market share	0.106%	0.111%
U.S.—All banks with deposits over $100 million		
Exchange Bank—total deposits	$ 114,465	$ 127,003
U.S.—total deposits	628,539,393	658,679,363
Market share	0.0182%	0.0193%

Source: Keefe Management Services, Inc.

**Table 47   San Diego Trust & Savings Bank
Deposit Market Share ($ Thousands)**

	December 31, 1974	December 31, 1975
California peer group—banks with deposits of $250–$500 million		
San Diego Trust & Savings Bank—total deposits	$ 276,432	$ 324,153
California peer group—total deposits	1,294,716	1,974,560
Market share	21.4%	16.4%
California		
San Diego Trust & Savings Bank—total deposits	$ 276,432	$ 324,153
California—total deposits	107,911,796	114,063,530
Market share	0.256%	0.284%
U.S.—all banks with deposits over $100 million		
San Diego Trust & Savings Bank	$ 276,432	$ 324,153
U.S.—total deposits	628,539,393	658,679,363
Market share	0.0440%	0.0492%

Source: Keefe Management Services, Inc.

this bank's gain in deposits was generally above average, and that it fared particularly well among banks of its size in California.

Table 47 shows the same groups of market share for the San Diego Trust & Savings Bank. According to this table, the bank's market share of deposits shrank among its California peer group and gained in market share in California and in the United States. The overall conclusion would be that this bank's increase in deposits was above average, but that it faced particularly severe competition among banks of its size in California.

For United California Bank, Table 48 shows that this bank's market share declined in all three categories. The decline in market share reflected the divergent trends of a decline in the bank's deposits, while deposits of the various markets in which the bank participates rose.

Performance Measures

Exchange Bank.   Based on data from the Bank Administration Institute, Tables 49 and 50 show selected comparisons of performance. Table 49 shows five selected measures of performance of the Exchange Bank compared with its California peer group of 32 banks with assets from $100 to $499 million in 1975. These five measures comprise only a small part of the complete information available from this source. The table indicates the value for the lowest decile, lower quartile, median, upper quartile, and upper decile. The values for the Exchange Bank are in italics. The bank was at the median point in the gain in

**Table 48   United California Bank
Deposit Market Share ($ Thousands)**

	December 31, 1974	December 31, 1975
California peer group—banks with deposits over $5 billion		
United California Bank—total deposits	$ 7,752,789	$ 7,288,021
California peer group—total deposits	90,280,301	95,400,185
Market share	8.59%	7.64%
California		
United California Bank—total deposits	$ 7,752,789	$ 7,288,021
California—total deposits	107,911,796	114,063,530
Market share	7.18%	6.39%
U.S.—all banks with deposits over $100 million		
United California Bank—total deposits	$ 7,752,789	$ 7,288,021
U.S.—total deposits	628,539,393	658,679,363
Market share	1.23%	1.11%

Source: Keefe Management Services, Inc.

income before securities transactions from 1974 to 1975. Return on assets ranked between the upper quartile and upper decile, indicating considerable strength in this key measure. The equity to assets ratio showed that the bank ranked a bit below the median, and the yield on loans and personnel expense as a percent of total operating income were above the median.

Then next, Table 50 shows a comparison of the Exchange Bank with its peer group of 824 banks in the U.S. The peer group position of the Exchange Bank in the United States was different in almost each instance from its position in the California peer group. The relative position of its return on assets and equity to assets dropped a notch in this second comparison, while the position on yield on loans and personnel expense as a percent of total operation income advanced.

The next two tables show another way of presenting performance ratios. Keefe Management Services show three comparisons within different peer groups. The California peer group shows 14 banks with deposits from $100 million to $150 million. In Table 51 the value for the return on assets of the Exchange Bank for the years from 1972 to 1975 are indicated, along with the median value for the California peer group. The difference indicates that the Exchange Bank has consistently shown a higher return on assets than its California peers. The next category of comparison shows that the Exchange Bank has a lower ratio of equity capital to total assets than its California peers, although the gap has narrowed in recent years. The final measure shown in the table indicates that the net interest margin on a tax equivalent basis of the Exchange Bank has been above the median of its peer group and that this advantage has widened in recent years.

Table 49 Exchange Bank
Comparison of Performance—California Peer Group of 32 Banks—Exchange Bank Shown As Percent in
Italics Peer Group Data for 1975—Exchange Bank for June 30, 1976

	Lower Tenth Percentile	Lower Quartile	Median	Upper Quartile	Upper Tenth
One year growth in income before securities transactions	−87.68%	−13.55%	10.96%	20.95%	999.99%
			10.96%		
Return on assets	0.09	0.30	0.60	0.85	1.03
				0.97%	
Equity to assets	4.06	4.68	5.85	7.60	9.23
		5.56%			
Yield on loans	8.49	9.18	9.48	10.01	10.26
			9.82%		
Personnel expense as a percent of total operating income	13.64	21.16	25.75	27.68	28.79
			25.90%		

Source: Bank Administration Institute.

Table 50   Exchange Bank

Comparison of Performance—U.S. Peer Group of 824 Banks—Exchange Bank Shown as Percent in Italics Peer Group Data for 1975—Exchange Bank for June 30, 1976

	Lower Tenth Percentile	Lower Quartile	Median	Upper Quartile	Upper Tenth
One year growth in income before securities transactions	−34.49%	−10.59%	6.00%	19.43%	37.71%
			10.96%		
Return on assets	0.32	0.59	0.81	0.99	1.18
			0.97		
Equity to assets	4.99	5.80	6.81	7.87	8.97
	5.56%				
Yield on loans	8.06	8.44	8.89	9.37	9.97
				9.82%	
Personnel expense as a percent of total operating income	14.31	16.39	19.27	22.73	26.25
				25.90	

Source: Bank Administration Institute.

Table 51   Exchange Bank
Comparison of Performance Ratios—California Peer Group
of 14 Banks $100–$150 Million in Deposits

	1972	1973	1974	1975
Return on total assets				
Exchange Bank	1.02%	0.97%	0.95%	0.98%
California peer group	0.61	0.64	0.26	0.79
Difference	+0.41	+0.33	+0.69	+0.19
Equity capital and reserves to total assets				
Exchange Bank	5.29%	5.21%	5.32%	5.59%
California peer group	6.61	6.41	6.21	6.02
Difference	−1.32	−1.20	−0.89	−0.43
Net interest margin on a tax equivalent basis				
Exchange Bank	5.39%	5.38%	5.61%	5.59%
California peer group	4.73	4.73	3.49	3.47
Difference	+0.66	+0.65	+2.12	+2.12

Source: Keefe Management Services.

Next, Table 52 compares the same three measures of performance with a peer group of 313 banks in the United States showing $100 million to $150 million in deposits. The comparison indicates that the Exchange Bank has a higher return on assets than U.S. banks in its size category. The table shows that the Exchange Bank has a much lower ratio of equity capital and reserves to total assets and also shows a higher net interest margin on a tax equivalent basis than banks in this peer group.

San Diego Trust & Savings Bank.   Tables 53 and 54 show a comparison of performance measures for the San Diego Trust & Savings Bank. Table 53 shows comparisons with the California peer group, and Table 54 shows comparisons with the U.S. peer group. The tables show important similarities between the peer groups. The bank's return on total assets rose from 1972 to 1975, while that of the U.S. peer group declined. The bank's comparative position with this measure rose and ended the period significantly above the average for the peer group. The bank's ratio of equity capital and reserves to total assets showed similar trends when measured against the California and U.S. peer groups, and in both instances, the shortfall in the bank's ratio diminished from 1972 to 1975. The bank's net interest margin on a tax equivalent basis rose more rapidly than did the margin for either peer group, and the bank's comparative advantage of this margin increased from 1972 to 1975.

United California Bank.   Tables 55 and 56 show comparisons of measures of this bank's performance based on its California and U.S. peer group. The

Table 52 Exchange Bank
Comparison of Performance Ratios—U.S. Peer Group of 313
Banks $100–$150 Million in Deposits

	1972	1973	1974	1975
Return on total assets				
Exchange Bank	1.02%	0.97%	0.95%	0.98%
U.S. peer group	0.83	0.88	0.82	0.80
Difference	+0.19	+0.09	+0.13	+0.18
Equity capital and reserves to total assets				
Exchange Bank	5.29%	5.21%	5.32%	5.59%
U.S. peer group	8.07	8.04	8.14	8.17
Difference	−2.78	−2.83	−2.82	−2.58
Net interest margin on a tax equivalent basis				
Exchange Bank	5.39%	5.38%	5.61%	5.59%
U.S. peer group	4.39	4.47	4.60	4.67
Difference	+1.00	+0.91	+1.01	+0.92

Source: Keefe Management Services, Inc.

Table 53 San Diego Trust & Savings Bank
Comparison of Performance Ratios—
California Peer Group of Banks $250–$500 Million in Deposits

	1972	1973	1974	1975
Return on total assets				
San Diego Trust & Savings Bank	0.53%	0.76%	0.89%	0.90%
California peer group	0.57	0.57	0.38	0.57
Difference	−0.04	+0.19	+0.51	+0.33
Equity capital and reserves to total assets				
San Diego Trust & Savings Bank	5.06%	5.08%	5.17%	5.32%
California peer group	6.24	5.96	5.81	5.93
Difference	−1.18	−0.88	−0.64	−0.61
Net interest margin on a tax equivalent basis				
San Diego Trust & Savings Bank	4.85%	5.25%	5.90%	6.14%
California peer group	4.59	4.50	3.97	5.02
Difference	+0.26	+0.75	+1.93	+1.12

Source: Keefe Management Services, Inc.

Table 54   San Diego Trust & Savings Bank
Comparison of Performance Ratios—U.S.
Peer Group of 175 Banks $250–$500 Million in Deposits

	1972	1973	1974	1975
Return on total assets				
San Diego Trust & Savings Bank	0.53%	0.76%	0.89%	0.90%
U.S. peer group	0.83	0.83	0.79	0.69
Difference	−0.30	−0.07	+0.10	+0.21
Equity capital and reserves to total assets				
San Diego Trust & Savings Bank	5.06%	5.08%	5.17%	5.32%
U.S. peer group	6.64	6.50	6.57	6.70
Difference	−1.58	−1.42	−1.40	−1.38
Net interest margin on a tax equivalent basis				
San Diego Trust & Savings Bank	4.85%	5.25%	5.90%	6.14%
U.S. peer group	4.40	4.44	4.61	4.73
Difference	+0.45	+0.81	+1.29	+1.41

Source: Keefe Management Services, Inc.

Table 55   United California Bank
Comparison of Performance Ratios—California Peer
Group of 5 Banks Over $5 Billion in Deposits

	1972	1973	1974	1975
Return on total assets				
United California Bank	0.49%	0.39%	0.37%	0.29%
California peer group	0.48	0.42	0.39	0.40
Difference	+0.01	−0.03	−0.02	−0.11
Equity capital and reserves to total assets				
United California Bank	4.55%	4.16%	3.67%	3.79%
California peer group	4.25	3.92	3.52	3.67
Difference	+0.30	+0.24	+0.15	+0.12
Net interest margin on a tax equivalent basis				
United California Bank	4.43%	4.08%	4.30%	4.53%
California peer group	3.77	3.48	3.62	3.91
Difference	+0.66	+0.60	+0.68	+0.62

Source: Keefe Management Services, Inc.

Table 56   United California Bank
Comparison of Performance Ratios—U.S. Peer
Group of 18 Banks Over $5 Billion in Deposits

	1972	1973	1974	1975
Return on total assets				
United California Bank	0.49%	0.39%	0.37%	0.29%
U.S. peer group	0.56	0.53	0.51	0.50
Difference	−0.07	−0.14	−0.14	−0.21
Equity capital and reserves to total assets				
United California Bank	4.55%	4.16%	3.67%	3.79%
U.S. peer group	5.13	4.54	4.05	4.22
Difference	−0.58	−0.38	−0.38	−0.43
Net interest margin on tax equivalent basis				
United California Bank	4.43%	4.08%	4.30%	4.53%
U.S. peer group	3.64	3.40	3.53	3.77
Difference	+0.79	+0.68	+0.77	+0.76

Source: Keefe Management Services, Inc.

California peer group includes only five banks, while the U.S. peer group includes eighteen banks. The small number of banks in the California peer group would indicate that these comparisons would have less validity. Nevertheless, the two comparisons indicate similar trends. The bank's return on total assets declined more rapidly than either of the peer groups, and the bank's comparative position declined from 1972 to 1975. The bank's comparative strength in its net interest margin held fairly steady in the interval on the basis of both comparisons.

However, there was an important difference in direction in the ratio of equity capital and reserves to total assets. United California Bank's ratio declined more rapidly than the ratio for the California peer group, but the bank's ratio dropped less rapidly than the ratio for the U.S. peer group. Thus United California's equity ratio position weakened when viewed from a California base, but improved on a U.S. basis.

Measures of Market Share

San Diego Trust and Savings Bank.   Table 57 shows selected measures of the California market share of the San Diego Trust and Savings Bank. Seven categories of real estate loans, loans to farmers, and four other selected components of loans are shown. Total loans are also indicated to provide a measure of overall market position.

The table shows a wide variation of market penetration among the various categories. The bank had no position in loans for multi-family residential property insured by FHA, had a small share of loans to farmland, yet had better-than-average positions in multi-family residential property not insured by FHA and one-to-four family residential property guaranteed by the Veterans Administration. Moreover, the bank showed an exceptionally strong market share in individual installment loans to repair and modernize residential property and individual installment loans for autos. These observations are based on the comparison of market share of loans in each category with the market share for total loans. For example, on December 31, 1975, the bank's modernization loans for residential property showed a market share of 2.60 percent of loans of this type in the state of California. This market share was seven times larger than the market share for all loans of the bank, indicating the strong emphasis that the bank placed on this type of lending activity. In contrast, commercial and industrial loans accounted for 0.19 percent at year-end 1975, well below the bank's total loan average of 0.37 percent. This

Table 57 San Diego Trust & Savings Bank
Selected Measures of Market Share of
Loans and Deposits (Compared with All California Banks)

Loans	December 31, 1974	June 30, 1975	December 31, 1975
Real estate Secured by farmland	0.07%	0.07%	0.08%
Secured by 1–4 family residential property, insured FHA	0.32	0.33	0.30
Secured by 1–4 family residential property, guaranteed by VA	0.52	0.49	0.50
Secured by 1–4 family residential property, not insured or guaranteed by FHA/VA	0.35	0.36	0.35
Secured by multi-family residential property, insured FHA	0	0	0
Secured by multi-family residential property, not insured FHA	0.42	0.46	0.54
Secured by nonfarm, nonresidential property	0.55	0.55	0.49
Loans to farmers	0	0	0
Commercial and industrial loans	0.16	0.17	0.19
Loans to individuals—check credit and revolving credit plans	0	0	0
Loans to individuals—installment loans repair/modernize residential property	2.83	2.74	2.60
Loans to individuals—purchase of private autos on installment plan	1.00	0.99	1.04
Total loans	0.35	0.36	0.37
Total time and savings deposits	0.28	0.33	0.31

Source: Keefe Management Services, Inc.

comparison indicates that the bank did not place major emphasis in lending to corporate customers.

These comparisons of major types of loans and deposits provide a useful indication of the marketing and management direction of the San Diego Trust and Savings Bank. Although the table is abbreviated, it indicates a strong emphasis in consumer borrowing and a selection of those consumer markets it prefers to emphasize. The ratios were comparatively steady over the 1974 to 1975 period, giving an indication that the lending policies of the bank remained steady.

United California Bank. Table 58 shows the market share for the same types of loans for United California Bank. The table shows a different position of emphasis in lending activities. At year-end 1975, this bank showed a 42.08 percent market penetration in loans secured by multi-family residential

**Table 58   United California Bank
Selected Measures of Market Share of Loans and
Deposits (Compared with All California Banks)**

Loans	December 31, 1974	June 30, 1975	December 31, 1975
Real estate Secured by farmland	1.82%	1.51%	1.37%
Secured by 1–4 family residential property, insured FHA	0.69	0.94	0.97
Secured by 1–4 family residential property, guaranteed by VA	2.28	2.62	2.86
Secured by 1–4 family residential property, not insured or guaranteed by FHA/VA	6.59	5.79	5.35
Secured by multi-family residential property, insured FHA	40.83	15.08	42.08
Secured by multi-family residential property, not insured FHA	18.55	20.67	20.66
Secured by nonfarm, nonresidential property	11.90	12.58	11.52
Loans to farmers	5.32	4.53	4.69
Commercial and industrial loans	8.00	6.99	7.30
Loans to individuals—check credit and revolving credit plans	53.46	54.58	49.82
Loans to individuals—installment loans repair modernize residential property	7.49	6.27	5.07
Loans to individuals—purchase of private autos on installment plan	3.44	3.66	3.25
Total loans	8.16	7.67	7.64
Total time and savings deposits	6.29	5.58	5.68

Source: Keefe Management Services, Inc.

property, insured by the Federal Housing Authority. This ratio was more than five times larger than the 7.64 percent market penetration in California of the bank's total loans. Loans to individuals through check credit and revolving credit plans accounted for more than six times its market penetration of total loans. In contrast, loans for one-to-four family residential property, insured by the Federal Housing Authority, were a small fraction of the market share of the bank's total loans.

A review of the market share penetrations of each bank shows its own particular pattern. United California Bank, for example, gave greater emphasis to loans to commercial and industrial organizations than did the San Diego Trust and Savings Bank. Although both banks were interested in consumer lending, there were differences in areas of special emphasis. United California Bank gave relatively little concern to auto loans, in contrast to the considerable interest in these loans by the San Diego Trust and Savings Bank.

INTERNATIONAL COMPARISONS

There are approximately 160 banks in the United States that have significant overseas banking operations. These banks are among the nation's largest, and their relatively small number belies their importance. They provide the basis for major loans to the largest corporations and governments and act as headquarters banks for the network of U.S. correspondent banking.

There are two major markets for international banking. The first is the market for loans to overseas corporations and governments. These major borrowers are able to attract the interest of international banks through their public reputation, large size, and proven ability to earn profits or generate tax revenues. The large international corporations include such companies as General Motors, American Standard, and Royal Dutch Shell. The large governments and agencies include such examples as the Kingdom of Norway and the British Steel Corporation. Loans and deposits to these customers are usually denominated in U.S. dollars, indicating that changes in currency exchange rates are a principal concern to customers. Most people usually think of this market when they think of international banking.

A second market for U.S. international banking includes all the indigenous banking services of a U.S. bank in a host country. This market includes all loans and deposits of such customers as small shopkeepers, individuals, businessmen, and corporations that are denominated in the local currency. These customers usually, but not always, do not have international prominence.

The two periods of major expansion in U.S. international banking were from 1900 to 1914 and from 1955 to the present. Both expansions were supported by the successful efforts of many major U.S. corporations to expand their operations to a worldwide scope. The earlier expansion reflected the development of tropical agricultural products in the Caribbean and South American areas. Sugar, rum, cigars, bananas, and rubber formed the basis of that banking expansion. Most of the banks that participated in this earlier phase are located in New York and Boston.

The second phase of expansion in international banking reflected the overseas growth of U.S. manufacturing and fuel producing corporations following the Second World War. The expansion of U.S. banks filled a financing vacuum left by the Second World War in Europe and the waning British colonial and mercantile trade in the rest of the world. The banks that participated in this development were principally located in New York, Chicago, and San Francisco.

Overseas operations have been important to banks because they have represented an important source of earnings growth. The international operations have also been important because they have permitted U.S. banks to circumvent some of the rigor of U.S. banking regulation. In fact, many of the major U.S. banks would show a reduction from one-half to one-third in the size of their earnings if their international banking services were not in operation.

Sources of Information

Despite the importance of international banking, there is little information concerning international banking activities that is useful in making comparisons. The international operations of banks have not regularly reported much information to the public. In fact, relatively little information has been collected and organized in a manner that makes comparisons possible, especially comparisons involving policies of banks.

Fortune Magazine. Each year the August issue of *Fortune* magazine surveys the 50 major commercial banks outside the United States for the previous year-end. This review follows the regular survey in July of the 50 major domestic banks. The survey of the banks shows the basic financial measures of assets, earnings, loans, and shareholders' equity. Data are shown in U.S. dollar equivalents. The editorial offices are located at Time and Life Building, New York, New York 10020, telephone 212–JU6–1212.

American Banker. Each year the *American Banker* magazine prepares a list of the 500 largest banks in the world. The ranking shows deposits in U.S. dollar or dollar equivalents for the previous year-end. Exchange rates—and deposits in indigenous currency—are shown if the bank is located outside the United States. The magazine's address is 525 W. 42 Street, New York, New York 10036, telephone 212–563–1900.

"World Financial Markets." This monthly report from Morgan Guaranty Trust Company presents a wide variety of international financial information, including monthly estimates of Eurocurrency bank deposits and loans. The report uses benchmark data based in large part on information from the Bank for International Settlements, the World Bank, and the Bank of England and adds market information from its own sources to prepare monthly estimates. The timeliness of the report gives it special value. The report is available from the Morgan Guaranty Trust Company of New York, 23 Wall Street, New York, New York 10015, telephone 212–483–2323.

World Bank. The World Bank prepares annual and quarterly estimates of Eurodollar borrowings. These estimates show new borrowings, but do not show totals. The estimates are based on the World Bank's various sources of information, including the financial press in various areas of the world and its association with financial and other institutions.

There is no legal requirement to report Eurocurrency loans. In fact, there could be reasons why certain borrowers or lenders would not want to publicize a transaction or its terms, and any estimates should be viewed in light of the difficulty in preparing the totals. The World Bank is located at 1818 H Street N.W., Washington, D.C., telephone 202–393–6360.

Sample Comparisons

One of the most frustrating aspects of observing banking developments is the inability to use the fragmentary information that is available. The data are, in most instances, not comparable. As a consequence, bank analysts must grope in the dark, and in the absence of information, rely on their own judgment to provide missing pieces.

For example, the information on Eurodollar deposits (available from the Bank for International Settlements) provides little help in making comparisons of market share with Eurodollar deposits of U.S. banks because the banks usually do not separate Eurodollar deposits from indigenous deposits. A bank analyst can do little more than guess concerning the proportion of Eurodollar to indigenous deposits. In another instance, information concerning international lending from the World Bank shows only the flow of loans (Table 59).

Table 59 Borrowing in International Capital Markets by Category of Country, 1973–75 (New Borrowings for Each Year, U. S. $ Millions or Equivalent)

	Publicized Eurocurrency Credits		
	1973	1974	1975
Industrial countries	11,671.7	17,243.2	5,090.2
Developing countries	8,296.9	9,741.5	12,429.1
Oil exporters	2,797.6	789.0	3,207.9
Others	5,499.3	8,952.5	9,221.2
Higher income	4,550.4	7,041.0	7,860.5
Middle income	702.7	1,620.2	1,289.4
Lower income	246.2	291.3	71.3
Socialist countries and organizations	735.5	1,116.9	2,692.4
International organizations	—	14.0	65.0
Development institutions	—	14.0	65.0
Others	—	—	—
Borrowers unallocated by country	159.5	416.8	298.5
Total	20,863.6	28,532.4	20,575.2

Source: Borrowing in International Capital Markets, World Bank.

This information provides little help in viewing the outstanding loans to the areas, and it is the volume of outstanding loans that is the key to understanding risks of exposure and market position. Nevertheless, Morgan Guaranty Bank made the attempt, in a limited way, to show this information for OPEC, Communist, and less developed countries (LDCs) in the December 1976 issue of "World Financial Markets." The information could provide the basis of more complete estimates.

No figures exist for international comparisons that can provide information about market share which are similar to the figures that are available domestically. To obtain these figures, all international banks would be required to report basic information in a common manner. This type of reporting would provide an international version of a call report and an international version of a report on income. Although the Bank for International Settlements and other organizations are actively promoting such a reporting procedure, banks are reluctant to support the effort. Banks are concerned that the additional information could bring greater regulation, and additional regulation could bring less flexibility to service customers and would likely lower profits.

The table shows the information concerning foreign loans that recently has been available from two major banks. The classifications are from the World Bank and are based on each country's annual per capita income. The high income LDC category included countries with annual per capita income between $375 and $700. Middle LDC countries had per capita income between $200 and $375, and low-income LDC countries had per capita income under $200.

The following countries are included in the principal nonindustrialized categories.

Oil Exporting Countries. Algeria, Ecuador, Gabon, Indonesia, Iran, Iraq, Nigeria, and Venezuela.

Higher-Income Countries. Argentina, Brazil, Chile, Republic of China, Colombia, Costa Rica, Cyprus, Dominican Republic, Fiji, Greece, Guatemala, Guyana, Israel, Jamaica, Malaysia, Malta, Mexico, Nicaragua, Panama, Peru, Portugal, Singapore, Spain, Trinidad and Tobago, Tunisia, Turkey, Uruguay, Yugoslavia, and Zambia.

Middle-Income Countries. Bolivia, Botswana, Cameroon, Congo, Egypt, El Salvador, Ghana, Honduras, Ivory Coast, Jordan, Korea, Liberia, Maritius, Morocco, Paraguay, Philippines, Senegal, Swaziland, Syria, and Thailand.

Lower-Income Countries. Afghanistan, Bangladesh, Burma, Burundi, Central African Republic, Chad, Dahomey, Ethiopia, Gambia, India, Kenya, Lesotho, Malagasy, Malawi, Mali, Mauritania, Niger, Pakistan, Rwanda, Sierra Leone, Somalia, Sri Lanka, Sudan, Tanzania, Togo, Uganda, Upper Volta, Vietnam, and Zaire.

Table 60   Foreign Loans As a Percent of Shareholders' Equity December 31, 1976

	Chase Manhattan Corporation		Citicorp	
	Percent of Foreign Loans	Percent of Equity	Percent of Foreign Loans	Percent of Equity
Industrialized countries	58.5	420	54.2	186
OPEC countries	6.2	45	8.8	39
High-income LDC	27.5	198	27.9	167
Middle-income LDC	4.3	31	6.7	40
Low-income LDC	0.5	4	1.4	2
Centrally planned economies	3.0	21	1.0	9
Total	100.0	719	100.0	443

Source: 1976 Annual Reports of Citicorp, Chase Manhattan Corporation.

International Loan Exposure.   Table 60 shows one method of comparing loan exposure. Foreign loans as a percent of capital (shareholders' equity) shows the relative importance of loans in each of the World Bank's classifications. The table indicates that developed countries accounted for the major international loans of these two banks at year-end 1976, with these loans accounting for 58.5 percent of international loans of Chase and 54.2 percent of Citicorp. These loans represented approximately four times the equity of the Chase and less than twice the equity of Citicorp. In contrast, the low income of LDCs accounted for 0.5 percent of Chase's foreign loans and 4 percent of this bank's equity capital. These loans also represented a small proportion of Citicorp's foreign loans and equity.

These comparisons are primitive, but they represent a beginning, and they will become more meaningful as information for subsequent years becomes available, and bank analysts would be able to track changes over time. Nevertheless, changes can occur in international banking with remarkable speed, and data that are reported once a year or at irregular intervals provide only benchmark information. For example, in 1976, the low-income LDCs faced serious balance of payments difficulties, which were largely financed by the international banks acting as intermediaries between deposits of the oil exporting countries and loans to the less developed countries. This major transfer of financial obligations increased the importance of loans to low-income countries of most major international banks.

To keep abreast with the rapid increase in borrowings by less developed countries, bank analysts would want to make adjustments to the benchmark figures that some banks provide. This is not a satisfying conclusion, and it points up the need to seek and use all kinds of information from trade sources, business associates, and other information that may be available from the banks themselves. It also points up the importance of judgment in sifting and evaluating this additional information.

CHAPTER 11

ECONOMIC INFLUENCES

The economy, in its broadest context, determines the size of a bank's operations. Other factors also affect the size of a bank's operations, including a bank's various internal policies and the number of competitors regulatory agencies permit in an area. Yet the most important factor affecting the size of a bank is the economy of the area that it serves.

The perimeter of the geographic area that a bank serves represents the first major economic factor affecting banks. This perimeter is determined by statutes. Interstate branch banking is, for all practical purposes, prohibited by the McFadden Act, which permits new interstate banking only if two states pass enabling legislation. The statute has been in force for over 50 years, no reciprocal legislation has been enacted. Thus as would be expected, the states with larger economies also are the locations of the largest banks.

Despite these various geographic limitations, many banks have managed to expand the scope of their market beyond their boundaries. These banks have taken three directions to reach out beyond their home base.

International banking represents the most widely recognized route a few of the large banks have taken to expand the scale of their operations. A second route is through Edge Act subsidiaries, which permit a bank to open an office beyond the bank's immediate geographic boundaries. Although an Edge Act office is not permitted to accept deposits, and is restricted in other ways, it offers a useful presence to banks that service large national corporations.

A third way that banks have sought to move beyond the geographic restrictions of U.S. banking is to expand into areas of financing that do not have these restrictions. Banks with subsidiaries provide the legal vehicle to accomplish this step. The nonbank activities include factoring, leasing, personal finance services, as well as other activities that provide intermediary financing.

An expansion in the scale of banking operations does not necessarily make a bank more profitable. Despite considerable economic theory that would

244

suggest that larger size provides the basis for economies of scale, there does not appear to be clear evidence of economies of scale in banking. In fact, after a certain size has been reached, there may be diseconomies of scale, and in many comparisons, larger-sized banks tend to be less profitable than smaller-sized banks. Banking is a service business, and its basic unit is the relationship between a banker and a customer. This relationship is not easily made more efficient, because personal discussions cannot always be compressed as can production schedules in manufacturing, and the relationship may be a basic constraint on an effort to obtain economies of scale. Although there have been many ways of improving the efficiency of handling the paperwork of banking, these efficiencies are generally available to banks of almost all sizes.

A second major way the economy influences banks is through the price of its shares on the securities markets. As was discussed in an earlier chapter, capital provides the vital link between the financial world and a bank. The link serves as a long-term stimulus or a constraint on the size of operations.

The price of shares of banks is most determined by decisions made outside the control of a bank. The decisions to buy or to sell or the implicit decision to hold shares of a bank's stock are made mostly by persons not employed by the bank and reflect an independent assessment outside the control of its management. These decisions of buying or selling stock reflect a bank's financial performance, as well as conditions in credit markets, the rate of inflation, and many other general economic issues. A relatively high price of a bank's stock has the effect of lowering its cost of capital and providing it with an incentive to expand its operations. The incentive reflects the ease by which a bank may be expected to obtain funds to support expanded loans either from credit or equity markets.

DEPOSIT AND LOAN MARKET SIZE

Local Market

The size of the local market for loans and deposits in which a bank operates has a major bearing on the size of its operations. Table 61 shows the relation-

Table 61 Arizona, Maine and New York Comparison of Personal Income with Bank Assets 1975

State	Total Personal Income	Total Bank Assets[a]	Ratio Bank Assets to Personal Income
Arizona	11,908	7,125	0.60
Maine	5,071	2,255	0.44
New York	118,958	170,587	1.43

Source: Federal Deposit Insurance Corporation.
[a] All insured commercial banks.

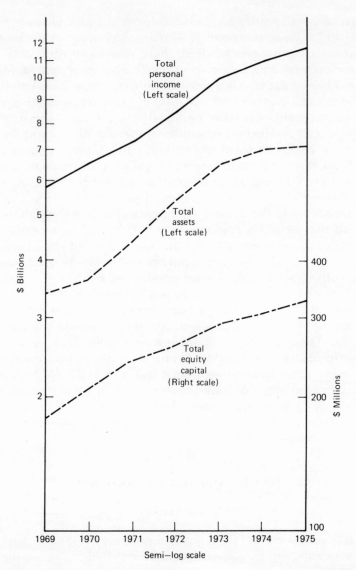

Figure 63 Arizona—Growth of economy and banking activity. *Source:* U.S. Department of Commerce, Federal Deposit Insurance Corporation.

ship of bank assets to personal income, which is used here as an indicator of the volume of general business activity. In both Arizona and Maine, statewide banking is prevalent. Statewide branch banking is now permitted in New York, and the totals for the whole state of New York can be used here for broad comparative purposes.

The table shows that an important relationship exists between personal income of a state and the total assets of the banks of the state. The differences among the three states mainly reflect differences in types of banking. Banking in Maine tends to reflect consumer, farming, and small business customers, while banking in New York includes the headquarters of a major portion of large corporate and government customers. Thus the ratio of bank assets to personal income in 1970 was 0.44 for Maine and 1.43 for New York, representing one of the widest differences in the United States. The ratio of 0.60 for Arizona is closer to the average of 0.73 for the nation as a whole.

The ratio for New York probably represents the upper limit that a bank community may expect to achieve, for the present, from a change in the economic base of its customers, if such an option were open to pursue. This would mean, for example, that if Maine were to transform its economy from an agricultural to a highly commercial and industrial base, it might expect its bank assets per dollar of personal income to triple. Of course, such a possibility is not likely, but it does illustrate the importance of a commercial and industrial base to the size of a banking community's operations. Moreover, commerce and industry attract large concentrations of people. They also raise per capita income. For example, in 1975 per capita income in Maine was $4,786, while it was $6,564 in New York, 37 percent higher (not shown in table).

Figures 63–65 show the pace of expansion in personal income, total bank assets, and total bank equity for the three states. The charts show that the rate of expansion of personal income in each state has an effect on the rate of gain in banking assets and equity capital. For example, income gained most rapidly in Arizona, as did bank assets and equity capital in that state. New York

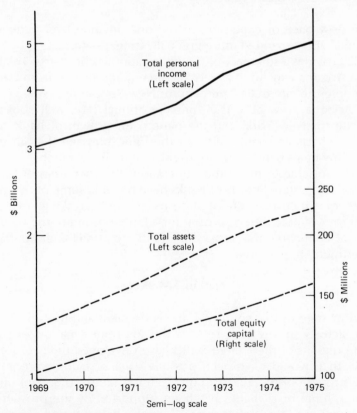

Figure 64 Maine—Growth of economy and banking activity. *Source:* U.S. Department of Commerce, Federal Deposit Insurance Corporation.

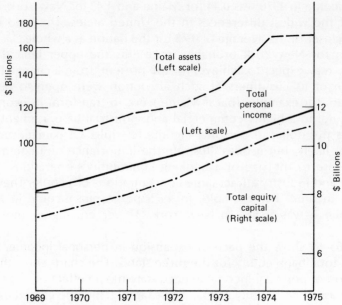

Figure 65 New York—Growth of economy and banking activity. *Source:* U.S. Department of Commerce, Federal Deposit Insurance Corporation.

showed a slow pace of expansion in personal income, and bank assets and equity capital also expanded more gradually in that state.

Table 62 provides a summary of the information in the charts. Total personal income in Arizona expanded at a 12.70 percent annual rate from 1969 to 1975, almost double the rate of 6.67 percent for New York in the same period. Bank assets in Arizona grew at a 13.27 percent annual rate, well above the 7.58 percent rate for New York, and the pattern for growth of bank capital was similar. The charts and table indicate the same message that an expanding local economy helps banks increase the size of their operations.

Banks are not able to move their operations to other areas of the country, much less across a state line. Thus banks have become some of the most active supporters of the expansion of industry in their banking areas. Banking personnel for example, often account for a large portion of the road shows of chambers of commerce that cross the country to attract attention, and hopefully, investment in their area.

National Market

No region or state of this country is an economic island to itself. The level of economic activity in any area reflects the enormous market of the United States. The regions of the United States have developed their resources more intensively than would have been possible if each region were a market to itself. The strength of the U.S. economy is important to U.S. banks in all locations. The volume of all banks has been supported by the prosperity of the United States, and the volume of all banks has suffered when the U.S. economy has faltered.

The chart shows U.S. gross national product (GNP) and domestic U.S. bank assets from 1896 to 1975 (Figure 66). Gross national product is the most inclusive measure of aggregate economic activity available. The chart shows that the volume of banking activity, as measured by domestic assets, has fluctuated with movements in gross national product. For example, banks experienced lower activity during the depression of the 1930s. Subsequently, banks showed a marked expansion in their activity, as the U.S. economy entered a prolonged span of expansion.

The chart also shows that the relationship between U.S. domestic bank assets and gross national product has remained almost steady throughout the past eight decades. On the whole, bank assets have amounted to more than one-tenth of the value of the gross national product. During periods of weak business conditions, such as the late 1930s, bank assets tended to represent a higher ratio to gross national product, reflecting the unwillingness of bank customers to use banks for borrowing as fully as they would have done under ordinary conditions. During periods of business confidence, the ratio declined to lower levels, reflecting increased use of banks by customers. Overall, the level of U.S. economic activity has been an important factor affecting the size of the market for banking services and an important factor affecting the size of banks.

The U.S. economy has undergone important changes during the past decade, and these changes may have affected its sustainability. These changes include an erosion in the proportion of income going to corporate profits, and a shift from private domestic investment to personal consumption expenditures and government purchases. Banks have been affected by these changes because they affect the types of loans, deposits, and services demanded by sectors of the economy. Moreover, the aggregate effect of the

**Table 62 Arizona, Maine and New York
Comparison of Compound Annual Rates of
Gain for Personal Income, Bank Assets and Bank Equity**

	1969	1975	1969–1975 Compound Annual Rate of Gain
Total personal income			
Arizona	$ 5,811	$ 11,908	12.70%
Maine	3,039	5,071	8.91
New York	80,765	118,958	6.67
All insured commercial banks—total assets (millions)			
Arizona	$ 3,374	$ 7,125	13.27%
Maine	1,285	2,255	9.83
New York	110,049	170,587	7.58
All insured commercial banks—total equity capital (millions)			
Arizona	$ 178.4	$ 329.4	10.77%
Maine	103.6	159.4	7.45
New York	7,298.8	11,355.3	7.64

Source: Federal Deposit Insurance Corporation, U.S. Department of Commerce.

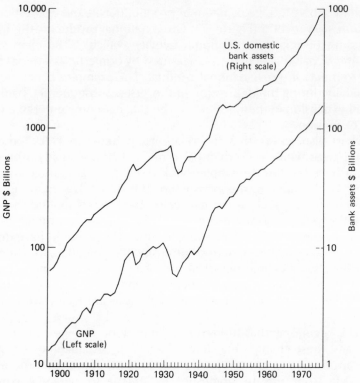

Figure 66 U.S.—Trend of economy and domestic bank assets, 1896 to 1976. *Source:* Federal Reserve Board, U.S. Department of Commerce.

changes also has an impact on the overall level of economic activity and thus on banking activity.

U.S. industrial output, a measure of basic economic activity unaffected by distortions of inflation, has appeared sluggish and recession prone in the decade of the 1970s. From 1969 to 1975 industrial output rose 6.3 percent, compared with gains of 11.8 percent for Germany, 15.3 percent for Italy, 18.6 percent for France, and 26.3 percent for Japan. Only England showed slower growth in output with a 4.5 percent gain for the period. The recent recession affected the United States and Japan most severely, with declines in industrial output from 1973 to 1975 of 9.2 percent for the United States and 14.7 percent for Japan, compared with more moderate reductions in industrial output of 7.2 percent for Germany, 6.7 percent for France, 6.6 percent for England, and 4.5 percent for Italy. The figures suggest that U.S. economic performance is not as vital as it might be. The comparatively stronger showing of U.S. industrial output in 1977 largely reflects a large federal budget deficit approaching $50 billion and a balance of payments deficit which may amount to $25 billion. These deficits have provided a major but unsustainable stimulus.

An important factor in explaining this slower pace of economic expansion appears to be the growing weakness of corporate profits in the United States. A lessened proportion of corporate profits would indicate that the profitability of investment in U.S. industry was slackening. Table 63 shows that in

1965 pretax corporate profits (net of adjustments) accounted for 13.6 percent of total national income, while compensation of employees accounted for 70.1 percent and interest and other income 16.3 percent. By 1974 the proportion of profits had dropped to 7.5 percent, while the proportion of compensation for employees had risen to 77.1 percent. The figures for 1976 show a moderate gain in the proportion of national income attributable to corporate profits, but not enough to indicate a change in the basic direction. The proportion of these profits has steadily declined in each of the recessions shown in the table: 1967, 1970, and 1975.

These figures show the performance of corporate profits after two key adjustments: the inventory valuation and the capital consumption. Both adjustments reflect an effort to show corporate profits net of the effects of inflation. The inventory valuation adjustment removes the effect of gains (shown as a subtraction) or losses from changes in the price of inventories. Inventory gains or losses are not ordinarily considered to represent true manufacturing profits. The capital consumption adjustment shows an estimate of the cost to business of buying new production facilities compared with the depreciation that companies have taken for that equipment. A higher replacement cost than depreciation is shown as a negative number and reflects one of the crucial effects of inflation on corporate profits.

U.S. pre-tax corporate profits in 1965 amounted to $75.2 billion. The inventory valuation adjustment reduced that figure by $1.9 billion, and the capital consumption adjustment added $3.8 billion, providing net profits of $77.1 billion. In 1975 pretax corporate profits amounted to $114.5 billion. The inventory valuation adjustment reduced that amount by $11.4 billion, and the capital consumption adjustment lowered that figure by $11.5 billion, giving net profits of $91.6 billion. Thus in 1975 these two adjustments, which reflect the effects of inflation, reduced reported pretax corporate profits by 20

Table 63   Distribution of Major Components of National Income

Year	Total National Income	Compensation of Employees	Pretax Corporate Profits— Net of Adjustments	Interest and Other Income
1965	100.0%	70.1%	13.6%	16.3%
1966	100.0	70.6	13.3	16.1
1967	100.0	72.0	12.1	15.9
1968	100.0	72.8	12.0	15.2
1969	100.0	74.4	10.6	15.0
1970	100.0	76.3	8.5	15.2
1971	100.0	75.8	9.0	15.2
1972	100.0	75.1	9.7	15.2
1973	100.0	75.1	9.3	15.6
1974	100.0	77.1	7.5	15.4
1975	100.0	76.9	7.6	15.5
1976	100.0	76.2	8.8	15.0

Source: U.S. Department of Commerce.

percent. The impact of these adjustments for inflation has continued to grow, and in 1976 they reduced reported corporate profits by 22 percent.

An important impact of lower profits on the U.S. economy has been a lower proportion of private investment. A high proportion of investment is essential to the economy to provide the basis of increased productivity, since it is gains in productivity, not gains in population or working force, that are principally responsible for increasing output and gross national product on a long-term basis. The lower proportion of investment in the U.S. economy would tend to reduce the ability of the economy to expand.

Table 64 shows that gross private domestic investment accounted for 16.3 percent of gross national product in 1965 and declined to 12.1 percent in 1975. In the interval, personal consumption expenditures increased in the share of gross national product as did government purchases after consideration for the effects of the Vietnam War. In 1976, private domestic investment remained significantly below the level of the mid-1960s or the early 1970s as a percent of gross national product. The proportion going to investment has steadily declined in each of the three recent recessions: 1967, 1970, and 1975.

The table also shows that the markets for banking services have shifted toward the consumer and government sectors of the economy and away from the investment sector that would provide rapid expansion in total business activity. Thus while the U.S. economy remains the largest in the world, it has shown signs of important structural changes that would appear to limit its possibilities for a major expansion.

International Market

The greater expansion possibilities of many foreign economies has been a principal factor in the development of the international business of U.S. corporations. Since the major international corporations have been the customers of the largest U.S. banks, the development of international banking

Table 64   Distribution of Major Components of Gross National Product

Year	Total GNP	Personal Consumption Expenditures	Gross Private Domestic Investment	Government Purchases	Exports and Imports
1965	100.0%	62.5%	16.3%	20.1%	1.1%
1966	100.0	61.7	16.5	21.1	0.7
1967	100.0	61.6	15.2	22.6	0.6
1968	100.0	61.7	15.1	22.9	0.3
1969	100.0	62.0	15.6	22.2	0.2
1970	100.0	63.0	14.3	22.3	0.4
1971	100.0	62.8	15.1	22.0	0.1
1972	100.0	62.6	16.1	21.6	−0.3
1973	100.0	62.0	16.8	20.6	0.6
1974	100.0	62.8	15.2	21.5	0.5
1975	100.0	64.2	12.1	22.4	1.3
1976	100.0	63.7	14.3	21.6	0.4

Source: U.S. Department of Commerce.

Table 65   Sales of U.S. International Corporations (Sales by Majority-Owned Foreign Affiliates of U.S. Companies, Billions)

1966	$ 97.8
1967	108.5
1968	120.8
1969	134.3
1970	155.9
1971	184.4
1972	211.9
1973	291.4
1974	437.7
1975	580.0 estimate

Source: U.S. Department of Commerce.

has been largely restricted to the largest banks. In fact, the major dozen banks in 1975 held more than two-thirds of total foreign assets of U.S. banks. In 1975 total foreign assets held by U.S. banks amounted to $138 million, and these assets amounted to approximately 13 percent of all domestic and foreign assets of U.S. banks.

The expansion in foreign banking has reflected the growth of foreign sales and profits of U.S. international corporations. The tables show that foreign sales and profits of U.S. corporations have significantly risen in the past decade, especially in the 1970s (Tables 65 and 66). The figures for earnings for the latter part of the 1960s may have been understated, because during that period federal government regulations required repatriation of earnings as a means of reducing the U.S. balance of payments deficit. These requirements were removed in 1971 when the U.S. adopted fluctuating exchange rates. The decline in international earnings of U.S. comporations in 1975 reflected the worldwide recession.

The international corporations provided the basis to establish an infrastructure of international banking by U.S. banks. The oil cartel of OPEC provided a new dimension for its use. The international banks accepted

Table 66   Foreign Profits of U.S. International Corporations (Pretax Profits with Inventory Valuation Adjustment, Billions)

1965	$ 3.2
1966	2.7
1967	3.0
1968	3.2
1969	3.7
1970	3.8
1971	4.5
1972	4.9
1973	6.8
1974	11.1
1975	6.1

Source: U.S. Department of Commerce.

deposits from OPEC nations and made loans based on the deposits to nations that were required to borrow to maintain their standard of living and continue their economic development programs.

Table 67 shows the increased foreign indebtedness of governments of major developing countries. This debt rose sharply following the increased price of oil in 1974 and the worldwide recession of 1974–1975. Approximately one half of the sharp increase in debt of these countries in recent years has been financed by international banks. This debt has been funded ironically by the principal cause of the increased debt, the OPEC controlled oil prices. Thus there has been a growing indebtedness of the developing countries to the major U.S. international banks.

Yet something has been added to the classic intermediary banking function. The growing role of a few large U.S. banks in brokering funds among countries has changed from being a commercial banker to what usually has been associated in the past with governments and government agencies. The change may have major implications for these banks. It may force them into the position of assessing more than the creditworthiness of a loan. They may be called on to consider essentially governmental questions of whether a country's standard of living should be sustained or reduced. Major banks may deny that this consideration would be given any weight or even be considered. Yet the issue so pervades lending to the less developed countries that it would be difficult to avoid, even by a purposeful effort.

The new responsibility also could push international banks into a relationship with the U.S. government that neither would necessarily prefer. The repercussions of decisions to deny an expansion of credit to virtually any less developed country affect the foreign and military policy of the U.S. government. The implications of this potential new alliance between the large international banks and the U.S. government have yet to be made clear, but they could affect the market for international banking services.

SECURITIES MARKETS

The broad direction of the U.S. economy also affects the volume of activity of banks through the securities markets. These markets affect the cost of new

Table 67   External Public Debt 86 Developing Countries (Billions)

1967	$ 50.6
1968	57.1
1969	64.3
1970	74.2
1971	87.0
1972	101.2
1973	121.9
1974	151.4
1975	185.0 estimate

Source: World Bank.

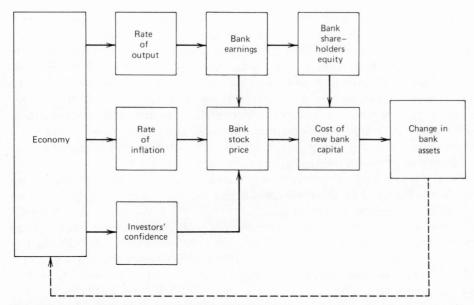

Figure 67   Relationship of economy and bank assets.

capital of banks and through this linkage, act as a brake or an accelerator on the pace of overall banking activities.

Figure 67 illustrates the linkages. On the left side it shows decisions made by government, and on the right, decisions made by banks. The U.S. money supply is affected by the exchange rate of the dollar, the Eurocurrency market, domestic fiscal policy, and high-powered money (which is total domestic currency publicly held and deposit liabilities of the Federal Reserve). In turn, money supply affects the rate of inflation. The rate of inflation and investors' opinions affect the cost of new capital. The relationship between the cost of new capital and the return on existing capital indicates whether a bank will likely add or relinquish assets. Finally, completing the cycle, changes in assets of a bank have an effect on government policies.

The Economy and Stock Prices

There is widespread belief that the condition of the economy is a major factor in determining stock prices, although opinions and theories vary concerning precisely how this occurs. Figure 67 shows that the relationship between aggregate U.S. economic activity and stock prices flows through three chan- nels. The level of activity of the economy affects the level of earnings of a bank. The pace of output can be measured by such broad measures as real gross national product (gross national product adjusted to eliminate changes in price levels) or industrial production. Banking services are used more inten- sively when real output rises—a basis for higher bank earnings—which in turn, have a favorable effect on bank stock prices.

In addition, the rate of change of general price levels, either inflationary or deflationary, affects the price of stocks of banks. Rising price levels usually depress stock prices of banks, as well as stock prices of companies in other industries. The higher rate of inflation acts to raise interest rates, which increases the discount of future earnings and lowers the present value of those earnings. It also pushes up yields of debt securities and makes them more attractive compared with stocks than they were previously. Declining price levels have occurred only rarely in this century and have been associated with severe dislocations in overall economic activity. Bank stock prices have suffered in these periods. Slowly declining price levels have often been associated with periods of major capital formation and have not had an unfavorable effect on the stock prices of banks.

Steady prices and rising levels of economic activity are best for bank stock prices. Investors then usually expect rising earnings, and the value of those earnings is expected to remain intact.

Investors follow economic developments with great interest, since a large part of their evaluation of securities portfolio policy is based on economic factors. For example, if inflation is increasing and economic activity is leveling, investors may be expected to lighten their holdings of bank stocks, as well as stocks in general.

Cost of Capital

The *cost of capital* is the cost a bank must pay to obtain additional shareholders' equity. It may be measured by the ratio of recent earnings to the price that investors in the stock market will pay for those earnings. For example, if the stock market believes that the earnings of a bank are valuable, the price of the stock will rise relative to the earnings, and the ratio of earnings to the stock price will decline. Thus the cost of capital, measured by this latter ratio, will drop.

It would be helpful—and more precise—if it were possible to develop some measure of the return on the increment of new equity for each period. Unfortunately, there is no clear way of determining the return on an increment of new equity. Thus the chart compares an average relationship (return on shareholders' equity) with a marginal relationship (earnings-price ratio). The presumption is that the marginal and average costs of these two measures are not widely different and in most instances this assumption is probably correct. More practically, these are the two best measures available. Nevertheless, it would be a mistake to press them too far or neglect to keep in mind that any measurement of the cost of capital is only an approximation.

The cost of capital is the key part of the overall process that affects banking volume. It is the point at which the external economy and internal operations of a bank meet. Share prices are completely or almost completely out of the control of a bank. Earnings are almost completely under a bank's control. At all other points where a bank and the economy meet, there is usually considerable room for a bank to select options, reflecting some degree of the bank's control of operations. For example, if a bank seeks funds from money markets and finds the rates high in comparison with its return from the assets it is funding, it usually has options such as selling the assets or funding the assets with shorter-term and lower-cost liabilities. However, with cost of capital, there is little room to maneuver.

The cost of capital is often highly volatile, sometimes doubling or halving within a year. This volatility adds uncertainty in a part of a bank's operations, and the uncertainty has an unsettling effect on bank managements that pride themselves on running operations that show stability and predictability. Sometimes managements deny the importance of capital markets to the cost of capital. Even some highly technical internal accounting systems of banks will use debt measures of the cost of capital to avoid the volatility of the cost of capital as measured by equity prices. Yet volatility is a part of capitalist system and a part of the cost of capital. Virtually all other factors affecting a bank change more gradually or are more predictable.

Tables 68 and 69 show the cost of capital for Wells Fargo and Morgan. The earnings per share are shown quarterly, on a seasonaly adjusted basis. The earnings of both banks rose fairly steadily from the fourth quarter of 1968 to the second quarter of 1975. The table also shows the average share price for both banks. The average share price is calculated using the high and low price of trades for the months of each quarter.

In contrast to the steady gains in earnings per share, the average share price of Wells Fargo fluctuated sharply. For example, shares were traded at an average price of $30.20 in the fourth quarter of 1968 and fell about 40 percent to $17.80 one and one-half years later. The cost of capital for Wells Fargo rose from 5.4 percent to 9.4 percent in the interval, went higher during 1973, and reached 20.9 percent in the final quarter of 1974. The average share price for Morgan held fairly steady during the late 1960s and early 1970s, then rose in the mid-1970s. Morgan ended the period with about the same cost of capital that it began. In the fourth quarter of 1968, its cost of capital was 6.7 percent, and it was 7.2 percent in the second quarter of 1975.

The cost of capital of most banks followed the pattern of Wells Fargo and increased sharply in the 1970s as the stock prices of these companies fell. The decline in prices reflected higher rates of inflation and increased yields of debt securities.

The example of Morgan represents an exception and is shown to illustrate one way that investors' opinions can offset the general direction of economic influences. During the first half of the 1970s, investors became impressed with the ability of Morgan to manage its operations in a prudent manner and still show strong earnings gains. They were also impressed with Morgan's close relationship with the major international corporations, which were showing major sales and earnings gains. These opinions benefited Morgan's stock and helped keep its cost of capital lower than that of most other banks.

Cost of Capital and Return on Existing Capital

A comparison of the cost of new capital and the bank's return on existing capital (return on shareholders' equity) is important in evaluation of whether the scale of its operations is appropriate. When the cost of new capital is below the return on existing capital, it is worthwhile for a bank to expand operations. A reversal of this relationship indicates that new capital would be

Table 68 Wells Fargo and Company
Cost of New Capital As Measured by Earnings—Price Ratio

Year	Quarter	Earnings (Seasonally Adjusted at Annual Rate)	Average Share Price	Cost of New Capital (Earnings-Price Ratio)
1968	4	$1.64	$30.20	5.4%
1969	1	1.66	27.90	5.9
	2	1.68	26.70	6.3
	3	1.66	23.70	7.0
	4	1.76	25.50	6.9
1970	1	1.70	20.80	8.2
	2	1.68	17.80	9.4
	3	1.70	19.20	8.9
	4	1.76	19.20	9.2
1971	1	1.78	21.80	8.2
	2	1.71	21.60	7.9
	3	1.87	19.40	9.6
	4	1.81	20.80	8.7
1972	1	1.86	21.10	8.8
	2	1.99	24.10	8.3
	3	2.11	27.20	7.8
	4	2.15	27.70	7.8
1973	1	2.25	25.10	9.0
	2	2.22	21.60	10.3
	3	2.11	22.60	9.3
	4	2.16	23.30	9.3
1974	1	2.15	24.60	8.7
	2	2.59	21.20	12.2
	3	2.42	13.70	17.7
	4	2.65	12.70	20.9
1975	1	2.79	15.60	17.9
	2	2.62	18.00	14.6

Source: Wells Fargo and Company, quarterly reports, Standard and Poor's Corporation.

costing more than the return, on average, from its deployment. This deficit would indicate that the bank would hold back its capital from use as a base for further expansion in assets, until the deficit were eliminated.

Figure 68 shows the return on equity and the cost of new capital for Wells Fargo from the fourth quarter of 1968 to the second quarter of 1975. From the beginning of the period through the first quarter of 1974, the cost of new capital was below Wells Fargo's return on equity. The gap represented a surplus, which acted as an incentive for the bank to expand its operations. New capital could be obtained cheaper than the return from its use by the bank. From the second quarter of 1974 to the end of the period, the cost of new

**Table 69   J. P. Morgan & Co., Incorporated
Cost of New Capital As Measured by Earnings—Price Ratio**

Year	Quarter	Earnings (Seasonally Adjusted at Annual Rate)	Average Share Price	Cost of New Capital (Earnings-Price Ratio)
1968	4	$2.11	$31.30	6.7%
1969	1	2.23	30.00	7.4
	2	2.33	28.00	8.3
	3	2.18	28.00	7.8
	4	2.43	29.80	8.2
1970	1	2.46	31.80	7.7
	2	2.65	29.50	9.0
	3	2.92	32.80	8.9
	4	3.13	32.50	9.6
1971	1	3.37	33.40	10.1
	2	2.47	33.80	7.3
	3	3.17	32.30	7.3
	4	3.02	35.10	9.1
1972	1	3.20	38.30	8.4
	2	3.21	45.20	7.1
	3	3.21	50.50	6.4
	4	3.41	53.20	6.4
1973	1	3.76	50.80	7.4
	2	3.95	51.00	7.7
	3	3.83	64.80	5.9
	4	4.01	66.50	6.0
1974	1	4.13	63.90	6.5
	2	4.65	61.20	7.6
	3	4.93	49.00	10.1
	4	4.87	51.30	9.5
1975	1	5.03	59.40	8.5
	2	4.65	64.60	7.2

Source: J. P. Morgan & Co., Incorporated, quarterly reports, Standard and Poor's Corporation.

capital for Wells Fargo rose above its return, indicating that new capital could not be put to use and show a sufficient return to pay its cost. The incentive would be to pare operations, and if the relationship were to continue, to shrink the assets of the organization.

Figure 69 shows the same comparison for Morgan. In this example the return on equity remained well above the cost of new capital. In fact, on an overall basis, the surplus widened as the period progressed. The return on equity increased throughout the period, and after rising in the initial part of the period, the cost of new capital eased downward. Throughout the period, there was a strong incentive to expand the size of this bank's assets.

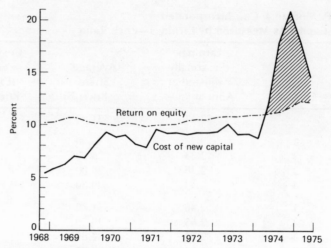

Figure 68 Wells Fargo and Company—Comparison of profitability and cost of new capital. *Source:* Wells Fargo and Company, quarterly reports, Standard and Poor's Corporation.

A bank might think that it can increase its return on equity by increasing its leverage. Thus it would appear that the comparison between the return on equity and the cost of new capital can be manipulated. For example, if a bank saw its cost of new capital were rising, it could offset this increase by increasing leverage, which would enable its return on equity to rise perhaps sufficiently to keep a favorable gap between the two series.

Yet the increased leverage also increases the risk to equity holders. The higher leverage means that the bank has added new debt and the new debt would be supported by the same equity base as earlier. Equity holders would tend to downgrade the value of the stock, and its price would tend to be below the price that it would have been if the leverage had not been added. The lower price, in turn, would tend to raise the cost of new equity, and in so

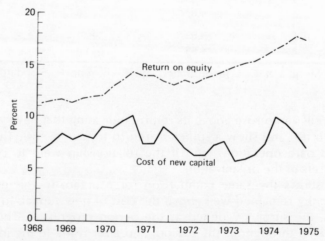

Figure 69 J. P. Morgan & Co., Incorporated—Comparison of profitability and cost of new capital. *Source:* J.P. Morgan & Co., Incorporated, quarterly reports, Standard and Poor's Corporation.

doing, would tend to neutralize the benefit that had been hoped to be obtained through the use of higher leverage. Despite the involved reasoning, there is no doubt that investors do make such adjustments. The profitability of a bank as measured by return on total assets and the risk because of leverage appear to be basic guides that investors use in assessing the value that they place on equity of a bank. Thus the use of the comparison of the return on equity with the cost of new capital may be regarded as a stable relationship not likely to be materially changed by financing techniques of a bank.

Changes in Capital and Assets

Banks do not always heed the signals of the relationship between capital and volume. And they are not required to do so in the short term. They may decide to hold their assets under tight rein when the capital comparisons are favorable because other factors may give them concern. Or as has also happened, banks may expand their assets in the face of major deficits in their capital comparisons. Nevertheless, on a long-term basis, banks may be expected to be responsive to the guides of the cost of capital.

Table 70 shows the surplus or deficit of return on equity compared with the cost of capital, as well as average total assets from 1969 to 1975 for Wells Fargo. This relationship is called the "capital comparison." If the return on equity is higher than the cost of capital, the difference is shown as a positive figure. For example, in 1969, the return on equity for Wells Fargo was 10.5 percent, and the cost of capital was 6.5 percent, leaving a difference of 4.0 percent. This difference indicated that the bank could use additional capital and show a surplus. Consequently, there would be an incentive to expand its assets.

From 1969 to 1973 the capital comparison for Wells Fargo was positive, indicating an incentive to expand assets. Assets increased during each of the years, rising from an average of $5,569 million to $10,320 million in the interval, representing an average annual growth rate of 17 percent. In 1974, the capital comparison for Wells Fargo turned negative and continued nega-

Table 70   Wells Fargo and Company
Capital Comparison and Average Total Assets

Year	Capital Comparison (Surplus or Deficit of Return on Equity Compared with Cost of Capital)	Average Total Assets (Millions)
1969	+4.0%	5,569
1970	+1.2	5,822
1971	+1.5	6,970
1972	+2.3	8,004
1973	+1.5	10,320
1974	−3.5	11,741
1975	−3.9[a]	11,669

[a] Two quarters.

**Table 71   J. P. Morgan & Co., Incorporated
Capital Comparison and Average Total Assets**

Year	Capital Comparison (Surplus or Deficit of Return on Equity Compared with Cost of Capital)	Average Total Assets (Millions)
1969	+3.6%	10,955
1970	+3.9	11,627
1971	+5.5	12,635
1972	+6.4	13,410
1973	+8.0	17,115
1974	+8.2	22,176
1975	+10.0[a]	25,119

[a] Two quarters.

tive during the initial two quarters of 1975. Average total assets declined slightly from $11,741 million in 1974 to $11,669 million in 1975.

Table 71 shows the same relationship between the capital comparison and assets for Morgan. Morgan's relative cost of capital showed a positive spread throughout the period, as assets rose steadily.

The two comparisons for Wells Fargo and Morgan cover two recessions and two expansion periods of general business activity. During the 1970 recession, both banks showed gains in assets, while during the initial part of the 1975 recession only Morgan showed a gain in assets. Of course, these comparisons should not be pressed too far. As has been discussed, other factors affect the level of assets, and these factors may offset, temporarily, the direction that would be indicated by capital comparisons.

CHAPTER 12

REGULATORY PRESSURES

Banks are regulated by a collection of agencies, and to a large extent the character and the structure of banks reflect the interests of these regulators. Banks are regulated because it is widely believed by most legislators that they are too vital to the public to be left to the chance that they will always operate satisfactorily. As a consequence regulatory agencies have a primary responsibility of preventing bank failures. In an industry that numbers more than 14,000 units, this responsibility involves major tasks.

METHODS OF CONTROL

Regulators use three principal methods of controlling banks. The first method is to know the exact condition of banking activities in each bank and to take steps to keep each bank sound. The regulatory agencies employ a large number of bank examiners who perform examinations on a year-round basis. The examinations range from the traditional counting of till cash in branches to subjective evaluations of the way senior management conducts itself. A major part of the examination covers a close review of the quality of the loans of a bank. Repayment records, collateral, the thoroughness of a credit review, the amount of the current financial information about borrowers, the conditions of the records themselves, as well as other factors are taken into consideration in evaluating the quality of the loans. The examinations are unannounced, and examiners make great efforts to keep their presence anonymous prior to the examination. For example, some examiners register in hotels under assumed names when they travel to distant locations.

The second method regulators use to control banks is through their authority to grant charters, mergers, or permit the opening of new branches. In this manner, regulators control the amount of competition in the banking industry. Overall, they attempt to walk the line between monopoly and so much competition as to risk bank failures. These yardsticks are not clear and precise, and the proper dose of competition is a difficult measure to determine. The third method is news leaks.

In its broadest scope, regulation confers both constraints and benefits upon banks. The constraints are designed to curb banks from taking major risks. Banks are restricted in the types of lending and other business activities they may engage in. They are constrained in their contact with the public through the number of new branches or mergers they are to make. They are constrained in pricing through ceilings on interest rates for various types of deposits. There are constraints on the sum a bank may lend to a customer, and there are minimum requirements for cash and government securities.

There is, of course, another side to the regulatory hand. Banks receive two major benefits from regulators. Both of these benefits set banking apart from other industries.

One benefit of banking regulation is the implicit assurance that if a bank runs a sound operation, it will be aided in the event of an unexpected difficulty. Members of the Federal Reserve System may borrow at the discount window. The Federal Reserve regards this borrowing potential as a privilege. Actually, in most recent instances the Federal Reserve has been generous in opening its discount window to almost all member banks. The discount window has been closed only when a bank has deliberately taken action that runs counter to the wishes of the Federal Reserve, and the Federal Reserve almost always gives a warning before it closes the discount window to a bank. Although a large number of banks are not members of the Federal Reserve System they are covered by lines of credit, in almost all instances, with banks that do have the insurance of the discount window. Nevertheless, banks that are not members of the Federal Reserve System are not completely without remedies, should they face difficulties. The Federal Deposit Insurance Corporation may make advances to a bank. In the past quarter century depositors have not been hurt in any efforts to support or salvage a bank. No firm in any other industry has such an option for instant liquidity.

As another benefit from regulation, the financial community interprets the close supervision of regulators as a proxy for safety and is willing to lend funds to banks far more liberally than to companies in most industries that are not so regulated. This assurance is critical to banking, because, by its nature, money lending is a business involving risk, and lenders and investors tend to avoid risk. Thus the constraints and implicit assurances of regulatory agencies benefit banks by enabling them, with a relatively small amount of capital, to expand the scale of their operations to an extent that otherwise would not be possible.

COMPETITION AMONG THE REGULATORS

The outstanding characteristic of U.S. banking regulation is the intramural competition among its major regulators. The Federal Reserve Board, the Comptroller of the Currency, the Federal Deposit Insurance Corporation, the

Securities and Exchange Commission, and the various state banking commissions share the overall regulatory control of banks. Many of the responsibilities of these agencies overlap, and banks find that in many instances they actually can choose which agency they would prefer to govern them. In turn, the regulatory agencies find themselves in the position of competing for the customers whom they regulate.

Dislike of Strong Regulators

Banking regulation in the United States is an unusual environment that reflects the special nature of U.S. banking development. Banks and the public have shown a history of dislike of central money power. The regulatory structure of banking in the United States reflects the extreme lengths that a government and the governed are willing to go to avoid monopoly power on either part.

Each major banking problem in the United States has been solved by the creation of a new government agency, which has overlapping jurisdictions with other agencies already in existence (Figure 70). The initial effort to develop a strong central supervisory authority in the form of the First and Second National Banks was rejected early in the nation's history. Prior to the Civil War, U.S. banking was virtually unregulated except for a loose regulation by state banking commissions. The need to provide a stable basis for banks in order to finance the Civil War brought the national banking system and the Comptroller of the Currency into being. The state-chartered banks were expected, but not required, to join the national banking system. The state banks lived on, and the national banks represented a new tier to regulated banks.

The Comptroller, nevertheless, did not attempt to regulate the supply of money or control of the availability of credit for the banking system. Following the panic of 1907, the Federal Reserve System was created to remedy that shortcoming. It was given powers of examination of banks that overlapped the examinations of the Comptroller of the Currency. However, the Federal Reserve System did not act to prevent the collapse of nearly two-fifths of the banks in the early period of the depression of the 1930s, to solve this problem the Federal Deposit Insurance Corporation was created. This new regulatory agency, in turn has powers that overlap the other agencies.

Recently, following the demise of Franklin National Corporation, the Securities and Exchange Commission increased its requirements for additional information in a bank's prospectus. The growing concern of the Securities and Exchange Commission reflects its belief that investors should be given enough information to determine independently the soundness of a bank. This responsibility, of course, overlaps the responsibilities of the other bank regulatory agencies.

This brief summary of the development of regulatory agencies in the United States also points out that all significant banking legislation in this country has followed major debacles in the banking industry or has reflected the special needs of government. During the intervening years there has been considerable discussion and debate about proposed changes in banking regulation,

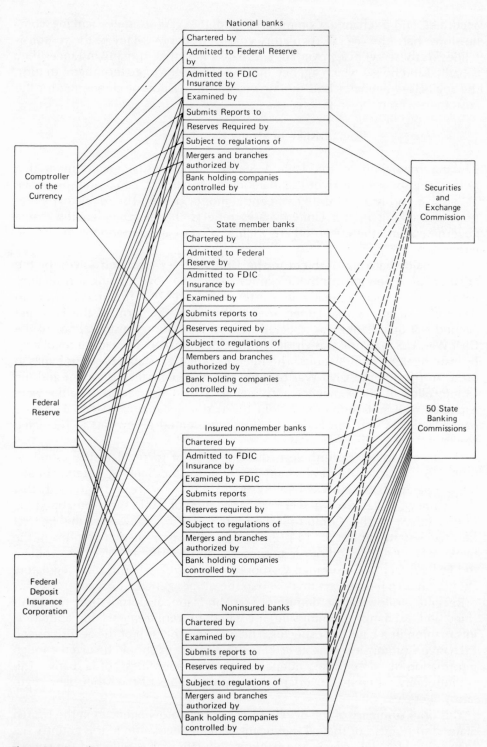

Figure 70 Regulatory powers.

but there has been virtually no change in the powers of the regulatory agencies. For example, recently there have been proposals to concentrate banking regulation into one agency and recommendations to permit a much greater competition among various types of financial service companies. The past pattern of banking regulation would indicate that little would develop from these proposals unless there were a major financial debacle. Thus the competition among regulatory agencies appears to be a situation that may endure for an indefinite period in the future.

Attempt of Regulators to Gain Pre-eminent Power

Figure 70 shows the five major regulatory entities and their principal areas of regulation. It gives a visual image of conflicting or at least overlapping agencies. The chart shows, for example, that national banks are subject to the regulations of the Comptroller of the Currency, the Federal Reserve, the Federal Deposit Insurance Corporation, and if they are a bank holding company, the Securities and Exchange Commission. Other government agencies, such as the IRS, are also involved in the affairs of banks, but they are not as specifically concerned with banks as are these four agencies.

During recent years, each of these banking agencies has sought to increase its power, and each has engaged in a mild kind of feudal warfare to gain a top position in regulatory control. In the mid 1960s the Comptroller of the Currency began to emphasize new advantages of a national bank charter over state bank charters, including lenient approvals of branch applications, new bank charters, a de-emphasis of the traditional guidelines on liquidity and capital, and support for diversification into new fields of business. Chase Manhattan Bank switched from a state to national charter in 1965 and demonstrated the importance of a bank to choose its regulatory agency rather than to accept its historical regulatory agency.

The development of bank holding companies in the late 1960s reflected another instance of regulatory competitiveness. The Bank Holding Company Act of 1956 had exempted single bank holding companies from regulation on the basis that they were primarily shells. Nevertheless, in the late 1960s Unionamerica Corporation recognized that single bank holding companies represented an almost completely unregulated vehicle for acquiring nonbank businesses and financing these businesses with commercial paper. Once opened, many banks rushed through the door. In 1969 more than 200 one-bank holding companies were formed, comprising about one half of the U.S. banking system's total assets. The holding company approach also provided a way for a nonbank to raid a bank. Leasco Corporation almost gained control of Chemical Bank through a raid on its holding company.

Regulatory agencies and Congress also saw the loophole in regulation that the one-bank holding company legislation had opened. The Nixon Administration in 1969 sought to have the power of the then-pending bank holding company legislation vested in all three principal agencies on an equal basis. All of the principal agencies lobbied to obtain the major responsibilities exclusively. Congress followed the bidding of the Federal Reserve and in 1970 placed the central bank in sole charge of bank holding companies. This was important legislation, since the vast majority of all bank deposits are tied to holding companies, and banks at the time looked to holding companies as a key source of their future growth.

Through this legislation, the Federal Reserve has acquired a preeminent regulatory authority, but this position may not be easy to maintain. Bank holding company regulation is certain to be unpopular with banks, and at the flanks of the Federal Reserve, the other regulatory agencies still remain intact. Already, the struggle between the Federal Reserve and the banking industry on the issues of admissible bank holding company activities has created a rift. Partially as a consequence, an effort by the Federal Reserve to extend its regulatory control in 1975 and 1976 never moved beyond the speechmaking stage.

The record indicates that in a competitive regulatory environment it is not possible for any regulatory agencies to obtain a hegemony of power on a permanent basis. The pendulum of power has swung back and forth among the agencies, reflecting changed conditions and new attitudes. Where regulatory competition has been most prominent, such as during the later half of the 1960s, banks have been able to use this competition to their advantage and expand along lines where regulation was weakest. During periods of stricter regulations or when regulation was centered on one of the agencies, banks have built support in Congress to limit the power of the agency that appeared to be restrictive.

Banks want competition among regulatory agencies, since it provides them with more freedom than if there were one regulatory agency with plenary power. Moreover, the pattern of competition of regulatory agencies, which has endured for over a century, appears to be ingrained in the politics of U.S. banking. Efforts by special committees to unify regulatory control, such as the recommendations of the Hunt Commission and the FINE study (a congressional study titled "Financial Institutions and the Nation's Economy"), make their case on logical grounds. Yet the will to carry out the changes has been lacking. There has been no strong unified interest on the part of the public, bankers, or other financial institutions to bring about integrated regulation.

TECHNIQUES OF CONTROL

Regulatory agencies use three techniques to control banks. Examination, persuasion, or censure—the first method—is the most widely practiced method. The second method is the response of regulatory agencies to a change in a bank's franchise, such as a request for a new branch or an acquisition. The third method is news leaks to the press.

Examination, Persuasion, and Censure

The basic method of control of banks is the use of information obtained from an examination. As has been noted, the examination process includes verifying the accuracy of the bank's financial statements, a review of the quality of its assets, a review of its basic measures of performance, such as liquidity, capital and earnings results, and an overall assessment of its management. The examination provides a focus for the review of the bank by its own management, and the process of reviewing the results of an examination makes the management of a bank more fully aware of what has been happening within its organization.

When there are differences in opinion over an issue that arises from an examination, the agencies try to persuade a bank to change its ways. The Federal Reserve Banks historically have carried a major share of this responsibility. Senior officers of Federal Reserve Banks have always kept an approving eye on their examiners who have been able to spot difficulties and present them to a member bank's management in a way that elicits a cooperative attitude and a correction of the problem. In fact, a large number of the presidents of the Federal Reserve Banks have been from the ranks of examiners because of the importance of persuasive talents. Outside bank analysts do not have knowledge of these discussions.

If persuasion fails and a problem is serious, a regulatory agency has powers of censure, which range from a refusal to provide the facilities of its discount window to a refusal of membership with the regulatory agency. Bank analysts are not aware of these discussions and decisions between banks and regulatory agencies, except where membership with an agency actually has changed.

Response to a Request for a Change in Franchise

The second method of control used by regulatory agencies is their response to a request of a bank to change its franchise. A change of franchise involves some fundamental change in how the bank conducts its activities and includes new branches, acquisitions, or mergers with other banks, and the undertaking of new nonbanking activities.

In handling requests, for example, the Federal Reserve Board acts as a judicial review board and even writes its opinions using the precision of legal phrases and language. As has been mentioned, the Federal Reserve System has control of bank holding company activities. The strength of the Federal Reserve's position is not only its authority to make a decision, but also its ability to publish the reasons for its decision. The latter privilege is probably more important, since these decisions provide a platform to reveal the current thinking of the Federal Reserve Board to other banks and to the general public as well. The power of the Federal Reserve carries even further, since it can make a decision, and then make further comments that carry far beyond the issues which prompted a bank's petition. Thus the decisions of the Federal Reserve Board have the weight and scope of a high court.

For example, in November 1975, the Federal Reserve rejected the proposed acquisition of three consumer finance companies by Citicorp. The finance companies were located in Seattle, Washington; Los Angeles, California; and Dubuque, Iowa. Citicorp had intended to acquire the three companies through its subsidiary, Nationwide Financial Services Corporation. In denying the proposed acquisitions the Federal Reserve Board said that they would have had an "undesirable effect" on the growth of competition in the consumer finance industry. In addition, the Board attached special attention to the fact that the proposed acquisitions would have required about $28 million of Citicorp's capital funds and commented that "a proposal which would divert funds to expansion, when those funds would be better utilized for improvement of the financial position, must be accorded adverse weight." Presumably, the Board would have preferred the bank to improve its equity capital ratios, retaining the capital that would have been paid for the proposed acquisition. These two parts of the decision—the effect on potential growth of competition and a recommendation to shore up capital—have importance far beyond the immediate issues of whether Citicorp should acquire a relatively insignificant addition to its operations. By making this decision, all banks were again notified to watch out for the doctrine of potential competition. Moreover, the Board's opinion provided an additional opportunity for it to restate its position that banks should build up capital.

Like many judicial decisions, the Board's decision also included a dissenting opinion. The dissenting opinion indicated that there was "no public purpose" in discouraging Citicorp from undertaking this venture. This dissenting opinion also noted that the Federal Reserve had encouraged bank holding companies to enter the consumer finance industry. Since the decision to deny the proposed acquisition was carried by a five-to-one vote (with one abstention), the dissenting opinion carried little importance. This decision of the Federal Reserve Board did not represent a landmark decision. It merely reaffirmed positions that had been established in other decisions.

In another instance, in 1976 the Federal Reserve Board turned down a proposed acquisition of the Citizens Bank of Bunnell by Florida National Banks of Florida. This instance illustrates the complexity and long periods of negotiation that are often a part of negotiating with regulators. The Citizens Bank of Bunnell was a small, profitable bank and was important to Florida National in its plans to expand into areas of the state that had shown growth in banking activity. At an earlier period, Florida National had been ordered by the Federal Reserve Board to divest itself of its nonbanking subsidiaries. All these assets were part of a trust set up to handle the estate of Alfred I. du Pont, heir to the chemical fortune.

The bank attempted to comply with this request through the creation of a trust, which held slightly less than 25 percent of the shares of Florida National. Florida National considered that it had complied with the divestiture requirement and could proceed to make acquisitions. At first, the Federal Reserve allowed two acquisitions, but then requested that the trust should divest itself of the remaining interest in Florida National and in effect issued an acquisition moratorium. The principal officers of the trust planned various methods to bring this about, but a depressed market for bank stocks held up completing the plans. At this time, the officers of the trust were presented with the possibility of buying Citizens Bank of Bunnell, but were apparently concerned that they would lose the acquisition prospect if the Federal Reserve Board made a decision after a lengthy period of deliberation. Thus the principals of the trust purchased the stock of the bank for their own account in hopes of subsequently selling it to Florida National after Board approval.

The Federal Reserve Board was apparently not convinced that the officers of the trust had acted in good faith. The Board indicated that it intended to judge the petitioners on a moral basis and stated that "'managerial resources' does not . . . refer solely to the business abilities of management or its past financial success. The legislative history . . . makes it clear that this factor relates not only to management's competence but also to management's integrity . . . the board believes it should not approve an application to retain the illegally acquired control position and thereby allow the offending party to reap the fruits of the violation."

Bank analysts viewing these developments might have been confused at the backing and filling of petitions and decisions, many of which were not mentioned in this brief summary. Nevertheless, the issue that stands out is the Board's decision that the spirit of its wishes was being thwarted. The Board then passed a moral judgment on the management's actions. The issue was clear for Florida National. In addition, other banks and the public were notified that the Federal Reserve Board was prepared to tell bankers that they must have integrity. The decision sounds simple in an old-fashioned way. But in making its decision the Board reaffirmed the importance of key ethical issues to banking and probably won quiet widespread support.

News Leaks

The third way regulatory agencies communicate with banks is through news leaks. This method of communication represents a new approach. News leaks convey information to the banking industry and to bank analysts previously kept secret. The information purports to have contained facts and opinions concerning banks that had been used by a regulatory agency. In one instance, the *Washington Post* on Sunday, January 11, 1976, published a front-page story, headlined "Citibank, Chase Manhattan on U.S. 'Problem' List." The report stated:

> Two of the three largest banks in the United States have been placed on a supersecret list of problem banks by the U.S. Comptroller of the Currency.
>
> New York's First National City Bank (Citibank) and Chase Manhattan Bank, with combined assets of $100 billion were placed on a problem list—until recently code named "Victor"—after bank examinations disclosed "inadequate" capital at both banks and sharp increases in assets of questionable value compared with previous examinations.
>
> Typically some 200 of the nation's 14,500 banks at any given time are given the special supervisory attention the "Victor" program was designed to provide.
>
> There is no indication that either of the giant banks, which hold $1 of every $10 on deposit in U.S. banks, faces any immediate financial difficulties. Citing the respect that both banks command, the examiners rated Citibank's future prospects "excellent" barring a world-wide catastrophe, while Chase's prospects were listed as 'fair'.

The report then showed the specific measures used to reach the conclusion that the banks should be placed on a problem list. Some of the information in the article had never been made public previously, such as the ratio of "classified" assets to gross capital funds, total classified loans, as well as opinions of bank examiners concerning the quality of each bank's management.

James E. Smith, the Comptroller of the Currency at the time, said that he would not acknowledge that the two banks had been placed on the problem list. Smith was quoted as saying that they were "strong, well managed banks." The presidents of the two banks declined to confirm or deny that either of the two banks was on the problem list. Both presidents gave strong endorsements to the strength of their respective banks.

Needless to say, the information was received by most readers as a shock. Subsequently, it was revealed that the Federal Reserve also had its own special list of problem banks, and this list was subsequently published. The list named 35 bank holding companies, including both large and small companies. The Federal Deposit Insurance Corporation also was shown to have a list.

An important issue to bank analysts involves the conditions under which the original information was leaked from the Comptroller of the Currency to the press. This question opens one of the more interesting speculations in current banking regulatory issues. Nor did the series of unusual events cease. For example, subsequent to the press disclosure of January 11, the files of the Comptroller of the Currency were broken in, and the burglary involved bank financial information. Reportedly, the FBI investigated.

A second example of a news leak perhaps should be titled a news fumble. On August 20, 1976, the *New York Times* reported:

> The Federal Reserve Board yesterday rejected a proposed acquisition by the Bankers Trust New York Corporation, the nation's eighth largest bank, citing "financial difficulties" at the New York bank. After the announcement produced an uproar in financial circles, the board issued a late afternoon statement declaring Bankers Trust "sound".
>
> The morning announcement of the decision, which involved acquisition of a small upstate New York bank, caused the outcry not because of the rejection but because the Federal Reserve seemed to imply concern for Bankers Trust's financial viability. It is highly unusual for the board to cite publicly a particular bank's financial problems.
>
> However the Federal Reserve, in its clarification, said that the decision represented only a continuation of an existing policy of denying acquisitions by banks that have been under financial pressure.
>
> Both the original statement and the clarification produced wide conjecture over why the Fed had chosen wording that could have caused large withdrawals of deposits from Bankers Trust. While some analysts believe the choice of words was a blunder on the Fed's part, others suggested that it was intended as a warning to other banks to pursue acquisitions less vigorously.

Bank analysts were left with less than clear evaluations of these news leaks. If the regulatory agencies were intending to prod the banks into a course of action, they ran a risk—admittedly remote—that they might precipitate a loss of confidence in the banks, with a run on the banks by depositors. This possibility involved a risk no regulatory agency would want, because the basic purpose of regulatory agencies is to prevent such an occurrence.

The data provided by the leaks were old. The leaks referred to information from one or two years previous to the news leaks. Nevertheless, the basic information the regulatory agencies made available provided bank analysts with both data and an evaluation previously not available.

REGULATORY ISSUES

The regulatory environment is one of almost continuous competition among regulators. The struggle is focused on several issues, and seven of the most important of these are briefly reviewed here.

Effectiveness of Audits and Examinations

A primary objective of bank regulation is the prevention of bank failures. The ability of regulatory agencies to perform this objective rests to a large extent on the quality of the information about the condition of banks under their supervision. According to the *Washington Post*, a recent draft report of the General Accounting Office criticized how the regulatory agencies perform their audits and examinations. The draft report indicated that the three principal regulatory agencies, the Federal Reserve Board, the Comptroller of the Currency, and the Federal Deposit Insurance Corporation, have been lax in monitoring the financial condition of banks, as well as have not acted to prevent them from violating various federal and state laws and regulations.

The report allegedly singles out the Federal Reserve Board for not satisfactorily monitoring the activities and the financial condition of bank holding companies. The draft is reported to carry its criticism a step further and recommend that the Federal Reserve System should attempt to identify and correct holding company problems before those problems affect the subsidiary banks.

The General Accounting Office's report is a draft version of a final report scheduled for future publication. The draft will be circulated among the three regulatory agencies for their comments, and most likely will be less critical before its official publication. Nevertheless, this report joins a new issue for regulatory agencies and cuts into the confidence that bank analysts place in their competence. The draft report, which includes the unexpurgated facts and opinions of the General Accounting Office's staff analysts, could be the basis of considerable discussion for a period ahead, regardless how mild the official version might appear.

Role of Nonbank Subsidiaries

To regulators, the nonbank subsidiaries are neither fish nor fowl. They do not fit into the mold of a bank. Yet regulators are not prepared to consider them as ordinary companies without any affiliation with a commercial bank. Regulators are concerned that bank holding companies might sacrifice a subsidiary bank to salvage a sinking nonbank subsidiary. The issue focuses on what standards should be used to measure the performance of nonbank subsidiaries.

This issue had been merely an interesting question until the Public Interest Research Group, an organization closely affiliated with Ralph Nader, submitted a memorandum to Congress in the summer of 1976 charging that bank holding company permissiveness on the part of the Federal Reserve Board had served to weaken banking. The memorandum indicated that certain nonbank subsidiaries of 23 major bank holding companies reported losses in 1974 and 1975 amounting to $107 million. The report stated that many bank holding companies absorbed these losses by transferring income from their strong bank subsidiaries to their troubled nonbank subsidiaries and that this use of subsidiary bank income to cover losses siphoned off potential capital from the subsidiary banks. In other cases, the memorandum continued, bank holding companies arranged for their subsidiary banks to purchase poor quality loans originated by the nonbank subsidiaries. By this method, subsidiary banks have absorbed the losses of nonbank subsidiaries without any explicit transfer of capital or income. The memorandum concludes that the subsidiary banks may disguise these losses for several years by failing to properly write down to market value the poor quality loans.

The issues raised by the Public Interest Research Group extend far beyond the specific concerns of the memorandum. Banks expanded into nonbanking subsidiaries hoping to find areas of profit greater than those they believed were possible from banking and also hoping to avoid regulatory scrutiny. The Public Interest Research Group is raising the question of whether nonbank subsidiaries should be subject to the same standards and tests as banks.

Several years ago, one bank correctly foresaw this issue and concluded that the outcome would be stringent for bank holding companies. At year-end 1973, Unionamerica, a bank holding company, split its holding company into a group of nonbank companies and a bank. The new organizations are called Unionamerica, now a nonbank financial service company, and Union Bancorp. Management believed that the 1970 bank holding company legislation would prove to be a heavy burden for bank holding companies and that the period of freedom and opportunity for bank holding companies to acquire nonbank subsidiaries and operate them profitably to the expectations of shareholders had passed. The issue concerning the role of nonbank subsidiaries is the question of whether Unionamerica's decision was correct.

Regulatory Disclosure

This issue involves the proper amount of information that should be made available to the public. The traditional position has been that the regulatory agencies have a special prerogative to judge which information about banks should be kept confidential. The position has been based on the assertion that regulatory agencies learn of information which could be damaging to the reputation of banks if made public. Nevertheless, the regulatory agencies stress, in almost all instances, that the errant banks have been capable of remedying their problems. Thus public disclosure might disturb public confidence in a weak bank and could make recovery of that bank a more difficult task. Some regulators have even warned in congressional testimony that this information could lead to a broad panic. Moreover, regulatory agencies are concerned that the mass media could sensationalize information, making the information appear to be more significant than it might be.

This traditional position has been challenged by a potentially significant lawsuit against federal regulators following the collapse of the U.S. National Bank of San Diego in February 1974. The suit charges that both the Comptroller of the Currency and the Federal Deposit Insurance Corporation knew that fraudulent loans, backed by fraudulent records, were being made by the bank at least since 1962, but that they failed to discharge their duties and stop the bank from these activities. The suit was brought in January 1976 by British Columbian Investment Company and 32 affiliated companies. The case alleges a large-scale cover-up, and the removal of a conscientious examiner from position of responsibility when he insisted that corrective action should be taken. The implication of the suit is that regulatory agencies may not be as effective in keeping banks sound as, perhaps, full public disclosure or the threat of disclosure.

Some banks are moving voluntarily to disclose information, which, as recently as five years ago, had been considered highly confidential. The Securities and Exchange Commission has been particularly active in pressing for fuller disclosure. At present, the principal bank regulatory agencies appear to be in a retreat from their position of keeping information as confidential as possible. There are limits to disclosure. Yet in the context of U.S. society in the latter half of the 1970s, these limits do not appear to have been reached.

Treatment of Foreign Banks in the United States

One of the unusual facts about U.S. banking regulation is that there is virtually no direct federal control of foreign banks located in the United States. This situation applies to representative offices, agencies, branches, and subsidiary banks of foreign parent banks. The only federal regulation is a requirement that subsidiary banks need to be accepted for Federal Deposit Insurance Corporation insurance. Other foreign bank compliance is on a voluntary basis. Since June 1973, for example, foreign banks operating in the United States have been asked, but not legally required, to maintain reserves against increases in their negotiable certificates of deposit and Eurodollar borrowings.

The banking charters for foreign banks are granted by the various state banking commissions. Ten states have enacted legislation allowing foreign banks to operate within their jurisdiction, including California, New York, and Illinois. Sixteen states explicitly prohibit foreign banking operations of any kind, and the remaining twenty-four states have taken no position.

This regulatory situation of foreign banks provides them with a potential loophole in federal regulation that could prove to be one of the most important future issues in U.S. banking. Foreign banks are not restricted from expanding their operations on an interstate basis. These banks have the potential of establishing a banking network of operations in the principal commercial banking states, while U.S. banks are prohibited from doing so. The value of such a banking network cannot be underestimated to wholesale banks that serve nationwide U.S. corporations.

Most legislation which has been introduced by regulatory agencies has stressed the need to bring foreign banks under the same regulations that apply to U.S. banks. This legislation has languished for years, despite repeated efforts of regulatory agencies, including the Federal Reserve, to win support for the regulations. Perhaps surprisingly, it is not entirely clear that all U.S. banks would favor such legislation. There is some support to permit the foreign banking companies to be the leading edge to break down the barriers to interstate banking. It could be reasoned, with this point of view, that U.S. banks should be allowed the same privileges as foreign banks.

Control of U.S. Banking Abroad

In recent years U.S. banks have looked overseas as the principal way of expanding their activities to expand profit opportunities and avoid regulatory control. Profits of the major U.S. banks that have developed strong international operations have risen sharply in recent years, and several major international banks now obtain more than one half of their earnings abroad. In many instances their international earnings have been gaining more rapidly than domestic earnings. Moreover, banks are not restricted from corporate securities underwriting in most overseas countries as they are in the United States.

Regulatory agencies and many bank analysts have become concerned about the activities of U.S. international banks. Because U.S. banks maintain a greater distance between themselves and regulators than in most other countries, there is doubt among some bank analysts that the U.S. regulatory agencies are as fully aware of foreign developments as they should be. The interest in expanding regulatory controls of international banking of U.S. banks has recently been given additional weight by the growing recognition that international banking companies—those of the United States and other major industrial countries—have become principal lenders to the nonindustrial countries of the world. These countries are finding their foreign debt service has increased sharply and become more burdensome since the OPEC countries raised the price of oil.

There have been many proposals to tighten all aspects of international bank reporting, from requirements of complete reports of nonearning loans to foreign exchange trading activities. There have been proposals to tie together the deposit insurance systems used throughout the world. There have been efforts to obtain further information concerning the source of deposits. All these proposals have neither brought about much increase in the authority of regulatory agencies over foreign banking activity, nor much additional information to bank analysts. Nevertheless, the issue of control over U.S. international banking could surface quickly as a major issue if there were any new important difficulties from international banks.

Regulation of Electronic Banking

Banking has always been one of the slowest industries to understand how to use new technology and even slower in permitting it to be used. Legal issues of jurisdiction have been a major factor in delaying the fuller use of electronic equipment in banking. Regulatory agencies share with the courts and

Congress the power to authorize the use of much of the new electronic equipment.

Many banks in states that prohibit branch banking have pressed for a definition of customer bank communication terminals (CBCT) which would set them apart from branches. These banks could then expand their presence of banking services. Currently, court rulings have interpreted customer bank communication terminals as branches, and the Comptroller of the Currency has issued guidelines supporting the findings of the courts. Nevertheless, regulatory agencies have probably only begun to wrestle with the issues of electronics in banking.

Carried to its farthest, electronics has the potential to provide instant execution for virtually all types of transactions. A customer could use a telephone, a leased wire, or possibly a personal transmitter to communicate with a bank. The traditional use of a bank or a branch would then change meaning, and the communicator terminal—either a phone, wire, or personal transmitter—would perform many of the services of tellers and customer service officers. There would be considerable need for personnel under such a system to install and maintain the electronic equipment and to serve as a liaison with customers, but the total number of personnel required for a group of customers would most likely be much lower than for the traditional methods.

Of course, this future possibility has not arrived and may never arrive or even be approached. Nevertheless, all the electronic developments and experiments are steps in a direction that could lead to this outcome. The role of regulatory agencies would be greatly changed and could include responsibility for such new areas as maintaining, auditing, and servicing equipment, maintaining standards of confidentiality of information, and daily audits of transactions. How all of these activities might be administered in a regulatory environment of competitive regulators could be a difficult issue to resolve.

Additional Banking Powers for Near-Banks

Near-banks are all financial institutions offering various kinds of deposit and lending services. They include mutual savings banks and savings and loan associations. If the definition of near-banks is given more latitude, it would also include personal finance, sales finance companies, industrial finance companies, and credit unions, as well as most other financial intermediaries. These companies usually accept deposit type liabilities, although some obtain a portion of their funds from institutions and underwritings. Banks are unique in that they can issue checks, accept demand deposits, and lend for a broad spectrum of purposes.

The line between banks and near-banks was respected by both groups in a kind of gentlemen's agreement until the early 1970s. Then, mutual savings banks became concerned that their market position was slipping. As a response in 1974, mutual savings banks, savings and loan associations, and cooperative banks in Massachusetts and New Hampshire obtained permission to issue drafts against interest bearing savings accounts. These drafts are called negotiable orders of withdrawal or NOW accounts. This action not only eliminated the uniqueness of checking accounts of banks, but it also provided the mutual savings banks with a competitively superior service. They could offer interest on funds left on deposit, while banks could not.

Two regulatory agencies had certain powers to control NOW accounts, but chose to avoid the issue. The Federal Deposit Insurance Corporation regulates interest rates of the mutual savings banks that it insures and could have imposed a zero interest rate ceiling on NOW accounts. It could have thereby eliminated their competitive advantage over the regular checking accounts of commercial banks. However, only 8 of the 167 mutual savings banks in Massachusetts were insured, and the Federal Deposit Insurance Corporation was reluctant to act. The Federal Reserve could have affected the negotiability of NOW drafts by classifying them as noncash items for clearing processes. However, there were legal and political problems with this approach. The regulatory agencies were unable to reach an accord among themselves, and armed by a favorable state court decision that cleared the way of any state legal problems, mutual savings banks brought the issue to Congress. Congress acted and granted the request of the mutual savings banks, as well as extended the authority to other depository institutions except credit unions in the two states.

Subsequently, NOW accounts have been authorized for mutual savings banks in Connecticut and New York, although the accounts in New York do not earn interest. Federal savings and loan associations are permitted to offer NOW accounts in all six new England states. The barrier between banks and near-banks further blurred in October 1974 when the National Credit Union Administration began authorizing credit unions to issue share drafts for payment of members' funds to third parties. These share drafts are used and accepted as being interchangeable with regular checks.

Member banks of the Federal Reserve System are required to carry financial burdens not required on their near-bank competitors. Federal Reserve System membership requires that reserves be held in vault cash or noninterest bearing reserve bank deposits, while many state regulators count certain interest bearing securities as reserves. The difference in accounting for reserves can be substantial. For example, Baystate Corporation of Massachusetts recently withdrew five banks belonging to its Baybanks, Inc. subsidiary from the Federal Reserve System. The organization estimate that the change would increase its earnings about 12 percent from what earnings otherwise would have amounted if it had remained in the Federal Reserve System.

The near-banks have, understandably, not found cooperation from the Federal Reserve System to expand their services beyond the narrow boundaries of a few states in the northeast. Their efforts have been focused on Congress, which has acted in a sympathetic way in the northeast area where most mutual savings banks in the United States are located. However, Congress has not acted with much vigor to aid them outside the northeast area. The issue is important to the Federal Reserve, since the growing privileges of near-banks tend to weaken the System's control over its membership.

Changed Accounting Rules

Two major changes in accounting rules proposed for banks include price level accounting and restructured debt accounting. Neither of these changes has been proposed by the three principal regulatory agencies. Nevertheless, the proposals have reflected interest on the part of the Securities and Exchange Commission. The Financial Accounting Standards Board (FASB) considers these issues to be its responsibility and has proposed position papers on both issues.

The position paper on price level accounting recommended that supplementary financial reports should be available for banks and other companies which would show earnings statements and balance sheets after adjustment for inflation. The position paper was released in 1974 and created considerable discussion by banks, most of it opposed to the adjustments. Subsequently, nothing significant has happened, and the FASB has apparently let the issue drift.

The FASB position paper on restructuring debt was released at year-end 1976 and proposed, for all practical purposes, to allow most banks to continue to retain their present method of accounting for bad debts. The draft paper draws fine lines, for example, and distinguishes between restructurings of "substance" and of "form," with an accounting recognition of loss needed only if the change is of "substance." Most banks claim that the majority of their restructurings are of "form" only and that ultimately the full debt will be repaid. The FASB has proposed hearings on the topic and presumably will issue a final position paper after the hearings. Since there is not likely to be much pressure on the part of banks to make the draft more stringent, the final report might look much like the draft.

RESPONSE TO REGULATORS

Within broad scope, the overall requirements of regulatory agencies cover most banks similarly. Nevertheless, banks are able to make numerous decisions about how regulatory controls affect their organizations. Banks have developed three principal approaches in responding to regulatory controls—acquiesence, challenge to regulators, and exploitation of regulatory loopholes.

Acquiescence

The first response is to accommodate regulatory agencies in their requests and to acquiesce to the requests. Most banks operate with this policy. It takes considerable time and often expensive legal talent to take any other policy. Most banks are content to live with an ambience with regulators that does not involve challenges, arguments, and legal petitions. Bank managements will state an issue forcefully, but not press matters beyond a decision by a regulatory agency. In turn, regulatory agencies have developed considerable sensitivity to the level of discomfort that their constituents feel toward them and are adept at keeping the discomfort level below a boiling point. Often, when difficulties arise from a contentious issue, the regulatory agencies provide compensation by granting concessions to banks in other matters. Thus there is a balance between control and discontent, and most banks acquiesce to the bulk of regulatory pressures.

Challenge to Regulators

A few banks have challenged regulatory agencies in their decisions. In some instances they have aggressively made challenges. The instance of the Bank of the Commonwealth, noted in an earlier chapter, illustrates the difficulties of this approach. The manner in which the Bank of the Commonwealth pursued its efforts to circumvent the controls of the Federal Reserve System probably were as important as the issues themselves. The Bank of the Commonwealth openly flaunted its challenge to regulators and this carried risks beyond the issues of contention. Nevertheless, most banks that challenge regulatory agencies do so suavely and with great care.

The word *challenge* is used here to refer to any significant legal effort to change a decision by a regulatory agency. For example, on November 10, 1975, Citicorp's original request to acquire West Coast Credit Corporation of Seattle was turned down by the Federal Reserve Board, as was noted earlier in this chapter. Nevertheless, Citicorp persevered in its request and petitioned for reconsideration. West Coast Credit's financial condition was judged to have weakened, and on March 23, 1976, the Board reversed its earlier decision and granted permission for the acquisition. Citicorp challenged the regulatory agency, and was at least partly successful in that challenge.

Not all challenges are carried forth in ways that involve newspaper publicity or even press releases. For example, CIT Financial Corporation, a broadly based conglomerate corporation, acquired the National Bank of North America in May 1967. CIT had previously established a strong position in a wide range of financial services, as well as owned a group of manufacturing companies. The nonfinancial parts of CIT were significant. If all of the financial parts of CIT were excluded, the remaining manufacturing parts would have been large enough to make the company qualify as a Fortune 500 manufacturing corporation.

Since CIT was technically considered to be a bank holding company, it was obliged to divest those subsidiaries acquired after June 30, 1968 in areas of business not on the list of approved activities of the Federal Reserve System. Earlier acquisitions might be retained under a grandfather clause. Nevertheless, the Federal Reserve had power to rescind the grandfather exemption, if it chose to do so. The CIT activities under review that qualified for the exemption included North American Company for Life and Health Insurance, with gross assets of $225 million in 1975, North American Company for Property and Casualty Insurance, with gross assets of $66 million, and a group of manufacturing and merchandising operations, with sales of $515 million in 1975. The manufacturing operations included All-Steel, a furniture manufacturer, Gibson Greeting Cards, and Raco, Inc., which manufacturers electrical boxes and fittings. Picker Corporation and certain consumer finance companies were acquired subsequent to the cutoff date of June 30, 1968.

The Federal Reserve Board decided on December 20, 1976, to permit CIT to keep all of the operations owned prior to the cutoff date. Thus CIT was entirely successful in its efforts to retain its organization intact, within the interpretation of the 1970 Bank Holding Company Act. The discussions between CIT and the Federal Reserve were completely private and confidential could have been some. A literal reading of the Bank Holding Act would permit CIT to hold the bulk of its nonfinancial subsidiaries. Nevertheless, the Board's decision permitted an important exception to the division between banking and nonbanking activities, which underlay the purpose of the Act.

Exploitation of Regulatory Loopholes

Banks sometimes exploit opportunities that appear as a result of loopholes in the overall regulatory system. These loopholes may reflect gaps in regulatory control or differences in requirements among regulatory agencies. The loopholes invariably represent temporary advantages, but while they last, they can be important to banks.

For example, in 1967 Union Bank determined that there was a major loopholes invariably represent temporary advantages, and while they last, they pany called Unionamerica. At this time, one-bank holding companies were virtually free from regulation and could diversify into nonbanking businesses. As has been noted, the discovery brought about an avalanche of banks which turned themselves into one-bank holding companies. Eventually, in 1970, Congress passed legislation that brought bank holding companies under Federal Reserve Board regulation, and the legislation indicated that diversification of bank holding companies would have to be closely related to banking. The loophole was closed. By being first, Unionamerica gained precious time to make acquisitions in the areas of its interest.

PART FOUR
VIEWING
THE MANAGEMENT
OF A BANK

CHAPTER 13
BANKING STRATEGIES

An earlier chapter discussed banking profitability from an accounting point of view. Nevertheless, profitability is not the result of accounting measures. *Banking profitability* is the result of how bankers and customers conduct their business. The accounting measures record only whether or not these day-by-day business decisions are being conducted profitably, and they have limited usefulness in explaining why certain banks are more profitable than others. This chapter looks at the business strategies that banks use, which in turn, have a major influence on their profitability.

IMPORTANCE

The link between a bank's strategy and profitability represents one of the basic factors in evaluating the company's longer-term prospects. It is important because there does not appear to be any other way of making this type of evaluation. Certain strategies have been regularly associated with sustained high profitability, and the identification of these strategies provides an important factor in assessing whether a bank's profitability is likely to be sustained. Other strategies have been associated with lower levels of profitability. Nevertheless, many banks actively pursue strategies that have never successfully achieved high profitability. These banks hope that they will be unique and have put together a program on paper which appears reasonable and logical. The record indicates, however, that these programs are usually impractical, do not provide significant or sustained gains in profitability, and are quietly forgotten after a few years. Still other banks have not developed an explicit strategy. They believe that day-by-day attention will provide a route to adequate profitability, and they are sometimes right and other times wrong in this approach, depending on which of several strategies they actually practice.

The assessment of a bank's strategy represents a method of analysis different from the usual numerical approach. Accounting information has been designed to show information important to regulatory agencies and shareholders, but not to managers of banks. For example, there is plentiful information concerning assets and liabilities according to various types of risk for regulators to review, and there is information concerning overall profits and shareholders' equity for shareholders to consider. However, there is virtually no accounting and little marketing information concerning the superiority of a bank's services to various types of customers. Yet even if this information were available, it would be a measurement of a skill. It would not be a direct perception of the strategy itself.

The assessment of a bank's strategy represents a personal evaluation. It is based on observations concerning how a bank responds to its customers' needs and how it awakens customers to their own needs. It is a selective process of refining a large number of apparently different observations to find a common element. Perhaps, more aptly, it is much like the description of how a team plays on a field.

The strategy of a bank is not a plan. Plans represent formalized proposals and projections of future activities. They emphasize a forecast of the usual accounting measures of performance, such as assets, deposits, and profits. The development of plans represents an important step in the understanding of the components of a bank, but plans are not always realistic, and they do not attempt to show patterns of behavior that banks will typically follow under widely different circumstances. For this reason, plans are of less value to bank analysts—and perhaps to banking companies themselves—than strategies.

STRATEGIES OF SELF-DETERMINATION

Only a few banks are able to develop their organization entirely the way they would like. These few banks which follow strategies of self-determination are able to do so because they show such superior profitability that they are self-funding, or if they make securities offerings, the offerings are matters of choice. By doing so, they avoid the constraints that regulatory agencies or shareholder groups often apply. The self-determination of a bank reaches deeper into the organization. These banks provide their own terms for conducting business, either through their proprietary skills or by their ability to control their banking environment sufficiently so that they retain oligopolistic benefits of low unit costs. Either strategy can be successful in keeping profitability high. However, only specialty skills can both keep profitability high and provide the basis for significant further growth of the organization (Table 72).

Proprietary Skills Strategy

"Proprietary skills" in banking represent a capability of performing services in a superior manner for customers. These are specialty skills. In doing so, a bank is able to charge a premium and earn a profit above the typical profit of banks that do not provide such skills. The approach to proprietary skills used here cuts across marketing, operations, research and development, yet focuses the

Table 72   Banking Strategies

Strategies of self-determination	Proprietary skills strategy
	Oligopolistic strategy
Strategies of drift	Outflank strategy
	Serendipity strategy
Strategies of retardation	Archaistic strategy
	Purge strategy
	Militant strategy
	Contraction strategy
	Speculative strategy
	Futuristic strategy

characteristics of all three into patterns of behavior. It stresses the importance of a unique service, lowest unit costs, and the use of innovation.

Such a simple description. Nevertheless there are spectacular results when it is successfully practiced. Yet, for all of the common business sense that it reflects, the importance of proprietary skills appears not to be well understood by many businessmen, and perhaps less well understood by bankers. In any event, programs for the development of proprietary skills are not widely practiced.

The explanation for a lack of interest in developing proprietary skills may lie in the quasi-public image bankers have of their business. Bankers clearly like to earn a profit. They recognize the importance of earnings in an organization that requires the generation of capital to sustain itself. Yet service to customers, rather than a drive to increase earnings represents the primary goal of most bankers. Bankers believe, correctly, that profits are the result of a service well performed. Yet most bankers traditionally have been reticent concerning any attempt to press these profits to the maximum, perhaps because in the minds of many bankers this goal could conflict with the primary goal of serving customers in ways that promote their best interests. Many bankers believe that their customers still need an admonition now and then about prudence in the use of debt. There is still a belief among many bankers that left entirely on their own, many customers would reach out for too much debt, much like a child in an unattended candy store. The expansion of corporate borrowing in the past three decades has not changed this belief, since many established corporations have faced difficulties in recent years that were the aftermath of unwise borrowing.

The traditional caution of bankers has been replaced in a few instances by an aggressive expansionist approach to profits, and the goal of service is swept forward in the enthusiasm of placing loans. The effort of many banks to finance real estate investment trusts in the early 1970s was an example of this effort. Nevertheless, this expansionist approach to profits largely has been limited in scope and does not represent the prevailing direction of efforts to earn profits.

Service to customers never has been able, taken alone, to provide the impetus to the development of a superior bank. Special skills have always been a key factor among those banks that have developed rapidly with high profitability.

Bankers with proprietary skills have projected their entrepreneural temperment to their customers, evaluated the response of their customers, and supported those customers who understood their own entrepreneural goals. These bankers invariably sought those areas of the banking business where their activities were not easily duplicated by competitors. The skill of these bankers became regarded as a special and rare capability, and customers sought these banks to participate in the benefits from this skill. Banks that possessed this skill in their leaders and institutionalized its practice into their organizations have made unusual and important contributions to banking and have rewarded their shareholders. Their potential for future development has been and will always be enormous.

Mellon Bank.   The development of the Mellon bank by Andrew W. Mellon represents an example of the successful use of proprietary banking skills. From 1874 when he joined the bank until 1921 when he became U.S. secretary of the treasury, Andrew Mellon developed a small, inconsequential bank into one of the nation's major financial institutions. This development was possible because the bank was highly profitable and was able to add to its capital and show a strong return to its shareholders.

Andrew Mellon possessed two outstanding capabilities. He understood the effects of business cycles and the opportunities that ensue from the cyclical ebb and flow of profits. He also understood how to differentiate between those very few venture capitalists who were likely to succeed from the multitudes of inventors who are only intelligent dreamers. He positioned his bank so that it could use those two skills, and only during the latter years of his life, when he undertook government responsibilities, did the powerful expansion of this bank begin to ease.

Mellon was frail, reserved, and analytical, hardly the qualities usually associated with bank presidents. He attended a small local college in the Pittsburgh area and helped as an assistant to his father, Thomas Mellon, who had started a bank named T. Mellon & Sons several years earlier. The strain was too great, and to avert a breakdown, Andrew Mellon quit college.

Andrew Mellon's father then advanced the 17-year-old young man $40,000 which he used to build and stock a lumberyard. The lumber business had barely been established when Andrew saw that business conditions were turning weak. Sensing severe troubles ahead, he completely sold out the business. It took courage for a young man not yet 20 years of age to liquidate a business that he had just started. Yet this was the right decision, because the U.S. economy had reached a speculative peak in 1873. The following five years of depression were, for the times, as severe as the depression of the early 1930s. Andrew Mellon protected his capital from the devastation of that depression, a feat that almost none of his business contemporaries accomplished.

Mellon then joined his father's bank, and for a decade watched as his father used the bank to support Henry Frick in his effort to establish a strong position in the developing coke business. Coke was essential to steelmaking, and steel was still an expensive specialty metal at the time. Andrew Mellon watched how a bank could obtain fees, take options, and benefit from backing a leader in what was then an emerging industry. The development of the Bessemer process of steelmaking in 1880 assured Henry Frick of financial success, and provided a handsome profit to the Mellon bank. The lesson of backing the right entrepreneur at the right time with sufficient funds from loans and equity participations left a strong impression on Andrew Mellon. Frick's expansion in 1880 also was launched early in a period of expanding business conditions. In 1882, the father, Thomas Mellon, gave the management of the bank to Andrew Mellon and subsequently gave him and his brother ownership. The pattern of specialty skills had been set.

In 1889, after Andrew Mellon had spent a decade apprenticing in the bank and another decade and a half operating it, three strangers to the bank applied for a loan. They came directly to Mellon's desk, located in easy access to all of the bank's customers and staff on the first floor at the front of the bank. One of the men, Arthur Vining Davis, described the characteristics of aluminum, and the other two, a metallurgist and a chemical engineer, explained a new electrolyte process of extracting aluminum, which had been developed by Charles Hall. This process was the basis of a company called the Pittsburgh Reduction Company. Then, as now, banks preferred to lend to established customers, preferably those who were engaged in businesses that could be easily understood, which in those days included industries such as retailing or railroads. The purpose of the meeting was to refinance a $4,000 loan from another bank which had been called. The company had $20,000 in original stock subscription that had largely been exhausted.

Andrew Mellon looked at the plant which was a shack filled with pots. The collateral for a loan clearly was not worth much. Nevertheless, he was impressed with the lightness of the new metal and that this nondescript company had reduced its price from $8 to $2 per pound through new cost savings methods. He called the three men back for a meeting and told them that they needed $25,000, not $4,000, if the operation were to succeed. He was prepared to take stock for that money, as well as subsequently provide additional loan funds. This step in the development of the company was undertaken during a period of business expansion. Mellon supported the company during a subsequent recession. Five years later, in 1894, as business conditions turned from recession to expansion, he analyzed the economics of the company's operations and purchased a part of the bonds that were issued to pay for moving the company to Niagara Falls, where electrical power was cheap and plentiful. The company, which subsequently became Alcoa, never again worried about money, and word was passed in business circles that the Mellon Bank was a place where new technologies were given careful consideration.

In 1900, another stranger called at Andrew Mellon's desk. This inventor held a dark colored stone of silicon carbide in his hand which he called a "diamond." The material was fused using ordinary sand, coke, and salt at temperatures that were considerably higher than any previously used in commercial production. An electric furnace was the only method of obtaining these temperatures. Mellon knew the facts of electric power from his knowledge of aluminum. He took an equity interest and bought a large part of the bonds that were used to move this second company to Niagara Falls. The company was to become the Carborundum Company.

The discovery of oil in western Pennsylvania had opened Mellon's interest in that business, and for many years he was engaged in financing and owning oil exploration, refining, and transportation companies. Yet Mellon was more interested in the possibility of developing oil resources far away from western Pennsylvania, which lay in the middle of Standard Oil's home territory. He invested in oil exploration in Texas and was one of the principals of the Spindletop discovery in east Texas in 1902. Through his knowledge of the oil business and the lack of any bank at the time in Texas which could develop the discovery, he was able to turn his new oil interests into an organization that was later Gulf Oil Company.

There were many other ventures which were based on the same pattern of investing in ventures of new technology with capable management at a time during business expansions. For example, he organized the New York Shipbuilding Corporation, which built ships completely out of steel, using new construction techniques that had been developed by builders of steel bridges. These activities were supported not only by the original bank, T. Mellon & Sons, a private bank, but increasingly by the Union Trust, a national bank largely controlled by Mellon, but which also had public shareholders.

There were limits to Mellon's talents. Whenever he stepped beyond his specialty skills, he did not perform well. For example, Mellon's entry through Koppers into the public utility field was not successful. He did not understand the special ways of public utility regulation. In another instance, Mellon did not understand the problems of consolidating declining industries or of running monopolies, and an entry into coal mining proved costly. Most of these less successful ventures occurred after he had left active control of the bank and had become secretary of the treasury.

Mellon had a talent to pick winners from a parade of inventors, promoters, and others who passed his desk. In addition, for the men he chose, he also projected an image of what they could accomplish. He understood the importance of developing companies which provided unique products, and stressed the importance of keeping these companies as the low cost producers. In turn, this strategy reflected how he approached his own bank.

Valley National Bank. Walter Bimson of Valley National Bank provides a contrast to the methods of Andrew Mellon. Bimson was raised in Colorado at the turn of the twentieth century and worked as a commodities loan officer for Harris Trust and Savings Bank in Chicago. An open, friendly man, he liked the companionship of the West more than the formal relationships of a large city bank.

Bimson possessed two special characteristics. He held a belief that his bank should be a place for ordinary people. Most banks at the time catered to merchants and businessmen and had little understanding or interest in personal loans or home improvement loans. Bimson also had confidence that an expansionist government policy would prevail and enrich the country.

At the beginning of 1933, during the worst part of the depression, Bimson became president of Valley National Bank. The connection between Valley and Harris had been made through the purchase of agricultural loans by the latter bank, and Bimson was selected to see this small local bank through its difficulties. At the time, deposits were less than $7 million, which represented a small bank even for those days.

Bimson began to find ways of developing bank business based on the needs of ordinary people. He was concerned about repairing residential and other neglected properties, and he authorized loans to refurbish these properties, thus providing employment as well as income to the bank. He worked closely with many Mormon Church members who prided themselves on their earnestness in honoring loan agreements, and he made a special effort to assist all customers who had fallen on the hard times of the depression and who showed intentions of good faith in their business dealings. Through his personal contact with these people, he conveyed a close sense of fellowship and projected an image of confidence. He reassured his customers that he would not foreclose on them and that he trusted them to begin the repayment of their loans as soon as they could do so. In a simple and small way, Bimson captured the essence of the philosophy of the New Deal even before it had been formed. When the New Deal programs were enacted, Bimson understood them and knew how to use them more effectively than any other banker in Arizona.

For example, in the fall of 1934, Congress passed the National Housing Act, which among other things provided a program for government insured household loans. Most bankers were not interested in the act. They believed that home improvements for ordinary people were risky, in view of the uncertainties of the depression. Many bankers also believed that the act would be struck down by the U.S. Supreme Court and that they would be left with many doubtful uninsured loans.

Bimson had none of these doubts. He assisted furniture companies, paint dealers, appliance distributors, roofers, and other suppliers in promoting and advertising their wares and trades. Valley National Bank supplied representatives who explained the new law, provided application forms, and helped people fill out the applications. Where local banks would not sponsor the programs, Valley offered an arrangement whereby it would provide funds for the loans and take all risks, as well as provide a fee to the local bank which would handle the application. Valley thus developed a customer base in virtually all areas of Arizona, and as soon as possible, opened small branches to directly serve these newly won customers.

The FHA mortgage program further accelerated the development of Valley National Bank. This program provided a government guarantee for home mortgages. By featuring the program, Valley quickly became Arizona's major mortgage banker. Most bankers believed that the new government program would be declared unconstitutional and that the government guarantees would be worthless. Bimson quickly ran out of deposits to fund the mortgages, but was able to sell them at a discount to Occidental Life and still show a profit. Acting as a broker, he was able to further expand his branch system and lay the foundation for regular banking services which were to come later.

Bimson pioneered the development of direct automobile loans and personal loans in the Southwest. This development brought an accompanying analysis of the costs of handling each type of loan so that it could be priced to show a profit. Competitors had neither Valley's cost analyses nor Valley's volume.

Valley National Bank grew from a small organization of less than $7 million in deposits in 1933 to $2.5 billion in deposits in 1975. Shareholders' equity, which in 1975 mostly showed cumulated retained profits, grew from a negligible amount to $153 million in 1975. The bank had used its high profitability to become the largest bank in the state and the largest between Texas and California.

Oligopolistic Strategy

A banking oligopoly occurs when a few major banks control the banking market. Often, one of these major banks, usually the largest, dominates the market, sets pricing standards, lending terms, and generally provides the prevailing direction to banking activities sometimes described as "banking leadership." The oligopolistic structure of banking is common throughout most areas of banking competition in the United States.

The oligopolistic strategy is designed to keep one bank in a dominant market position, primarily to keep the bank's unit costs as low as possible. The low unit costs are critical to the ability of an oligopolist to keep its profitability high. The oligopolistic strategy is usually, but not always, undertaken by branch banks. Oligopolistic strategy is important for these banks, since their branches are usually a source of low-cost individual deposits. They would also represent a potential problem of costly overhead, if the volume of banking activity shrank. The special advantage of the dominant bank would be neutralized, if competitive banks increased their activities. The oligopolist would face its competition without its special cost advantage. All of this assumes that none of the banks possessed particularly effective specialty skills.

The oligopoly strategy of a bank often follows a period of a major expansion when the bank had possessed, but lost its specialty skills. All service skills can be copied. If the bank does not develop new specialty skills, it may find itself in a defensive position, protecting its major position. It may then follow an oligopolistic strategy to hold the presence it inherited from an earlier period.

STRATEGIES OF DRIFT

The proprietary skills and the oligopolistic strategies reflect programs designed to change banking activities or protect a competitive advantage. However, not all banks have taken deliberate steps to determine the direction of their profitability. In fact, most banks have no strategies to change their profitability, and the strategies they do follow may be characterized as strategies of drift.

Banks following a strategy of drift do not look at profitability as a gauge of success, rather they often look at earnings per share, or in some cases, an expansion of balance sheet aggregates such as deposits or total assets. These banks have not taken major steps to improve their profitability because they perceive no need to take such strenuous measures. They perceive themselves as doing well enough, and they believe that the risks of following more aggressive strategies outweigh possible benefits.

Two strategies of drift are described here. They cover most banks in the United States and are noted without specific examples.

Outflank Strategy

The "outflank strategy" exploits temporary weaknesses in the strategy of a dominant bank. Nevertheless, it does not involve a commitment to basic proprietary skills that could form the base of a steady, ongoing strategy. The outflank strategy represents an effort to move programs quickly into position when they could be successful and dismantle them whenever the bank could no longer use them to advantage.

For example, one bank used this strategy to exploit a dominant bank's low interest rate on passbook savings accounts. At the time, the legal limit for these accounts was 5 percent, and all competitive banks were paying 4-1/2 percent. By raising the interest rate on these deposits from 4-1/2 percent to 5 percent, the bank with the outflank strategy hoped to gain a temporary advantage of attracting additional deposit funds. Moreover, this bank was able to substitute the passbook savings deposit funds for higher cost certificates of deposit. In this manner, the maneuver would not only expand the deposit base of the bank, but also reduce its cost of funds.

An important assumption was that the competition, including the dominant bank in the area, would not follow the move. If this had occurred, the move would have had no competitive benefit to the bank with the outflank strategy, and instead, all banks would have raised their cost of funds. The assumption proved to be a successful guess, and for approximately one and one-half years, the insurgent bank alone, among principal banks, paid 5 percent for passbook savings deposits and predictably accomplished its objectives. Nevertheless, the competitive banks eventually raised their interest rates for these deposits, and the temporary advantage of this strategy was eliminated.

Sometimes an outflank strategy can have important lasting effects, if other banks do not respond. For example, in the 1910s, one midwestern bank saw the telephone as an important technical innovation to banking organizations, and not simply as an aid in conducting business or as a substitute for letter writing. This bank used the telephone as a key to the expansion of its branch banking operations. Other banks did not follow this lead and lost an important advantage when the state legislature subsequently set up major restrictions on branch banking.

Serendipity Strategy

The serendipity strategy makes fortuitous discoveries accidently. This is a strategy of keeping an open mind and hoping that business developments outside the bank will bring benefits. In its simplest, this approach represents a continuation of the past ways of conducting business. It usually involves no difficult choices. A large number of banks have pursued this strategy, and it is perhaps the most typical strategy in the banking industry.

For example, one major bank was neither the first nor the last bank in its banking area to begin an overseas expansion of branch operations. It turned itself into a bank holding company after a number of competitors had done so and developed its currency trading activities along the lines of its principal competitors. All of these activities were undertaken in response to requests of customers. None was pursued to develop a unique position or an advanced degree of excellence.

The advantage of a serendipity strategy is its flexibility and its quickness of response. Banks pursuing this strategy always seem to survive and often survive quite well. Yet they never are outstanding banking organizations as measured by a high level of profitability.

Perhaps there is a kind of collective merit in the prevalence of the serendipity strategy among banks. A smoothly running banking system requires a large number of banks that are flexible and responsive to customers' needs. It could be a major weakness in a banking system if a large number of banks attempted to undertake difficult or risky strategies which were significantly different from the prevailing ways of banking. There would be no guarantee that most of these more adventuresome strategies would be successful, and many would not work out well. Thus the widespread practice of this strategy may provide a measure of stability to the banking system.

STRATEGIES OF RETARDATION

Not all efforts to direct the efforts of a bank are fruitful. Six strategies are noted here that have shown a pattern of impeding the improvement of profitability. The irony of these strategies is that they are often adopted in hopes of improving earnings and eventually improving profitability. There is no theoretical reason why they could not be successful, and in an exceptional instance, one could be successful. Nevertheless, a review of banks which have adopted these strategies indicates that they do not usually fulfill their expectations.

Archaistic Strategy

An "archaistic strategy" attempts to turn the calendar back to an earlier period. This strategy represents a conscious effort by a bank's management to either preserve the ways of doing business of an earlier age or roll back contemporary changes and reconstruct the bank along the lines of an earlier period.

A bank may pursue an archaistic strategy simply from habit. The senior managements of many banks have grown comfortable over a period of years and have accumulated personal estates that enable them to forget the problems of balancing a weekly budget. Some banks that are family owned or are predominately controlled by a board of directors consisting of a large number of management have followed an archaistic strategy.

A bank may pursue an archaistic strategy because it may believe that contemporary banking trends are leading the industry down misguided paths. One major East Coast bank has followed an archaistic strategy for this reason. This bank believes that many of the banking trends of the past decade are misguided and that these trends have led to excesses such as low levels of liquidity and poor quality in loan portfolios. This bank believes that these trends will need to be corrected in the future. By not embarking on programs that would lead to these supposedly erroneous ways, this bank expects to be spared the harsh consequences of a future day of reckoning.

Purge Strategy

The "purge strategy" represents an effort to replace major portions of the management of a bank with a new managing group. The purge strategy involves much more than the hiring of a new president or the addition of several outside members of senior management from outside a bank. The addition of outside members to a management team is a common occurrence among many banks and may indicate little change in the policy of the bank. A purge occurs where there is a deliberate effort to rid the bank of the presence and the thinking of an earlier management.

For example, one western bank had become less competitive, and its earnings and profitability had declined. The bank's board was concerned that the price of this company's shares had declined and that programs had been directed in unproductive directions and were ineffective. The board sought a new chief executive who would provide the bank with better direction. A new chief executive was hired and concluded that the major problem with the bank was inept managers. The bank had been largely built through a series of mergers during the previous two decades, and this new chief executive believed that the gentlemen's agreements to keep all of the incumbent management had been a serious mistake.

The bank was reorganized, and virtually all of the senior managers were told to find other work, or they took early retirement. The purge strategy reached into middle management as well. Most of these managers who were retained were assigned to new responsibilities. The process of changing management took almost two years, and managers were relieved of their assignments as their replacements were hired. Despite these and other efforts to improve earnings and profitability, the subsequent performance of this bank has been mediocre, and it is difficult to ascribe benefits from the purge strategy.

The purge strategy has an important weakness. It cuts off the regular line of succession and gives a taint to having been a member of management prior to the purge strategy. Many middle managers believe that they no longer have opportunities for advancement. It is essential that these persons retain a sense of accomplishment and some hope for advancement throughout their career. Without the support of middle managers, young men and women cannot be trained effectively, information cannot be organized, analyzed, and transmitted upward in an organization properly, and the policy directions decided by senior management cannot be passed to tellers and clerks with endorsement and conviction. In banking, middle managers perform these crucial roles in determining the productivity of the overall organization. The purge strategy runs a risk of demoralizing and alienating this group, and its members are not likely to seek employment elsewhere because of their age and loss of benefits. A successful and profitable bank always treats this group with deference and respect.

There is a second difficulty with the purge strategy. To benefit a bank, the assumption that the major difficulty of the bank was weak management must be correct and the new group of managers have to be effective in a way that the previous managers were not. If the difficulties of a bank are more complicated than weak personnel, as is usually the case, the complicated personal overtones of pursuing the purge strategy can obscure these other issues, and the bank may not make the progress toward solving other, more difficult, problems.

Militant Strategy

The "militant strategy" is an effort to meet competitors head-on, with no differentiation between the services of the banks. It represents an effort to directly challenge the ongoing business relationships between a competitor bank and customers. The militant strategy invariably involves major expenditures with personnel, facilities, and equipment to support an aggressive effort to capture business from competitors. The most effective method is by offering reductions in the price of banking services. Followers of the militant strategy are aware of the negative impact of price cuts on profitability, but they aim to recoup enough additional revenue to offset the effect of price declines. Eventually, the bank would raise prices to competitive levels.

For example, one bank had branches mostly concentrated in one half of a state in which branch banking was permitted. This bank began to open a number of new branches in the other half of the state, fully aware that they would not be profitable immediately. It was anticipated that the branches would quickly gain regular loan and deposit business and within a few years would reach levels of profitability of the older branches in the other half of the state. The impact of the new branches was met with a counterchallenge by another bank, which expanded its branches into the home territory of the original bank, and cut prices on a number of banking services. The effect was damaging to the earnings of both banks. The bank initiating the militant strategy subsequently abandoned it.

The example shows that the major flaw to the militant strategy is the likelihood of a counterchallenge by either a competitor of equal strength of a group of banks. This flaw could be costly and involve a major erosion in overall profitability, which could be difficult to restore.

Contraction Strategy

The "contraction strategy" is a program to reduce the size of assets of a bank so that it could be more profitable. The main effort of the contraction strategy may be an outright contraction of loans in line with changes in loan requirements of customers. The effect may also be a winnowing of the assets, so that the least profitable assets are disposed and the total of the remaining assets would be smaller, but show a higher average return. The contraction strategy is often avoided by bank managements, because they believe, perhaps erroneously, that the public attaches considerable importance to asset totals that constantly increase.

In one example, a bank followed a strong expansionist approach in loans to a major industry which had been rapidly growing for more than two decades. The expansion in the industry turned to contraction, and the bank found itself unable to expand its loans and keep the loan quality and pricing margins it required. The decision to contract represented a willingness to mirror the changed conditions of its customers.

A much more difficult aspect of the contraction strategy is the decision to deliberately reduce loan volume and trim overall assets. In an example of this type of situation, a major bank on the East Coast reduced its loans moderately, following a period a major loan losses, and widespread concern over the quality of its assets. The difficulty in following this approach to profitability is that the weakest loans and the least attractive municipal securities are the most difficult to divest. For all practical purposes weak loans cannot be sold, and they tend to be self-perpetuating rather than self-liquidating. Securities of state and local governments under a financial cloud are also difficult to sell, because there is usually a thin market for them, and their sale would almost always require the bank to show a loss in its income statement. Moreover, some banks show relatively little variation in profitability among various classifications of assets. A divestiture of any group of these assets would have only a small or a negligible improvement in the bank's return on assets.

Speculative Strategy

The "speculative strategy" positions assets of a bank so that they would fluctuate in value as a result of changes in financial markets. The basis of the speculative strategy is that the management of a bank has superior forecasting skills to the markets in which it operates.

In one example, a small bank sought to expand its lending to construction and real estate borrowers. This bank was unable to attract deposits as rapidly as its loan requirements and the bank's parent company issued short-term commercial paper to fund the loans. This bank implicitly speculated that the future course of interest rates would not move sharply upward and that credit markets would not tighten. If those developments occurred, the bank would be placed in serious difficulties, and perhaps would be insolvent. In this instance, the speculation had an unfavorable conclusion. But many banks have taken speculative risks of this type which have shown favorable results.

In other instances, banks have taken unhedged positions in foreign currency transactions. These banks have, in widely publicized examples, lost considerable sums. However, many of the same banks have made considerable profits in foreign exchange positions at other occasions, and the results have not been widely publicized.

How banks can speculate is almost endless. The central issue to a speculative strategy is that its promoters are more capable of assessing future financial markets than others. This assumption represents a major assertion that may not be clearly recognized by the managers of banks that engage in the strategy.

It is on this issue that the speculative strategy has a flaw. In most instances, banks are not superior forecasters of future financial trends. In fact, a strong case can be made that their forecasts would show less-than-average results, because bankers are placed in a public position to convey an optimistic outlook whenever possible. This position reflects the quasi-public responsibilities of banks to look hopefully toward the future. Even if a bank were to possess special skills in forecasting, because of a unique computer forecasting model or special prescience on the part of the senior financial officer, the issue of speculation involves odds, as well as risks. If the risks are major and the bank continues a speculative strategy over a period of years, even remote odds can be worrisome, because any odds indicate that at some time the forecast of this bank will be in error, and a major loss could occur. The speculative strategy requires either great personal courage to overcome this knowledge or a lack of realization of the full implications of the strategy.

Futuristic Strategy

This strategy represents an attempt to position the bank according to conditions at some future period. It represents a strategy based on an anticipation of events and makes a bank's present organization fit this future scenario. To some extent, most banks continuously make adjustments to their organization with an eye to the future. The futuristic strategy differs from the incremental approach in that it attempts to rigorously change a bank to fit a fundamentally different banking environment, not yet experienced.

In one example, a major bank believed in 1948 that there was going to be a major depression in the 1950s and that the banking industry would face deposit runs and huge loan losses. This bank did not accept consumer loans, held virtually no municipal securities, accepted no loans from new companies which had been established during the Second World War because they had not experienced the difficult times of the depression to prove their capabilities, and spent no money training new employees because it expected many employees of competitive banks would be available for hiring. In this instance, the bank attempted to retain the liquidity that had been built up during the Second World War. This strategy was subsequently abandoned, but major opportunities had been lost in the meantime.

The flaw of the futuristic strategy is similar to the flaw of the speculative strategy. It bases its success on political and economic assumptions that may prove to be incorrect, and it makes major changes in its organization that can be justified only if its assessment of future trends is correct. There is always a possibility that a bank's futuristic strategy could be correct. Moreover, it is a matter of record that major changes in business conditions usually occur without anticipation, and banks that could have positioned themselves to benefit from the changed financial conditions would have accomplished a major competitive advance, at the vert least. Nevertheless, the futuristic strategy involves major risks that a bank could also position itself into a weak or noncompetitive position.

REGENERATION

Most banks keep the same strategies for decades. Yet banks are not locked into their past strategies, except as they wish to be. The willingness of a bank to change its strategy represents an important consideration because a change in strategy presents perhaps the most fundamental challenge a bank will ever encounter.

Changes in the strategy are not always announced in clearly defined terms to the bank itself or to the public. It is often important for a bank to give an indication of continuity with past ways of conducting business, with hopes to preserve ongoing business relationships or keep a staff intact and dedicated to its work. In fact, most staff and close customers quickly perceive changes in strategy. Nevertheless the broader public, including more remote customers, and securities holders, may not be aware of the change.

There are sometimes indications of a change in strategy when a new chief executive is installed, and this person desires to show a break in continuity with the previous management. A new chief executive from outside the banking organization may serve as an indication of a change in strategy. Sometimes a member of an ongoing management may become chief executive and bring about an important change in strategy. The only certain guide is a review of letters to shareholders, public statements, and a review of the policies of the bank.

CHAPTER 14

MANAGEMENT CONTROLS

Previous chapters have discussed ways banks show results of their activities and ways policies and strategies provide ideas that serve as guidelines. Management controls provide the ways these ideas are acted on. Controls represent how ideas are made real and are turned into the daily life of a bank.

Management controls focus on people, and involves the conduct of individual employees. Control is often considered to be a financial procedure, and numbers are ordinarily thought to be the scope of control. Numbers are a part of management control, or perhaps more correctly, they are one way of measuring control. But numbers, audit sheets, and examinations do not cover the scope of management control. The numbers are records of behavior. How personal behavior is directed and encouraged is the basic issue of management control.

Control involves the intercommunication of all persons of a bank. It operates most effectively when all persons of a bank fully and completely understand the goals of the bank. The paradox of control is that effectively controlled organizations have almost always been least able to adapt to new circumstances. Control limits freedom, and change requires some element of freedom. This paradox is particularly important to banking, because there are important reasons why banks need effective management controls. Yet few banks can keep tight controls on the thought and action of their employees and expect to understand their customers if the needs of these customers are rapidly changing (Table 73).

Banks need effective management controls because the money of customers is fungible and without controls could be improperly transferred. Banks with tight management controls may be expected to have records which mean exactly what they say. Strict controls, however, can easily become a way of life and can involve personal conduct in broader ways than a correct procedure of entering numbers into a ledger. The image of a hidebound

Table 73   Checklist of Management Controls

External controls

1. *Financial reporting*—Is there quality, quantity, internal consistency, and accuracy of published numbers?

2. *Auditing*—Does the chief auditor report to the board or to line management? Is he identifiable as a senior officer?

3. *Planning*—Is budgeting used as a basis of management? Does long-range planning fit with the bank's strategies?

4. *Promotions*—Do promotions reflect the strategies?

5. *Operations officers*—Are these persons situated in all departments? In key departments? Do they bring about effective compliance?

Internal controls

6. *Code of conduct*—Are the strategies of the bank given first consideration?

7. *Image of bank*—Is the image clear? Is it used to direct the many small decisions which never are formally reviewed, but are collectively important?

8. *Image of chief executive officer*—Is the image clear? Is it appropriate for the needs of the bank?

9. *Art and architecture*—Do they give a clear image of the bank?

banker, with a punctilious and over precise bearing may reflect an over concentration of control. Nevertheless, the encouragement of freedom to bring new policies and new ideas into banking has always been suspect by bankers and nearly everyone else, because no one knows for sure whether the controls over funds might continue to be effective enough in a more permissive organization. The hidebound banker may appear restrictive, but the accuracy and control of his operations are usually welcomed by depositors and debt holders as well as investors.

Some banks have attempted to combine a freer attitude in meeting customers' needs, while retaining a tough core of management controls to insure the accuracy of accounts. Other combinations of freer attitudes with central controls have also been proposed. This effort at solving the paradox of management control in banking reflects the results of new management theory. The solution appears interesting, although it is not certain whether the solution will work for a long period. The harboring of two distinctly different management points of view in a single organization requires an exceptionally strong senior management and one that remains poised and balanced.

METHODS OF MANAGEMENT CONTROL

Banks use two methods to exercise management control. The "external approach" uses methods for controlling persons within a bank which are brought about through other persons. The internal methods of control refer to ways the employees of a bank impose self-selected controls upon themselves and believe that they are acting on the basis of their own volition.

External Controls

External controls include the ways that a banking company measures or reports what an employee has done. These controls include the usual types of financial records that are most widely associated with management controls.

Audit Controls.   The most common type of external control of management is audit and examination. These procedures involve the verification of a bank's figures to insure that the basic figures shown in the reported financial statements are correct. Auditing involves the checking to see, for example, if there is a loan agreement—a physical piece of paper—to back up the financial reports in the balance sheet showing the total loans outstanding. Audit procedures also involve communicating with a debtor to verify, for example, that a loan agreement is the same as it is in the files of the bank. The examination may involve such traditional procedures as counting the till cash of a branch to determine whether the amount of cash is the same as is indicated on the daily cash sheets of the branch. The audit and examination procedures involve one person's responsibility if the bank is small or a department of many persons if the bank is large.

It is important that the auditing and examining department be antonomous from the rest of the bank so that its objectivity remains unimpaired and unquestioned. Outside bank analysts have no way of determining this independence directly. Nevertheless, one indication would be whether the chief auditor reports directly to the board of directors. This arrangement provides the tightest management control.

Perhaps of greater day-to-day importance are the verification procedures of the daily activities of a bank. An example of these procedures is whether two signatures are required to execute a foreign currency transaction. Such an arrangement makes it more difficult for an improper transaction to occur. Bank analysts may sometimes learn of audit methods from a bank's reports, although the usual way of determining these methods is by questioning management.

Financial Reports.   The financial reports submitted to regulatory agencies and shareholders, as well as various other internal financial reports, are a second type of management control. These reports are discussed in Chapters 2 and 3.

Planning.   The use of planning is a relatively recent development in banks. Most planning programs provide banks with three services. The programs include long-range projections of what a bank might achieve, a short-term annual plan, which in other industries is called a budget program, and a formal basis for discussing these plans. The benefits of long-range plans have yet to be determined, because they have been used in most banks for only a short period of a few years.

Nevertheless, the short-term plans or budgets provide a near-term management tool of great power when used effectively. A comparison of actual performance with a budget prepared annually, with semiannual revisions, gives banking management an effective way of reviewing current developments and questioning where performance falls short or exceeds expectations. A key to the effectiveness of budget or short-term planning is whether the bank holds regular monthly meetings with its major department heads to review progress. Despite its importance, there is no way that outside bank analysts can be completely certain how a planning process is used.

Promotions.   The most obvious method of external control is promotion. The selection of personnel in a bank provides a direct and tangible method of communicating to all employees and bank analysts the values most highly esteemed. Perhaps no other topic occupies the attention of banking personnel as much as the anticipation of a promotion, and after the event occurs, an analysis of why the selection was made.

Most banks make promotions in their ranks or hire an outsider on the basis of one or a combination of three factors—service to a senior person, assessment of a person's market value, and loyalty. The service to a senior person involves the time-honored method of being a good assistant, without being a potential threat to the senior person. The assessment of market value involves the interest of a bank in providing a measure of compensation for personal achievement, as well as a protection to retain the most attractive candidates for senior management. Loyalty is important to banks because there is considerable cost in selecting and training persons in the management of a bank. Again, outside bank analysts are not easily able to observe these aspects of control.

Board of Directors.   The policies of a bank are controlled by its board of directors. Nevertheless, as was discussed in an earlier chapter, bank directors sometimes do not exercise their full authority, either because they may be members of the bank's own staff and thus are already under obligations to the management of the bank, or because the information that they receive has been filtered by the bank's management and lacks information that might challenge it.

Boards of directors of banks originally comprise the principal owners. However, most large banks today have boards whose ownership of all members may total less than a few percent of the outstanding stock. These board members sometimes do not have the proprietary interest that they might have if they held major stock positions. Nevertheless, many boards of directors of banks have functioned effectively without the incentive of personal interest. These boards usually have a strong sense of mission for their bank and act in earnest out of their dedication to that mission. Thus it is not possible to conclude that because a bank does not have a board with a major interest of shares that the board will not exercise its responsibilities. Of course, many small- and medium-sized banks have ownership positions in the hands of a few families, who are the principal board members.

Outside bank analysts cannot observe how the board of a bank operates.

They would need to observe the board's reports, which are not publicly available. They are left with little more than opinions, based on their knowledge of the business associations of the board's members.

Operations Officers. Another method of providing external management controls of a bank is to observe the activities of its operations officers who are charged with the responsibility of making sure that there is full compliance with the operating procedures of the organization.

The presence of operations officers can bring about important other aspects of management control. They observe and report on many other developments beside verification procedures and often administer a personnel administration's salary-and-hours responsibilities. They provide the presence of the interests of senior management. They are alert to unusual activities in a department such as those that could lead to lower output or to unionization efforts. They are the first line of report concerning information whenever difficulties occur. Banks require a certain amount of discipline and control, and although there are audits, examinations, personnel reviews, and financial reports, there still is benefit to an element of observation and control for a bank which shows itself on a daily basis, year in and year out.

Outside bank analysts have no way of determining the effectiveness of operations officers. Nevertheless, it is often useful for bank analysts to examine the organization charts of departments to see if operations officers are present in areas where control is important. Some banks will permit the bank analysts to look at organization charts on their premises.

Internal Controls

The methods of providing internal management controls for the personnel of a bank are a matter of equal importance to external controls. *Internal controls* are those patterns of behavior that each individual believes is important and voluntarily conforms to them in his or her daily behavior. The subject is seldom discussed, and the topic almost never appears in articles about banking.

Code of Conduct. Most bankers consider themselves as being part of a professional code of conduct by which they respect the bank's needs and wishes. Some banks encourage this code of conduct and have built this code into their organization as an important management control. If it is effective, this code of conduct is a part of all activities. At the highest levels of the bank, this code of conduct involves a gentlemanly toleration of differences of opinion and an unswerving dedication to the needs of the bank.

This code of conduct stresses the needs of the bank as a first loyalty in innumerable other ways. It is a part of the way that thinking is carried on meetings, conversations, and in memos. There is no document that an outside bank analyst might obtain which would indicate the effectiveness of this method of internal control. Bank analysts usually develop their impressions on the matter from their personal association with members of the bank.

Image of Bank. A second way that banks control the thinking of their employees is through the image of the organization. Images of banks as perceived by employees are, at best, difficult to define. Nevertheless, in a simple, yet significant way, banks project the image of their organization through their name. Bank analysts would be interested in the clarity of the image of the bank's name and how the image is used to control the activities of employees.

The name of a bank receives more attention than any other designation. Most managements of banks at one time have spent considerable time on the selection of the name for their organization, making sure that it was completely appropriate. Most names of banks are prosaic and describe the organization as serving the needs of a local community. And they are usually exactly what their names imply: solid, community-oriented banking organizations.

Nevertheless, some names of banks raise important issues that observers might otherwise pass over without much attention. For example, Marine Midland Banks, Inc., describes three images in its name. One image is a bank engaged in international trade, especially trade beyond the shores of the United States. Another image is that of a bank of the midlands, refering to the landscape of the state of New York, with its local businesses, shopkeepers, and farms. Still another image is a bank that is a collection of banks which have been brought together under one corporate roof. The name "Marine Midland Banks, Inc.," conveys these images each time it is used in conversion, writing, or on a letterhead or building.

A bank analyst might wonder whether the name for Marine Midland Banks conveys an image of a collection of disharmonious parts. The differences between the world of international trade, which involves foreign currencies and letters of credit are completely apart from the landlocked businesses of small- and medium-sized towns. Moreover, a collection of banks involves considerably more management effort than a branch network under a single overall management or a unit bank.

These observations form a part of the image of Marine Midland Banks, Inc., and the image suggests a way of thinking which may be practiced by employees of the organization. This form of internal management control would appear to indicate an emphasis on maintaining a fragmented organization, without an emphasis on a single, overriding corporate purpose. Such an image does not reflect what is usually considered to be management control.

Another example of the significance of names is J. P. Morgan & Co., Inc. There is little doubt that this name refers to the financing of large corporations. As is well known, John Pierpont Morgan was the major financier in the United States at the turn of the century, when the dominance of the corporate form of business ownership and management was being established.

The name of J. P. Morgan & Co., Inc., suggests a bank with a single purpose of helping large corporations. It also suggests the importance of close personal associations, since the name of the bank is a personal name. The name would appear to provide considerable direction to employees in their efforts to promote the services of the bank. For example, Morgan provides checking accounts to a limited number of persons who fulfill certain qualifications. One qualification is simply to agree to keep on deposit a sum of several thousand dollars. This qualification is handled by account officers in discussions with customers in a gentlemanly manner, almost as a casual afterthought. Moreover, Morgan is interested in the personal accounts of those who are or could be important to Morgan in its corporate business. The procedure is exactly as J. P. Morgan would have wanted it, and his name acts as an image to perpetuate the style of organization he built.

Image of Chief Executive Officer. Bankers make personal judgments. Reflecting their service orientation, they are sensitive to the wishes of their customers, as well as to the image of their chief executive officer. On the whole, bankers probably respond with greater willingness to accommodate the wishes of their chief executive than in most other industries. The strength of image is a major factor in the internal controls of all banks. The impact of the image of a chief executive officer is difficult, at best, for an outside bank analyst to evaluate, since most are not associated in a business relationship with the chief executive officer of the bank they may be reviewing. Outside bank analysts, again, are mainly concerned with the clarity of the image and how the image is used to control the activities of employees.

The retirement of Gaylord Freeman as chairman of First Chicago Corporation and the appointment of Robert Abboud to that position in 1974 represented an example of a major change in the tone, style, and manner of management of that organization. Considerable discussion has occurred in the press concerning the diferences of personality between these two men. Gaylord Freeman is described as being erudite and courtly, and permissive in allowing innovation and development. In contrast, Robert Abboud is described as being direct, abrasive, and authoritarian in manner. Although there is often considerable assertion that one or another particular management style is best for a bank, it has never been proven. The important issue appears to be whether the chief executive has a clear image that is appropriate for the times and is effectively communicated to all levels of the bank so that it can be a part of the internal management control.

In the example of First Chicago, there is no reason why the organization could not operate as effectively under the reportedly benign leadership of Gaylord Freeman than under the rigorous leadership of Robert Abboud, if indeed those terms accurately describe their image within the bank. Each approach has strengths and weaknesses. A benign leadership may stimulate new thinking, but it usually is not discriminating and can permit developments into areas of business that may not stand up well under tests of adverse markets. One difficulty of First Chicago in 1975 and 1976 has been a large exposure in real estate investment trusts. Yet is was a permissive attitude, in the early 1970s, that allowed the bank to move quickly and aggressively to make loans to real estate investment trusts when they were thought to be a part of the new wave of banking opportunities.

Robert Abboud's reputed rigorous approach is more suited to sorting out real opportunities from hope and winnowing the many directions of activity so that the most durable will remain and prosper. Yet rigor can narrow the scope of the mind and limit opportunities. So long as both men are reasonably consistent in their methods and are able to project their images successfully, there would be good reason to believe that each respective image would be effective in directing and controlling the activities of employees.

Art and Architecture.   Art and architecture are a reflection of ideas and decisions of a bank's management. They provide clues to ideas that are often not clearly articulated or that may even be deliberately obscured in the use of language or numbers. Nevertheless, in most instances, they confirm other observations.

It may appear unusual to consider art as a part of banking. The practice of banking is perhaps the most ascetic and least tangible business in the world. Banking does not involve the shaping or creation of a product, such as is done in the manufacturing industries. The function of banking appears to lack the material from which it could fashion its product in an artistic manner. Banking is primarily involved with credit and confidence and is only incidentally involved with the physical transactions of a financial exchange. In fact, the headquarters buildings of many new banks have been designed so that it is not possible for the public to cash a check. The headquarters have been designed to enable decisions concerning credit and confidence to be reached with greater ease and accuracy.

Yet banking is closely connected with art and architecture exactly because it lack. a tangible product. The ability of art and architecture to convey ideas is important in an industry based on the ideas of confidence and credit. Banks have long recognized this association and have acted to use art and architecture to further their purposes.

A few examples illustrate the point. At the turn of the century, most banks in the United States were built of the most solid construction possible. They featured floors and interiors of marble and domed skylights flanked with gold leaf. Offices were often panneled with the finest hardwoods. These styles were chosen to convey an impression of wealth and solidity for banks, precisely because everybody knew that the banks at that time were risky. During the latter part of the nineteenth century, banking panics were frequent. The banks chose a style of art and architecture which attempted to allay that fear.

Art and architecture continue to be important ways of internal control. One western bank that had expanded rapidly in recent years and specialized in a few types of commercial lending recently faced major loan losses. It was a new bank in a community of established banks, and it attempted to create an impression of long-established wealth. The bank filled the waiting room outside the office of its president and chairman with New England period furniture and hung pictures of European artists. The decoration apparently was designed to overcome feelings customers might have about doing business with a newcomer to the banking establishment. Nevertheless, neither the furniture nor pictures was authentic. The chairs and tables were replicas of Boston colonial styles, and the pictures were not paintings, but lithographs in expensive frames.

Another bank in the West, the most profitable of the major dozen, is housed in unpretentious quarters. The main office is in a building over 50 years old with an annex not quite level with the main building, so that on each of the connecting floors everyone walks up or down a few steps dozens of times each day. The cafeteria is in the basement. It is too small for the number of employees it serves, which acts as a reminder to be busy even with the business of lunch.

The anteroom to the chairman's office is small and filled with a secretary's desk and file cabinets. The chairman's office is a medium-sized corner office with structural pillars that cut the room into compartments. There is a large, old oak desk, a number of nondescript chairs, and a large davenport with its back to a window. The Spartan image is reflected in the close control over the bank's costs.

Most banks would consider their annual report to be their most representative artistic product, and annual reports can provide insight into the thinking of management. Most banks' annual reports use graphics showing their employees or buildings in an informal, candid manner.

For example, the 1975 annual report of a medium-sized bank in a mountain state showed pictures and biographies of persons who had been a part of the bank's management training program. The graphics lacked technical precision. For example, the photographs of some persons showed reflections of light bulbs on their glasses, and some photographs were out of focus. Nevertheless, the people in the pictures appeared in natural, untutored positions. The graphics message was completely consistent with other information about the bank, which had expanded rapidly and profitably on the basis of an efficient operation and employees who promoted the bank in the communities it served.

A major southeastern bank showed a completely different graphic impression to bank analysts in its 1975 annual report. This bank showed photographs in color of its six principal officers. Each of these men was dressed in a solid or pin-striped dark blue or gray suit. All six wore conservative foulard or rep ties. The composure of all six faces was similar, conveying a uniform image of quiet confidence and strength. This impression was further emphasized by the chairman, who stood with his arms neatly crossed, giving a picture of a solid and tough combatant. The impression of this bank's senior officers reflected its conservative, aggressive, and profitable approach to banking.

Integration of Controls

Banks operate with a variety of external and internal controls and need to keep their various control systems operating in a cooperative manner. In this way, all of the external and internal controls can reinforce each other, making the total control of the bank fully effective. Banks organized in this manner are able to focus the energy of their employees. In contrast, banks showing some control systems working in one direction, and other systems working against that direction, may face serious difficulties. There is no perfect or best set of controls for any banking organization. The key sought by bank analysts is to learn how well they blend.

Table 73 provides a checklist of the principal methods of control in a bank. It indicates the breadth of the issue of control and that controls are a larger issue than a matter of preventing fraud and defalcations. The latter two issues cannot be minimized. They invoke basic issues of control and reflect matters in which there can be fairly clear decisions of acceptable or unacceptable behavior. Nevertheless, the table suggests that fraud and defalcations may be only the tip of the iceberg of control and that they should not be regarded as self-contained issues, but as related to the larger issue of control.

The table also illustrates the difficulty in making an analysis of control of a bank by an outside bank analyst. One approach would be to prepare an appropriate comment covering each issue. The next step would be to compare these notes to see if they indicate a congruence or a conflict of controls. The final step would be to determine whether the controls would be appropriate in light of the broader strategy of the bank. The task requires a bank analyst's total perception.

TWO EXAMPLES

The following examples provide an overview of management controls in two banks that encountered major difficulties.

Overvaluation of Bonds at Chase

On October 2, 1974, Chase reported serious irregularities in the bank's bond-dealer operations. The report, carried in the *Wall Street Journal* and other newspapers, indicated that Chase's bond trading inventory had been valued on its internal records at about $34 million above the estimated market value. The senior vice-president in charge of Chase Manhattan Bank's bond-dealer activities resigned immediately prior to the announcement. The Securities and Exchange Commission stated that this person was responsible for overvaluing the bank's portfolio and causing erroneous public financial reports. He was subsequently enjoined, under a consent agreement, by the Securities and Exchange Commission, from "further violations of the reporting, registration and antifraud provisions of federal securities laws." This person made a statement, which was reported in the *Wall Street Journal* on September 21, 1976, that "I am innocent of any wrongdoing," and added that he had consented to the action "to avoid the onerous cost of litigation."

How was it possible that Chase could have allowed its securities holdings to have been falsely valued? Chase was audited at the end of 1973. The false valuation occurred over a nine-month span and involved large sums. Most banks and bond dealers have control systems under which securities valuations are made on a daily, weekly, or monthly basis. Some banks have tighter controls and require an operations officer to initial all trades and keep a separate set of records, which are compared daily with the accounts of the traders. In its review of the case, the Securities and Exchange Commission found that Chase's control procedures prior October 1974 regarding trading account securities "weren't adequate to review the accuracy of values placed upon the securities." It added that Chase had subsequently strengthened its controls, and it ordered the bank to continue to comply with safeguards against the possibility of future fraud.

Retail and Wholesale Banking at Marine Midland

Marine Midland Banks had been formed in 1929 as means of establishing a statewide banking organization in a state that did not permit statewide branch banking. The management controls were originally designed to keep these independent banks in good condition and yet obtain whatever benefits were available from organizing them into a single corporation.

By the mid-1960s this collection of banks had begun to develop into two rival camps, each with its own goals and its own internal controls. At this time, there were 50 banks, and the New York City bank began to consider itself a major international bank and opened a London office. The dowstate bank had caught the spirit of expansion in banking which was developing in New York City. Not all of the upstate New York banks in the Marine Midland group agreed with these programs. Increasingly, their criticisms of the expansionist plans began to disrupt the concensus of how the overall organization should be managed. From 1966 to 1976 three men unsuccessfully tried to resolve the cleavage. In the struggle to bring about overall control, the headquarters was shifted twice from Buffalo to New York City. Marginally priced, but high-risk, loans in both domestic and international markets were placed, and earnings fell so sharply that the bank's dividend was halved. At the end of 1976 a new heir apparent was installed as president.

Nothing basic had changed in the decade from 1966 to 1976. The cleavage in control between the more conservative, retail, and small business orientation of the upstate banks was set against the expansionist and international approach of the New York City bank. The upstate banks provided most of the funds, and the downstate bank was reported to have made most of the decisions that lowered the overall profitability of the organization. The bank has undergone a civil war which has been devastating. Yet its potential for earnings and asset expansion is enormous, if it were to unify its organization and establish integrated internal and external controls.

PART FIVE
PREPARING
AN EVALUATION

CHAPTER 15
FORECASTS

Forecasts are an attempt to make the future visible. They are important information for banks seeking to improve their performance. Since proposals for current changes in a bank's direction will have an impact in the future, the usefulness of various proposals for change is based on a comparison of forecasts. For these purposes, forecasts assume a level of importance approaching that of the organization's current performance or its record.

DEVELOPMENT OF FORECASTING

The traditional banker never used formal forecasts and seldom made general forecasts except as a banquet speaker or when a few words of confidence seemed appropriate following the news of a very good or a very bad event. The comments about the future were intended to gather support or inspire confidence among listeners more than they were intended as an appraisal of future events. This traditional use of forecasts is not without merit. There clearly is a time and place for encouragement and confidence. No bank has ever developed into a major institution without a strong sense of confidence. Without this sense of direction, the best that could be expected from a bank would be solid mediocrity.

Yet there is more to confidence in the future than rhetoric. Confidence in a bank is built on a pattern of successful experience. The ability to peer ahead, to look at how the world will appear to a bank at a future time, requires special talents. Without these talents, the fortitude of strong character soon appears hollow. Similarly, without the ability to show conviction, the most perceptive forecasts would lie dormant.

The pressures for forecasting have usually not come from the senior management of banks. These managers have traditionally emphasized accuracy and timeliness of information about their banks. They have acted on the belief that if they had good current information, they would make the

313

best decisions possible about each day's business, and they would be able to respond to any emergency quickly enough to avoid serious difficulties. This philosophy of keeping the banker's ear close to the ground was reflected, if not encouraged for many years by bank examiners, who rated this skill highly. In fact, until recently, the research activities within the Federal Reserve System were almost exclusively directed to the analysis of historical and current developments, and forecasts were frowned on.

Investors were the first group to seek forecasts about banks. In the late 1960s, when large banks began to be listed on the New York Stock Exchange, banks began to be subjected to the same type of queries about their future that industrial companies had encountered for many years. Since banks did not usually provide forecasts, the securities industry began to make forecasts for them. Earnings per share were the main interest, but since this measure involved many other factors, it became increasingly clear that the business of forecasting was complicated and required specialists. To meet this vacuum, security analysts found a waiting market for their skills.

The impact of forecasts on banks was probably greater than on securities holders. To test their projections, or perhaps in hopes of getting a clue about any possible forecasts that the bank might have, the security analysts began questioning the senior management of banks about forecasts. Since security analysts were in a position to affect the opinion about holders of stock, bank managements became concerned about the opinion that a security analyst might hold of their forecasting capabilities. It became clear that highest marks went to those senior managers who handled questions involving future directions, future contingencies, and forecasts in general with greatest ease. Since high marks for management skills might be worth a fraction of a price-earnings multiple for the bank's stock, it made good sense for senior managers to brush up on their forecasts. Once the skill was learned, banks found many other uses where it could be employed, including acquisitions, budgeting, and planning.

A second prod to forecasting in banks came from the need to develop a defense against new pressures from the Federal Reserve System. During the period of high interest rates in 1974, the Federal Reserve approached banks to keep a lid on the prime rate at 12 percent. The cost of marginal funds was greater than 12 percent, which placed banks that were financing loans with nondeposit, short-term sources of funds in a profit squeeze. For several years prior to that squeeze, the conventional wisdom in banking had supported this method of expanding operations as a way of avoiding the limitations of a slowly growing deposit base. The Federal Reserve System's action pointed up a flaw in this earlier simple reasoning. It also pointed up the need to think through all possible contingencies in any new program. The process of thinking about new programs and the impact of various possible future events is forecasting.

STRUCTURE OF FORECASTS

All forecasts share the same structure and may be divided into four parts: the selection of the key information to be forecast, assumptions, elements of change, and the forecast of a series. Whether all of the parts of a forecast are explicitly shown or are implicitly indicated, they all are necessary. In fact, a forecast that has been explored carefully will show as much attention to the selection of the series, assumptions, and elements of change as to the forecast of the series.

Selection of Series

The interest of security analysts and investors for forecasts of earnings per share is well known. Most investors in equities of banks are also interested in a forecast of dividends, which represent another source of payout from stocks and have shown a greater degree of certainty than capital gains.

Liquidity is a series that has become more important in recent years to a wide group of bank analysts, including investors, regulatory agencies, and depositors, as well as major borrowers of banks. Since the credit crunch of 1970 and the credit squeeze of 1974, bank analysts have increased their interest in the liquidity of banks.

Another series that has attracted recent interest is loan loss experience. In 1975 and 1976 the provision for loan losses was an important factor in earnings and represents an important part of forecasting earnings per share. There also has been interest in the future direction of risk policies, because there may be a level of risk that certain bank analysts might want to avoid.

Assumptions

The assumptions of a forecast are factors influencing the outcome of the forecast series, yet which are expected to remain unchanged in the forecast period. The assumptions need to be related to the series. They represent the forces of continuity that would be expected to hold the present or historic relationships steady.

Elements of Change

The elements of change are those factors expected to change a forecast series. They represent forces that, if left entirely to themselves, could remake a bank into a different organization.

The same factor may be either an assumption or an element of change. The judgment of the forecaster is crucial, because there is no formula which can make such a decision. It is at this point that forecasts that turn out to be accurate often may be separated from forecasts that prove to be faulty. The problem for bank analysts in separating assumptions from elements of change has become an increasing challenge in recent years. Almost each year has brought a questioning of at least one area of banking that the year earlier had been considered an assumption of no change. Several examples illustrate the point.

In early 1974, most financial forecasts looked for declining interest rates. Three month treasury bills had reached a high of more than 8-1/4 percent in the late summer and had declined to a range from 7-3/4 percent to 7-7/8 percent in December. On the basis of past cyclical patterns, a forecast of declining interest rates appeared reasonable. Many banks converted their maturing longer-term liabilities with short-term obligations and were preparing to ride down a projected drop in interest rates on those liabilities to improve earnings. However, short-term interest rates reversed their decline and rose to a second high of more than 8-1/4 percent in the late summer of 1974. The effect was to penalize severely the earnings of banks that had bought short-term funds. A critical difference between a bank that moved through the period unscathed and one penalized was interest rate forecasts.

In another example, for more than 40 years banks had regarded municipal securities almost as secure as government securities. They were usually considered more secure than most loans. Municipal securities that were given a low rating were not seriously thought to involve appreciably greater risk, and the municipal securities of the nation's major cities were traded almost as a currency in themselves.

It is difficult to determine the precise time when the financial issues facing New York City became a crisis. It was clear that a crisis had been reached in early 1975 when the city's bonds could not be sold at any reasonable—or unreasonable—price. On March 13 and 20, 1975, the city, through its underwriters, offered for sale to the public $912 million of short-term notes at tax exempt rates up to 8 percent. Weeks following the offering, the underwriters could sell only $375 million of the notes, despite vigorous marketing efforts. From that time on, the city was threatened with the possibility of default, and one plan after another was developed to prevent a default from occurring.

The difficulties of financing the debt of New York City appeared as a major shock to many banks, which had considered the securities of that city as one of their more secure assets. Not only was the income reduced from these securities, but their market value dropped sharply. During certain periods there was virtually no market for the securities, reducing the effective liquidity of any bank holding them.

The debacle of the New York City securities raised the question of whether that occurrence represented an isolated event or the beginning of a new direction in municipal securities. If a forecaster believed that the New York City difficulties would resolve themselves, then it would be appropriate to make the assumption of stability in municipal securities markets. This view might be supported with the belief that New York City's difficulties had acted as a valuable lesson for that city and other cities, and the cities would correct the difficulties. However, if a forecaster believed that New York City's difficulties represented the first wave of a growing problem in municipal financing, then there would be an important element of change in the forecast of virtually all of the key forecast series for a bank.

In another instance, the major international banks have provided the links that have tied together the three major economic blocks of the world in recent years. These economic blocks include the industrial nations, the major oil exporting nations, and the nonindustrial nations. The current account deficit of the balance of payments of the nonindustrial nations rose from $11 billion in 1973 to about $41 billion in 1976. Higher prices for oil have been a major factor in the growing gap.

Although the governments of industrial nations and multilateral agencies have increased their financial assistance to the nonindustrial nations, this move has not been enough to close the gap. At the same time, the major oil exporting countries have been building up large currency deposits, as a result of their surplus from their oil exports. The large international banks have acted as the intermediaries between the deposits and loans. By the end of 1976, banks were providing about 50 percent of the financing needs of the nonindustrial countries, more than double their proportion of the early 1970s. Total external debt of the nonindustrial countries probably amounted to about $180 billion at the end of 1976, with the banks accounting for perhaps $70 billion of that total.

Banks have been interested in expanding their lending to the nonindustrial countries, because it has been highly profitable. The maturity of bank loans to these countries are typically for five- to seven-year periods, usually at 4 percent or more over what the banks pay for their Eurocurrency souces of funds. Amortization and interest payments on the external debt of the nonindustrial countries amounted to about $18 billion in 1976, double the payments in 1973. Three quarters of the $18 billion was due to the major international banks and represented an important contribution to income from loans and fees to these organizations.

The rise in loans and earnings to the nonindustrial countries might continue for many years and could represent an important assumption in making a forecast concerning the outlook for an international bank. Some financial economists look for the expansion of this business for a period of many years and cite a strengthening of export prices of the mid 1970s of the nonindustrial countries as a principal factor in the ability of these countries to sustain increased borrowing.

Other financial economists look for the past trends to soon end, representing an element of change in a forecast of an international bank. One group expects that borrowing by nonindustrial countries soon will level and that this source of expanded banking activity will continue to be an important source of earnings and loans, but will remain comparatively static. Another group expects that the present burden of debt cannot be sustained through another worldwide recession, which possibly could occur during the latter years of the 1970s. This possibility would represent an *element of change* that could have a serious negative impact on the future performance of international banks, just as the *assumption* of continued expansion in their activity could have a strongly positive impact on performance.

Another example of the difference between an assumption and an element of change would be the future role of welfare activities of the U.S. government. The welfare activities of the federal government are shown in the health and income security sector of the federal budget outlays. These welfare expenditures rose from $4.7 billion in fiscal 1967 to $160.5 billion in fiscal 1976 and are projected at $172.7 billion in fiscal 1977. In fiscal 1967, health and income security outlays amounted to 3 percent of total U.S. government outlays and rose to 44 percent in fiscal 1976. The principal factor accounting for the increase in federal outlays from $158.3 billion in fiscal 1967 to $365.6 billion in fiscal 1976 has been the sharp increase in health and income security outlays. Most other major sectors, such as national defense and international affairs, also increased in the period, but at a much slower pace.

The figures show that the federal government has accepted major new social commitments in the 1967–1977 decade. At the same time, however, the federal government has been reluctant to finance fully the increase in outlays by increasing taxes to provide sufficient receipts. In fact, the reverse situation has occurred, and tax rates have been reduced by various rebates and tax credits. As a consequence the gap between receipts and outlays rose from $8.7 billion in fiscal 1967 (and actually showed a surplus of $3.3 billion in fiscal 1969) to a deficit of $65.6 billion in fiscal 1976. These deficits proceeded in a series of waves during the period, and the deficits grew larger in each wave. An important factor in these waves was an economic philosophy that deficits were not necessarily inflationary and that, in any event, highest priority should be placed on programs that stimulated economic activity. There was concern that either raising taxes or reducing outlays could depress economic activity.

The assumption of a continued pattern of rapid welfare spending and larger federal deficits would have important implications on credit markets and the performance of banks. The assumption of a growing pattern of deficits would point to a period of accelerating inflation, a crowding out of the private sector in debt markets with only the largest, most creditworthy corporations having access to medium or long-term debt financing. Other borrowers would be forced to turn to banks for their borrowing needs. The higher inflation would raise interest rates, which would depress the prices of long-term bonds, and would, for all practical purposes, freeze the liquidity of banks indicated by long-term securities portfolios. It could also stimulate demand for loans, much as a similar occurrence in 1974 and 1975 accelerated the commercial demand for loans.

If the pattern of ever-increasing waves of federal government deficits were broken, it would likely bring less pressure on debt markets by the federal government, and borrowers might find less need for funds, as well as many alternative sources of funds beside banks. A major reduction in inflationary pressures could bring about a reduction in economic activity. The level of economic activity might simply remain at a moderate but nonexpanding pace for a period, and then resume an expansion. Banks would experience a period of slack loan demand under this element of change, much as they experienced in 1976. If the cutback were sharp or prolonged there could be a possibility of a surplus in federal expenditures and a drop in overall price levels. An economic slump might accompany this possibility, which could bring about a period of losses among corporations and considerably higher loan losses for banks, as well as some difficulty in attracting deposits. Thus each of these implications could bring about different, but important, forecasts for banks.

Forecast of Series

The final step in a forecast is to make a "forecast of a series." The forecast reflects the combined effect of assumptions and elements of change on the series that has been selected. The forecast represents the interrelation of these factors.

After the forecast of the series has been completed, it is useful to review the complete forecasting process to be certain that each of the parts is relevant to each other. There is no way to prove relevance. Reviewing factual information that bears on the forecasting process is usually helpful in confirming relevance. In reviewing the overall structure of a forecast, it is also useful to review the specific assumptions and the elements of change that make an important difference in the outcome of the forecast.

FORECASTING METHODS

Bank analysts typically use five methods in making forecasts. These methods are an interpretation of comments by management, judgmental models, endogenous models, exogenous models, and integrated models. Virtually all forecasts reflect one of these five methods.

Interpretation of Comments by Management

The managements of most banks are usually reluctant to offer specific forecasts of their performance to bank analysts because of their own uncertainty about the future. Forecasts about the specific future direction of their organization, which may turn out to be inaccurate, run a risk of making a management appear foolish. Moreover, there may be only limited benefits if the forecasts prove to be accurate.

Banks, like other organizations, are also concerned about the legal issues of disclosure when they make a forecast. The issue involves the obligation of the management of a publicly held company to inform all persons simultaneously who have an interest in the company of any new information. The outlook for a bank represents one of its most critical issues. For this reason alone, many in banking management would prefer to remain silent concerning projections of their organizations.

Nevertheless, some banks have made informal forecasts of their operations available to the public. Usually, these forecasts include projections of earnings, loan losses, and net interest margins. These forecasts have usually been made in response to pressure from institutional holders of stock, who seek to be informed of the most current status and outlook for their holdings. The managements of most major banks are aware of this interest and an increasing concentration of ownership of their shares among institutions. Some banks have provided the press with forecasts, and a very few have carried the matter a step further and have announced goals for broad measures of their performance.

Judgmental Forecasts

A *judgmental forecast* is one that uses the best estimates of a forecaster for the future period. The approach relies on the perception, skill, and intuition of an analyst and represents a compilation of how generally held assumptions and elements of change affect a particular bank. A judgmental forecast is sometimes called a "naive forecast," because of the open and eclectic way it uses information. Nevertheless, it is not necessarily an unsophisticated method. In fact, a carefully crafted judgmental forecast may reflect more decisions than any other method.

Tables 74–75 show one of a set of judgmental forecasts for J. P. Morgan & Co., Inc., which was prepared by William M. Weiant and David C. Garvin of First Boston Corporation in a report released on February 3, 1977. The tables show a carefully reasoned projection of the key factors that form a judgmental forecast. The overall objective of the report is to determine whether J. P. Morgan & Co. could achieve a long-term earnings expansion of 12 percent or more. The tables shown here are part of an overall forecast which supports the view that an earnings expansion of that magnitude could be attainable.

In original context, a narrative accompanies each of the tables showing background information in support of the forecasts. This type of information is useful in reviewing judgmental forecasts, since the analyst's reasoning process is important to the forecast. A brief exerpt follows:

"Our projection of domestic net interest income requirements was derived by subtracting estimated foreign net income from the overall level of net interest in Table 3 [Table 74]. (We will be using the increased leverage scenario shown in Table 3 [Table 74] as the more logical expectation for the next five years.) Projecting foreign net interest yields is difficult, especially as the mix between loans and redeposits can change significantly. We have used an average net interest yield of 1.30% for the five-year period. While this rate is below that recorded in 1975 of 1.56% (as we calculate it) and in the first half of 1976, it is roughly level with the rates being recorded after this period. . . . It should be remembered that 1975 and 1976 foreign net interest yields were partially aided by funding benefits. These opportunities are not present now, as interest rates have probably bottomed. A 1.30% foreign net interest yield also assumes that overseas pricing will remain firm over the five-year period, though it should be noted that there have been some pricing pressures recently.

"To provide a benchmark for the amount of improvement required for domestic accounts under the preceding assumption, we have calculated future loan yields using the current prime formula and an average cost of interest-bearing funds of 6.50%. In other words, to maintain the domestic net interest income needed to allow corporate earnings growth of 12%, Morgan would have to improve the gross yield on loans above and beyond what the current pricing situation would suggest. Morgan does not operate on a "formula" basis, but this exercise is used to characterize the current general pricing structure in the industry.

"This exercise suggests trends that are typical for the industry as a whole. Banks will have to improve their net interest yields by improved pricing through increases in the formula and by differentiating more as to what various kinds of customers must be charged. As Morgan will likely maintain its strategy of concentrating on the highest-quality customer base (the accounts that can dictate and obtain lower prices), it becomes apparent that other efforts may be needed if an earnings growth rate of 12% is to be achieved."

Judgmental forecasts are the typical method used in making projections in the banking industry. Many banks prepare judgmental forecasts for internal purposes either on an annual or on a quarterly basis, and a few make monthly revisions of the forecasts. These forecasts begin with the latest data for each of the lines forecast and include an estimate for each line based on a survey of all information within the bank concerning the line. These lines are totaled, and the earnings and key balance sheet lines are evaluated for their overall reasonableness. Usually, the totals are thought to require some modification, and the analyst who prepares the forecast reviews each line, and its reasoning to make adjustments to the original projections. New totals are prepared and are again reviewed for their overall reasonableness. Often this process is repeated several times before the overall totals and individual lines of the forecast are considered to be in balance and reasonable.

The process of developing judgmental projections by banks and securities analysts is similar. Both use the same methods of thinking. However, outside bank analysts almost never have an opportunity to review the internal forecasts of a bank. Since projections represent an earnings forecast by management, banks regard these forecasts as confidential information. In fact, many banks confine the distribution of these forecasts to only a few employees.

Bank analysts may obtain forecasts about major banks from securities analysts, such as was shown earlier in an example, or they may prepare their own. The preparation of a forecast by an outside bank analyst involves considerable time, but is often the only way of obtaining a judgmental forecast about a bank, especially if the company is a small or regional organization.

Endogenous Forecasting Model

Endogenous forecasts are based on the principle that all or nearly all of the information needed to make a forecast is contained within the data of the company. They are focused on the internal relationships of a bank. Rigorously logical, endogenous models are built on a basis of a series of relationships and ratios. Because computers have vastly expanded the mathematical capabilities of analysts, they were quickly put to use in endogenous model building.

Most endogenous computer models give little attention to the broader financial and economic environment in which a bank operates, and this neglect represents an important limitation to their scope. To remedy this drawback, some of the more recent computer programs for endogenous forecast models incorporate an input to determine banking volume by using an overall measure of business activity, such as gross national product.

Table 76 shows a simplified endogenous forecast model for Citicorp, and was prepared by Robert B. Albertson of Smith Barney, Harris Upham & Co. It shows the rate of reinvestment on equity for Citicorp. This measure indicates the bank's internal capacity to increase its equity and is a measure of the sustainable rate of expansion of operations. The table shows the key ratios of income and expense to earning assets, pretax return on these assets, and an adjustment to pretax return on total assets. Factors for taxes, securities transactions, dividends, and leverage are applied, and the rate of reinvestment on equity is shown in the final line.

In making a forecast from this model, an analyst would begin with a set of ratios and the forecast year, and determine that the ratios are internally

Table 74 J. P. Morgan & Co. Inc. Judgmental Forecast

Income Statement and Asset Projections Assuming Increased Leverage, 1975–1981P
(Millions)

	1975R	1976R	1977P	1978P	1979P	1980P	1981P	Annual Growth Rates	
								1976–1981	1970–1975[a]
Profit after taxes	$192	$203	$227	$255	$285	$319	$358	12.0%	13.7%
Tax rate[b]	58.4%	58.0%	58.5%	58.5%	58.5%	58.5%	58.5%		
Profit before taxes[b]	$462	$483	$547	$614	$687	$769	$863		
Noninterest Income									
Trading profits	3	29	12	12	12	12	12	—	—
Trust	92	101	109	117	125	134	143	7.0	7.7
Foreign exchange	32	34	40	46	54	64	74	17.0	43.1
Other	82	88	104	122	145	171	201	18.0	25.0
Total	$209	$252	$265	$297	$336	$381	$430	12.2	11.6

Noninterest expense									
Staff	182	204	230	260	294	333	376	13.0	12.4
Occupancy	34	38	44	50	58	66	76	15.0	17.1
Equipment	14	16	19	22	26	30	35	17.0	16.4
Other	53	67	78	90	105	121	141	16.0	15.8
Total	$283	$325	$371	$422	$483	$550	$628	14.1	13.6
Provision for loan losses	97	68	40	54	59	66	75		
Net interest income[b]	633	624	693	793	893	1,004	1,136	12.7	18.0
Retained earnings[c]	—	$ 138	$ 156	$ 174	$ 195	$ 218			
Shareholders' equity[a]	$ 1,162	$ 1,362	1,498	1,645	1,810	1,994	2,200		
Leverage	21.6X	18.9X	19.4X	19.9X	20.4X	20.9X	21.4X		
Total assets[d]	$25,119	$25,724	$29,061	$32,735	$36,924	$41,674	$47,080	12.8	16.2
Net interest yield	2.52%	2.43%	2.38%	2.42%	2.42%	2.41%	2.41%		
Return on assets	0.76	0.79	0.78	0.78	0.77	0.77	0.76		

Source: First Boston Corporation report, February 3, 1977.

[a] Exponential Regression.
[b] Taxable Equivalent.
[c] Dividend Payout Ratio of 39%.
[d] Average.

Table 75 J. P. Morgan & Co. Inc. Judgmental Forecast

Projected Domestic Balances and Net Interest Income, 1975–1981P
(Millions)

	1975R	1976R	1977P	1978P	1979P	1980P	1981P	Compound Growth Rates 1976–1981
Total net interest income[a]	$ 633	$ 624	$ 693	$ 793	$ 893	$ 1,004	$ 1,136	
Less: foreign (estimate)[b]	127	145	152	175	202	232	266	5.0
Domestic net interest income[a]	$ 506	$ 479	$ 541	$ 618	$ 691	$ 772	$ 870	
Domestic balances								
Loans and other	8,130	7,227	8,087	9,049	10,126	11,331	12,680	11.9%
Investments	3,283	3,616	3,797	3,986	4,186	4,395	4,615	5.0
Total	$11,413	$10,843	$11,884	$13,035	$14,312	$15,726	$17,295	9.8
Interest-bearing liabilities	7,508	6,996	7,819	8,734	9,755	10,895	12,167	11.7
Noninterest-bearing funds	3,905	3,847	4,065	4,301	4,557	4,831	5,128	5.9
Net demand deposits	$ 2,991	$ 3,024	$ 3,144	$ 3,270	$ 3,402	$ 3,538	$ 3,679	4.0
Residual	914	823	921	1,031	1,155	1,293	1,449	12.0

Interest Income							
Loans and other	665	514	691	810	930	1,066	1,226
Investments[a]	329	341	358	376	395	414	435
Total[a]	$ 994	$ 855	$ 1,049	$ 1,186	$ 1,325	$ 1,480	$ 1,661
Interest Expense	488	376	508	568	634	708	791
Net Interest Income[a]	$ 506	$ 479	$ 541	$ 618	$ 691	$ 772	$ 870
Rates							
Loans and other	8.18%	7.11%	8.54%	8.95%	9.18%	9.41%	9.67%
Investments[a]	10.02	9.43	9.43	9.43	9.43	9.43	9.43
Total	8.71	7.89	8.83	9.10	9.26	9.41	9.60
Interest expense	6.50	5.37	6.50	6.50	6.50	6.50	6.50
Net interest yield[a]	4.43	4.42	4.55	4.74	4.83	4.91	5.03
Spread of loan yield vs. average cost of interest-bearing funds (basis points)	168	174	204	245	268	291	317

Source: First Boston Corporation report, February 3, 1977.
[a] Taxable equivalent.
[b] Projected net interest yield of 1.30%.

Table 76 Endogenous Model of Citicorp

	1975	1974	1973	1972	1971
Net interest income ÷ earning assets (plus)	3.58%	3.12%	3.02%	3.09%	3.21%
Other operating income ÷ earning assets (minus)	0.98	1.07	1.17	1.09	1.04
Staff expenses ÷ earning assets (minus)	1.37	1.30	1.34	1.42	1.53
Other operating expenses ÷ earning assets (minus)	1.08	1.06	1.09	1.10	1.11
Loan loss provision ÷ earning assets (equals)	0.70	0.35	0.20	0.16	0.15
Pretax return on earning assets	1.42	1.49	1.56	1.51	1.46
Pretax return on total assets	1.17	1.23	1.31	1.27	1.20
Tax factor	52.2	52.0	53.0	53.8	53.1
Securities transactions factor	100.5	99.8	98.9	100.0	100.5
Dividend factor	68.8	68.5	65.7	62.7	57.3
Total leverage (multiple)	25.3x	24.5x	21.2x	17.8x	20.x
Reinvested on equity	10.7%	10.7%	9.6%	7.6%	7.3%

Source: Smith Barney, Harris Upham & Co.

consistent. These ratios may be obtained from the year immediately preceding the forecast period or some average of the ratios for recent years. Estimates of income and assets for the forecast period might be derived from the rate of reinvestment on equity. These steps would be continued throughout the forecast period.

The endogenous forecast points a spotlight on the internal dynamics of a bank. It focuses on how a bank has made its decisions to use its resources and gives little or no attention to the business and financial conditions around it. An endogenous forecast assumes that the economic environment of a bank will remain unchanged or will not change in a significant manner.

Exogenous Forecasting Model

Exogenous forecasts of banks are based on developments that lie outside their immediate control and are usually tied to a model of aggregate economic or financial activity. These models link the economic or financial environment with a bank through a number of key points, such as interest rates, loan volumes, and income statement or balance sheet.

Exogenous forecasts also developed rapidly when computer models of the economy were formulated. Exogenous models may be considered as spin-offs from these larger, more complicated models. Exogenous forecasting models are sometimes referred to as derivative models, because of their primary relationship to models of aggregate economic and financial activity.

Table 77 illustrates the principle of the exogenous approach to forecasting. It shows the gross national product of the United States from 1970 to 1975, a preliminary estimate for 1976, and forecasts for 1977, 1980, and 1985. The forecasts are based on the growth rate of U.S. gross national product from an econometric model. The next line shows a numerical relative for U.S. gross national product for each of the years. The numerical relatives provide a way of comparing the projections in the forecast on a common basis. The forecast series shows aggregates of 15 principal U.S. banks that are strongly tied to international markets. Thus the gross domestic product for Germany and Japan are also shown and serve as proxy for the economic activity of the international operations of 15 major banks. The measures of output for Germany and Japan are each weighted 20 percent, and the output for the United States is weighted 60 percent to reflect an estimate of the proportion of the importance of the economies to the banks in the forecast period. A line shows the composite gross national product from 1970 to 1975. The next line shows the multiple by which a change in U.S. gross national product is forecast to reflect a change in output in Germany and Japan. The multiple of 1.06 is based on the 1970–1975 period, indicating that output of these two countries is expected to continue to move upward at a faster rate than that of United States. The next line shows a forecast of the relative of the composite output of the three countries.

The assets of the 15 banks are shown next. Immediately above the dollar total of the assets is a line showing the ratio of these assets to the composite output of the three countries. This ratio showed a steady increase from 1970 to 1975, indicating that the assets of these banks increased more rapidly than

Table 77 Fifteen Major U.S. Banks[a] Exogenous Forecast 1975–1985

Assets, Shareholders' Equity, and Earnings

	1970	1971	1972	1973	1974	1975	1976	1977	1980	1985
U.S. GNP (Dollar billions)	982	1,063	1,171	1,307	1,413	1,516	1690p	1785E	2208a	2976a
Relative 1970 = 100	100	108	119	133	144	154	172f	182f	225f	303f
Japan GDP (Yen billions)	70,890	79,369	90,594	111,031	132,725	144,915				
Relative 1970 = 100	100	112	128	157	187	204				
Germany GDP (DM Billions)	687	763	835	928	996	1050p[b]				
Relative 1970 = 100	100	111	122	135	145	153				
Composite GNP of Three Countries with U.S. Weighted 60%, Japan 20%, Germany 20%	100	109	121	138	153	164				
1970–1975 Change of U.S. GNP to GNP of Japan and Germany						1.06	1.06f	1.06f	1.06f	1.06f

Forecast of composite GNP (assumes 5% Inflation in 1980, 4% in 1985)

157	160	166	180	197	197.5	182f	192f	239f	321f

Ratio
Assets of 15 banks ($billions)

157	160	166	180	197	197.5	197f	200f	210f	230f
157	174	201	249	301	325	359f	384f	502f	738f

Ratio
Shareholders' equity of 15 banks ($Billions)

85	83	79	75	73	77	78f	78f	77f	76f
8.5	9.0	9.6	10.3	11.2	12.7	14.2f	15.0f	18.4f	24.4f

Ratio
Earnings of 15 banks ($Billions)

104	97	95	95	99	96	82f	88f	89f	88f
1.04	1.06	1.15	1.31	1.52	1.59	1.49	1.68	2.13f	2.82f

Return on assets					0.49%	0.42%f	0.44%f	0.42%f	0.38%f
Return on equity					12.5%	10.5%f	11.2%f	11.6%f	11.6%f
Capital ratio					3.93%	3.96%f	3.91%f	3.67%f	3.31%f

[a] Banks include Citicorp, Chase, Morgan, Manufacturers Hanover, Chemical, Charter, Marine Midland, Bankers Trust, Western Bancorporation, Crocker, Wells Fargo, Security Pacific, First Chicago, Continental Illinois, and Mellon.
[b] f = forecast, p = preliminary estimate, E = estimate based on 5.5% gain, a = forecast based on model.
Source: 1975 annual reports, U.N. Statistical Yearbook, U.S. Department of Commerce.

output. The ratio is forecast to continue to rise to 1985, although at a much more moderate pace. The next two lines show similar information for shareholders' equity. In this example, shareholders' equity shrank relative to output in the 1970–1975 period and is forecast to hold almost steady in the 1975–1985 period. The two lines showing earnings before securities transactions and its ratio to output point to a slightly rising trend in the forecast period, reversing the pattern of recent years.

Integrated Forecasting Model

An "integrated forecasting model" is a blend of both endogenous and exogenous models, so that both approaches have impact on the forecast series. This type of forecast represents an effort to replicate as closely as possible how a bank would likely perform in a future period. Integrated forecasting models are sometimes referred to as ambient models, reflecting their interrelationship between a bank's programs and the environment in which the bank conducts its business.

The critical part of an integrated forecasting model is the feedback between the external and the internal factors of a bank. The feedback or iteration in the model reflects how the management of a bank and financial markets respond to other. The pattern of action and response provides the dynamics of integrated forecasting models.

In many respects an integrated forecasting model represents a more formalized method of handling a judgmental forecast. Both forecasting methods attempt to look at important parts of a bank and its environment and make changes in a forecast series on the basis of the effect of changes in each of those factors. Both methods are concerned with the fact that each decision to change a factor on the part of a bank or each change in the overall direction of financial markets redefines both the position of a bank and the financial environment, even if the change is small. The integrated forecasting model differs from the judgmental model in that the integrated model selects key factors considered to be most important and formally organizes them. The judgmental approach does not have such a formal organization of key relationships, but relies on the skill of the forecaster.

Figure 71, which is divided into three sectors, shows an example of an integrated forecasting model. The shaded parts represent economic factors that lie outside the bank. They include the business cycle, the long-range trend of measures of economic and financial markets, the market for a bank's services, the trading price of the bank's stock, and new equity funds from investors. These factors represent key aspects of forecasting a bank's performance that lie completely or mostly outside the control of a bank.

The second sector includes the policies that lie in the figure between the dashed lines and the shaded sector. These include the capital, credit risk, profitability, liquidity, and interest rate policies. Those five policies represent the basis of operating decisions made throughout a bank. They include those factors over which managements of banks have complete or almost complete control.

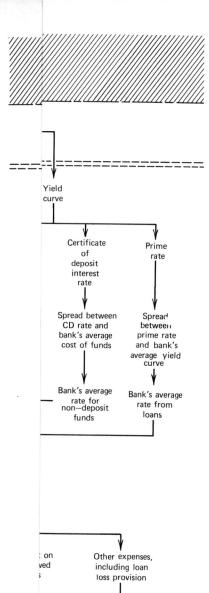

Yield
curve

Certificate
of
deposit
interest
rate

Prime
rate

Spread between
CD rate and
bank's average
cost of funds

Spread
between
prime rate
and bank's
average yield
curve

Bank's average
rate for
non—deposit
funds

Bank's average
rate from
loans

on
ved

Other expenses,
including loan
loss provision

The third sector includes the financial series of a bank from interest rates charged for loans to net income. These series respond both to changes in the bank's economic and financial environment and the policies of the bank's management. The forecast series are interdependent, and a bank analyst may select those series which may be most useful.

The figure shows an integrated model's interrelationships as if there were one pass through or iteration. The operation of an integrated model involves many iterations. For example, if a run of the model showed a drop in net earnings of 20 percent, one reaction could be a reduction in employee expenses and a reduction in staff. Another reaction could be to seek lower quality loans, which could have a short-term benefit of increasing net interest income. Another reaction could be to obtain higher levels of income from longer-term securities. Still another response could be to make no change in operations. The decision of which change, if any, would be appropriate would reflect the policies of the bank.

The example shows that there are many qualitative aspects to forecasting which should not be overlooked in using forecasting models. It shows that the limits of quantitative forecasting techniques are not always greater numerical detail, but in understanding which alternative a bank would select when a change occurs in its financial condition. Finally, the example points out the importance of looking at banks as responding, as well as in a few instances challenging their environment, and the central position of the management of a bank. These observations sometimes have been overlooked in an effort by some bank analysts in their development of mathematical methods of forecasting.

ACCURACY OF FORECASTS

Bank analysts look to forecasts as a method of pushing away an indeterminate future. The rewards for being able to accomplish this feat are enormous. If bank analysts had accurate information about the future of banks (and if only a few of them possessed this information), they might be able to meet or anticipate the countless events that appear as surprises. With an accurate forecast of key series of a bank, an analyst would be better informed to handle stock or debt holdings or would be better able to manage deposits or loans.

The obvious difficulty in using bank forecasts is that a bank analyst can never be sure of their accuracy. A user of forecasts does not know whether a particular forecast will be close to subsequent results or wide of the mark. The same forecasting technique or same forecaster may be completely accurate at one time, and not so at another time. Despite these limitations, bank analysts continue to seek and use forecasts. As inadequate as they are, a forecast is often considered to be better than none at all.

The need to provide a way of handling the accuracy of forecasts is a problem that will not go away—and probably never can be solved. Nevertheless, bank analysts often use three methods to control forecasts so that they may be used to full advantage: a provision for a range of accuracy, the use of alternative forecasts, and an appraisal of the record of a forecaster.

Range of Accuracy

The first method of handling the likely variation between a forecast and subsequent developments is to show a range for a forecast. For example, many securities analysts will forecast earnings per share for a bank in a range from, for example, $4.00–$4.40. This type of forecast gives more information than a forecast of a single number, such as $4.20. The range indicates the forecaster's belief that the estimate could possibly be in error approximately 5 percent on either side of the most likely estimate of $4.20. Although the probability of results occurring in a range of plus or minus five percent of $4.20 is not specifically indicated, there is an implicit assumption that the bulk of the odds favor the results falling in the range.

Some bank analysts prefer forecasts that are expressed in a range. However, many prefer not to show ranges in their forecasts because they are considerably more difficult to use, especially if detailed income statements or balance sheets are a part of the forecast. Numbers expressed in a range are usually awkward to use if these forecasts are further adjusted and modified. Nevertheless, for a simple forecast of one or two series, showing forecasts in a range can provide a way of working with the problem of accuracy.

Alternative Forecasts

Alternative forecasts represent another method of handling uncertainty concerning the accuracy of forecasts. Sometimes two or more forecasts are shown without any indication which is the most likely forecast, and the bank analyst may regard these forecasts as points on a range.

The alternative forecasts are usually complete, self-contained projections with income statements and balance sheets. The forecasts differ according to certain assumptions, which are usually kept simple and basic, such as differences in interest rates or leverage. Bank analysts may review each of the forecasts and observe the effect of changes in the assumptions or elements of change on the forecast.

Alternative forecasts provide more information than a single forecast, and they provide more precise information than most forecasts which use a range of values. Moreover, alternative forecasts provide a way of reviewing the key assumptions or elements of change and the results of a forecast in a fairly simple manner. Most bank analysts have found this approach to be a useful although a time-consuming method of working with the problem of accuracy.

Record of the Forecaster

The practice of making forecasts requires an element of personal judgment. Prior to the development of computer models, the importance of a forecaster's skill in applying various techniques was usually taken into consideration in appraising a forecast. The development of computer models tended to eclipse this type of appraisal. The printouts of computers were always exact. There were never pencil smudges, erasures or crossed out figures on worksheets. The computers provided much greater detail than most traditional forecasts showed, and the greater detail erroneously has been considered to be an indication of greater forecasting precision.

Yet the overall record of computer models in forecasting in many fields has not been better than the record of individual forecasters, and in certain fields, such as economics, computer models have not done as well as many individuals. Recently, there has been a return to the view that forecasting is an art, and a reconsideration of the forecaster, rather than the method of forecasting, as the essential factor in assessing the likely accuracy of a forecast.

Some forecasters have a consistent record of being more nearly correct than others. To some extent, the difference in the record among forecasters can be explained by chance, although that factor does not appear to be able to explain all of the differences. The skill that forecasters use appears to be an important ingredient in forecasting, even if that skill cannot be precisely defined. Perhaps certain individuals possess a special perception of current events that enables them to see trends more clearly than others. Whatever the reason, a forecaster who has shown a good track record should be valued by bank analysts as a precious resource indeed.

CHAPTER 16
MARKET VALUATION

The previous chapters have discussed banks from the point of view of their specialized activities, including banking policies, the impact of various types of environment, and the key elements of management. In addition, the techniques of control and forecasting were reviewed. All of these considerations are important parts to a valuation of a bank.

The purpose of valuation, however, is different from that of the analytical efforts discussed earlier. Valuation provides an assessment of the worth of a bank. It combines the analytical information in a way so that a bank analyst may arrive at a conclusion which places a value on a bank. How this valuation may be accomplished is considered in this chapter and the following chapter.

IMPORTANCE

The purpose of making an analysis of a bank is to value that bank. For example, a simple comment about the net loan losses of a bank carries with it an implicit valuation of the bank. If the loan losses were large, the valuation of the bank might be low. This valuation likely would not be appropriate for most needs of a bank analyst. But an evaluation would have been made, indicating that evaluations are a basic part of all discussions of banks.

In many instances, valuation is related to price. In the United States, most bank analysts have become accustomed to considering all valuations in terms of a market economy, which uses the price of securities as a measure of value. The connection between valuation and price is useful for most purposes. Valuation is concerned with utility, and price usually serves as a proxy for utility in a market economy.

Nevertheless, price is not always useful as a measure of utility. To illustrate this point, suppose that wage and price controls were again instituted in a far-reaching program of government controls. They would require a revision in our valuation measures. The government could require banks to finance the redevelopment of housing in selected neighborhoods, and banks might have access to funds in proportion to their fulfillment of that objective. In this simple example, the more traditional measures of utility of a bank, such as profitability, would be subordinated to the newer government directives. The government, in this instance, might decree that banks would be measured by their social utility, as determined by the government, rather than their economic utility, as measured by market forces.

Current opinion does not expect that there would be such sweeping changes in government regulation of banking. The example does serve, however, to illustrate that there could be changes in the way the utility of a bank might be measured.

PERCEPTION

It may appear unusual that a review of the subject of valuation of a bank would include a discussion of the importance of perception, but the issue is fundamental. Most errors in judgment of banks have been made from faulty perception rather than from mistaken numbers. For example, the difficulties of Franklin National were available for bank analysts to observe months before its demise, but the perception of these facts was not clear to countless hundreds of analysts who purchased stock of Franklin during that period.

A bank analyst needs to learn of the information needed to form an evaluation. It is often tempting to begin the other way, which is to find the information which is available and use it as the basis of an evaluation. The latter approach runs a major risk of overlooking the importance of information not readily available.

No simple test exists to determine the information a bank analyst needs to know to make an evaluation of a bank. This information will vary according to the size, markets, location, and other factors of a bank. For example, the outlook for agricultural products and land values would be important to a bank in Iowa, but less so to a wholesale bank in a money center.

In another instance, there is no reliable information showing possible speculative transactions in real estate. Banks need to be aware of speculation in the real estate market, because they could be vulnerable to the effects of a break in the speculation and its impact on borrowers, depositors, as well as shareholders. The recent difficulties of the real estate investment trusts indicated that many banks were not aware of the speculative elements in this real estate market when they made loans.

SECURITIES

Except for a handful of private ones, all banks in the United States have issued equity shares, which may be traded occasionally. Many of the larger banks also have issued notes and debentures, which also may be traded. The price for these securities reflects an opinion of the markets for the securities. In turn, this market value may be used as a proxy for a valuation of a bank represented by the securities.

Market valuations of securities reflect information primarily of interest to short-term or long-term shareholders and debt holders. The position of these shareholders and debt holders is outlined in Chapter 1, which discusses the various types of bank analysts who can use this book. A market valuation usually reflects a broad point of view of many different market makers. It often may be interpreted as representing an impersonal, independent view and reflecting the aggregate opinion of all holders of the securities.

There are three possible limitations to the use of securities markets in valuation. In some instances a market for a bank's securities may not be broad enough to provide a balanced cross-section of opinions. For example, a small bank might find that there would be only a handful of persons who might be interested in the stock of the bank.

A second limitation to market valuations is that sometimes even large markets can lose balance. This is a condition of speculation or depression. It occurs when assets or securities are valued not on their economic usefulness, but on expected further changes in their price. The price of most bank stocks reflected the speculation of 1929, as well as the depressed outlook for stocks in 1946. Both periods represented extremes when stock prices were at unsustainable levels. Thus even broad markets cannot always be relied on to provide an accurate valuation of banks.

A third limitation to the use of market valuations is that changes in the valuation of any particular bank's securities often reflect the policies of the U.S. government more than changes of the bank itself. For example, an increase in interest rates, reflecting a shortage of funds in money markets, would have the likely effect of lowering the value of debt securities of a bank that had been issued at an earlier period of lower interest rates. The decline in the value of the bank's debt securities would occur even if there were no change in the fundamental position of the bank.

Equity Measures

Price-Earnings Multiple. The price-earnings multiple is the most common measure of valuation of banks. This is the ratio of the current price with the most recent earnings expressed on an annual basis. The price-earnings multiple shows how much a given dollar of current earnings is valued. Banks with comparatively high price-earnings multiples usually reflect strong past earnings performance or strong future earnings prospects.

Table 78 shows the price-earnings multiples of Citicorp, Chase, and Morgan from the fourth quarter of 1968 to the second quarter of 1975. These three banks were selected for comparison because they represent three major international banks located in New York City and wholesale banks with similarities in lending and deposit characteristics. The multiples of all three declined on an overall basis from the beginning to the end of the period. The multiple for Citicorp declined from 19.6x to 13.3x, the multiple for Chase dropped from 15.6x to 5.6x, and the multiple for Morgan declined from 14.6x to 13.0x.

Table 78 Citicorp, Chase and Morgan
Comparison of Price-Earnings Multiples of Each Bank with the Average of the Group

Year	Quarter	Citicorp Price-Earnings Multiple	Citicorp Ratio to Average Multiple	Chase Price-Earnings Multiple	Chase Ratio to Average Multiple	Morgan Price-Earnings Multiple	Morgan Ratio to Average Multiple	Average Three Banks' Price-Earnings Multiple
1968	4	19.6X	118	15.6X	94	14.6X	88	16.6X
1969	1	18.3	118	14.5	94	13.7	88	15.5
	2	16.9	118	13.7	96	12.4	87	14.3
	3	16.1	115	13.3	95	12.7	91	14.0
	4	15.0	106	14.4	102	13.0	92	14.1
1970	1	15.4	108	14.0	98	13.5	94	14.3
	2	14.0	109	12.5	97	12.1	94	12.9
	3	14.1	108	12.2	97	12.6	97	13.0
	4	13.6	111	11.6	94	11.6	94	12.3
1971	1	13.8	112	11.9	97	11.1	90	12.3
	2	13.7	109	12.7	101	11.3	90	12.6
	3	13.2	112	11.7	99	10.6	90	11.8
	4	15.3	115	12.9	97	11.7	88	13.3
1972	1	16.9	117	13.8	95	12.9	89	14.5
	2	18.8	121	13.6	87	14.3	92	15.6
	3	21.1	121	15.1	87	16.0	92	17.4
	4	21.7	125	14.0	81	16.3	94	17.3
1973	1	21.7	132	12.9	78	14.9	90	16.5
	2	20.3	136	10.1	69	14.2	95	14.9
	3	22.6	133	11.0	65	17.3	102	17.0
	4	22.1	129	12.1	71	17.1	100	17.1
1974	1	18.7	121	11.8	76	15.9	103	15.5
	2	16.6	121	9.8	72	14.6	107	13.7
	3	12.2	121	7.1	70	11.0	109	10.1
	4	11.2	122	5.6	61	10.9	118	9.2
1975	1	12.7	125	5.8	57	12.0	118	10.2
	2	13.3	125	5.6	53	13.0	123	10.6

Source: Citicorp, Chase Manhattan Corporation, J. P. Morgan & Co., Incorporated, quarterly reports, Standard and Poor's Corporation.

337

The average of the multiples of the three banks may be regarded as an overall indicator of how much value the equity securities market placed on current earnings during each of the quarters of the period. This average multiple declined overall from 16.6× in the fourth quarter of 1968 to 10.6× in the second quarter of 1975. The decline of this average may be regarded as a reflection of the difficulties of equities to withstand the negative pressures from money markets and a persistent upward direction in the long-term trend of inflation. Thus an important part of the decline of the price-earnings multiple of each of the three international banks reflected changes in the basic structure of financial markets and the U.S. economy and not necessarily the banks' condition.

The ratio of each bank's price-earnings multiple to the average multiple for the group represents a measure of how well that bank's multiple performed relative to the others. This is a measure of the relative strength or weakness of the multiple and serves as a way of eliminating the effects of changes in the multiples because of the events in financial markets and the U.S. economy. It represents an effort to obtain a measure showing how shareholders assessed the strengths and weaknesses of similar banks.

The ratio of the price-earnings multiple for Citicorp to the average multiple of the group of three banks was 118 percent in the fourth quarter of 1968. The ratio remained above 100 throughout the period shown in the table and ended the period with 125 percent. There was a moderate upgrading in the relative value of Citicorp by shareholders in the period.

In contrast, the ratio for Chase began the period at 94 percent of the three banks' average and improved on an overall relative basis in the subsequent two years. The ratio for Chase reached 102 percent in the fourth quarter of 1969 and 101 percent in the second quarter of 1971. Thereafter, the ratio steadily fell and reached a low of 53 percent at the end of the period. Shareholders reduced the value that they placed on the earnings of Chase toward the end of the period.

The ratio for Morgan followed a different pattern. In the fourth quarter of 1968, the ratio for this bank was 88 percent of the three banks' average. The ratio subsequently rose on a gradual and fairly steady basis, rising to 123 percent of the average. Shareholders increased their relative value of this bank's earnings as the period progressed.

Dividend Yield. A second measure of the value of equities is a bank's dividend yield. This is a traditional measure widely used during the period prior to the Second World War. The measure shows dividends per share, expressed at an annual rate, divided by the trading price of a share.

Dividends represent a clear return to a shareholder, and during that prewar period, shareholders often looked on generous dividends as an indication that their shares were with a productive organization. At this time little information about earnings was available to shareholders. During recent years, as information concerning earnings has become plentiful, most shareholders have become convinced that earnings represent a better measure of the profits from an equity holding.

Nevertheless, the traditional measure of dividend yield still is used by a small group of shareholders in valuing stocks. This group includes persons who require income from their securities holdings and who see a dividend check as a benefit which can be immediately converted to cash. A second group includes persons who are not completely convinced that the earnings of a bank represent an accurate assessment of the profits of a bank's shares. These shareholders look at the assumptions that underlie many of the accounting rules used in estimating earnings. They prefer to rely on dividends as a key measure in valuing shares, because they believe dividends represent harder evidence of performance than earnings.

In Table 79 the dividend yield of three major international banks in New York City in the second quarter of 1975 is shown. The average price is estimated by averaging the monthly high and low transaction price for the stock of each bank, and the dividend rate is indicated by showing the quarterly dividend per share at an annual rate. Chase showed an average dividend yield of 6.5 percent during the period, Morgan showed a 2.8 percent yield, and Citicorp showed a 2.4 percent yield. In this measure of return to shareholders, Chase ranked first, followed by Morgan and Citicorp. This ranking was the reverse of that of the banks according to price-earnings multiple.

Multiple of Market Value to Book Value

This comparison is another measure of value of the stock of a bank that was widely used in assessing banks prior the Second World War. "Book value" represents total shareholders' equity. For ease of comparison book value is placed on a per share basis and compared directly with the trading price of a share.

Market value for a share above its book value may be regarded as a surplus for shareholders, indicating that the securities markets value the shares of the bank more highly than their asset value. Similarly, a shortfall would indicate that the securities markets did not appraise the shares as highly as the value of the equity.

This measure of the value of a bank is used frequently as a basis of establishing the trading price of shares by small banks that do not have an active market for their equities. In many cases, the cashier or treasurer of the bank serves as a market maker. Persons who wish to buy or sell shares indicate their interest to this officer of the bank, and arrangements are made to bring the interested parties together. Sometimes the cashier or treasurer will handle those transactions out of treasury stock, using book value as the basis of establishing the price of the shares.

Shown in Table 79 is the multiple of market value to book value of the three banks in the second quarter of 1975. The multiple in calculated by dividing the average price per share by the average book value per share. Morgan showed a multiple of market price to book value of 2.4x during the second quarter of 1975, Citicorp showed a multiple of 2.1x and Chase showed a multiple of 0.8x. In this measure of value, Morgan ranked first, followed by Citicorp and Chase.

This ranking of the value of stock is different again from the ranking of dividend yield. The multiple of market value to book value is perhaps the

**Table 79   Citicorp, Chase, and Morgan
Comparison of Three
Measures of Equity Valuation Second Quarter 1975**

Bank	Price-Earnings Multiple	Dividend Yield Percent	Multiple of Market Value to Book Value
Citicorp	13.3X	2.4%	2.1X
Chase	5.7	6.5	0.8
Morgan	13.0	2.8	2.4

most conservative measure of value of a bank's shares. It purports to show the sum a shareholder would be left if the bank were liquidated.

Rates Paid for Large Certificates of Deposit

Large certificates of deposit include certificates issued in amounts of $100,000 or more. The interest rates paid on these certificates are not regulated by the Federal Reserve System and reflect market forces. The Federal Deposit Insurance Corporation insures only an amount up to $40,000 in the name of any one person or group of persons. Thus the remaining amount, is uninsured, and interest rates for that amount or larger amounts would reflect market evaluation of risk by depositors.

Unfortunately, this information is not regularly reported to the public on a comparative basis. There has been a strong reluctance of banks to provide this information. A rumor of difficulties with a major loan or difficulties in earnings or unexpected pressures from various foreign governments could lead to fears by some depositors, which would be quickly reflected in the higher rates a bank would need to pay for its new certificates of deposit. At present, this information is not organized in a way that provides a quick and easy comparison for depositors.

A few major money market houses make secondary markets in certificates of deposit. These market makers provide a general commentary to their institutional and wealthy individual customers. At best, this information is imprecise and often is based on relatively few transactions.

Nevertheless, from time to time, the results of these market makers are collected and published, usually one or more months after the period described. Here in Table 80 is one of these results, published in London by the *International Currency Review*. The table shows that between November 1974 and June 1976, there were important changes in the ranking of banks in rates paid for large certificates of deposit. This period covered the time from the collapse of Bankhaus Herstatt to a later period when the shock of that demise had become accepted as an isolated event. Several major banks, described as four prime U.S. banks and the top three New York City prime banks, dropped in rank from first to second position in the interval, while the Japanese banks moved from the bottom of the list to a rank above major U.K. merchant banks and Italian banks. The report indicated that the top tier was usually separated from the bottom tier by three-quarters of one percent, except for deposits from Arab countries, where the difference was considerably larger.

RATING SERVICES

Over many years rating services have developed techniques of evaluating debt offerings from municipalities and corporations, including bank holding companies. These ratings are provided to investors, including underwriters of new securities to aid in the pricing of the securities and to help market them to their final purchasers. The two principal rating agencies are Moody's Investors Service, Inc., and Standard & Poor's Corporation, both located in New York City.

For many years, these two rating services did not publish ratings for banks. Recently, this policy has changed. Standard & Poor's began rating bank holding company commercial paper in 1970 and the long-term debt of bank holding companies in 1974. These ratings are made only at a bank's request. This practice gives banks the right to refuse the ratings. If ratings are agreed on, they are then made public (Table 81).

Table 80   Ranking of International Bank Premiums Paid for Large Certificates of Deposit

November 1974

1. Four prime U.S. banks
2. One prime U.S. bank
3. Remaining top 10 U.S. banks
4. Second tier U.S. banks in major cities
5. Canadian and certain medium-sized West Coast banks
6. London clearing banks and regional U.S. banks
7. Wholly owned American merchant banks
8. Medium-sized consortium banks
9. Italian banks
10. Japanese banks

June 1976

1. A large U.S. West Coast bank
2. Top three New York City prime banks
3. Prime U.S. banks
4. Second tier
5. Japanese banks
6. Major U.K. merchant banks
7. Italian banks

Source: International Currency Review, Volume 8, Number 3.

Table 81   Comparison of Quality Ratings of Selected Banks According to Rating Services

Bank		Moody's (February 1977)	Standard & Poor's (February 1977)	First Albany (July 1976)
J. P. Morgan & Co.	8s Notes '86	Aaa	—	I
Manufacturers Hanover Corporation	Debentures 8⅛ 2004	Aaa	—	II
Manufacturers Hanover Corporation	7.60s Notes '81	Aaa	—	II
Manufacturers Hanover Corporation	8⅜s Notes '82	Aaa	—	III
Chemical New York Corporation	6⅝s Notes '80	Aaa	—	III
Chemical New York Corporation	7.80s Notes '82	Aaa	—	III
Chemical New York Corporation	Debentures 8.40s '99	Aaa	—	IV
Bankers Trust New York Corporation	Debentures 6⅜s, B, '78	Aaa	—	IV
Bankers Trust New York Corporation	Debentures 8⅛s, C, '99	Aaa	—	IV
First Bank System	6¾s Notes '79	Aa	AAA	I-A
First Bank System	8¾s Notes '83	—	AAA	I-A
Northwest Bancorporation	6⅞s Notes '78	Aa	—	I-A
Northwest Bancorporation	7⅞s Notes '86	—	AAA	I-A
Mercantile Bancorporation	Debentures 8½ 2004	Aa	—	I-A
Citicorp	8.48 Notes 2007	Aaa[a]	AAA[a]	III

[a] Rated in March 1977.

The March 1977 offering of $350 million of notes of Citicorp were rated Aaa by Moody's and AAA by Standard & Poor's. These ratings were the highest on the rating scales of both services. Published reports from these services provide an insight into the reasoning underlying these conclusions.

Moody's describes its position in the March 14, 1977, issue of its weekly publication "Moody's Bond Survey." The discussion under the section of quality and rating briefly notes that Citicorp holds Citibank, the second largest commercial bank in the world in terms of total assets and total deposits and the largest commercial bank based on total equity. It notes that the nonbank subsidiaries account for less than 20 percent of assets, revenues, and income. The report then discusses the strong growth of net interest revenues in recent years. The expansion of earnings is reviewed, with particular emphasis placed on the relatively high and stable return on average total assets. The ability of

Citicorp to develop capital internally is given attention, and its ability to provide an excess of provision for loan losses than actual net charge-offs is reviewed.

Standard & Poor's discusses its rating of the Citicorp offering in the March 26, 1977, issue of its weekly publication, "Fixed Income Investor," noting the large size of the bank, its strong earnings performance, a high return on equity, and an ability to generate capital internally. In addition, Standard & Poor's pointed to the ability of Citicorp to tap capital markets when the banking industry was under scrutiny. This rating service also commented on the quality and depth of the management team as part of its assessment.

A newcomer to the rating of banks is First Albany Corporation, a regional brokerage firm, which predominately handles retail accounts. First Albany takes a position on the safety of bank debt that differs from that of Moody's and Standard & Poor's. Unlike the latter two, First Albany believes that banking is essentially a risky business. In its report "Bank Holding Company Debt Ratings" of July 1976, the firm asserts that the quality variations among bank holding company debt issues are wider and the necessity for selectivity is greater than most investors and rating agencies assume. Nevertheless, this report claims that in 1975 most banks reversed a trend toward lower quality in their financial condition.

Unlike Moody's or Standard & Poor's, which publish mostly a discussion of their reasoning about quality ratings, First Albany's report on ratings consists largely of pages of ratios, although it notes that its credit ratings are not based only on these numerical compilations. This rating service considers its judgment of the numbers is an important step in arriving at its conclusions. The numerical basis of the rating for each bank is the result of 23 ratios covering capital adequacy, leverage, profitability, loan portfolio quality, accounting practices with respect to loan losses, the investment portfolio, liquidity, interest coverage, and possible problem areas. These 9 categories are heavily weighted to emphasize balance sheet analysis and give less emphasis to earnings.

The rating systems of the three services are not entirely comparable and require some explanation. Moody's uses a rating system for corporate bonds with nine categories, ranging from AAA to C. The category AAA is judged to be of best quality. These bonds carry the smallest degree of investment risk and are generally referred to as "gilt edge." Interest payments are protected by a large or by an exceptionally stable margin and principal is secure. The category C is the lowest rated class of bonds and includes elements of danger with respect to principal or interest. Often these bonds are in default. This rating also indicates a bond has extremely poor prospects of ever attaining an investment standing.

Standard & Poor's uses a similar ranking system for corporate bonds with a range from AAA to D. The bonds rated AAA are the highest grade obligations. They possess the highest degree of protection as to principal or interest. In contrast, all bonds rated D are in default.

The rating categories of First Albany include the five categories of I-A, I, II, III, and IV. The category of I-A indicates the highest degree of financial strength and, for the bondholder, investment quality. Banks in this group are characterized by strong capital, high profitability, quality assets, and strong interest coverage. Banks in category IV exhibit serious deficiencies in most or all of the key tests. The bonds issued by these banks are regarded as speculative, and First Albany recommends that they should be avoided by serious investors. The lowest ratings for Moody's and Standard & Poor's may be regarded as being of a lower indication of quality than the lowest category of First Albany.

The table shows that Moody's and Standard & Poor's ratings are approximately the same in the four comparisons. In contrast, many of the comparisons between Moody's (as well as Standard & Poor's in four cases) and First Albany show basic differences in ratings. The difference in time periods—with the ratings for Moody's and Standard & Poor's occurring in February or March 1977, and the ratings for First Albany occurring in July 1976—is not regarded as being of major significance.

There is no basic disagreement among the three services for the ratings of Morgan, First Bank System, Northwest Bancorporation, or Mercantile Bancorporation. However, the highest rating given to Manufacturers Hanover by Moody's and Standard & Poor's is not reflected in the category II rating of First Albany. Moody's and Standard & Poor's also rate Chemical New York and Citicorp in their highest category, but First Albany rates them in category III. This group, according to First Albany, includes banks that exhibit more numerous or serious weaknesses, and because of this, First Albany recommends that investors should look for price concessions so that the acceptance of greater risk would be compensated. The widest difference among the rating services is for Bankers Trust, with Moody's and Standard & Poor's showing a highest rating and First Albany showing a lowest rating.

These differences represent an important issue in bond ratings. Apparently, the well-established rating services, Moody's and Standard & Poor's, do not perceive the risks that First Albany believes exist. Within the next few years these differences in opinion will be tested.

Most new debt issues are priced by the ratings of Moody's and Standard & Poor's, and most institutional investors in bank debentures are not concerned with the lower ratings of First Albany. Nevertheless, a fundamental issue is involved. The two different assessments of quality represent a recent major schism in debt ratings of banks. During the postwar years up to the 1970s most banks avoided issuing debt. Debt issues of banks increased in the 1970s as they sought to use long-term debt as a substitute for equity capital.

Banks had been considered to be completely safe, almost above the rating systems used for industrial corporations, and the major banks enjoyed untarnished reputations so far as creditworthiness was concerned. The demise of Franklin National and the concern over bank loans to real estate investment trusts created doubts in the minds of many investors, and rating services were called in 1974 to attest to the strength of banks. The singularly strong credit reputation of banks was reconsidered. A difference in opinion expressed by different ratings by the rating services developed. The fact that there could be wide differences of opinion in certain instances and the trend away from a unanimity of opinion suggest that the future course of ratings of bank debt securities could involve some difficult decisions by investors.

CHAPTER 17
COMPOSITE VALUATION

The methods of valuing a bank which use information from securities markets provide important conclusions for some bank analysts. Yet each of these methods has inadequacies. The securities market has imperfections, information about rates for large certificates of deposit is difficult to obtain, and rating services do not always agree among themselves.

There is a more fundamental difficulty with these methods of valuation. They do not provide information for all bank analysts. None of the methods, for example, indicates which bank would be most appropriate for a borrower, and none is particularly useful to a depositor. These bank analysts, and others, must look elsewhere for methods of valuation.

ORGANIZATION OF COMPOSITE VALUATIONS

An approach to overcome these difficulties is to show a composite valuation, which measures a bank according to key structural elements and organizes a conclusion according to the needs of various bank analysts.

Structural Elements

The principal parts of an evaluation of a bank include the liquidity, credit risk, interest rate, profitability, and capital policies, as well as the environment of a bank, the business strategy and controls, and an evaluation of the accounting reports the bank makes available to the public. Each of these policies and issues has been discussed in earlier chapters and is briefly reviewed here.

The liquidity policy refers to the program a bank follows to provide itself with cash funds. The credit risk policy includes how a bank insures itself that it will be repaid its principal and interest when due. The interest rate policy includes the management of interest rate spread. The profitability policy refers to how a bank's earnings compare with its resources. The capital policy covers the guidelines a bank uses to build its capital base.

These five policies may be considered to include the principal financial guidelines by which a bank manages itself. Virtually all of the financial programs of a bank relate to one or more of these policies. For example, earnings per share have been given prominence by many security analysts, and many banks manage their operations with earnings per share as a principal goal. Yet for purposes of analysis, earnings per share do not represent an elemental policy. They are a hybrid of several more basic policies, particularly interest rate policy and credit risk policy in the short-term and capital policy in the long-term. If these three policies are known, earnings per share can be better understood and better forecast.

Most banks do not have clearly stated financial policies and usually respond to questions about these policies with general or vague comments about the need to remain flexible. Nevertheless, a careful examination of the records of banks shows that most of them have followed a particular policy in a fairly regular manner for a period. The analysis of the structural elements of a bank attempts to identify and measure these patterns of performance.

The five financial policies serve as a balance to each other and cover the essential parts of a financial structure which all bank analysts are interested in. In many instances the parts work against each other, and this is precisely why they are all so important. The mark of a successful bank is its ability to show strength in all of the policies and not permit one or a few of the policies to fall into a shadow.

Ranking the Bank

The success of a bank in pursuing its various policies and issues provides a basis for evaluation. The use of comparisons to rank a bank's performance shows one yardstick of performance. Unfortunately, it is not always an easy matter to make banking comparisons. Data are not usually ranked or presented in a way that shows the performance of a bank on a comparative basis. Often, broadly based averages are the only data available for making comparisons, and at times even these averages are not available. The bank analyst often must work with less than ideal information.

An average provides only a crude indication of the rank of a bank among its peers. Other graduations of rank, such as quartiles, quintiles, deciles, and percentiles provide a better measure of rank. The latter show gradations running from 1 to 100. Often a bank analyst needs to combine data expressed in many of these ranking bases. The best approach is to convert all of the data to percentiles to avoid losing the detail of any part.

Often conflicting data result from more than one source. For example, some information might indicate that a bank ranked in the sixtieth percentile, while data from another source might indicate an eightieth percentile rating. The differences could reflect different peer groups, as well as different methods of calculating averages. The bank analyst would decide which set of data was more appropriate or would make an average of the data.

Bank Analysts

Chapter 1 discussed seven types of bank analysts, namely, directors, depositors, borrowers, short-term shareholders, long-term shareholders, debt holders, and employees. And most analysts of banks fit into one of these seven categories.

Bank analysts' interests vary considerably. For example, depositors place considerable importance in being able to obtain their funds either on demand or when a deposit is due. Liquidity would rank high in importance to them. In contrast, short-term shareholders are primarily interested in changes in earnings per share over a short-term period and would be interested in the credit risk policy.

The relative importance of each policy and issue varies according to the different groups of bank analysts, indicating that one bank might be appropriate for the needs of one type of analyst, and not as appropriate for another. Some might wish to select different weights for the policies and issues, basing their selection on needs as they might perceive them.

The results of a composite evaluation sum to a number for each particular group. For example, if a percentile scale is used, a bank under review might score in the sixty-fifth percentile for a bank analyst group. This result would indicate that the bank would probably be better than average, but not outstanding. The use of a single number for a valuation reflects the importance of simplicity to analysts at the completion of any valuation process, especially a complicated one.

Despite an effort to reach an objective appraisal of a bank, most bank analysts form evaluations of banks on their opinion of the people in the organization whom they know. One good friend in a bank is worth a thousand ratios in the eyes of most bank analysts. There is no question that the presence of a good friend in any situation is quite valuable. Yet even good friends may be limited in what they can accomplish for a bank analyst, who may wish to be aware of the limits that may be imposed on friendship by the structure of the bank itself.

FIRST NATIONAL BANCSHARES

First National Bancshares serves here as an example of a composite valuation. This bank was selected because it comes close to representing a typical U.S. bank. It has shown an overall good record to most bank analyst groups and it successfully repulsed a recent raid by a wealthy Arab investor.

First National Bancshares has been in business in Santa Clara County, California, for more than 100 years. It was organized in 1874 as the Farmers' National Gold Bank of San Jose, the principal city in Santa Clara County. Subsequently, in 1880 the bank's name was changed to the First National Bank of San Jose and most recently in 1975 to First National Bancshares. The First National Bank of San Jose comprises almost the total consolidated assets and operating income of First National Bancshares.

Headquartered in San Jose, the bank has 34 branch offices in Santa Clara and in the adjacent counties of San Mateo and Alameda. At year-end 1976, the bank had total assets of $421 million, deposits of $380 million, and loans and leases before deduction of reserves of $218 million. Based on deposits, it ranked as the fourteenth largest bank in California and the 264th largest bank in the United States. The chart shows that quarterly earnings per share, shown on a seasonally adjusted basis at annual rate, were approximately level from the first quarter of 1970 to the second quarter of 1974, but have shown significant, steady expansion from the second quarter of 1974 to the same quarter of 1977.

Review of Peer Group Rankings

Four measures of peer group rankings are shown here. The comparisons are based on California and United States competitors using banks with approximately the same size of deposits.

Keefe Management Services. An examination of Table 82 shows the peer group rankings of the First National of San Jose for five policies. The data are from various publications of Keefe Management Services. The California peer group includes eight banks ranging in deposits from $250 million to $1 billion. The United States peer group includes 132 banks with deposits from $300 million to $1 billion. All 1975 ratios of the Keefe services are calculated using an average of December 31, 1975, June 30, 1975, and December 31, 1974, domestic call report information related to 1975 income data from the income and dividend report. Ratios for earlier years are calculated on the same basis.

The first measure of liquidity policy is indicated by the proportion of core deposits to total deposits and borrowed funds. "Core deposits" refer to demand deposits and savings deposits and are regarded as being a stable base of deposits. The First National Bank of San Jose had 77.35 percent of its source of deposits and borrowed funds in core deposits in 1975, according to Keefe data. This ratio ranked second highest in eight banks. The valuation for this ranking is shown as 85 on a percentile basis. The valuation is determined by reducing the number in the peer group by one in making the comparison. Thus being first in rank would indicate a valuation of 100 and being second would indicate a valuation one-seventh lower or a valuation of 85. If a bank ranked eighth of eight, it would have a valuation of 0.

In contrast to the relatively high rank in core deposits, The First National Bank of San Jose ranked seventh among eight peer group banks the ratio of U.S. treasury and other U.S. government securities to average domestic assets, giving a valuation of 14. This measure of liquidity considers all types of U.S. government securities as assets that are close to cash.

The summary valuation for the liquidity of First National Bank of San Jose is shown as 30. This valuation is lower than a simple average of the valuation of 85 for the ranking of the ratio of demand and savings deposits to total deposits and borrowed funds and the valuation of 14 for the ranking of the ratio of U.S. government securities to assets. This lower summary valuation reflects the greater importance of the ratio of U.S. government securities to assets as a measure of liquidity.

The credit risk policy is indicated by two measures, both relating to loan loss performance. The ratio of net charge-offs to total loans in 1975 was 0.32 percent for the First National Bank of San Jose, according to Keefe data. This ratio ranked the bank fourth among eight banks in its California peer group, giving a valuation of 57. The bank's performance of net charge-offs to loans in the U.S. peer group of 1976 was better, with net charge-offs showing 0.26 percent and ranking 38 in 132 banks of its peer group. This performance indicated a valuation of 72. Among its U.S. peers, the bank showed a significant increase in rank from 1974 to 1976, with a rise in rank from 67 to 37 in the interval. This performance is valued here as representing 80, indicating a record well above average.

The "loan loss coverage multiple" represents a second measure of credit risk policy. This measure shows income before taxes, plus the provision for loan losses divided by loan charge-offs. It attempts to show the earnings power of the bank in relation to its loan losses. The presumption is that a bank with strong earnings can withstand a higher level of loan losses than a bank with modest earnings capability. The multiple for the First National Bank of San Jose was 8.39X in 1975, ranking it third of its eight California peers, and giving it a valuation of 71.

The average of these four valuations shown in the table—57, 71, 72, and 80—is 70. The simple average is used here as the summary valuation because each of the four measures represents an indicator of credit risk policy approximately equal in importance.

The interest rate policy is measured by the net interest margin on a tax equivalent basis. This measure of Keefe Management Services shows the sum of all interest income and expense on a fully taxable basis divided by loans and securities. It is a measure of how a bank manages its interest spread. The table shows that the First National Bank of San Jose had a net interest margin of 5.34 percent in 1975, ranking it third in a group of eight California competitors. This performance indicated a valuation of 71, which is shown rounded to 70 in the summary valuation.

The profitability policy is indicated by the return on total assets. This measure shows income before securities transactions divided by total assets, which are averaged in the manner described above. The First National Bank of San Jose showed a ratio of 0.86 percent in 1975, ranking it second in its California peer group for a valuation of 85. The bank's return on assets was 0.81 percent in 1976, ranking it 53 in 132 banks of its peer group in the United States for a valuation of 60. There was a slight decline in the bank's rank of this measure of performance from 1974 to 1976. A consideration of these offsetting factors led to a valuation of 50, indicating an average performance.

The average valuation of the three measures of profitability—85, 60, and 50—amounts to approximately 65, which is used for the summary valuation. Two of the three measures reflect the position and trend of rank in the United States, and the summary valuation gives greater emphasis to that peer group than the California peer group.

Table 82 First National Bank of San Jose
Keefe Management Services Peer Group Rankings

	California Peer Group—Deposit Range $250 to $1000 Million	U.S. Peer Group—Deposit Range $250 to $1000 Million	U.S. Peer Group—Deposits Less Than $1 Billion	Summary
1. Liquidity policy	Demand and savings (core) to total deposits and borrowed funds—77.35%—ranked 2 in 8 of California peer group Valuation = 85 U.S. Treasury and other U.S. Government securities to average domestic assets—ranked 7 in 8 of California peer group Valuation = 14			Valuation = 30
2. Credit risk policy	Net loan charge-offs to total loans—0.32%—ranked 4 in 8 of California peer group Valuation = 57 Loan loss coverage multiple—8.39X—ranked 3 in 8 of California peer group Valuation = 71 Net interest margin on a tax equivalent basis—5.34%—ranked 3 in 8 of California peer group	Net charge-offs to loans—0.26%—ranked 38 in 132 of U.S. peer group Valuation = 72	Significant improving trend of rank of charge-offs: 67 = 1974, 38 = 1975, 37 = 1976 Valuation = 80	Valuation = 70

3. Interest rate policy	Valuation = 71			Valuation = 70
4. Profitability policy	Earned on total assets—0.86%—ranked 2 in 8 of California peer group Valuation = 85	Earned on total assets—0.81%—ranked 53 in 132 of U.S. peer group Valuation = 60	Slight declining trend of rank in return on assets: 50 = 1974, 53 = 1975, 54 = 1976 Valuation = 50	Valuation = 65
5. Capital policy	Equity capital to total assets—5.93%—ranked 3 in 8 of California peer group Valuation = 71			
	Equity capital and loan loss reserves and long-term debt to total assets—7.10%—ranked 7 in 8 of California peer group Valuation = 14	Equity capital to total assets—6.13%—ranked 84 of 132 in U.S. peer group Valuation = 37	Major declining trend of rank in equity capital to assets: 67 = 1974, 84 = 1975, 101 = 1976 Valuation = 20	Valuation = 35

Source: Keefe Management Services, Inc. For California peer group—*Bank Operating Performance,* 1975. For U.S. peer group—*Year-End Report, Comparative Performance and Analysis,* 1976, except where noted.

The capital policy is indicated by four measures. The ratio of equity capital to total assets was 5.93 percent in 1975, ranking third in eight of the California peer group. The valuation was 71. The same measure showed a valuation of 37 in the U.S. peer group for 1976. The major difference between these two valuations reflected a difference in capital ratios between West Coast banks and eastern banks. West Coast banks typically have significantly lower capital ratios. Among its California peers, there was a low valuation of 14 for the bank's position in the ratio of equity capital, loan loss reserves, and long-term debt to total assets. This measure will probably be discontinued, since it shows loan loss reserves as a part of capital rather than as a contra-asset to loans, which is now preferred. Nevertheless, the measure indicates that taking a broad measure of capital, the bank ranked low.

The decline in the bank's position in the ratio of equity capital to total assets was fairly rapid. Compared with its United States peers, the bank's rank in the ratio declined from 67th in 1974, was 84th in 1975, and 101st in 1976 of a peer group of 132 banks. The decline represented a major erosion in position. This drop is ascribed a valuation of 20, indicating a valuation well below average. The summary valuation of the capital policy is shown as 35, representing approximately the average of the four valuations of 71, 14, 37, and 20.

Bank Administration Institute. A second approach to the ranking of the performance of the First National Bank of San Jose is provided by the Bank Administration Institute (Table 83). The Bank Administration Institute uses the call reports and income and dividend reports, which are the same original information used by Keefe Management Services. This organization uses a slightly different method of averaging than Keefe and includes data from four call reports in its averages.

The Bank Administration Institute arranges its peer group averages into five groups—lower decile, lower quartile, median, upper quartile, and upper decile. Thirty-nine ratios, yields, and other comparisons are presented for both a bank and its peer group. The table shows information for five policies of the bank according to a California peer group of 32 banks with assets ranging from $100 million to $499 million, as well as a United States peer group of 824 banks with the same asset range.

The liquidity policy is indicated by loans as a percent of total assets. The First National Bank of San Jose ranks as the median bank among its California peers in this measure and shows a valuation of 50. Among its United States peers, the bank ranked in approximately the 65th percentile in this measure of liquidity. Liquidity is inversely proportional to the ratio of loans to assets, and the ranking of this measure is inverted. Thus a ranking in the 65th percentile indicates a valuation of 35. The summary shows a valuation of 45, which represents approximately the average of the two liquidity measures.

The credit risk policy is measured by three indicators of loan loss experience, the loan loss provision as a percent of total operating income, net charge-offs as a percent of total loans, and the provision for loan losses as a percent of average loans. In all six measures of the California and United States peer groups, the bank ranked from about the 45th to the 50th percentile, providing a summary valuation which rounds to 50.

The interest rate policy is reviewed by eight measures, including the tax equivalent yield on earning assets, the yield on loans, interest expense as a percent of total operating income, and net interest margin on a tax equivalent basis. These measures are shown for both peer groups in California and the United States. The initial three measures represent only parts of the net interest margin. They include either measures of the yield on assets or the cost of interest. The net interest margin represents the only complete measure of interest rate policy of the group. Nevertheless, it is often useful to check the components of net interest margin to determine whether there is an unusual situation with one of the components.

The measures of interest rate policy among the California peer groups indicate a lower ranking than among the United States peer group. The summary average valuation of all eight measures would be approximately 70, and an average valuation among only the two measures of net interest margin would be 65. Since the measure of interest expense is represented only once in the table and is higher in rank than two measures of yield on assets, these measures may be biased on the low side, and the summary valuation of 70 is used.

The profitability policy is measured by return on assets and return on equity. Of these two indicators, return on assets is a better measure of profitability and is given most weight. Nevertheless, the strong showing of the bank's rank of return on equity tips the scales a bit upward, and a valuation for profitability is shown at 70.

The capital policy is indicated by the ratio of equity to assets. As was mentioned in the Keefe measurements, there is a basic difference in capital ratios between the West Coast banks and those in the East, with typically lower capital ratios prevailing in the West. The bank showed a valuation of 50 among its California peers and 25 among its United States peers. The summary valuation of 35 indicates the greater importance of the United States peer group.

Overall Review of the Ten Policies and Issues

The forementioned results for peer groups represent important information in forming an overall valuation of the First National Bank of San Jose. They provide the benchmark information concerning the ranking of the bank, yet in some instances they could be biased because of small sample size. Thus the results of the peer group rankings should be reviewed in light of broader and more complete information. Moreover, the five issues involving economic environment, regulatory environment, management strategy, management controls, and an evaluation of accounting practices do not fit into precise peer group rankings. Each of the ten measures is reviewed next.

Liquidity Policy. An overall valuation of the ten policies and issues for First National Bancshares (looking now at the total organization) is shown in Table 84. The liquidity valuations are shown for Keefe Management Services and the Bank Administration Institute, along with a separate valuation of liquidity based on a review of several other measures.

The maturity of securities provides a measure of the self-liquidating

Table 83   First National Bank of San Jose Bank of Administration Institute Peer Group Rankings

	California Peer Group—Assets $100 to $499 Million 32 Banks			
	Loans as a percent of total assets—57.08%—Median bank			
1. Liquidity policy	Valuation = 50			
	Loan loss provision as a percent of total operating income—2.32%—approximately 45th percentile	Actual net charge-offs as a percent of total loans—0.32%—Median Bank	Provision for loan loss as a percent of average loans 0.34%—approximately 45th percentile	
2. Credit risk policy	Valuation = 45	Valuation = 50	Valuation = 45	
	Tax equivalent yield on earning assets—8.86%—Median bank	Yield on loans—9.51%—approximately 55th percentile	Interest expense as a percent of total operating income—35.36%—approximately 70th percentile (inverted ranking)	Net interest margin on a tax equivalent basis—58.21%—approximately 55th percentile
3. Interest rate policy	Valuation = 50	Valuation = 55	Valuation = 70	Valuation = 55
	Return on assets—0.84%—approximately 75th percentile	Return on equity—14.43%—approximately 75th percentile		
4. Profitability policy	Valuation = 75	Valuation = 75		
	Equity to assets—5.85%—Median bank			
5. Capital policy	Valuation = 50			

Source: Bank Administration Institute.

U.S. Peer Group—Assets $100 to $499 Million 824 Banks				Summary
Loans as a percent of total assets— 57.08%— approximately 65th percentile (inverted ranking)				
Valuation = 35				Valuation = 45
Loan loss provision as a percent of total operating income— 2.32%— approximately 45th percentile	Actual net charge-offs as a percent of total loans— 0.32%—Median bank	Provision for loan loss as a percent of average loans— 0.34%— approximately 50th percentile		
Valuation = 45	Valuation = 50	Valuation = 50		Valuation = 50
Tax equivalent yield on earning assets—8.86%— approximately 75th percentile	Yield on loans— 9.51%— approximately 80th percentile	Interest expense as a percent of total operating income— 35.36%— approximately 90th percentile (inverted ranking)	Net interest margin on a tax equivalent basis—58.21%— approximately 75th percentile	
Valuation = 75	Valuation = 80	Valuation = 90	Valuation = 75	Valuation = 70
Return on assets—0.84%— approximately 55th percentile	Return on equity— 14.43%— approximately 80th percentile			
Valuation = 55	Valuation = 80			Valuation = 70
Equity to assets—5.85%— approximately 25th percentile				
Valuation = 25				Valuation = 35

Table 84   First National Bancshares Valuations of Policies and Issues

		Keefe Management Services	Bank Administration Institute	Other Measures	Overall Valuation
1.	Liquidity policy	30	45	40	40
2.	Credit risk policy	70	50	80	65
3.	Interest rate policy	70	70	70	70
4.	Profitability policy	65	70	70	70
5.	Capital policy	35	35	35	35
6.	Future economic environment			95	95
7.	Regulatory environment			50	50
8.	Management strategy			60	60
9.	Management controls			70	70
10.	Evaluation of accounting			60	60

approach to liquidity. Sixty percent of the bank's U.S. government securities, including both treasuries and agencies, were in the one-to-five year bracket at year-end 1976. Seventeen percent were less than one year and 23 percent were for a period longer than five years. The bank's holdings of obligations of states and municipalities were distributed so that 12 percent were less than one year, 30 percent were from one-to-five years, 29 percent five-to-ten years, and 29 percent over ten years. These proportions appear to have moved slightly to a shorter maturity over the 1971 to 1976 period, indicating slightly rising liquidity. Overall, the maturity of the bank's securities portfolio would represent a position that would be fairly long for government securities and about average for municipal securities.

The loan deposit ratio provides a measure of the asset saleability approach to liquidity. It shows a rough guide of how fully a bank is "loaned-up." The bank's loan deposit ratio generally has risen in recent years—68 percent in 1972, 66 percent in 1973, 70 percent in 1974, 72 percent in 1975, and 74 percent in 1976—on a year-end basis. This performance indicates a lessening in the bank's liquidity. A loan deposit ratio of 74 percent is not exceptionally high, although it does indicate that the bank may be unable to continue this trend for too many more years.

The volatile liabilities ratio measures how the bank approaches purchased funds in money markets. These funds do not provide as much assurance of liquidity as regular demand and passbook savings deposits. The first measure of purchased funds is the proportion of certificates of deposit over $100,000 to total deposits. This proportion has risen steadily in recent years, amounting to 4 percent in 1972, 5 percent in 1973, 7 percent in 1974, 9 percent in 1975, and 12 percent in 1976.

The second measure is the net position of the bank in federal funds. The position of the bank in federal funds is a measure of how fully the bank can provide for its reserve requirements from internal sources. Purchases of federal funds indicate greater dependence on money market forces outside the direct control of a bank and consequently less internally generated liquidity. The bank does not show figures for federal funds sold on the same basis as federal funds purchased, so it is not possible to calculate the bank's net position. Nevertheless, there appears to be a trend toward a small, but greater dependence on federal funds. Average federal funds sold as a percent of average total assets declined from 1.8 percent in 1972 and 1.9 percent in 1975 to 0.9 percent in 1976. From 1972 to 1975 the bank showed no federal funds purchased at year-end, but held $10 million of these funds at year-end 1976.

Considering these measures of liquidity—a somewhat long average maturity of securities, a rising loan deposit ratio, and a growing proportion of purchased funds—the bank appears to be following a policy of slowly relinquishing a part of its liquidity. Yet the decline has not been pronounced, and liquidity does not appear to be a serious concern for the bank. A valuation of 40 for these liquidity measures is shown in the table. This valuation is between the other two valuations, and a valuation of 40 is used as an overall valuation for the bank.

Credit Risk Policy.   Three measures of credit risk are reviewed in addition to the measures in the Keefe and Bank Administration Institute. The first of these is the trend of the ratio of loan losses to average loans. This measure shows a declining ratio for the bank, with 0.36 percent in 1972, 0.31 percent in 1973, 0.34 percent in 1974, 0.29 percent in 1975, and 0.22 percent in 1976. This trend indicates an increasingly high standard of quality for the bank's loan portfolio. The bank has not lent to a real estate investment trust, which can only help raise the opinion of its quality standards for loans.

A second measure is risk adjusted margins. This measure shows whether net interest margins have kept pace with loan losses. As will be reviewed later, net interest margins have increased in recent years. The decline in the ratio of net loan losses to average loans would indicate that the adjusted net interest margins most likely rose more rapidly than interest margins, indicating a conservative credit risk policy.

A third measure of credit risk policy is shown by the relationship between book value and market value of the investment securities. At year-end 1976, the book of investment securities showed an approximate market value of $81,098,000 and a book value of $80,599,000. Market value was one percent above book value at that time, representing an improvement over the 5 percent shortfall one year earlier. The bank does not hold any securities of New York City.

These measures of credit risk—the trend of the ratio of loan losses to loans, to risk adjusted margins, and the ratio of market value to book value of securities—indicate that the bank has pursued a credit risk policy that has emphasized quality. This record appears stronger than the rankings of Keefe and the Bank Administration Institute indicate, and this separate valuation is shown as 80. The overall average valuation of the three valuations—Keefe, the Bank Administration Institute and the separate valuation—is 65.

Interest Rate Policy.   Interest rate policy is concerned with interest rate spread and whether the maturity of the sources and uses of the bank's funds are in balance. An imbalance in the latter could lead to either a benefit or detriment to earnings as interest rates fluctuate. Three measures of interest rate policy supplement the peer group rankings.

The first measure is the net interest spread. This is shown as the net average percent yield over the average percent cost of deposits. This spread has risen in recent years. It was 3.65 percent in 1972, 3.57 percent in 1973, 3.87 percent in 1974, 3.97 percent in 1975, and 4.35 percent in 1976. This rising spread indicates a policy of keeping margins as strong as possible.

A second measure of interest rate policy is the matching of maturities of principal assets and liabilities. Excluding one-to-four family residential real estate loans and consumer loans, the bank's remaining loans primarily include commercial industrial and business loans, which amounted to 72.7 million at year-end 1976. Of this total, 66 percent had maturities of one year or less, 23 percent had maturities from one to five years, and 11 percent had maturities over five years. Twenty-nine percent were loans with fixed interest rates, and 71 percent were loans with floating interest rates.

Of course, the addition of residential consumer loans would tend to lengthen the average maturity and increase the proportion of loans with fixed interest rates. Against these maturities, the bank had 88 percent of its deposits in demand, savings, and time deposits. These deposits have proven to be

Table 85   First National Bancshares Factor Separation Analysis (FASAN) Averages for

	Equity ($ Millions) ÷	Capital Ratio ×	Interest Income Ratio	Other + Income Ratio −	Personnel Expense Ratio −
1972 factors	17.400	0.06677	0.04529	0.01293	0.02238
Introduce 1976 equity	22.265				
Introduce 1976 capital ratio		0.05767			
Introduce 1976 interest income ratio			0.05289		
Introduce 1976 other income ratio				0.00736	
Introduce 1976 personnel expense ratio					0.02265
Introduce 1976 loan loss provision expense ratio					
Introduce 1976 other expense ratio					
Introduce 1976 one-tax rate					
Introduce 1976 number shares outstanding					
1976 factors	22.265	0.05767	0.05289	0.00736	0.02265

stable over a long period. Twelve percent of the bank's deposits were large certificates of deposit with an average maturity of less than one year. These measures would indicate that the maturity of the bank's loans would likely be longer than the maturity of its liabilities, but not out of proportion to most other similar banks.

These two measures of interest rate policy—interest rate spread and the maturity of sources and uses of funds—indicate a bank with good control over this policy. The valuation for these two measures concur with the valuation indicated by the two sets of peer valuations, giving an overall valuation of 70.

Profitability Policy. The Keefe and Bank Administration Institute give special emphasis to return on average total assets, which is the profitability measure providing the broadest coverage of activities of a bank. It is also the best indicator of the concept of return on investment. The trend of the bank's return on average total assets declined moderately in recent years, but still was comparatively high. The ratio was 0.95 percent in 1972, 0.89 percent in 1973, 0.87 percent in 1974, 0.87 percent in 1975, and 0.84 percent in 1976. Most banks showed some decline in this measure.

Table 85 shows a factor separation analysis of First National Bancshares from 1972 to 1976. This analysis is designed to show the factors responsible for

Years

Loan Loss Provision Ratio	− Other Expense Ratio)	= Total Operations Ratio	× 1 − Tax Rate	÷ No. Shares Outstanding (Millions)	= Calculated Earnings Per Share	Dollar Change Attributed to Each Factor
0.00126	0.01426	0.02032	0.48027	1.250	$2.03	
					2.60	+$0.57
					3.01	+ 0.41
					4.14	+ 1.13
					3.32	− 0.82
					3.28	− 0.04
0.00194					3.17	− 0.11
	0.01734				2.72	− 0.45
			0.45586		2.58	− 0.14
				1.281	2.52	− 0.06
0.00194	0.01734	0.01832	0.45586	1.281	2.52	

Source: First National Bancshares, 1976 Annual Report.

changes in earnings per share, but they also have application in explaining the changes in overall profitability.

The analysis shows that the combined effect from 1972 to 1976 on earnings per share of additions to equity and greater leverage (shown by the lower capital ratio) amounted to additions of $0.57 and $0.41, respectively. These two factors represent the increased volume of activity or increased asset base of First National Bancshares. The interest income ratio, which is the net interest spread divided by average total assets, contributed $1.13 to the increase in earnings per share. This strong contribution to earnings per share reflects the strength in the interest rate policy just noted.

Offsetting these gains were six factors, which had the effect of reducing earnings per share. The ratio of other income to average total assets reduced earnings per share $0.82 in the interval. The bank's most remarkable achievement, nevertheless, must be the small reduction in earnings per share of only $0.04 because of the personnel expense ratio. The loan loss ratio reduced earnings $0.11 per share, the other expense ratio reduced earnings $0.45 per share, the tax rate $0.14 per share, and a larger number of shares outstanding reduced earnings per share $0.06 in the interval.

This analysis of the First National Bancshares indicates no special area of basic weakness. In fact, the major factor that held the gains in the earnings per share lower than they otherwise might have been was the category of other operating income, which rose significantly less rapidly than the gain in assets. Trust department income doubled to $379 thousand from 1972 to 1976, service charges on deposit accounts inched upward to $1.5 million, but other income was cut in half to $983 thousand in the interval.

Earnings per share rose on an overall basis in recent years. They were $1.62 in 1970, $1.95 in 1971, $2.03 in 1972, $1.96 in 1973, $1.97 in 1974, $2.22 in 1975, and $2.52 in 1976. The pattern of earnings per share, on a quarterly basis seasonally adjusted is shown in Fig. 72. The average annual rate of gain was 7.6 percent in the 1970–1976 period. The average annual gain in the most recent two years was 13.1 percent. A look at the seasonally adjusted earnings per share (Figure 72) showns the accelerated expansion in those years as well as less volatility.

The valuation of the profitability policy from all of these considerations is shown as 70. This rating is the same overall valuation for the bank's profitability policy, which is shown by the Keefe and Bank Administration Institute measures.

Capital Policy.   The capital policy shown by the Keefe and Bank Administration Institute measures indicate that this policy may have been given low priority by First National Bancshares. These findings are reflected by other considerations.

The capital ratio, as measured by the ratio of equity to assets, was 6.52 percent in 1972, 6.51 percent in 1973, 6.42 percent in 1974, 6.10 percent in 1975, and 5.78 percent in 1976. The decline from 1972 to 1974 was gradual, but the drop from 1974 to 1976 was more rapid. A broader measure of the capital policy shows the same pattern. The ratio of equity, plus capital notes, plus mortgage indebtedness to average total assets shows a measure of the funds of the bank that may be regarded as being placed on a long-term basis and

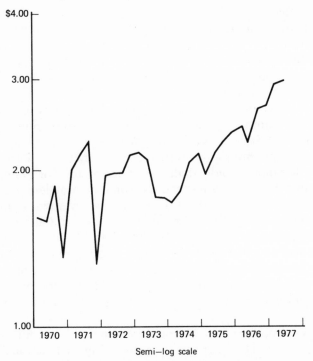

Figure 72 First National Bancshares seasonally adjusted earnings per share for each quarter shown at an annual rate. *Source:* First National Bancshares, quarterly reports.

represents a stable capital base. This ratio was 7.81 percent in 1972, 7.65 percent in 1973, 7.48 percent in 1974, and then dropped fairly rapidly to 7.00 percent in 1975, and 6.51 percent in 1976.

The dividend payout has been a factor in the decline in the capital ratio. On April 13, 1977, the annual indicated dividend rate was $1.30 per share, and the stock was selling on the over-the-counter market at bid $19, providing a 6.8 percent dividend yield. This yield would provide an attraction to many investors, and no doubt is an important factor in maintaining strength in the price of the bank's stock. (Book value at this time was estimated to be slightly more than $18 per share.) Nevertheless, this dividend yield carries an accompanying liberal dividend payout ratio, which is the proportion of dividends to earnings paid to shareholders. The dividend payout ratio was 52 percent in 1976, down from 54 percent in 1975 and 61 percent in 1974, but still a generous payout proportion.

An overview of the bank's capital policy would conclude that the present trends would need to be modified sometime in the future either through a slower expansion in assets, a higher retention of earnings, a stock offering, or a combination of these factors. A review of the trend of the bank's capital ratios and other considerations indicates an overall capital valuation of 35.

Future Economic Environment. First National Bancshares is located in San Jose and Santa Clara County. The city and county are one of the most rapidly developing areas in the United States. The area is the world's center of semi-conductor production, a rapidly expanding new industry. Semi-conductors are the critical components to new types of electronic equipment, permitting this equipment to be smaller, lighter, and more efficient. The area and industry have been described, perhaps only partly with exaggeration, as providing the same impetus to the electronics industry that Pittsburgh provided to the metals industry in 1880.

Tables 86–87 show brief measures of the business environment of Santa Clara County for comparison with California and the United States. These indicators show that Santa Clara County has expanded its population and a broad measure of income significantly more rapidly than California, which in turn has expanded more rapidly than the United States. For example, for Santa Clara County effective buying income (personal income less personal tax and nontax payments), increased at an 11.40 percent average annual rate from 1970 to 1975, compared with a 9.45 percent rate for California and a 9.00 percent gain in personal income in the United States.

There are indications that the economic development of Santa Clara County will continue to expand at a rapid pace because of the growing importance of semi-conductors in industry. This outlook would rank the economic base of the bank among the highest in the United States, with a valuation of 95.

Regulatory Environment. First National Bancshares is a bank holding company regulated by the Federal Reserve System. The First National Bank of San Jose is a national bank with primary supervisory authority from the Comptroller of the Currency.

There have not been any public statements from regulatory agencies concerning the bank holding company or the bank. Nevertheless, the Comptroller of the Currency apparently has an above average opinion of the bank, since it used the bank as one of its models in the development of new audit and examination procedures. The bank holding company also received preliminary approval of the Federal Reserve Board to proceed with a

Table 86   Measures of Business Environment

	1965	1970	1975	Average Annual Rate of Change	
				1965–1970	1970–1975
Santa Clara County, California					
Population (millions)	0.90	1.08	1.22	3.71%	2.47%
Effective Buying Income (billions)	$ 2.47	$ 4.39	$ 7.53	12.19	11.40
State of California					
Population (millions)	18.9	20.0	21.2	1.14%	1.17%
Effective buying income (billions)	$52.6	$75.9	$119.2	7.61	9.45

Source: *Sales Management*, U.S. Bureau of Census.

Table 87 Measures of Business Environment

| | 1960 | 1970 | 1975 | Annual Average Rate of Change | |
				1960–1970	1970–1975
California					
Population (millions)	15.9	20.0	21.2	2.32%	1.17%
Personal income (millions)	$ 42,900	$ 89,900	$ 138,900	7.68	9.09
Employees in nonagricultural establishments	4.90	6.95	7.82	3.56	2.39
U.S.					
Population (millions)	180.0	203.8	213.1	1.25%	0.90%
Personal income (millions)	$399,900	$808,200	$1,243,300	7.29	9.00
Employees in nonagricultural establishments	54.2	70.9	77.0	5.52	1.66

Source: U.S. Bureau of Economic Analysis, Bureau of Census.

proposed acquisition of Redwood Bancorp of San Francisco, although that proposed acquisition was subsequently terminated.

Despite these favorable indications, there would likely be some pressure by the Federal Reserve System and the Comptroller to review the capital policy of the bank with interest. In addition, the backlog of funds available for dividends without the special approval of the Comptroller shrank recently. At year-end 1976 the amount of these funds available for dividends was $2.7 million, down from $3.3 million one year earlier.

The overall evaluation of the regulatory environment is about average. A valuation of 50 is shown in the table.

Management Strategy. Historically, First National Bancshares appears to have followed three guidelines in its management strategy. It has jealously guarded its independence and resisted all efforts that would cause the management of the bank to lose control over its operations. It has primarily been a bank for selected consumers and proprietors of small business, strongly preferring loan customers who are regarded as very low credit risks. The bank has also been an innovator, but not a full-scale promoter of new banking services.

The strong presence of powerful competitors such as Crocker, Wells Fargo, and other major California banks has been a large factor in the importance First National Bancshares has given to innovation. The concept of controlled innovation is shown by the bank's development in 1953 of a regional credit card, the first such card west of the Mississippi. Further, the bank was the first to provide drive-up banking in the Santa Clara Valley, and the bank auto lease program, established in 1965, was one of the first programs of its kind. Apparently, the presence of major competitors has been a restraint on the bank's pace in expanding its activities. It was probably thought that too much expansion too quickly could lead to difficulties, which could lead to a loss of control. Overall, in past years this strategy appears to have been nicely balanced, giving sufficient differentiation of banking services from its large competitors, but not so strongly expansionary as to require major increments of capital or run risks of credit or liquidity difficulties.

This strategy may have changed, following the recent episode of the bank with Adnan Khashoggi, who offered to purchase a one-third equity interest in the bank in 1974. This interest would have been established through the sale of 300,000 new shares of the bank for $14.1 million. In approaching the directors of the bank with his offer, Khashoggi was reported to have indicated that if they did not approve the sale of the new stock issue, he would attempt to obtain control of the stock through open market purchases. The directors voted 12 to 15 to recommend to shareholders that they approve a proxy on the issue.

The issue became a major consideration of the area's businessmen and shareholders, and opposition to the proposal was led by one of the bank's directors who had voted against the offer. Among those who opposed the sale were Donald Glazer, executive director of the Jewish Federation of San Jose, Melvin Cotton, president of the same organization, and Fortney Stark of the United States House of Representatives, who added fuel to the fire by reportedly saying that a "pattern is emerging which indicates Arab interests are raising money through questionable arms deals and using the funds to buy banks." The proxies disapproved the sale by more than two-thirds (a two-thirds favorable vote was required for approval), and in January 1975, Khashoggi withdrew his offer and retired from the San Jose scene.

The Khashoggi incident may have shaken the bank into a new strategy. Many of the supporters of the bank in the proxy fight recognized that the old strategy of the bank fit the situation of Santa Clara County when it was an agricultural center. By emphasizing consumer loans, it had been missing the dynamic elements of the new wave of business growth in the semi-conductor business. In January 1975, the bank hired McKenzie Moss II as president, and five months later he became the chief executive officer.

The bank subsequently appears to have embarked on a strategy that retains one element of the old strategy and introduces two new elements. The old element is the strong desire for independence. The vote to approve the Khashoggi offer was either a mistake for the chairman of the time, or it was a ploy to gain time to develop support against the offer. Either explanation would be consistent with the desire for independence and could explain the installation of outside management as the fight ended.

A new element to the strategy has been for the bank to aggressively seek commercial loans with small, growth-oriented companies. Table 88 shows that the bank's California market share of commercial and industrial loans was 0.21 percent at year-end 1975, well below the bank's average loan penetration of 0.38 percent and sharply below the 2.73 percent market share of loans to individuals to repair and modernize residential property. Branches have been designated for this new purpose, and loan officers with business loan experience have been hired for these branches. It will require several years and at least one recession to determine the effectiveness of this program.

Table 88 First National Bank of San Jose Market Share

	12/75 Amount ($000)	California Market Share	6/75 Amount ($000)	California Market Share	12/74 Amount ($000)	California Market Share
Real estate Loans						
Secured by farmland	123	0.06	364	0.16	369	0.15
Secured by 1–4 family residential property insured by FHA	488	0.03	565	0.03	591	0.03
Secured by 1–4 family residential property guaranteed by VA	95	0.01	105	0.01	122	0.01
Secured by 1–4 family residential property not insured or guaranteed by FHA or VA	58,462	0.69	55,087	0.64	57,276	0.66
Secured by multi-family residential property insured by FHA	16	0.06	17	0.01	17	0.02
Secured by multi-family residential property not insured by FHA	1,941	0.22	2,042	0.17	2,136	0.16
Secured by nonfarm nonresidential properties	11,270	0.23	11,118	0.27	11,178	0.27
Loans to financial institutions						
Domestic, commercial, and foreign banks	0	0.0	0	0.0	0	0.0
To other financial institutions	0	0.0	0	0.0	306	0.01
Loans for purpose of carrying securities						
Brokers and dealers	0	0.0	0	0.0	0	0.0
Other loans for purpose of carrying stocks, bonds, etc.	40	0.03	42	0.03	62	0.04
Loans to farmers	604	0.04	503	0.03	199	0.01
Commercial and industrial loans	42,616	0.21	33,842	0.17	33,208	0.16
Loans to individuals for private autos on installment	35,245	1.13	34,291	1.10	30,499	0.97

Table 88 (Continued)

Loans	12/75 Amount ($000)	California Market Share	6/75 Amount ($000)	California Market Share	12/74 Amount ($000)	California Market Share
Retail credit card plans	13,292	0.79	11,021	0.76	11,248	0.78
Check credit and revolving credit plans	0	0.0	0	0.0	0	0.0
Loans to purchase mobile homes	1,946	0.22	1,565	0.19	1,396	0.17
Loans to purchase other retail consumer goods	19,030	1.46	6,156	0.89	3,812	0.62
Installment loans—repair and modernization of residential property	22,140	2.73	17,012	2.14	13,409	1.72
Other household loans—household, family, etc.	9,600	0.83	9,543	1.04	9,512	1.01
Single payment loans—household, family, etc.	0	0.0	0	0.0	0	0.0
All Other Loans	659	0.04	445	0.03	718	0.05
Total Loans	209,467	0.38	183,718	0.34	176,058	0.31
Cash and due from banks						
Cash items in process of collection	3,276	0.05	6,904	0.11	5,760	0.10
Demand balances with banks in U.S.	6,351	0.47	5,554	0.48	4,273	0.26
Other balances with banks in U.S.	0	0.0	0	0.0	0	0.0
Balances with banks in foreign countries	0	0.0	0	0.0	0	0.0
Currency and coin	5,373	0.48	5,699	0.60	8,120	0.83
Reserve with Federal Reserve Bank	20,225	0.36	19,382	0.45	16,106	0.39
Total cash and due from banks	35,225	0.23	37,539	0.28	34,259	0.26
Demand deposits						
Deposits of mutual savings banks	0	0.0	0	0.0	0	0.0
Deposits of other individuals, partnerships, and corporations	111,728	0.43	108,117	0.45	103,677	0.44
Total individuals, partnerships, and corporations demand deposits	111,728	0.43	108,117	0.45	103,677	0.44

Deposits of U.S. Government	1,006	0.34	1,541	0.60	1,592	0.52
Deposits of states and political subdivisions	494	0.06	391	0.06	365	0.05
Deposits of foreign government and officials	0	0.0	0	0.0	0	0.0
Deposits of commercial banks in the U.S.	0	0.0	0	0.0	0	0.0
Deposits of banks in foreign countries	0	0.0	0	0.0	0	0.0
Certified and officers checks, etc.	6,044	0.49	5,824	0.45	5,140	0.45
Total demand deposits	119,272	0.39	115,873	0.40	110,774	0.40
Time and savings deposits						
Savings deposits	123,318	0.66	120,704	0.70	107,108	0.71
Deposits accumulated for payment of personal loans	0	0.0	0	0.0	0	0.0
Deposits of mutual savings banks	0	0.0	0	0.0	0	0.0
Other time deposits of individuals, partnerships, and corporations	49,852	0.19	46,059	0.18	44,079	0.17
Total time and savings deposits of individuals, partnerships, and corporations	173,170	0.39	166,763	0.39	151,187	0.37
Deposits of U.S. government	0	0.0	0	0.0	0	0.0
Deposits of states and political subdivisions	29,873	0.47	16,658	0.30	17,545	0.27
Deposits of foreign government and official institutions	0	0.0	0	0.0	0	0.0
Deposits of commercial banks in the U.S.	0	0.0	0	0.0	0	0.0
Deposits of banks in foreign countries	0	0.0	0	0.0	0	0.0
Total time and savings deposits	203,043	0.37	183,421	0.35	168,732	0.33

Source: Keefe Management Services.

Table 89   First National Bancshares Valuation According to Seven Classifications of Bank Analysts

	Liquidity Policy			Credit Risk Policy			Interest Rate Policy			Profit-ability Policy			Capital Policy		
	Weight	Valuation	Factor	Weight	Valuation	Factor	Weight	Valuation	Factor	Weight	Valuation	Factor	Weight	Valuation	Factor
1. Directors	10%	40	4.0	10%	65	6.5	10%	70	7.0	10%	70	7.0	10%	35	3.5
2. Depositors	50	40	20.0	20	65	13.0	5	70	3.5	5	70	3.5	5	35	1.8
3. Borrowers	5	40	2.0	50	65	32.5	20	70	14.0	5	70	3.5	1	35	.4
4. Shareholders short-term	2	40	0.8	30	65	19.5	30	70	21.0	2	70	1.4	2	35	.7
5. Shareholders long-term	5	40	2.0	5	65	3.3	5	70	3.5	50	70	35.0	5	35	1.8
6. Debt holders	30	40	12.0	10	65	6.5	5	70	3.5	20	70	14.0	20	35	7.0
7. Employers	1	40	0.4	1	65	0.7	1	70	0.7	15	70	10.5	1	35	0.4

The other new element in the strategy was the establishment of a bank holding company in 1976. This step appears to indicate an interest in aggressively expanding the scale of the organization's efforts. The proposed acquisition of the Redwood Bank would have represented a first step in this program of the new strategy. Again, it will require some time to determine the effectiveness of this program.

An overall evaluation of the strategy would indicate that the bank may have lessened its use of its interest in proprietary skills and followed a course of action, which may reflect a serendipity strategy. As was noted in Chapter 13, which discussed strategies, this strategy reflects an interest in following widely practiced banking activities, but does not provide a unique niche for the bank. It would ordinarily be expected to lead to average results. An overall valuation of 60 is shown in the table, indicating that the risks and opportunities are tipped on the opportunities side for First National Bancshares, but that it is not assured that the new strategy will be as successful in its objectives of providing a major expansion in earnings and assets, as well as maintaining its independence.

Management Controls.   With a previous record of promoting from within, First National Bancshares, during its earlier years, had three members of the Clayton family, one of the founding families of the bank, as president. But as has been noted, the selection of McKenzie Moss II as president and chief executive officer in 1975 and the hiring of experienced commercial loan officers may have marked a new direction of management selection. The three other principal officers of the bank have been with the bank for more than 10 years.

The management selection of junior officers may not be a clear issue within the bank. This uncertainty could be a benefit, if it leads to a greater awareness of the staff that excellence could be rewarded. Control would then be enhanced. Nevertheless, the uncertainty could be a difficulty, if the senior management does not provide signals that excellence in performance is rewarded.

Future Economic Environment			Regulatory Environment			Management Strategy			Management Controls			Evaluation of Accounting			Valuation (Sum of Factors)
Weight	Valuation	Factor	Weight	Valuation	Factor	Weight	Valuation	Factor	Weight	Valuation	Factor	Weight	Valuation	Factor	
10%	95	9.5	10%	50	5.0	10%	60	6.0	10%	70	7.0	10%	60	6.0	61.5
5	95	4.8	1	50	0.5	1	60	0.6	1	70	0.7	1	60	0.6	49.0
15	95	14.3	1	50	0.5	1	60	0.6	1	70	0.7	1	60	0.6	69.1
30	95	28.5	1	50	0.5	1	60	0.6	1	70	0.7	1	60	0.6	74.3
5	95	4.8	5	50	2.5	15	60	9.0	3	70	2.1	2	60	1.2	65.2
5	95	4.8	1	50	0.5	1	60	0.6	1	70	0.7	7	60	4.2	65.8
5	95	4.8	5	50	2.5	50	60	30.0	20	70	14.0	1	60	0.6	64.6

The stock of the bank is moderately concentrated. No stockholder owned more than 4 percent of the 1,281,000 shares outstanding at year-end 1976. The 17 members of the board of directors owned 141,980 shares on March 12, 1976, representing about 11 percent of the total number of shares outstanding. Three directors owned 69,842 shares at that time, representing less than 6 percent of the shares. One of the directors with a major interest reportedly led the opposition to the Khashoggi offer, indicating that the board is not a rubber stamp of one man. This performance and the apparent decision to chart a new strategy suggest that the bank has a working board. The overall valuation for management control is shown in the table as 70, indicating a valuation well above average.

Evaluation of Accounting. An evaluation of the accounting records the bank makes publicly available provides an insight into the standards of logic that may be common within the company. Accounting systems that are available to the public, of course, show only a small part of the total accounting information used within the bank, but they do provide a sample of the standards of accuracy and reasonableness of information.

The report of the independent public accountants, Arthur Andersen & Company, in the bank's 1976 Annual Report indicated the usual unqualified opinion on January 14, 1977. The annual report and 10-K report include the usual financial statements and notes for a bank the size of First National Bancshares.

There are three niceties or fine touches to the accounting reports. The bank shows earnings only on a net earnings basis and does not show earnings before securities transactions. The bank does not engage in portfolio trading, and a line for the earnings before securities transactions would be redundant. More important, the focus on net earnings and use of this earnings measure in ratios represent a more comprehensive way of reporting earnings performance.

As a policy, the bank attempts to avoid placing loans on a nonaccrual basis. Loans of doubtful collectibility are normally charged immediately to the loan loss reserve as soon as the bank's management determines that the principal or interest payments are either unlikely to be collected or will be substantially delinquent. This represents a stringent approach to the management of loans, requiring difficult decisions quicker than allowing loans to remain in the limbo of a nonaccrual status. The accounting treatment suggests that the management may also hold stringent standards for other activities and may not be inclined to postpone unpleasant decisions.

The table in the 1976 10-K report showing interest rates and interest differential is advanced in concept. It enables a user to move from average volume to yields or rates to interest income or expenses smoothly and easily. Many major banks do not present such a table. This type of table deserves to be included in the annual report.

There are two small imperfections to the accounting information. The table described excludes certain small sources of funds. It only shows deposits as a source of funds, and the cost of federal funds purchased, mortgage expense, and interest expense of capital notes are not shown. Nevertheless, these three items did not appear to amount to 5 percent of the bank's deposits and do not distort the conclusions of the trend in net interest margins.

A second imperfection is that the federal funds sold are shown in a separate table and on a different basis than federal funds purchased. As a result, it is not possible to obtain a figure for the bank's net federal funds position. Nevertheless, the point is not of great practical importance, since neither federal funds position is significant.

An overall valuation of 60 for the accounting is shown in the table. This valuation indicates a standard above average for banks of First National Bancshare's size.

Summary of Valuations

Table 89 shows summary valuations of First National Bancshares according to the needs of seven types of bank analysts. The summary valuation for short-term shareholders was 74.3, indicating that the bank would appear strongest to these analysts. Of course, in determining the attractiveness of a holding, short-term shareholders would likely consider many other factors, such as the rate of inflation, the broad opinion of the banking industry that prevailed among shareholders, and the breadth of the market for the stock.

Borrowers would find the bank attractive to consider. The summary valuation of 69.1 for these bank analysts would indicate that the bank might nicely serve their interests under a wide variety of circumstances. Borrowers, of course, would want to consider other factors, such as convenience, their speciality requirements, and total loan requirements.

Debt holders and long-term shareholders showed a summary valuation of 65.8 and 65.2, respectively. These valuations would indicate that the bank would be attractive to these bank analysts. Employees showed a summary valuation of 64.6, indicating that their interests could be considered to be approximately as well served as debt holders and long-term shareholders.

The summary valuation for depositors was 49.0, approximately average. The valuation would indicate that the funds of these bank analysts are competently looked after. (Approximately one-half of the similarly grouped banks would not rank so high for depositors.) Nevertheless, the bank's strengths appear to be stronger for other analysts.

The summary valuation of 61.5 for directors represents a type of overall valuation. Directors are responsible for the total well being of the bank, and this valuation may be interpreted as serving as a proxy for the results of their management efforts. The valuation was well above average, but left room for improvement.

INDEX

373